Black Knight Alfa

The Most Feared Infantry Company

Also by Fred Steen

Team Shaka

Bluesman

Black Knight Alfa

The Most Feared Infantry Company

Fred Steen

JANUS PUBLISHING COMPANY LTD
Cambridge, England

First published in Great Britain 2001
by Janus Publishing Company Limited
The Studio
High Green
Great Shelford
Cambridge CB22 5EG

www.januspublishing.co.uk

A CIP catalogue record for this book
is available from the British Library.

ISBN 978-1-85756-468-6

Cover design Peter Clarke

Printed and bound in the UK by PublishPoint
from KnowledgePoint Limited, Reading

"The American soldiers who fought the war in
Vietnam did not lose that war.

The North Vietnamese Army sure as hell did not win it.

And Saigon did not fall!"

Black Knight Alfa.

**SOLDIERS, SAILORS, AIRMEN, AND TO ALL THOSE
IN OUR SUPPORT. I HAVE COME TO PRAISE AND
TO HONOR YOU FOR A JOB WELL DONE.**

To all those good combat soldiers who met the enemy in the mountains, in the flatlands, in the air, and on the water, I salute you. To all those young men and women who answered our nation's call to arms in the proud tradition of all of our brothers and sisters, gone on before us. Ours was not to debate the right or wrong of the political issues, but rather to answer the call when the dogs of war were released and someone yelled havoc.

Ours was the profession of arms and on our shoulders, just like always, rested the security of our great nation and its people, from sea to shining sea. Together we drank from the chalice of strength left to us by those who came before us. We shouldered the heavy load of adversity along with our clear and concise duty, which was to achieve victory, and victory was ours.

To all those glorious men of Black Knight Alfa – yesterday, today, tomorrow, and forever.
     And to:

Major	Horace Brooks
Captain	Alvin R. Norris
CSM	Gene Hudgens
CSM	Richard DeGeorge
CSM	H. T. Yamabayashi
SGM	Will Smith
MSG	Charles Davis

MSG	Leonard McKinnon
MSG	Bill Savage
SFC	D. Williams
SFC	F. Quientero
Mr	Harrel Jones

A special thank you to: Ms Deborah K. Currie for typing and editing. This story is fiction based on actual events that took place during my three tours in the Nam. Those tours extended to three combat units and across three major commands that made up the United States Army in the Republic of South Vietnam.

The major units with which I served were United States Army Vietnam (USARV), Military Assistance Command (MACV), and the proud, above-and-beyond men of the First Team, the 1st Air Cavalry Division.

Due to my eternal respect for all of my brothers- and sisters-in-arms, both living and dead, and their families and loved ones, I have deliberately made an honest effort to disguise the time frame, locations, names, and events that took place in the telling of my story. Any resemblance to actual persons, living or dead, is purely coincidental.

Contents

Retrospection   xiii

The First Step   1
Baptized in Fire   4
Via the Back Door   14
A Jungle Training Camp   34
Blocking Position   55
Ambush   68
Moving On   110
Packages from Home   128
Night Callers   135
Charley Alfa   141
Into the Valley of Death   161
Standing Down   250
The Flatlands   257
The Master of Ceremonies   276
Angels of Mercy   289
R-E-S-P-E-C-T   306
Go Tell it on the Mountaintop   320
JoJo is Down   328
Up on the Mountain   346
And Down to the River   353

Glossary   371
Notes   379

"ONE MORE TIME!"

Retrospection

Able Company, of the 371st Infantry Regiment, 92nd Division, was our company, and we were returning from a twenty-five-mile forced march with full field packs and gear. It was July in Alabama and as hot as hell. The sun was taking great pleasure in broiling us to a fare-thee-well. Thank God and our tired feet, the grueling forced road march was almost over.

We came out of the gap, pushing hard to reach our company area in the least amount of time possible. We still had a long stretch to go before reaching our area, which was located across the tracks in the colored section of the fort's cantonment area. Everyone was looking expectantly to a portion of high ground to the right of the road along our marching route. We were looking to see if our battalion commander was in his usual place, waiting to observe us as we came back through the gap.

Yes! There he was standing by his jeep, waiting to see us march by, but mostly waiting to hear us Jodie, or to hear us sing Jodie cadence. When we saw "the old man" (our colonel), we put our exhaustion right out of our minds.

It was time to pull our weary bones together and to do one of the many things that we did far better than any of the other companies in the entire black Buffalo Division. Master Sergeant Joseph Brown (we called him Sut) was our first sergeant, and old Sut could call Jodie as if he was Jodie himself. When Sut saw the old man waiting for us, he told us to "Get on it!" That was his way of telling us to get ready. Then he called the company to attention and began counting the regular cadence, as prescribed in Field Manual 22-5, to get everyone started on the right foot. "Hup, two, three, four," and we got ready.

Sut continued to count the cadence in the army-prescribed manner until the feeling was just right. Then he began to call old Jodie in a voice as clear as the ringing of a church bell.

Sut: "Well I know you're tired, you've been walking so long!"
We sang back: "Sit down!"
Sut: "Feet hurt so bad and you wanna go home!"
We sang back: "Sit down and rest a little while."

Oh, how I wish that you could have been there to hear us Jodie, because there are no words that come close to describing how wonderful it was to call Jodie. Our entire company was singing and raising our voices in perfect harmony, as we were rocking steady and letting our feelings of pride, passion, the profession of arms, and old Jodie carry us on in. The colonel was bubbling over with pride because he believed in our religion and shared our sacred feelings about singing Jodie cadence.

Fort McCellan, Alabama. In the old Brown Shoe "Colored" Army.

I remember and feel it today just as though it were yesterday. It was my first Sunday morning in my new unit, the 522nd Infantry Battalion. (The "Five Double Deuce" unit was a separate infantry battalion that came under the command of the Field Artillery.) Because we could sleep in on Sundays, I was lying in my bunk, feeling very happy to be back home once again in an infantry unit. In my last unit, I had held the most honored position of Chief of Smoke in an artillery battery. While I was an infantry non-commissioned officer (NCO), I also had the privilege of being a redleg and doing the cannon cocker's hop in artillery batteries ranging from 105 to 280 millimeters – and all that in actual firing batteries.

I was not sleeping, but rather lying in a mellowed-out state, daydreaming. At first, I did not hear the slight commotion that was going on outside the door of my NCO room. However, I became aware of what was about to happen when I heard the voices of the gospel quartet raised in soulful song. They began to sing that most beautiful, soul-stirring, old gospel song "I Got a Mother Done Gone":

"Well, I got a mother done gone, mother done gone on home,
Make me feel, like my time ain't long. Make me feel, make me
feel, like my time ain't long."

The quartet's singing was so beautiful. As they raised their voices in
perfect, down-home, soulful harmony, I imagined them singing in one
of those little white Baptist churches that sits in a grove of pecan trees,
surrounded by cotton fields, somewhere deep in the South. The quartet
was following a proud and honored tradition that had its birth
entwined in the fabric of the beginning – since the first time a black
man wore the uniform of the United States Army, since the formation
of the first "Colored Troops", since the days of the 10th Massachusetts
and the Buffalo Soldiers, since the times when we were relegated to the
farthest side of the cantonment area across the tracks, and since the
Buffalo Soldiers built Fort Sill, Oklahoma, with their bare hands.

During those times, it became a tradition for each company-sized
unit to form and maintain its own gospel quartet. It was customary for
the quartets to rise early on Sundays and to walk throughout the
company barracks singing those good-old, down-home country church
songs. In a way, it allowed us to remain in touch with our good-old
Southern upbringing of going to church on Sundays to sing and to
praise the Lord. I opened my door and began to sing along with the
quartet. There was no doubt that we had all "been down to the river".
As we sang together, "Mother don't you worry 'bout your son", they
smiled at me. The leader then sang:

"If you see my savior, tell him that you saw me, and when you saw
me,I was on my way. I say, dear Lord, take and use me, that is all
I can say.
And I give my heart to Jesus, how about you, how 'bout you, oh
how 'bout you?"

Memories of our mamas down-home and memories of the Delta
flooded our hearts, minds, and eyes as we returned in spirit to
Mississippi, Georgia, Alabama, and those other lands in the grand old
South that we could call "home".

Fort Sill, Oklahoma. Still the old Brown Shoe Army.

On my shoulder, I wore the insignia of the black buffalo – "ready and forward" Napoleon's helmet, "Vincent Amor Patriae" – and rode the golden dragon all the way to the right of the line, always in search of excellence, always just trying to be a good soldier.

From our foxholes in the snow, Smitty and I had often watched the sun rise over Mount Fujiyama, feeling the eerie quietness of "The Land of the Morning Calm". Sometimes I still listen with thirsty ears, hoping to hear Shirley singing "China Nights" just one more time. Oh, to break track again, to pull a pack when it is so cold even the gas freezes, to fly the geese, to call for Sabo, to hear the section leaders yell, "Up and shot out!"

Some time after Korea, the man who often said "The buck stops here" combined the separate and unequal military systems into one. After the President's order, I was finally assigned to the First Battalion of the 47th Infantry Regiment. After I paid my dues, I met a man who called everyone "hoss", and we walked across Germany, from the mountains to the sleeping villages.

There were many times, when in garrison and after a hard day's training when the feelings were right, we would go out in the company street and Jodie for a little while. That is what we liked to do, and we surely enjoyed the feeling of togetherness that came with the activity. We sang our joy like this:

> "Soldier, soldier, where've you been?
> Down in junk town, drinking gin.
>
> Soldier, soldier, have you heard?
> I'm going home, I got the word."

Sometimes, when the feeling was right and there were no orders against it in the company area, we would really get down and do "The Stockade Shuffle"."Now this was indeed a beautiful art form, passed down from the days of the Colored Troops. Some folks said that you had to be colored to shuffle correctly, but that was a gross misconception. Your color did not matter; you just had to have the right feelings and the right rhythm. As we shuffled, we sang:

> "I'm a thousand miles away from home, sleeping in the rain.
> A thousand miles away from home, just waiting for a train."

Once we were in the groove, we would move on up a little higher and do a little of Betty and Dupree, Train Time, and C. C. Rider. Sometimes we shuffled until it was completely dark.

Still the old Brown Shoe Army.

My heart is forever full of my comrades-in-arms and all of the yesterdays we shared. Together we loved to soldier, work, and sing. That is why I volunteered to go to Vietnam.

Now let me tell you about the best infantry rifle company in the entire world. Let me tell you about **BLACK KNIGHT ALFA.**

The First Step

I left Kagnew Station, MAAG Ethiopia, ending a most rewarding tour in Mother Africa, where I will forever have the heartfelt belief that I had visited my true beginnings. After my very long flight deposited me in Washington DC, I drove to the Military Personnel Center in Virginia. After a long wait, I finally had the opportunity to talk with a very nice lady about the purpose of my visit. I was not surprised to find that many of my old comrades-in-arms were also there with the same request that I had. Once my business was finished, I took a hop out to McGuire Air Force Base adjoining Fort Dix, New Jersey, and from there I traveled to Chicago to see my mother. From Chicago I flew to Frankfurt, Germany, where my wife, Heidi, was waiting to pick me up.

My new assignment was to be at McKee Barracks in Crailsheim, Germany. Before going there, I made a brief stop at the 7th Army Non-commissioned Officer Academy to visit some old friends and fellow instructors. Following those happy and memorable moments, I joined my new unit and the fine men and soldiers of the 51st Infantry.

Unfortunately, my stay with them was brief because I was soon transferred to the 4th Armored Division's NCO Academy at Ferris Barracks in Erlangen, Germany. There I served as the weapons instructor and later became the first sergeant. The men of that unit were outstanding. It was indeed rewarding to be there, working with them, and to have the opportunity to present instructions to the fine soldiers of our division and to give my favorite presentation of "Duty, Honor, Country".

At that time I was eagerly awaiting my requested orders to join the fighting in Vietnam. I constantly prayed that the nice lady at the Military Personnel Center would keep her word and assign me to the best division in the world – the 1st Air Cavalry Division, the First Team. Eventually, my clerk at Division called to say that my orders were coming down. That fine lady had kept her word. I was assigned to the 1st Cavalry Division. That was the best news I had received in years, and it became even sweeter when I had the orders in my anxious, hot hands.

Most of my dear, old friends were already in the Nam, some on their second trip because the turnaround time was very short for us grunts. As expected, some of my dear friends came home early in white pine boxes draped with Old Glory. Obviously, many soldiers returned home that way, but there were others who ran to Canada, Australia, and anywhere else they might hide to avoid going to Nam. Some even became "ministers". All the same, I am happy to say that I was among the many Americans who were doing all they could to get to Nam.

After I had completed my out-processing, I took Heidi and our children, Doris and Thomas, home to Mama (Heidi's mother) in Stuttgart, and very soon I was booked out and bound to go. The day before I left to go to Frankfurt and Rhein-Main, a friend brought me a copy of the *Army Times* and showed me the long obituary column. There were the names of four of my dearest friends, two of whom were in basic training with me. Somewhere in our shared past, we drank out of the same flip-top beer bottle, broke track, and ran our tanks down the gunnery ranges. We strolled down the Ginza, chased moose, and ate fish heads and rice together. Willie (Sfc. Williams) and I were like brothers in the truest sense of the word. I broke down and cried like a baby; then I cried like a man. I could not help it. The pain of the terrible news was overwhelming. So many of us were dying, but I still wanted to go to the Nam.

Dear God, I had to go. My dear brothers-in-arms, fellow soldiers, and members of the world's third oldest profession (the profession of arms) were fighting and dying, and my place was with them. I had soldiered with them in the sunshine, and by the grace of God, I would soldier with them in the shadows. None of us were sunshine soldiers or summer patriots. We may have disagreed with what was being said and done; however, we were prepared to defend to our death any American's right to speak freely.

My friends and I soldiered together in times of peace and during times of war. We stood firmly together as one – Blacks, Whites, Hispanics, Asians, Native Americans. We were one soldier, united in the common goal of victory over the enemies of our great country. We were the "old soldiers", and it was our sworn-before-God, sacred duty to make every effort to ensure that all of our brave young American men returned home alive to their mothers and fathers. We were the experienced – the teachers, the leaders, the professionals. United by democracy, we put our personal faith in our fellow Americans, and we never let them down.

A unifying force of dignity, pride, and honor held our brotherhood together. Most of us would still soldier our butts off, even if there were red lines drawn through our names on the pay roster. If we were busted on a Wednesday, we would simply "peel off" our old stripes and break starch on Thursday, soldiering to the max to get our stripes back and for the sheer love of soldiering. It was all this and much more that had inspired my honest desire to join my brothers-in-arms in the Nam. That was how it had to be. Soldiering was our life!

On the following day, Heidi drove me to Rhein-Main, and after I had signed in, I went to the main NCO club and found it tightly jammed with those going and coming. It was truly a family affair, a gigantic family reunion. Some of us went all the way back together to basic training, to forts McCellan, Jackson, Huachuca, Polk, and Benning. All the way back to the brown shoes, to A-burg, Kitzingen, and Baumholder, to the Ginza and Frozen Chosen. It was so good to be among so many of my dearest friends. We pulled tables together and with misty eyes, we raised our glasses high to those of us who had already given the full measure to our great country. Hail and farewell!

At least 75 per cent of the men on our flight from Frankfurt to McGuire were on their way to Vietnam, some for the third time. After we landed in New Jersey, I went home to 41st Street in Chicago to see Sis (my mother). After a brief visit with my family and some non-military friends, we had wheels up to Fort Lewis, Washington, where there was another "old soldiers' family reunion". There, we sadly raised our glasses to those who could only be with us in spirit.

Two days later and before first light, we had wheels up on the first leg of our journey, bound for the Nam.

"Mother, Mother, there's too many of you crying."[1]

Baptized in Fire

There were thousands of us at Cam Ranh Bay awaiting our orders. It was as hot as hell, but the tent and other accommodations were first-rate. The mess halls served outstanding meals; the food was much better than I could imagine any king has ever eaten.

Right after we had arrived at Cam Ranh Bay, I received my first shock, that is, aside from the heat. I was informed that my original orders to go to the 1st Cav did not guarantee that the Cav would be my final assignment. Oh man, I was plainly sick. I did not want to go to any other unit except the 1st Cavalry Division. Being Cav was my lifelong dream. I was also told that the units in most need of my rank and Military Occupational Specialty (MOS) would take precedence, and that meant my assignment could be changed right there in Cam Ranh. I could be assigned as a tanker, an artilleryman, or an infantryman in MOS 11B or 11C.

This revelation really jerked my chain. My heart was set on joining the First Team. In my mind, no other unit could be as great. Naturally, all of the combat units in the Nam were good units, but my unit of choice was the Cav. I really wanted to be assigned as a grunt because I felt most at ease in that MOS. Truthfully, I was an infantryman a long time before the MOS number designation came into being. I went back to the 1745 designation and then to the 11B designation of that time, which we often referred to as "Eleven Bravo" or "Eleven Bush". I had to smile when I thought of how I had been an infantryman since the only vehicles on the company property books were the old man's Jeep and possibly a mess truck or a wheelbarrow (a "Georgia buggy").

One of the other sergeants who had arrived earlier told us about the big tent at the end of the street. It contained a large board where all names and final units of assignment were posted and updated. After finding my name on the board, I watched it like a chicken hawk hungrily keeping surveillance on a fat, old hen. One night, shortly after 0200 hours, I checked the board and was overjoyed to see that my final unit of assignment had not changed. I was still going out there where the rubber meets the road, to beat the bush and to gain eyeball-to-eyeball contact with old Charlie.

On the following afternoon I was ready to go, along with many of the men who had come in on the same plane with me and some others who were already there when we had arrived. We were loaded onto three Charlie One Thirties (C-130 cargo planes) and flown into Tan Son Nhut Air Base. We were transported from there to Camp Alfa, where we began our in-country processing.

I do not remember how long I remained at Camp Alfa. I just remember being flown from the Saigon area north to An Khe, which was Cav Division Rear. During our stay at An Khe, we received our final issue of equipment. We also attended Remount training, where we were given some very important in-country training and briefings. We learned the fine art of jumping from a hovering helicopter and out of the window when caught in Sin City. A wiry, little ex-sapper gave us an important demonstration on those maneuvers.

Although I do not remember how many days I spent at An Khe or the deep-well indoctrination in that famous little city outside the wire, I do remember having our final family reunion in the senior NCO barracks. Some of the old-timers with poor hearing or bad eyesight stayed in An Khe, while the rest of us were flown north to I Corps and Camp Evans.

During our first night at Camp Evans, Charlie sent a welcoming party. His night probe hit the corner of one tent and took out one of our shithouses. None of us was hurt, but we certainly did hurt old Charlie. We grunts were pissed off about the attack, and we were on him like white on rice. When Charlie left, there were a few of his number who would not be making the return trip ... ever.

During my short stay at Evans, I met my new battalion commander and command sergeant major. Because of my background, they gave me a LURP team with whom I had the honor and privilege to serve among the first group of the finest American soldiers that I have ever known. However, I was later pulled in and reassigned to a line company, probably because of my age and the need for a senior sergeant first class.

The sergeant major took me to the orderly room of my new company, where I met the company's rear personnel who included the company clerk, the supply and mess personnel, and those men who had already served their time in hell and were just waiting to jump the freedom bird back home. It took some time for me to sign in and to have the necessary paperwork processed before I was ready to book out to meet my new company.

The supply sergeant gave me a ride to the helicopter landing pad, where I jumped on a slick and took off to meet my new company. We flew very high to stay clear of any artillery firing missions. The jungle below seemed endless. After passing a few mountains, the door gunner told me to take the rope and jump.

As soon as my feet hit the ground and I released the rope, the bird climbed into the sun and vanished quickly. The company was way out on top of a mountain as part of the security for a landing zone (LZ) or a firebase. Hereafter, I will call it LZ Mooney for ease of reference.

My new company commander was waiting for me, and as we went to the company command post (CP), I saw some of the men of the world's finest infantry rifle company, Black Knight Alfa.

In the old army, we called the company commander "the old man". Well, as soon as I saw my new commanding officer, it was plain to see that this term did not apply to him. I was a hell of a lot older than he was, but I could tell from the first moment I saw him that we would get along just fine.

After the CO and I talked for a few minutes, the outgoing first sergeant took me to the fighting positions to meet my new company. He was to be there for only a few more days before rotating back home.

Meanwhile, I was tasked with serving as the platoon sergeant of the First Platoon. I would hold that position until the old first sergeant went back to the company rear, and then I would take over. This was an excellent arrangement because it gave me the opportunity to get down in the holes[2] with the best fighting men and Skytroopers who had ever lived.

The leader of my first squad briefed me on the pertinent information regarding LZ Mooney. It was located on top of a mountain and sat alone, quite some distance from two other firebases that we could see when it was clear, though we could see little else. LZ Mooney had cost some lives to take and to hold. It was in the upper northern edge of I Corps and Quang Tri Province. When I arrived, LZ Mooney was securely locked in. We had batteries of 105s and 155s[3] ready and dug in, and there was an ammunition dump with enough ammo to keep Charlie in his place, which was incidentally all around the base of the mountain.

I purposely made eyeball-to-eyeball contact with each man in my platoon. Once I had finished talking with the last man, I had the heartfelt knowledge that I was fortunate enough to have the best infantry platoon in Vietnam. Although I did not know it at the time, this feeling held true for the entire company, which I later took over.

I must say right here and now that those fine young soldiers taught me how to survive in that hostile environment – the Nam. If not for them, I would surely have been pushing up daisies long ago. When they talked, I listened because I trusted their experience with old Charlie. Before I arrived, Black Knight Alfa had whipped off on Charlie whenever he was foolish enough to fight them, and they were still alive and beating Charlie at his own game. Naturally, I listened and that is why I am here today, telling you some of our story. Sweet Jesus, I owe them. I told them that one day I would tell the world about Black Knight Alfa, and by the grace of God and those fine young men, here I am, trying in my bumbling way to tell you our story.

We men of Black Knight Alfa were the true combat soldiers of our time, and we were out there where it counted in lives and the loss of lives. So many lies have been force-fed to the American people about how the North Vietnamese Army and their lackeys, the Viet Cong, were indestructible. Of course, that was all bullshit. Black Knight Alfa fought the enemy in his own yard – front and back – and whipped the hell out of him. The only thing that Charlie ever won was what we walked off and gave to him.

Anyway, we started off on the right foot together – my new platoon, my company, and I. I thank the Lord, my dear mother, and a lot of my real-world experience for instilling in me the good common sense to

7

listen to my troops. My listening to them encouraged them to listen to me. As a result, we developed excellent communication skills. We fully understood that "when two or more people are talking at the same time, there ain't no listening going on". So when they spoke, I shut up and listened. Our communication was so phenomenal that we could practically read each other's minds.

The first time I led my platoon, the First Platoon, past the red line into "Charlie's Country", we did not encounter any shit, and we succeeded in covering our entire assigned area without coming into contact with Charlie. That patrol was valuable for me because it allowed me to get my feet firmly on the ground, to get accustomed to working with my troopers, and most of all, to simply learn.

Our third patrol outside the LZ proved to be a completely different ball game. We had already searched our area of responsibility and were on our way back toward the red line along the outer perimeter. Old Charlie was waiting for us on our return trip. It was late in the evening, shortly before dark, which is when old Charlie did most of his homework. Unfortunately, he chose the wrong unit to hit. He was preparing to play one of his old tricks, which called for him to wait in ambush along our return route and to catch us just after we called our friendly positions and requested that he not pop caps or fire because we were coming in. That would be the best time for Charlie to hit and run, because our friendly positions would not fire for fear of hitting one of our own men.

I have to admit that Charlie had a good plan; it was tired but good. However, we were onto his shit and as my troopers had informed me, "You can feel Charlie's presence; you can really and truly smell his distinctive odor". We knew the enemy was waiting for us and to top that off, we knew exactly where he was waiting.

JoJo, our point man,[4] paused and sniffed the hot air like a good Mississippi coon dog. Then he turned to look at me and smiled as he gave us the heads-up signal. I passed the word back, and we continued to move along as if we were fat, dumb, and happy.

Without any orders from me, Pete, my radio telephone operator (RTO), pushed right up to Six (our CO), to let him know what was about to go down. We kept moving as if we did not know that old Charlie was waiting to bushwhack us.

Charlie thought he had us. The poor fool did not know that it was the other way around. In fact, "we" had Charlie where "he" wanted us, and when the time and our position were just right, I gave the signal.

It was show time!

JoJo opened fire right in the center of Charlie's concealed position. Our platoon boxed wide, and in that same instant, our thump gunners thumped and hit the trail behind and in front of us. Moving smoothly, they put four or five high-explosive grenades on the trail and began to hit the enemy ambush position. Jones and Caldwell, the best machine gunners in the business, had their M60 machine guns fully active.

Charlie had to fire early or risk dying without having fired a single round. I heard the enemy soldiers screaming painfully with the realization that their shit was on the fan. Charlie's game was up, which was unexpected because we were supposed to be the ones to die. Yet, there we were, devouring his ass. Certainly, Charlie must have known that there was a distinct possibility of his being caught between us and our quick reaction force (QRF), and if that happened, it was all over for his collective butt.

Old Charlie had been overconfidently licking his chops, thinking that he could take us cold. However, it was our trademark to do the unexpected. We had his shit "in the wind"! We did not intend to give him any opportunity that he sure as hell was not planning to give us. We did not cut him any slack.

I thank God and all the men in my wonderful platoon that we did not have any serious casualties. On the other hand, we made old Charlie pay dearly up front for fucking with us. As we blocked his planned escape route, we knew that those members of the enemy troops who were wise enough to book out would surely run directly into our QRF, which was on its way to help us. Charlie was due to pay, right down to the last fool.

You see, he could not run back up the side of the mountain; his only escape route was right down to us, and our box was strong and deadly. It was my first experience in that type of situation, and I was scared. Although I tried to hide my fear, it was major pucker time. It was not at all like acting in the movies or playing cowboys and indians. The bullets were REAL, and those who took a major hit were not about to get back up and continue living. Old Death came to satisfy his hunger, at least for the moment.

I called for Caldwell to shift his fire farther down the mountainside so that our QRF would not be in his line of fire. When I looked back toward the enemy ambush location, I saw a Charlie coming toward me, preparing to punch my ticket. Instinctively, I dropped and fired. All my years of training were right there when I needed them.

Sweet Jesus! Though my hands were shaking and my mouth was dry, I still managed to make my fear work for me rather than against me. Oh, the enemy unit who tried to ambush us ... we took them all down.

"Oh God, look at what I have done!"

Torn, bloody, and shattered bodies lay between the enemy's ambush location and us. The sight of slaughter was mind-bending. My first eyeball-to-eyeball firefight was over, and all of the Charlies were either dead or dying. I looked at the Charlie who had pulled on me, and I realized that my soul was scarred and blemished for life.

"Oh God, look at what I have done! I ... I ... I!" I cried like a tiny baby.

God, Father, Lord, forgive me! I was so ashamed and distressed because I was bawling like a baby in front of the fine men of my new platoon. I thought it was all over for me, until some of my troopers came over to me and told me not to be ashamed, acknowledging that they had experienced similar reactions after their first, horrific eyeball-to-eyeball firefights. Oh, I tell you right here and now, it is a terrible thing, seeing the face of old Death up close, smelling his breath and seeing his blood-red eyes. Some of my troops shook my hand and welcomed me into the exclusive club of Constant Nightmares, whose membership would forever haunt me with terrible dreams.

That night I could not eat any solid food, and I avoided the red Kool-Aid because it looked too much like blood. When I went to the nightly meeting at the company CP, I was still feeling very disturbed. The CO tried to reassure me by saying that my bawling episode was a normal reaction. He said that he would have been worried if my response had been cold and indifferent, and he affirmed that neither he nor my platoon thought less of me for reacting as I had. Then he acknowledged that I had endured my real baptism in fire, blood, and death by welcoming me into the society of Black Knight Alfa. I was somewhat relieved and tried to feel happy, but that emotion fully eluded me.

The next day we found ourselves in somewhat of a stand-down mode because we were moved back within the green line, and our sister unit was moved into our forward fighting positions. We slept a bit, and we replenished our supplies in preparation for our journey farther north into the mountains, somewhere near the earlier site of Operation Belt Tight. It was during that brief time within the green line that I had another opportunity to eyeball every man of my elite, well-oiled fighting machine.

I had never before met a finer collection of American soldiers and men. Some came from as far north as the rocky coast of Maine and others from as far south as Florida. Some were from California, and others were from the Atlantic seaboard states. One of my troopers was born in Cuba, and a few others were from Alaska, Hawaii, Guam, Puerto Rico, and the Philippines. I took all of them into my heart, and I believe they took me into theirs. In that way we became one platoon, one man, and one soldier.

We were truly a good cross representation of our great nation, the good-old US of A. We were one big family and damn proud of it. It is very important for me to tell you this: no matter what you have been told, we NEVER gave up on you, the American people. We loved you then as we love you now and forever!

Those times truly tried our souls. The problems and heartaches back home were grabbing most of the news headlines around the world. The great march toward freedom and equality for Black Americans was in progress. We saw news photographs of cowardly men who allowed dogs to attack and bite defenseless people. Some of those great "officers of the law" had clearly abused their power and had mercilessly clubbed down defenseless women and children.

I do not mind telling you that those painful scenes of such a tragic opera hurt us greatly as we fought a war with our nation's "other enemies". Perhaps if we had been given more time to think about the situation back home, we might have joined that sad parade of brother against brother, of hate and bigotry. Someone had released the dogs of war upon us, and we did not have time to choose sides. Hell no! Black or White, North or South, Brown or Yellow – we had to stick together or old Charlie would be more than happy to hang us separately. Our common goal was to live, and we had a common group of enemies who were trying their best to kill us. Out there in the bush, old Death made us either brothers or dead bodies.

I had the opportunity to observe what I call "the true men of that troubled time" – those fine young men and all-Americans of my platoon

11

and company. I looked into their eyes, heard what they said, and observed their body language. I listened and learned. Thank God, I had listened well. In truth, the good folks back home might well have taken lessons from those brave and dedicated lads of Black Knight Alfa who fought in the Nam. After all, were we not just an extension of the American people?

We were all soldiers – White soldiers, Black soldiers, Brown soldiers, Yellow soldiers, and Red soldiers. The binding word is soldier. Our first goal in life was to accomplish our military mission and to stay alive while doing our job. Victory, it was all about VICTORY!

We, the men of Black Knight Alfa, had to work as a team. Our survival depended on it. We had no time for Bloods and Rabbits; for dapping and giving up some love; for skagging, fragging, and blowing pot through the barrel of a shotgun. I made it quite clear to my troopers that if any of them wanted to fight, there were plenty of Charlies running around itching for a fight. In other words, we never had to fight each other. I warned that any man who wanted to fight any member of my unit was a cowardly bastard if he did not fight me first. I vowed to take on all challengers, individually or in groups; it really did not matter to me. I told this to everyone in my company from the start, and I was as serious as a major heart attack. My troopers took my message as gospel, and as far as I knew, no fighting ever occurred among us.

We were not in the Nam to die for our country. Hell no! We were out there to exert every effort open to us and to make sure that it was Charlie who did all of the dying for his country. Without a doubt, we knew that we must trust each other with our lives. True, essential brotherhood was the essence of our continued survival – make no mistake about it. There was absolutely no time for shucking and jiving or letting racial prejudice cloud our minds, eyes, and hearts. We had to stand together when we fought Charlie; otherwise, we would go out "dust-off", wrapped in a poncho liner and too proud to speak.

Our message to each other was quite clear: "You soldier for me, and I will soldier for you. You cover my ass, and I will cover yours. Brother, I will die for you!"

We did not waste time arguing with one another; every one of my precious Skytroopers knew damned well that to do so was counter-productive and stupid. It would have hurt our team and surely cost us some lives. Goodness knows, there were a whole lot of NVA (North

Vietnamese Army), Russians, Chinese, and others out there, waiting to take our lives.

I loved, respected, and was completely dedicated to each and every man in my platoon, and in my company after I became known as "Top", the first sergeant. Black Knight Alfa was a living part of me. When any of my men hurt, I hurt. When one of them died, I died. We walked through hell together, and I would do it again and again if necessary. May God bless them all, wherever they are today. Always and forever, Black Knight Alfa.

After the evening meal, all platoon sergeants were told to report to the company CP. Once everyone was present, we went with the CO to the Tactical Operations Center (TOC). Our battalion commander and his staff, along with some officers from Division and the Special Operations Group (SOG), were awaiting our arrival. As always, the briefing was straightforward with no bullshit. Our mission was clearly stated so that everyone concerned would understand it in the same way.

Battalion was sending us into Charlie's backyard. We took notes, asked questions, and received answers before we returned to our company CP. Once there, we laid out our maps and determined our best strategy. Finally, we went back to our platoon areas and relayed all of our plans and other information to our troops.

The good Lord willing and the creek don't rise.

The first light of the following morning found us spread out in our loading formations, waiting for our birds to lift us from LZ Mooney. We were going to make a Combat Assault – a Charley Alfa – and we were going up against one of the most respected NVA battalions in the area. SOG, who was dogging that NVA battalion, reported that the enemies were moving directly toward a Cav unit that was providing security for a new and most distant firebase, way out in the dead zone. That LZ was still in the process of being established, but a super-sensitive set of big ears was already operational, and those ears were extremely vital to many grunts operating in that area.

We were going out there to discourage Charlie from messing with that LZ, to slap him around a bit, and to detain his departure until another of our units could get in a position to destroy him.

13

Via the Back Door

Our lift of slicks was a tad late, but they were certainly looking good as they came in just over the trees and the patches of persistent fog. We popped smoke, brought them in smoothly, loaded up, and were away in very good time. Our birds flew just over the treetops again and along the valleys. They were trying to get as close to Charlie as possible, without letting him know that we were planning to drop in on him.

Once we neared the area where we planned to drop in, we made a false insertion. To do this, our birds dropped into the area and paused. If Charlie was watching (and we operated on the principle that he was always watching), he would see our birds loaded with troops who were sitting on the floor in the doorway. While our birds hovered, we lay down to hide on their floors, hoping that Charlie would think we had gotten off and were in that false insertion area. Then our birds turned and headed back in the direction from which they had come, appearing to be empty of troops.

Everyone felt a lot better when we reached our real insertion area and saw that Blue Max were there on station ready to fire Charlie up if required. As our birds went in, we did not have to fire a shot, and Black Knight Alfa was safely on the ground and moving. Our birds were off, climbing into the sun. Blue Max stayed on station like mother hens keeping watch, and the Charley-Charley[5] bird remained only to see us on the ground before following the slicks. Finally, our CO released Blue Max, and they flew off into the wide blue yonder.

We were alone and on our own.

It was my platoon's turn to be the point platoon,[6] and old JoJo was in typically good form. To get started, all he needed was for us to pinpoint our position on the map and for me to tell him where we were going. He was a born point man; he moved as silently as a ghost, his eyes seeing everything, his ears hearing everything, and his nose talking to him. Sometimes he would stop suddenly and stand as still as a statue until it felt okay to move on. Everyone knew that with JoJo on point, old Charles was never going to catch us flat and we were not going to walk into any shit.

Immediately after we made our second radical change in direction, the CO, Redleg, and their RTOs moved up to my position in our combat formation. Per the CO's instruction, I called a halt and the company automatically lagered. Our Weapons Platoon was always the hub of our lager. These men were ready to fire their 81s in any given direction; no commands or shouting orders were necessary. Whenever we stopped, we were up tight and ready to fight. That was our golden rule. Charlie was never going to catch us napping or tripping.

The CO and Redleg wanted to reassess our planned route because we were using some old, outdated French-made maps that our battalion intelligence officer (the S-2) had given us for our mission. The maps left a lot to be desired, especially when we were out there humping the bush.

We got our act together in record time, and I gave JoJo the signal to move out. Six-Alfa passed the word along to the other platoons via the radio. Soon we came to a place that required us to cross an open area, a valley floor bordered on both sides by high ridgelines. We stopped again, and I sent a squad forward to scout the safest and best route across. Normally, we preferred to travel the high ground just below a ridgeline, with our outguards right and left, high and low; however, this was not possible at that time.

My platoon was positioned to cover our third squad while they reconned for the best route. Meanwhile, the rest of the platoon and the company lagered and waited. While we were lying there waiting and looking across the beautiful valley floor, Pete called my attention to a drama that was about to unfold directly in front of us and across the valley on the other ridgeline. As I remember it, the drama happened almost in the center of the route that we had originally planned to take after crossing the valley floor.

A lone soldier was standing in the open. Using my field glasses, I saw that he was fully dressed in an NVA uniform. That Charlie was truly dressed to kill. He even wore a steel pot and a field pack, and he carried a well-preserved AK-47. He appeared to have everything except, as we soon learned, brains. When another player, a low-flying Loach – an OH-6A light observation helicopter – momentarily entered the scene, putt-putting along like a Sunday driver, that poor, foolish Charlie started popping caps at the lone Loach. His AK blazed away. Perhaps he was a new man who thought that little bird was fair game, or maybe he was simply a prime example of the 10 per cent who never seem to get the word.

We stood back, smiling in anticipation of what we knew would soon happen. It was like watching a tragic, one-penny opera. The Loach was merely bait on a hook; he was the little brother of a most unique team. Big brother was flying high and out of sight, tailing his little brother. The pair was just waiting for some foolish Charlie to do what the fool on the ridge was doing. Big brother was an AH-1G Huey Cobra, Blue Max. He was undoubtedly the meanest mother in the air, representing 10,000 pounds of instant death.

Naturally, little brother called upstairs to his big brother to say that a mean old NVA soldier was popping caps at him. Meanwhile, we watched as two other Charlies, all dressed up for the occasion, joined their foolish comrade. They also began shooting at the Loach, which danced around to avoid the rounds. Suddenly, the Loach pulled almost straight up, as if to poke fun and laugh at Charlie.

Soon, big brother made the scene. Poor Charlie was still too busy shooting at the Loach to realize that Death was approaching. By now, little brother was high in the sky, probably wagging his tail at the unfortunate fools. Big brother did not give Charlie any slack. When he started firing, the ground erupted in a cataclysmic explosion of hot steel, earth, vegetation, and human body parts. We heard Charlie's abruptly cut screams above the ordnance old Blue Max was putting on him. Man oh man, he lit up Charlie in a single pass. He was on him like stink on cat shit. Charlie did not even have time to kiss his ass goodbye. We saw body parts and one steel helmet fly through the air and fall to the valley floor. The Loach flew back over the smoldering ruins to check on the known damage, but that was obviously unnecessary.

That was how the happy brothers worked. It was customary for the Loach to diddy bop along in order to attract hostile enemy fire, and the

16

Cobra always flew back and high so that Charlie would think the Loach was alone or in trouble. Big brother was always armed to the teeth with machine guns, 40mm grenade launchers, and sometimes up to 70 2.75-inch rockets. That magnificent bird was also capable of achieving a speed of 350 kilometers per hour.

We quickly pushed up[7] to the Loach and announced that we had a ringside seat. We gave him our 20/20[8] so that he would not sic his big brother on us if he spotted some of our troops. The Loach buzzed around to see if there were any more Charlies near us. The two brothers promised us that if we hauled ass down to and across the valley floor, they would cover our butts as long as they had enough fuel to remain on station. We did just that.

"See you guys in the funny papers!" big brother called out as the pair flew down to the valley, still fishing for Charlies.

We ran as fast as we could, but we were still moving well below our normal running speed because our combat load was really slowing us down. Since we were in Charlie's backyard without any guarantee of artillery support, we were packing heavy with more than our normal 81mm mortar rounds. Going down the side of the mountain was not difficult, and we moved fairly well because we knew that the little Loach was watching over us. We rushed across the valley floor and did not leave a base of fire on the high ground as we usually did because the name of this game was to get across the open area as quickly as possible.

Once we were in the treeline on the far side, our guardian angels left us because of their waning fuel supply. By that time, we were already back into our preferred combat formation, moving up the side of the mountain. We were banking on the fact that if Charlie saw us, he would not pop caps on us for fear that our guardian angels would return to our aid. There was no way that Charlie wanted to fuck with Blue Max.

Black Knight Alfa moved up the side of the mountain well spread out, with JoJo back in the lead, doing what he did best. As we approached the top of the ridge line, we found evidence of Charlie. There were still open, hasty fighting positions oriented toward the valley floor, indicating that a large force had spent a night there ... but what night? Not wanting to be caught on that side of the mountain, we dared not stop to figure it out but instead pushed upward to just below the ridge line.

The CO decided that we would inspect the site where Charlie had been dropped by Blue Max because we might find some useful bit of combat intelligence there. Actually, Charlie had already provided us with some very important information. He had left us his NVA uniform and steel helmet, his well-preserved AK-47, and the knowledge that he was foolish enough to fire on the Loach. This suggested that the Charlies who were killed by Blue Max were new to the area as either outguards or perhaps the security for a much larger, well-equipped force. We were well aware that Charlie's method of operation while moving was to drop off a team of men to the rear. That team could be as close as five minutes to the main body or as far off as a full day behind them.

Very cautiously, we approached the site where Blue Max had annihilated Charlie. When we were in position with our company in a well-spread-out circle and ready to do whatever was necessary, only then did we physically move toward the site of death and destruction.

Everything was a huge mess; pieces of Charlie decorated the countryside. There was not enough left of any of the bodies for a proper burial. Even those good-looking AKs were nothing but hunks of junk, bent and twisted pieces of metal (definitely not good trading materials). Not wanting to spend any unnecessary time there, we quickly sifted through the remains and identified the NVA unit of the dead men.

While we were searching for more information, one of our other platoons reported that a platoon-size enemy unit was all over the side of the mountain. It was evident that they had moved in a hurry and in the same general direction that we were planning to go.

The CO wanted to move out quickly in order to catch up with the enemy unit. He figured that if we could move in on their tail, we might take them down, provided it was not too large a unit for us to handle. Of course, we would not know of the unit's size until we caught up with them. The CO certainly liked to live on the edge.

Fate intervened, however, and we had to make other plans. Darkness was rapidly approaching, and to follow the enemy would require us to break one of Black Knight Alfa's rules of survival: "Never move around at night except when you really and truly must. Otherwise, find a good place to hole up till the light of day comes." We decided to adhere to this rule by focusing on finding a good place to set up in a good defensive/ fighting position for the night, or in the words of our own code, "to move into a good FOB position".

As we moved along, we followed our normal survival procedures. We dropped off a blocking ambush team without stopping or pausing.

18

No one watching us would know that we had dropped off that team. We also dropped off men to act as connecting files; they would safely lead the blocking ambush into our FOB when we called for them.

We always used the terrain to our best advantage. After identifying a good location, we moved onto it and set up our mortars to fire in any direction near the area where the three Charlies had been dusted. We instantly put out the claymores and positioned them as only Black Knight Alfa could. We put them in the trees, with some far up and others only waist-high. We always backed up one claymore with another. When we put our claymores out, we always positioned them with their backs flat up against the base of a tree, log, or any other useful object. We improvised on occasion, but we always used the high-low technique when placing them. Placing a claymore with its back against the base of a tree made the little device even more deadly. Excluding our troopers, anyone who tried to retrieve one of our claymores would literally lose his head.

Once we were tightly locked up, the CO gave the word for our blocking ambush to come home. The connecting files guided them safely into our positions, and we settled in and waited to see what would happen.

The night passed peacefully without a peep from Charlie. The only excitement occurred when old two step dropped unannounced into the hole that Pete and I occupied. We called this beautiful, but deadly, little bamboo viper "two step" because once it bit you, you could move only two steps more before you were belly up for good. Needless to say, we promptly left the hole, temporarily giving up our position. The little bastard would not leave, and we refused to accept its stubbornness. If word got out that two step had taken our position, we would never again have our own hole. Although the snake continued to lay its claim on the hole, we finally gained an edge and persuaded it to leave by threatening its health.

After our little altercation with the snake, Pete and I crawled back into our hole and began making coffee for our supper. Over an hour later, SOG came up on our push to inform us that the enemy unit we were tailing had turned away from its original direction and was making tracks in an entirely new direction. SOG assured us that we could not possibly catch up to that unit before it was safely across the border into Laos.

Do not tell anyone, but we did not have to look hard before we saw the Demilitarized Zone (DMZ). We were already running into the small tributaries of the Ben Hai, so we just sat still and waited for the next day.

Early the next morning, Battalion confirmed our suspicions that we had been tail grabbing what was reported to be the most elite battalion in the North Vietnamese Army. Perhaps that is why they were moved into Laos. However, there were no indications that the elite NVA battalion knew that we had been dogging them, and that said a lot for us. Although they had gotten away from us, every trooper in Black Knight Alfa knew the day would come when we would lock horns with the K-5. We wanted them very badly!

Our original mission had been to bring down that battalion. Because they were good, they had been sent to snuff out a new temporary firebase. My CO believed that Hanoi suddenly pulled them back for a more important mission. In any case, we will never know the truth.

Battalion gave us a new mission because we were already far enough north and loaded for bear. Every man was humping 18 to 20 loaded magazines for our M16 rifles, in addition to his own stuff, C-rats, water, at least one bandoleer of 100 rounds of 7.62mm ammunition for our machine guns, two claymores, and two canisters containing 81mm high-explosive mortar rounds. We were also packing 40mm grenades for our M79 grenade launchers, which we called thump guns. We were carrying blocks of C-4 explosives, a number of M72 light anti-armor weapons (LAWs), and at least one M26 hand grenade per man.

Because our company worked so well in certain formations and certain platoons were at their very best when they were in particular positions, the CO decided not to switch the lead platoon. As a result, we left the FOB with JoJo as the point man for our company. Our line-up was the First Platoon (One-Six), the Headquarters section, our Weapons Platoon (Four-Six), the Second Platoon (Two-Six), and the Third Platoon (Three-Six). As always, Black Knight Alfa was well spread out; each platoon was staggered and each squad maintained the same configuration. We used a large diamond formation with Four-Six and Headquarters in the middle. When we faced open terrain where the trees were sparse, we often spread way out and maintained contact by radio. This prevented Charlie from catching all of us at once. We used the column formation when speed or the terrain was our governing factor.

After we were clear of our FOB area and we verified that no enemy was lurking nearby, we began to make good time despite our load and the wait-a-minute vines that were primarily responsible for slowing us down. We also had to travel rather slowly and cautiously because evidence of Charlie surrounded us.

We passed recent campsites where he had cooked his rice and spent the night. Fortunately for us, Charlie did not believe in good house keeping. Unlike Charlie, when we left an area where we had eaten and/or spent the night, we always dug holes to bury our garbage, leaving few if any traces of human disturbance (time permitting, of course).

We lagered and inspected one of the larger campsites. Did you know that we could determine with near accuracy the number of men who had been at the site, where they had slept, and their effectiveness as a unit? We could answer such questions as: Did they dig in? How well did they prepare their positions? Did they post security? We became so adept at reading Charlie's garbage that we could sometimes even tell what unit had stopped and how long they had stayed.

Charlie usually took his dumps on top of the ground. Did you know that a man's shit can tell you a lot about him? It certainly can, and we were not above digging in Charlie's shit to get to know him better. By examining his shit, we could assess details of time and number, such as how long it had been there and how many men had been there.

While examining the site, we found two freshly marked graves containing unripe NVA bodies. Later, Two-Six found a nice little rice cache, ammunition, and some items taken from American soldiers. We "fixed" the rice cache and took the personal items, which we later gave to our S-2 section. We could not resist leaving our calling card for Charlie. When he came back for his rice cache, he would get the surprise of his life. He would literally die laughing, compliments of Black Knight Alfa.

By that time, we were well out of the effective range of our artillery support, and we were moving under single jungle canopies, which greatly restricted but did not prohibit the use of our mortars. Our mortar men were the best in the world, and the lack of mask clearance did not stop them from shooting if that became necessary. They had written the book on hip shooting. When they fired from the hip, they damned well hit their targets.

The company was moving along nicely, well spread out. We were so quiet that we could not hear our own movements. This was very impressive considering that our company was almost up to organizational strength, with most of the squads having at least seven or eight men. The Weapons Platoon was short of ammunition carriers and handlers. However, the rest of the company compensated for the shortage because nearly everyone in Black Knight Alfa humped ammunition for our mortars, including the CO but excepting our medics and RTOs. You have probably heard of how Charlie was able to sneak through the jungle, but I must tell you that we were even sneakier than Charlie ever dared to be, and it helped us to stay alive.

For most of the morning, we continued to move along very nicely. We stopped once, lagered, and waited for the Third Platoon to deliver its personnel who were assigned to watch our tail. After we checked our maps and our route, the CO suggested that I change point men. Chico volunteered to take the point position, and JoJo dropped back behind me.

Around 1300 hours, I checked my map again. We were heading due east towards the South China Sea. All of us sensed Charlie, and our shared feeling was not a good one. We felt the enemy all around us, but instead of panicking, which was not our style, we accepted the situation and continued on our mission.

We were a bit different; you might even call us oddballs for several reasons. We liked working in the highlands and mountains, and we preferred to work alone. We would rather fight the NVA than any other Charlie because those guys were soldiers like us. If I had to take a shot that would be my one-way ticket to hell, I definitely wanted it to come from the rifle of a soldier like me rather than from a Charlie Cong. While fighting the Viet Cong in the flatlands, we had found them to be little more than a mob in black pajamas.

The VC would rarely stand and fight. Their tactics were to ambush, to bushwhack, and to hide in the villages behind the skirts of old women. Sometimes they even dressed like women so they could shoot us in the backs before they ran away and hid. That is why we never cut Charlie Cong any slack when we encountered him, and we did everything possible to guarantee that he died for his cause. We learned very well one of the prime rules of survival during the Vietnam War, a rule that was as old as warfare itself: "Always do the unexpected, never do the predictable or the same thing twice in a row, and obscure the obvious. Damn the book, fight to win." We fought Charlie Cong like he wanted to fight us, but we did it with style and grace, giving a completely new meaning to the expression "shoot and run".

JoJo asked to take the point position again because he could smell and taste the enemy's presence. He switched places with Chico and took only a minute to adjust before we were up and moving again. The CO tightened our formation because the jungle was dense. The trees were old and big, and the canopy seemed to have two layers, which made the environment much dimmer. JoJo slowed down a lot, and I knew that we were getting closer to Charlie. Boy oh boy, we could really feel Charlie's presence. Everyone in the company knew with certainty that we were going to hit some shit. By that time, the Second Platoon was running drag, and the Third Platoon had pulled up behind the Weapons Platoon. We were ready for Freddy.

Charlie was so close to us that we could smell him. His odor was so overpowering that I distinctly felt we were too close. JoJo stopped dead. He stuck out his tongue and tasted the hot, murky air. I stopped when he signaled me to hold. He wanted to move forward alone, but then he changed his mind as he seemed to pick up a new scent off to his right. Pete and I caught the same scent, which was borne on the heavy air. Then, I believe that we saw the same thing simultaneously. A Charlie was squatting in some high grass near a tree, taking a dump, with his trousers around his ankles.

He was a big guy, and his face registered shock and surprise when he saw us. He was so scared that when he tried to shout a warning, fear clogged his throat and only a squeak came out of his mouth. Without attempting to pull up his trousers, the stunned Charlie grabbed his AK-47, which had been leaning against the nearest tree, and he brought it up into firing position. In an instant, JoJo dropped him with a clean shot to his head. That shot brought another Charlie into view, after he thrust aside a camouflage curtain.

Imagine our surprise when we saw a huge, old bunker behind the drawn curtain. It had been carefully built to withstand a lot of pressure. There were large bundles of commo wire[9] leading in and out of one side, and there were radio antennas hidden high in the trees.

It was of little wonder that we had so strongly sensed Charlie's presence. We were practically on top of his mother lode; we were behind the rear of a big-ass enemy bunker complex. Sweet Jesus, we had found the objective of our new mission. Never mind that we had done so in an unorthodox manner. We were sitting on top of something so big that I had to make a conscious effort not to be intimidated by its size and to focus on what we must do next.

The second Charlie appeared to be a high-ranking, field-grade North Vietnamese officer. Even from our position some distance away, it looked as if he said "Oh shit!" Of course he must have said it in Vietnamese, but none of us had time to worry about what language he was speaking. It was show time! We popped the second Charlie before he could jump out of the way. Then, we heard several other voices within the bunker, yelling and screaming orders. We were now in shit up to our sweating necks!

In all honesty, we were temporarily lost when we had discovered the bunker. The CO, his RTO Danzig, and Redleg and his RTO ran up to my location to evaluate the situation. It was obviously too late for us to run like hell in the other direction. Frankly, our best option was to bluff our way out of this big mess by attacking and making our larger, well dug-in foes believe that we were not alone. Although we were unsure about whom we were up against and how many there were, we believed that we were greatly outnumbered.

Our CO cursed those old French-made maps and probably even the little corporal[10] himself. Using the radio, he designated the Second Platoon to cover our asses by serving as our base of fire. I instructed my platoon, the lead platoon in contact, to maneuver into attack position. The CO told the Third Platoon to hold its drag position, and the drag platoon automatically became our rearguard/maneuvering element. However, the Third Platoon was already under fire from our right side, having one hell of a fight with the NVA troops who were securing their positions. Meanwhile, my second squad was lighting up the enemy bunker complex. They had already put two LAWs directly into the rear door of the central bunker. It looked as if the body of the dead NVA officer was preventing those inside from closing the door, and my troopers were putting everything they had into that open door. Actually, the original door was gone because someone had thumped the entrance, blowing the door off its hinges. Part of the timbers collapsed and turned the big bunker into a death trap. We heard a lot of screaming, crying, and yelling going on inside the main bunker.

We were hitting the enemy from the rear. With our foot in his ass, pandemonium reigned supreme. Charlie's firing ports and positions were designed and oriented to the front, directly opposite us. Apparently, he had thought his rear was secure because he had no security posted there. Yet, there we were, as large as Death. Black Knight Alfa was doing a job on Charlie as he was trying to figure out how we had gotten there. Old Charlie was as confused as a bastard on Father's Day. He did not know who the hell we were or how we were able to get so close to him. Although we had some similar unanswered questions, we did not waste time wondering about them. We were busy doing what we had to do. As we rolled over the few posted enemy sentries, we saw them die in a state of bewilderment, looking at us as if we were ghosts. Some of them died with accusing expressions that suggested we had not played by the rules.

We were involved in a real-world situation and nothing more. The time called for action, and our men were making it happen. We hit Charlie with all that we had. Black Knight Alfa moved smoothly in its role as a well-oiled fighting machine. Each of our men knew his job well and performed with maximum efficiency. There was no yelling between us; we were too busy working as a team, kicking off on old Charlie.

Despite his confusion, Charlie put up a fight. It was not as if he had thrown in the towel when he saw us. He really did believe that we were part of a much larger force. It did not make sense for a lone rifle company to be stupid enough to hit a unit as large as his. We simply could not be there all alone. Surely, Charlie was expecting to be hit by our big brother. Perhaps he was fooled by this thought because we were operating under a canopy where the sky was not visible. Although we did not have a big brother at that time, we had God with us and bold as brass, we had our big pair of balls. Sometimes, that is all you need to survive.

We realized that it might not be long before Charlie got his shit together enough to figure out our game. By that time we were hoping to have the upper hand, but if we did not, we had an alternative plan of action. Throughout our fight we never forgot the most important rule: "Never underestimate the power of your enemy". We knew that Charlie still had the potential to turn the tide of the battle in his favor, and we were trying to keep him off balance until we could go for his throat and end it.

Our wonderful mortar men were shooting from the hip – there was no other way. The canopy and close trees made hip shooting a nightmare, but our guys rode their mares as if they were in the Kentucky Derby. They put hot steel where it was most needed and tried to keep Charlie from rallying his confused and scattered troops. Meanwhile, Three-Six kept Charlie off our rear.

The enemy soldiers who were in direct contact with us were almost suicidal in their attempts to keep us away from their main bunker, as if it were full of whores or rice. They kept running out and shooting at us, and they were dying like flies. Charlie's behavior made it easier for my second and third squads to make it into their trenches and fighting positions surrounding the main bunker. Simply given that Charlie's positions were manned in the wrong direction was advantageous for us. His reactions to us had been much too slow, and we were fighting like madmen. However, we were not truly mad because we never lost sight of our common goal, to take the enemy out and to stay alive while doing it. We went for Charlie's throat with all of our might.

More than half of my platoon were already in their fighting positions in the trenches. Their positions were excellent – well organized and stocked. Once we gained control of the enemy, our troops took the weapons off the dead Charlies and used them on the live ones. Charlie would have to fight like hell to retake his position. We had hurt him too badly for him to cut us any slack. It was do or die.

We soon learned that using the enemy's AK-47s was not such a good idea. We were already familiar with the distinctive firing sounds of M16s and AKs. Therefore, when our troopers started firing Charlie's AKs in an attempt to save our ammunition, the sounds of the AKs firing right next to us caused some confusion within our ranks because we could not tell where the bad guys were. I passed the word to my men not to use the AKs except in an absolute emergency, and our problem was solved.

Our medics were doing a great job as usual. I saw Doc B., our platoon medic, going about his job of caring for our wounded. Heroically, he went from one wounded man to the next, displaying efficiency and a devotion to duty and our men. I watched that grand young man attending to one of our troopers who had been badly hit, and he worked with complete disregard for his own safety. By the way, Doc B. was a "C O", a conscientious objector, to the Vietnam War and to the act of killing, yet there he was displaying a lot more guts than many of those who were gung-ho.

Doc B. was a quiet, well-mannered young man from the Midwest. Every day he humped the bush with the rest of us, carrying two large medical bags, extra water, bandages, and his ever-present Bible. I know he read his Bible every day. Doc B. was a wonderful, God-fearing man. I humbly ask God to bless him wherever he is today. Doc B., I am doing this for you and Black Knight Alfa. Thank you.

I had often witnessed our medics saving the lives of the enemy soldiers who had been trying to kill us before they were hit. Maybe they had even tried to kill the same medic who later attempted to save their lives. It is indeed a tragedy that most (if not all) of the stories that you have heard, read, and seen on television and the silver screen about us and our role in the Vietnam War depicted us as drug-heads, deadbeats, and a lot of other unfavorable things. The media so conveniently ignored stories such as the one I have just told you about Doc B. Sadly, it was more acceptable for them to tell you that we were "ALL" degenerate hop-heads, high on drugs. They also falsely told you that when we were not raping babies, we were killing each other. Although I am not denying that some of those horrible incidents took place, I am saying that it was not a universal affliction. We were not all junkies. The members of Black Knight Alfa certainly were not. My fine young American soldiers and I did not have time for such shit because we were constantly hard at work, trying to stay alive while fighting our enemies.

Pete moved closer to my side and informed me that Redleg was trying to obtain naval gunfire for us. I had not given it any thought, but maybe we were close enough to the South China Sea to bring in naval gunfire. They had said in our briefing that the Grand Old Lady, the USS *New Jersey*, was on station on the gun line. At that time, she was going to add the awesome firepower of her 16-inch guns to our defense. We certainly needed the help because Charlie was getting his shit together.

Joyfully, I told Pete to pass the word that help was on its way in the form of the Grand Old Lady, the USS *New Jersey*. Over the din of the battle, our guys cheered at the news. We were really going to put Charlie's shit on the fan this time.

The CO also passed the word and re-formed our company into a solid blocking position, with the company headquarters near my platoon headquarters' position. By that time, my whole platoon was well within the former NVA fighting positions and not too far from the main bunker. I had a very good view of the bunker and the left end of the Third Platoon. We kept firing on the bunker so that no one could slip out if anyone were still alive inside. We had Charlie by the short hairs.

I was close enough to our CO to see in his eyes some of the pride that he felt for his company. No one could know better than he that he was in command of some of the finest soldiers our country had ever produced.

"Roger, wait," I heard Redleg say into his microphone with a smile in his voice. He said something to the CO, and the CO spoke into his microphone.

Then the CO yelled to me, "One-Six, the countdown is in progress!"[11]

All hell was about to break loose. Meanwhile, Charlie was rallying around the cause and trying to gather enough survivors to counter-attack. His timing was piss-poor and unfortunate.

To the front of the bunker and some distance away, the CO and I observed through our field glasses an NVA officer and an NCO hastily forming to attack us. I was not sure where they had come from, but there suddenly appeared to be plenty of fresh troops in full uniform. I could not help but think that we had bitten off more than we could chew and that the *New Jersey* was preparing to save our asses.

"Shot out!" our CO called, and we signaled our men to get down.

The marker round was inbound. Like a fast-moving freight train, the 16-inch messenger of death wearing its steel jacket crashed squarely in the middle of the enemy troops as they were getting ready to fire upon us. Perhaps our enemies had held high hopes of winning their Red Stars, but alas, the fickle finger of fate gave them a one-way group ticket to hell. All of the Charlies inside the exploding radius disappeared in a flash of fire and smoke. The earth burst open, and trees and vegetation rose up and flew in every direction. What was left of Charlie rained down upon the jungle floor like paper confetti at a ticker-tape parade down Fifth Avenue.

That first round really got and held Charlie's attention. Loudly and clearly, big mama told Charlie that she was shooting for us. That beautiful, old girl was fixing to put more hot steel in Charlie's butt. Now Charlie might have been a little crazy, but he was not stupid. He did not want any part of what the *New Jersey* was putting down. Clearly, it was not his day. Redleg was already calling in the correct adjustments, which would put the shit on Charlie and keep him away from us.

You must understand that we normally had 105mm and/or 155mm artillery support available or on call. In our position, we always had to remember the bursting radius[12] of the different sizes of millimeter rounds when they exploded. Often it was a matter of life and death – our life and death – as to how close we could have those rounds fall to our positions. Sometimes it was necessary for us to bring those rounds in almost on top of us, especially when we were up against a half-wise Charlie. If he were caught in one of our hot steel showers and if he could close in on us, he might live to tell the tale. So, we brought our artillery in so close to our positions that the shrapnel would kill us if we did not know when to duck. We even did the same thing with our 175mm support. However, with the *New Jersey* shooting 16-inch projectiles and those projos having a much wider bursting radius, we did not dare to play around with them. That is why the Grand Old Lady had previously shot a marker round for Redleg, so that he could become familiar with her capabilities. Unlike Redleg, we were unfamiliar with her until that moment.

I watched some of the destruction take place. The shockwaves from the explosion blew my helmet off and rattled my brains. That marker round was so close that I suffered a temporary loss of hearing, which was probably the reason I did not hear Pete shout a warning to me. A Chicom hand grenade landed squarely in the former NVA firing position – with Pete and me! Fortunately, because the position was correctly dug and the flooring was tilted, the grenade rolled under the log flooring directly into what must have been a grenade sump.[13] The force of the exploding grenade helped to throw us clear of the hole. Though we were not hurt, we were shook up. Both Pete and I are grateful to the NVA soldiers who dug and built that particular fighting position because the grenade sump saved our hides. Thanks, guys! Way to go!

The fast, hellbound freight train of screaming death landed farther out and terribly damaged the Vietnamese countryside and the NVA. I do not know how many 16-inch rounds were in that salvo, but it was like Armageddon. If you think the marker round was awesome, you should have been there to witness a salvo of projos landing all at once. Thank God, Pete and I had the presence of mind to quickly jump back into what was left of our borrowed hole. The ground opened up and consumed a lot of NVA soldiers. Hell on Earth was right there before us. The remaining Charlies decided to haul ass in an attempt to put as much distance as possible between themselves and the *New Jersey*, leaving behind some Charlies who were caught in between that one salvo and Black Knight Alfa. Oh, it took only one salvo to make a believer out of Charlie and us.

A great hole had been torn in the jungle canopy, and sunlight shone upon the jungle floor, like a spotlight shining down on the stage of life. In this case, it was the stage of destruction. Uprooted trees and vegetation and all kinds of debris floated slowly down like some weird rain in a science fiction movie. Only that was a real-life episode in a live stage play, and although it was a long way from Broadway, that opening act was a real mother. No wonder old Charlie decided not to stick around for the next act.

Pete retrieved my helmet, and we turned our attention to the clean-up, which as I remember, presented something that seemed radically wrong. Instead of the NVA fighting us in an attempt to break contact so that they could get away, they were fighting us in an entirely different way, still as if they were guarding something of great value in their main bunker, which was starting to smolder. Both Pete and I immediately thought of gas, and we did not have our masks with us. We noticed that all of the dead Charlies seemed to have gas masks, but their masks were of very poor workmanship.

Pete and I thought about that matter as we looked about, assessing our situation. We spied the cover of a spider hole being raised slowly. Two Charlies sprang out of it with their AKs blazing away. Unfortunately for them, my troopers spotted them immediately and blew them away. We had figured correctly that the spider hole served as the escape route from the main bunker. The rats were now escaping because they had no other options. The third man to come out of the spider hole was a brown-haired white man of medium build, wearing a different uniform. He came out firing at us with his new AK-47 with folding stock. As we lit him up, he dropped his AK and screamed. Two of the three other Charlies who next appeared from the spider hole grabbed the white man and dragged him off while the third man fired wildly to keep us away. That brown-haired white man was a senior Russian officer. We wanted him badly, but we decided not to risk losing any of our men to chase after his body.

Jones and his machine gun caught the third Charlie and cut him in half. The two Charlies dragging the Russian officer were both hit, but they continued to get away with the Russian's body. Soon, however, they fell down the side of the mountain and out of our line of sight. Our troopers who were nearest to the incident identified the Russian officer as the equivalent of a US Colonel. We later found the bodies of the two Charlies who had dragged the Russian away, but the Russian was no longer with them. According to the blood trail, he was dead too.

Other Charlies tried to escape from the spider hole, but we were waiting for them. It was like nailing ducks in a shooting gallery, until someone thumped the spider hole and it collapsed. The few enemy soldiers still alive outside the bunker lost their taste for the fight and surrendered.

Battalion informed us by radio that air support was on the way and would be on station within minutes. Also, Garry Owen[14] was coming in to help us. Suddenly, everything was looking better, and good news was pouring in. We also received some other news that made us think.

Aerial Sensor and Surveillance Aircraft (Snoopy) reported its observation of a large NVA unit moving rapidly toward the fight at the bunker complex. However, when the *New Jersey* entered the scene, the unit changed its mind and ran like hell in the opposite direction. The battleship *New Jersey* had indeed pulled our chestnuts out of the fire.

Given that the remaining visible NVA soldiers had the fight knocked out of them, they were all ours. Of course, a few were still holed up inside the bunker, stubbornly holding on to their territory. The bunker was very well constructed and a formidable opponent. A lot of smoke billowed from its firing slits and seeped through the logs covering its roof. The LAWs we had managed to get inside were causing some of that smoke, and the rest of it came from the NVA soldiers inside as they burned their documents to prevent them from falling into our hands.

My platoon tried to get inside the bunker, but the enemy within stubbornly fired at us through the openings between the logs. We sent our ARVN scout forward to tell them that their situation was hopeless and that they had no support waiting on the outside. They hit our scout (just a minor wound), making it clear that they were not going to cooperate with us.

After Charlie hit one of our officers who also tried to convince him to surrender, the CO decided to prevent any further hits on our men by having us pop the bunker. We used our brains and all of the C-4 we were packing. We sent troops on top of the bunker, piled the C-4 into the form of a shaped charge and covered it with some of Charlie's sandbags to drive the blast straight down. Then, using an M57 firing device, we ducked and popped the bunker, driving a section from the top down onto Charlie's damned head. It was all over for him, and all that remained for us to do was to dig out his remains. This took only a few minutes because we had a lot of help.

We discovered the remains of an old enemy of ours – the original Charlie from the People's Republic of Red China. He was a Chinese "advisor" and the dude who had shot our scout and one of our officers. He was still carrying some of his official papers and awards he had received for killing Americans in Korea. His time of killing American soldiers had obviously ended.

Our S-2 had a field day with our discoveries inside the bunker. We found physical evidence that the Russians and the Chinese were not only advising but also trying to kill us at every opportunity. Our enemies were falling all over each other in a feeding frenzy; all were anxious to take our lives. We were literally surrounded by people who wanted us to die, even some of the "good" folks back home.

Later, most of the other troops who had been lifted in to help us were withdrawn. However, TAC Air remained and planned fire support from the Grand Old Lady of the Seven Seas. Yes, the *New Jersey* was still on the gun line and would shoot for us all night if necessary. We spent the night on the ground, all alone at the bunker site. G-2 thought Charlie would return to retrieve the Chinese body and some of his own men. However, we waited all night and nothing happened. All of that bullshit about Charlie coming back to retrieve his dead was just that – bullshit.

That day, we had not lost one man killed in action (KIA). We merely had to dust off three of our wounded – two enlisted men and one officer – and all of these men lived! One of them eventually returned to Japan, another went home to the States, and the third returned to our company.

For us, the fight was over and the day was saved. We had gone up against a full battalion – the best they had – and we had kicked ass. God and the *New Jersey* were truly with us. I am still so very proud of our fine troopers for that day's work. Our grand team had scared Charlie into thinking that we were the lead element of a large force. We had blown away the enemies' minds and butts, and they died thinking that we were a battalion, when in reality we were only an infantry company. Then again, we had one distinction: "We were Cav."

Black Knight Alfa. Alpha and Omega!

A Jungle Training Camp

On the following morning we waited for daylight before we started moving around. None of our trip flares, traps, or claymores showed any signs of tampering. Without any reservations, I can tell you that Charlie did not come anywhere near our area that night. If he had, we would have known it. I am not saying that Charlie was afraid of us, but he was scared shitless of the USS *New Jersey*. He showed a lot of good common sense by not repeating the great misfortune that had befallen some of his comrades the day before.

We thoroughly checked the area but held our new positions, just in case Charlie did something stupid. Around 0930 hours we were still waiting, and there was still no peep out of Charlie and the NVA. All of our probe teams on their search and security missions returned with the same story. The only Charlies they had seen were dead Charlies. Of course, we were very careful not to send any of our teams beyond the planned fire support line.

S-2 made a special trip back to commend us on a job well done and to inform us that our original mission had been declared a great success. We had gathered so much information that Battalion was still adding up the score. It also helped that our new prisoners were singing like the Mormon Tabernacle Choir. Our little operation had truly hurt Charlie.

We were resupplied with ammunition, water, and medical supplies. However, we were not brought back up to personnel strength, and no officer was available to replace the one we had lost during our fight for the main bunker.

Our sister unit moved into our new positions and also those that we had taken from the NVA. Around 1400 hours we saddled up and moved out in the original direction from which we had come. That night we set up in an excellent FOB position and took full advantage of the available terrain. We were especially careful because we figured that old Charlie must be jawed up tight about the licking we had given him. After the ass-kicking, some of our guys left calling cards so that Charlie would become painfully aware that it was Black Knight Alfa who had done the job on him during the fight at the bunkers.

The next day we pushed out of our FOB heading in a slightly new direction, although we were still heading back and mostly west. Later we learned that Battalion was moving us to a different location in preparation for a new mission.

After almost a day of pushing west, we were past the *New Jersey*'s shooting range, which saddened many of us. After we doubled back on our trail a second time and found it clean, we headed more south than west. We knew that if we kept pushing hard in that general direction, we could get the marines at Khe Sanh to shoot for us if necessary.

Battalion gave us a new direction and shackled the coordinates to a location where we were ordered to move by the most direct route. Once we were there, our instructions were to cut an LZ and wait to be extracted. Already there were two other Cav units working that area of operations (AO), and thankfully, our headquarters did not allow our units to work too closely to the other units. The grim specter of friendly fire accidents was all too real.

Because my platoon was a drag platoon and the lowest in personnel strength, we hoped to go into stand-down mode soon in order to sleep, resupply, and get some new personnel to replace the men we had lost to injuries. We were still amazed that we had not suffered any KIAs from our recent fight with Charlie.

Once we reached our extraction location, we lagered, posted security, and began to hack out an LZ. During the night we had spent at the site of the NVA bunker complex, Battalion had given us a squad of engineers, and those "cave killers" were still with us. Their chainsaws helped us to cut the LZ in half our normal time.

Everyone was dog-tired, and we reeked. I smelled so bad that the skeeters did not bother me, unless they were wearing gas masks. I was so filthy that I had crud on my crud. I was with one of my squads on security, lying there watching a little trail. A big leech was heading my way. When he got a good whiff of me, the bastard turned up his nose and passed me by.

Let's face it, if Charlie could not smell us, he needed to see a doctor. Besides, those chainsaws made such a racket that it really did not matter where we were. Charlie could easily find us, but he chose not to for reasons unknown to us.

Our birds came in on time, the CO popped smoke, and we slicked out. We were airborne in minutes, and the birds carried us back to LZ Miguel, which was then the farthest forward Cav LZ. It was located much farther north than Evans.

Once we were on the ground in our assigned positions, our log men[15] came to our aid with a complete supply of everything we needed. Some of our 81mm mortar ammunition was banged up, and we would not fire it unless there was an emergency.

That night we finally had hot water for washing, hot chow, and a fresh supply of jungle fatigues. Doc B. wanted to send Tran, our Vietnamese scout, to Evans or Phu Bai for better medical attention, but Tran refused to go, just as he had refused to leave on the first dust-off birds. It was nice to hear why Tran would not leave us. He was afraid that if he left, we would get someone to replace him. He said that Black Knight Alfa was the best company he had ever worked with. We made him know that he was a part of us, and we were a part of him. Brotherhood goes a long way when you are out there eyeball to eyeball with old Death 25 hours every day.

Our battalion commander made a special trip to LZ Miguel to congratulate us and to spend time visiting with us, and that made us feel very good. We were behind the green line, so it was possible for him to talk to everyone in the company at the same time. He told us that the things we had found in the main bunker and the supply bunker were "extremely valuable". He also praised our victory over the enemy, referring to the prisoners who had rolled over and sung their hearts out, to the Russian officer who would advise no more, and to the Chinese advisor who was so vain that he had kept a little red book on himself that contained enough evidence in his own handwriting to convict him in any court of law for murdering American soldiers.

After the fight at the bunkers, we had also collected quite a big haul of war booty, or trading supplies as we called them. We had a good supply of AK-47s, communist flags, racing slicks, and other things that we could trade to the navy, air force, and anyone else who was willing to trade with us. Money was never involved in our trades, and we mostly traded for steaks, ribs, and other commodities that were difficult for us to get.

Can you believe that most of the objects worth taking from the bunkers were made in America? There was even a case of our protective masks, as well as American cigarettes, toilet paper, candy, batteries, and much more. I wondered where the enemy had gotten that stuff, or more importantly, who might have supplied it to them.

Some of the items that we had recovered from the bunker were on their way back to Pentagon East. Our S-2 and G-2 were having a ball. Even some of the half-burned documents were yielding up great amounts of information, which our battalion commander said was already saving American lives. He also told us that it did not matter that we had been lost when we found that bunker. What mattered was that we had not fallen. We had recovered nicely and had gone on to lock up with a well dug-in unit four times our size. Most importantly, we had almost wiped them out without having casualties of our own. Our battalion commander told us that Snoopy, our own Cav LURPS, and SOG reported that between the navy and us, we had really hurt the NVA. Our little showdown at the OK Bunker Corral had encouraged the remaining Charlies to scatter all over the jungle and to run back toward their areas of control.

Battalion also announced that they had positive evidence that an entire NVA regiment had been moving to assist the besieged bunker, until they were called back when the Grand Old Lady of the Seven Seas interceded on our behalf. The SOG officer with the battalion commander informed us of the reason for the delay in our receiving the requested naval gunfire. An SOG team had been dogging that NVA regiment, so it was necessary for the team to be pulled back before the *New Jersey* could shoot for us.

Upon hearing the battalion commander's praise for us, our morale and fighting spirits rose considerably. It meant a lot to us grunts. It was also nice to know that our Grand Company was part of a wonderfully efficient team, which included those in command and control who planned the operations, as well as the pilots who flew us into enemy-held territory.

Our troops were also happy because our battalion commander delivered our mail from home. After we received our mail, we enjoyed a wonderful hot supper. Our cooks came out and prepared most of the meal in front of us, using portable grills. We ate steak, potatoes, fresh green salad, and apple pie, and we drank cold beer and soft drinks. The steaks were the result of some of our on-hand trading materials, previously received.

Before it was too late, our log personnel and cooks slicked out to go back to our company's rear position. They left some of the heavier and bulkier stuff behind for transport on the next day. The battalion commander and the SOG officer stayed to eat with us. Then they flew back to battalion headquarters.

After our rear personnel left, we settled in for a long-awaited, good night of sleep. Of course, we did not get to sleep. Around 0300 hours, old Charlie decided to be a complete nuisance by running on that most distant firebase. We had already been instructed to stay put if the bastard made a run on the firebase because we were unfamiliar with it. We were simply supposed to wait for a signal from the base security unit. If they popped a green star cluster straight up, then it was time for us to duck. If they popped a red star cluster, we were supposed to take our assigned defensive positions for "show time"! Soon, they popped the green star cluster and we ducked.

The American security unit allowed the sappers to penetrate the wire on the north end of the firebase, before the 105mm artillery batteries began their devastating salvos of canister shots fired low and directly into the sappers' surprised faces. The thousands of buckshots and the satchel charges the sappers were carrying contributed to their express trip to hell.

The infantry unit guarding the firebase was not all Cav, but they definitely had their shit together. They kicked off on old Charlie like he was a stepchild. Old Charlie was painfully aware that he was in Cav Country, and it was not long before he picked up his marbles and diddy maued the area.

By the time Charlie left, it was too late to go back to sleep. We started to get ready for the long day ahead of us. Some of our troopers' ponchos and poncho liners were torn to shreds by the canister shot because they had been placed too high above the ground. We were okay with that, though, because it was a small sacrifice to make in exchange for seeing a lot of sappers cross barbed wire for the last time.

After breakfast we slicked out to LZ Mooney. Once there, we were given positions along the green line. By the time we were set up in our positions, it was chow time. After we ate, the platoon sergeants were called to the company CP for a meeting and a briefing. We received confirmation on the Chinese soldier in the main bunker; however, one other Chinese soldier had managed to escape. That escapee was so badly chewed up that he was sent all the way back home. The one whom we had killed, however, was one of Charlie's very best men. So much for his very best.

Our success in taking out the bunker complex certainly did not go to our heads. We knew that circumstances might not have worked in our favor and that our continuing salvation remained in our own hands and depended upon our ability to do the unexpected, to be where we were not expected to be, to always fight as a team, and never to underestimate Charlie. That way we could always be ahead of him and continue to survive.

After two days on the green line, we received haircuts, shaves, baths, good hot chow, and any mail packages that we had holed up in the company rear. Two days of stand-down time was enough for us because we did not want to lose our fighting edge, which had always stood us in good stead when we came up against our enemies – Charlie, the Cong, the Russians, and the Chinese. The word on the vine was that we were going back north into the mountains, where we would be working our AO alone. We liked it that way because anyone not with our team was obviously the enemy, giving us no qualms to light him up as quickly as possible.

The CO said we were going up against a well-known NVA battalion of seasoned regulars. We had previously crossed swords with members of this battalion, having fought them in the Ia Drang Valley and having locked up with some of their seasoned veterans on the plains at Bong Son. We had also seen some of their handiwork applied to defenseless civilians after the Battle of Hue. Every Black Knight Alfa Skytrooper who had "been there before" was looking forward to our next meeting with the NVA.

Just before dark on our last evening at Mooney, the outgoing first sergeant flew back to the rear on our last log bird. His tour of duty was over, and he was going to catch that big old freedom bird back to the good old US of A. At that time I became the new first sergeant of the best infantry company in the world. I was Alfa Five, but my troops called me "Top". We were going to surf the outer regions of hell together and then come back together. Black Knight Alfa. Alpha and Omega!

After the outgoing first sergeant said goodbye, I took a few minutes to really talk to my new company. (This is something we did in the old Brown Shoe Army.) I kept my speech brief because it was not safe to bunch up together, even on Mooney and behind the green line. As I had been taught by the Buffalo Soldiers many years ago, I talked to my troops on an eye-to-eye, heart-to-heart level. Rank was an absent factor because I knew better than to talk down to my troopers. I could feel them listening to me, and I knew that they heard everything I said. The last thing I did at that time was to teach them our new statement of truth:

> Before us there were none,
> While we are here there are
> no others.
> After we are gone there shall be
> no more!

We ended that meeting with our battle cry:

BLACK KNIGHT ALFA. ALPHA AND OMEGA!

At that point, I knew with certainty that we would walk the road to hell and back and that we would do it as a team. Knowing that made me feel good.

On the morning of our departure from LZ Mooney, the first rays of the morning sun found us already marshaled into our lift formation. We were going out by Hooks and when the word was passed "Birds inbound!" I looked in the direction of approach and saw the familiar outline and the twin rotors of the incoming flight of Boeing Vertol CH-47 Chinook helicopters. The Chinooks, or Hooks as we called them, were the workhorses of our division. This was also true for most of the American and South Vietnamese units in the Nam. I guess you could say the Hooks were very much like those big rigs that are a normal sight on America's highways.

We were airborne in record time, and without a hitch, the Hooks took us to LZ Barbara. From there we were going to Charley Alfa into our first insertion point/LZ. We waited in the area of Barbara's landing pad for our lift of slicks to take us the rest of the way in. During our wait, I asked the CO if I might run down to the TOC to see an old, dear friend of mine, and he said okay. When I reached the TOC, I found a sergeant major standing outside, smoking a cigarette. I decided to make my first inquiry with him. I asked if he knew Master Sergeant Smith (Smitty) and if Smitty was on duty.

The sergeant major's face took on a very sad expression, which aged his appearance a bit. He asked if I were a relative of Smitty's because we looked so much alike. I responded no, and then I told him that Smitty and I had been young soldiers together at Harmony Church, Fort Benning, and also back in the days of the old Brown Shoe Army.

The sergeant major looked even sadder and older then. He slowly pointed toward a neat row of dead soldiers lying wrapped in their ponchos or poncho liners. When I first arrived at the TOC, I did not notice them because I was so excited at the thought of seeing my old friend Smitty again. I do not remember how many bodies were there, but they were lying closely together in a neat row, waiting to begin their last long journey home to America.

"Sergeant Smith is the one next to the last on the far end," the sergeant major whispered. He then turned and quickly walked away from me.

My legs turned into lead, and I could hardly walk the distance to where my friend was lying, dead. I grew numb and speechless, and my hands shook as I stopped by Smitty's body, trying to decide whether to look at him or to remember him as he had appeared when I had last seen him alive.

Dear God! Dear God! The pain was all-consuming, and my head ached. I thought about when I had been a young lad and everyone had said that "a man ain't supposed to cry". I guess I ain't a man, because that is just what I did. I told myself just to walk on back up to the landing pad because it would be better that way. However, I could not do that. I had to say goodbye to my dear, old friend. My head was so foggy, and I felt as if I were floating in another world. I fought for control because it is not good to let yourself fly apart.

In that time and place, there was just Smitty and I. I knelt down near his head and gently moved the poncho aside to look into his face "One More Time". I could not hold back the moan of pain that escaped from my lips and racked my whole body. Oh my dear Lord, he must not have been wearing his steel pot. That dreadful sight of him haunts me to this day. Smitty and I used to sing Jodie cadence to our basic training companies as we returned from the ranges at forts Leonard Wood, Jackson, and Polk. We had soldiered together in A-burg, Munich, Ulm, Kitzingen, and in "The Land of the Morning Calm". It was so heartbreaking to see him lying there in that condition. I covered his face again and prayed to God that when my time came, I would go out with dignity.

A young soldier saw me kneeling by Smitty's body and came over to tell me what had happened. Smitty had volunteered for a night patrol, and old Charlie had waited and caught the patrol unit just as they were about to come back through their lines. That time, Charlie's tired old game had worked, and my dear friend was dead as a result. The pain, oh the pain!

At that moment, I resolved always to wear my steel pot. I also made up my mind that I would exact a terrible vengeance on Charlie wherever and whenever I might encounter him. My days of possibly cutting Charles some slack were over.

It was a saddening occasion to begin the new day by having to look into the dead face of one of my dearest friends and to see what Charlie had done to him. When I stood up, my hands were no longer shaking, and my tears were frozen on my face.

Pete ran down the hill to get me. "Top, our birds are inbound," he said.

Because there was no replacement for me as the First Platoon sergeant, I asked if I could retain that position, and the CO said yes. So, I was the first sergeant and the platoon sergeant of One-Six.

It was not a good time to shift leadership positions, and I was definitely the senior NCO in our company in age, rank (I was still a sergeant first class), and time in grade. The CO and I felt confident about our decision because the immediate situation called for us to face a strong, dedicated enemy, who would be working the killing grounds, trying to send our souls to hell. To win, we had to get there first with the most.

The job of bringing in our birds was normally that of the first sergeant, so I said goodbye to Smitty and ran back with Pete to pop smoke and bring in our birds. As I waited for the lead bird to touch down, I promised Smitty that we would stand reveille again, side by side, either on the streets of heaven or hell.

The CO left on the lead bird, and I rode on the drag bird. Shortly before we slicked out, Battalion gave us their recent report from our Cav LURPS. There was enemy activity within our newly assigned AO. Therefore, we would have to search and destroy on the way to our main objective.

Once we were all in the air, we linked up with two other companies from our battalion. There were a lot of birds in that lift because we had a long way to go and the birds had to maintain enough fuel to get back to their bases after they dropped us off. This limited the number of men that each bird could carry.

Once we were near our LZ and our insertion point, we cheered at the ever-beautiful sight of the fighting Cobras. Blue Max took up their positions to escort us on the final leg of our flight. There were two flights of Cobras, and they were packing heavy. Old Blue Max were the absolute boss wherever they happened to be.

Under the many watchful eyes of Blue Max, we went in, and as usual, the skids of our birds never touched the ground. We jumped on the move, and the birds were gone, up, up and away. The loud whump-whumping of the rotor blades biting into the warm, humid air sounded like the musical notes of a gigantic symphony orchestra, playing the opening music to a sold-out play. It was a long-running play in which we had performed our parts many times before. The curtain was slowly rising for the first act.

When we reached the ground, we were already formed and in motion. The other two companies went together in one direction, and we fell in behind them for a short run. Then, we took off in an entirely different direction. Our troops were in good spirits, and we could feel one another's presence everywhere, even though we were very well spread out. I could still feel each platoon as if I could actually see them.

When the time was right, we paused to become one with our surroundings. It was a matter of becoming acclimatized to our new AO. For all of our survival senses to function properly, we had to adjust to the new sounds, smells, winds, and general feelings. Once we were acclimated to our new environment, we noticed anything that was out of place, and we reacted accordingly. Our quick reaction time kept us in good health. It did not take us long to adjust, and before long we were on our way again. I once heard one of our troopers say that we had reverted back to our basic animal nature, to our caveman beginnings. The more I thought about it, I could not agree more.

I do not think that modern men could have existed in the Vietnamese jungles of that time, at least not under the conditions that we survived. Naturally, many of those jungles were Charlie's home – his back and front yards – and a young American lad from the streets of Philadelphia was totally out of place. He had to adjust, to acclimatize himself to his new environment, to become one with his surroundings. When he could taste the wind, see everything, hear the flutter of butterfly wings, and smell and feel the nearness of Charlie, only then did he have the potential to survive. We developed these senses and became creatures of nature and of the jungle because we were determined to survive.

One-Six was designated to be the drag platoon, which placed me at the rear.

In our battalion, it was standard operating procedure (SOP) for the first sergeant to push the bush right along with his troops. I am not certain, but I think it was that way with all of the line infantry companies in the Cav Division.

The situation confronting me and the brave young men of One-Six was instrumental in helping me to cope with the loss of my dear friend Smitty. My men were my bridge over troubled waters and would prove to be that same bridge over all the troubled waters we were destined to cross. Sweet Jesus! They were the finest of the finest young men, and I felt good to be out there with them. One young trooper in my third squad started calling me Top even before I was moved into the position of first sergeant on our official company manning charts. He said to me, "Top, you got to put the sad memories of your dead friend in your pocket, because you gotta have a clear mind out here dealing with Charlie, or he'll get you, too. And we don't want that to happen. We don't want anything to happen to you. You gotta admit your buddy was pushing it. Maybe he was thinking of home, a cold beer, or something, and that's when Charlie got him."

That young soldier's words rang true and snapped me back to the business at hand. I thanked him and quickly regained control of myself. I put my mind, my heart, and all my senses to the task at hand, which was to accomplish our mission without losing any men.

That damned war had already cost me the lives of many dear, old friends, and every day that number grew. Dear God, I did not know it then, but the number of my dear old friends who were killed would, in the end, make me an orphan. Thank God, I was surrounded by the magnificent young men of Black Knight Alfa. It made me proud beyond mere words. My cup was running over.

After some long, hard hours of humping the bush and fighting those wait-a-minute vines, the CO signaled that the first of our objectives was near. Visibility was poor in some places because of the jungle canopy, and the heat was almost unbearable. It felt like we were in a huge pressure cooker. The canopy seemed to be double, which greatly restricted our mortar men's chances of effectively hip shooting our mortars. They had perfected the ability to "shoot through" some single canopies when those canopies were not too dense with large branches. When a canopy was sparse,[16] our mortar men would shoot through the holes and put their rounds down on top of Charlie, who was busy thinking that we could not shoot because of poor mask clearance on the canopy. Meanwhile, we were putting his shit on the fan. Naturally, some rounds occasionally hit a branch and went off, but we sure as hell gave it a try. If we got some rounds through,[17] then old Charles picked up the tab.

Needless to say, it was pure hell as we pushed on. The air seemed to grow hotter with every passing second, but each of us continued humping to the max. I was carrying two 81mm high-explosive rounds and two bandoleers of 100 rounds each for our machine guns. The CO was packing a similar amount. In our company everyone packed heavy when we were on such a mission, and none of my men ever complained about it.

Sweat burned my eyes and made it hard to see at times. Unfortunately, we could not carry towels around our necks to wipe the sweat from our eyes because the only ones available were white, and we certainly did not want to give Charlie some easy shooting targets. We had to hit the ground a number of times, and the leeches were all over us. We knew to wear our sleeves down and to tuck in our trouser-leg bottoms, and it was so miserably hot that these clothing restrictions made the heat even worse. Four-Six reported that one of their men was wearing old two step around his neck. Two step had dropped down on the poor guy (a common occurrence in the Vietnamese jungles). Faith

45

was still humping with us though, because the man managed to throw the snake off himself before it bit him. What luck! Maybe that old two step had sweat in his eyes, too.

We slowed down and got ready to rumble because everyone was starting to smell and feel Charlie. Although there was no wind, our method of approach made it possible for us to smell him a long time before he could smell us. Once we knew where he was positioned, the CO signaled for the company to move into a large diamond formation. The Second Platoon was leading in a diamond formation. The Third Platoon split with two squads right and two left, with the Weapons Platoon and the Headquarters section occupying the center. The drag platoon was in a diamond formation to the rear of the Weapons Platoon. As usual we were spread way out and staggered. We used our radios to maintain contact, but only when it was necessary. If some wind had been present, we might have operated differently. Fortunately, the lack of a breeze made it harder for Charlie to pick up the scent of our bug juice.

We approached Charlie with caution so as not to disturb the birds and the monkeys in the jungle. The Second Platoon already had a security team posted forward because we did not know the size of the enemy position. We maintained our spread-out posture in case Charlie had active security posted. After we had Charlie fixed, we would go into another formation. Pete informed me that the Second Platoon had a man down in a punji pit. All of our platoons reported that there were traps all around, so we had to slow down and be extra alert.

We had no way of knowing if Charlie's traps were backed up with other traps or if someone was guarding them. We waited while Two-Six got their man out of the punji pit. The punji pit was one of the cowardly traps that Charlie used to wound, demoralize, and/or kill us without having to face us. The punji pit was a deeply dug hole with bamboo stakes driven into the ground with the sharpened ends pointing upward. Often, similar stakes were driven into the sides of the pit with the sharpened ends pointing outward. When Charlie finished the inside of the punji pit, he concealed its opening with a light covering of branches, leaves, and dirt. When someone stepped on the flimsy covering, he would crash through and land on the sharpened stakes. Occasionally, death came instantly to a punji pit victim, but most of the time, the only thing instant was the pain. Charlie fashioned the pointed ends of his bamboo stakes to be very sharp, and he hardened them in a fire and covered them with human shit to poison the pierced victims. I had seen a few fellow soldiers impaled in those cowardly traps, but they had refused to cry out because doing so would have given away the location of our entire company. Sometimes old Charlie marked his traps, so his own people would not fall in, and we knew most of his markings. Our man who was just caught was the first one in a long time. Sometimes we found Charlie's traps and made an adjustment to them. I do so hope that our little changes hurt Charles as much as he was always planning to hurt us.

While we waited, our security team moved forward, looking for Charlie. They discovered him moving steadily away from us, and the team leader reported his opinion that Charlie did not know we were dogging him.

The CO directed security to wait and hold what they had. By that time, our trooper was out of the punji pit, and fortunately, his wounds were not life-threatening. That punji pit was an old one, and time had lessened its bite. That is when we discovered that all of Charlie's traps were old and, therefore, no longer deadly.

Because the enemy was ahead of us and the surrounding jungle was "trap heaven", the CO decided that we would take an avenue.[18] We moved easily into our column formation and out along the same trail that Charlie was using. When we picked up our security team, they told the CO everything they knew about the enemy. We strung out with good distance between units and individuals, and we moved along quietly that way for an hour or so.

I realize that you may have been told that using a trail was a no-no; however, we found that it was sometimes the best way to go, and this was one of those times. We also liked to do the unexpected.

Suddenly, I had a gut feeling that something was wrong! Oh man, I had let something slip through the cracks, and it was haunting the hell out of me. When I realized what I had forgotten to do, I moved up close to Hansen and told him to take JoJo and drop back to sweep our tail and see if Charlie was dogging us.

You see, it was the drag unit's responsibility to drop a team off to sweep our tail, and I had let it slip for too long. My thinking about Smitty could have been detrimental to us. Out there, you had to keep your head or lose it to Charlie. I recalled my young soldier's recent advice, and I felt rather sick. He was right on the money.

Our usual procedure was for the team (or the man) who was selected to drop back, while other platoon members took their (or his) load. Then they would pick a good position, fall out of the formation, lie dog, and wait for our tail to come along. When the team dropped out, the rest of us kept walking so that anyone watching would not notice the change in our formation. This technique worked very well for us.

I informed the CO that our team was out, and he told me he would stop the forward movement on my signal. From positions of maximum concealment, our team waited in ambush for anyone who was dogging our trail. The rest of the company proceeded along our route until I gave the signal to hold up. Upon my signal, the company lagered, and we waited. We were wise to Charlie's tricks. He would often assign a single Charlie to follow an American unit and report back to his puppet master, or that Charlie would follow the unit until they set up for the night and then he would point out their FOB to his unit so that they knew where to attack.

The team we dropped off had to be good, quick, silent, and totally deadly. They traveled lightly most of the time because their mission was not to engage in fighting but to take out the person(s) dogging us without so much as a whisper. Once our company stopped and formed a defensive/fighting circle, they could (with the added defense of our mortars) fire in any given direction and shoot for our drop-off team if necessary. The SOP for when we were hit called for our thump gunners to automatically thump any trail that was near us and to thump the front and rear of the trail that we were on.

If our team caught a Charlie dogging our tail, they always tried to take him out as silently as possible. Like the best game hunters, they did not let their quarries gurgle. Most of the time, they had to use knives. JoJo was our best knifeman; he was silent, efficient, and as deadly as they come.

Sure enough, we had a tail, which was my fault, plain and simple. I had let my mind wander too far from my job. Maybe that is what happened to Smitty. I promised to kick my own butt after the deal went down.

Our team already had the tail in hand and was waiting to determine if he was alone. After about five minutes, I told them to come on home. Once they pulled in, I sent a machine gun-heavy team a short way down the trail to ambush the same. The CO wanted to talk to Charlie, so we moved to a better and more easily defended position, with our machine gun-heavy team running drag. We were not taking any chances.

After the company lagered and our drag team came home, the CO, Tran, and Redleg, who spoke very good Vietnamese, came to "talk" to our prisoner. I must tell you how we did it because it will help you to better understand the modus operandi of the Grand Company of Black Knight Alfa.

At first, we just looked at Charlie. Naturally, he had already been strip-searched. By simply looking at him, we could tell that he was not hardcore. Rather, he was scared, and the leeches had eaten up his young ass. Therefore, we already had his undivided attention. The CO nodded his head, giving the okay for Doc B. to attend to the young man's many leech bites and God knows what else. Hansen gave the young NVA soldier a candy bar. In this way, we got on the young Charlie's good side, and he began to sing.

We were very happy to learn that he had been dogging us only for about 20 minutes before JoJo and Hansen brought him down. We had not passed him; instead, he had caught up to us, coming up on our rear all the way. Knowing that he had dogged us for just a short time did not make me feel any better about my mistake. If I had been paying attention instead of having my head up my butt, that Charlie would have been behind us for no more than 10 minutes before we would have brought him down. I promised myself that I would never make that mistake again. I admitted to the CO that it was solely my fault that Charlie had dogged us for that long. The CO just smiled and said that it was no big thing "as long as there was a lesson learned." Yes indeed, there was.

Fortunately for that Charlie, when Hansen put the habeas grabeas on him, they decided not to do him in, as long as he cooperated. The young Charlie never got cute with them and did as he was told. Therefore, they brought him home with the hope that he might shed some light on the situation.

We already knew that when the NVA dropped off a man to dog an American unit, they always chose a man like this Charlie for the job because if he were caught, he could only provide us with minimal information. On the other hand, we knew the chances were good that Charlie knew much more than his superiors realized. With this in mind, we questioned our prisoner.

We were as nice as pie to him, and he swore to Tran that he was alone. Although there were others with his same mission, they were not working with him. He was a hard hat[19] and a regular, even at his young age. Of course, we did not believe what Charlie said just because we were smiling at each other and he was working on his second candy bar. We observed "how" he spoke as he started talking to Tran and Redleg with assistance from JoJo and his sharp knife. Still smiling, Tran explained to the young Charlie that if he wanted to retain possession of his balls, he must tell us the truth. Otherwise, JoJo would cut off his balls and feed them to him on a banana leaf. This threat made the little Charlie sing like a hopped-up canary. He swore that he was telling us the whole truth and nothing but the truth. Of course, we still did not believe everything he told us, but we were able to extract some valuable information from the young lad before we turned him over to our S-2 section.

Most importantly, we learned that originally there had been two Charlies and when they had located us, the other one skirted wide around the high ground and ran ahead to tell the main body that we were following them. Supposedly, they did not have a radio. Without the enemy soldier having to tell us, we figured out that we were up against a wise and resourceful enemy who was a full cut above some of the more recent Charlies we had smeared.

We had acquired real information from the young Charlie just by watching him and seeing his limited equipment. We examined his AK-47 and asked ourselves the following questions: Was it Russian- or Chinese-made? How much ammunition was he carrying? What was the condition of his ammunition? How much rice was in his rice bag? How much water did he have, and was it good water?

There was something that made us sit up and take notice of that smiling little Charlie. He was well smeared with an ample supply of our good old American, US Army bug juice. The implications of that were enormous. Try this on for size. The little guy was hardly dirty, yet covered with open sores from leeches. He did not stink. He was wearing a lot of our bug juice and had almost a full bottle on him when Hansen brought him down. Wearing the bug juice would have allowed him to get real close to us because we would have been unable to pick up his distinctive NVA or Viet Cong scent. Although the little bastard smelled a lot like us, there was a noticeable difference between our smell and his that was hard to detect at first.

Everyone stopped talking to Charlie and began to study him more carefully and with greater respect. Naturally, we were not respecting him so much as whoever had put him on our tail.

The little Charlie saw that we were on to him, and his expression changed into one of greater fear. His eyes grew very large and cloudy. Not one of our troopers said a word to him. He sat on the ground while we stared at him in silence. He asked Tran if we were going to torture and kill him. He said that his superiors told him if we caught him, we would cut off his dick and his ears. Yet there was Doc B. tending to his leech bites, and we were feeding him. He knew that Hansen could have killed him. He said that the working conditions and fringe benefits were lousy on the other side, so he wanted to roll over if we would let him.

Now was the time for us to do the unexpected, but first, the CO, Redleg, and I had to put our heads together. We fully realized that to remain where we were was pushing it. Yet, something of great value had been thrust upon us suddenly, and we had to make a decision quickly.

The key to the whole mess was our new friend Charlie. First, we considered whether we had caught him or he had caught us. That is why we already had security teams out in four directions. We would not be caught napping. Here is what it boiled down to:

a. The Charlie was wearing a clean uniform and his rice bag was empty.
b. His AK-47 was in mint condition, Russian-made, and not dirty enough for his situation.
c. He was clean and did not stink, yet his body was covered with leech bites.
d. His ammunition was clean and of the same lot number.[20]
e. He had bug juice.

When Tran asked Charlie which direction he had come from, the little man automatically said that his unit was in front of us, which was at least 100 degrees away from the direction of his first instinctive glance. The CO, Redleg, Tran, our RTOs, and I moved some distance away from and behind the little Charlie.

"Top, what do you think?" the CO asked.

51

"Sir, I think we got us a live one. I know you already noticed that Charlie is wearing shoes instead of racing slicks, and from the looks of them, he has not been in the bush too long. So wherever he came from is not too far. Due to the size of our AO, where he came from might very well be in our AO. Also, I think his offer to roll over stinks."

Everyone basically agreed with me.

Tran said, "Sir, I think I can get him to come clean, 'cause I feel that he is unhappy with his position or status in his unit. He doesn't want to be here. He isn't hardcore."

"Okay, Tran, you've got five minutes. Tell him to come clean, or we'll ice him and leave his ass to rot," Redleg said.

The CO nodded. Of course, we would not do that, but we were hoping to bluff Charlie. Besides, the horror stories that his superiors had already told him might work on our behalf.

Tran rattled at Charlie for about three minutes before Charlie said, "Yes!"

Charlie agreed to do what we asked, and in return, we promised to get him safely to Saigon. With some reluctance, he led us to his unit. We were originally heading almost due north, but now Charlie was pointing us in a south-easterly direction.

The CO got on the radio and told our battalion commander what was going down. Battalion had some reservations; however, we were doing what we were told to do. If the enemy unit we were following had maintained the same pace, they would be long gone by now. So Battalion gave us the green light, and we were told to keep them up to date on our location. There were other American units operating in that general vicinity. If everyone was where they said they were, we were still alone and could do our thing.

Actually, the camp was only about an hour's push away, or perhaps less than that considering that we were moving very slowly and carefully. We were uncertain as to whether or not we were falling into a trap that Charlie, the little teacher, had been instructed to lead us into. We soon learned that our little friend was, in fact, a school teacher. How about that for a coincidence!

NVA University

The Second Platoon remained in the lead, the Third Platoon was moved to drag, and the First Platoon was pulled up to the rear of the Weapons Platoon. Our formation was designed to facilitate rapid reactions just in case the lead element came under accurate fire. If that happened, my platoon would become the base of fire, and the Third Platoon would become the fire brigade.

We were close to the training camp, which was so well camouflaged that we almost missed it. Clearly, Charlie had done an excellent job of hiding his special little university. What had helped our lead platoon to find it was the enemy's version of a fire brigade moving into their outlying defensive positions. I might add that we caught them "in between".

The camp defenders were hard hats and Viet Cong. Although they put up a good fight, they lost. We sent the Third Platoon down to the edge of a creek that ran along one side of the camp. Once there, they held the surprised defenders while we whacked them. The enemy fought us hard and fast, but their best was not good enough. In a short time, we took over their camp, but unfortunately, some of them slipped our grasp.

Once in charge, the CO told Battalion what we had, and Battalion called for help, although they had no idea where the camp was located. We posted our security team and assigned one man to guard our little teacher friend while we searched the place. It was not large, but its contents were very good.

The jungle training camp sat in a big circle under the jungle canopy, which was expertly hidden from our spotter aircraft. It was so well camouflaged that unless someone made noise within the camp, no one would know it was there. You could pass within 50 meters and not see anything unusual or out of place.

According to our little song bird, the reason there was only a skeleton force guarding the camp was that Charlie had received word that two of our Cav companies (the two who had come in with us) were heading in the direction of their camp. Therefore, the bulk of the staff, faculty, and student body had run off to try to turn our other two companies around. That is probably where the unit we were originally dogging was headed. That was also why it only took us a few minutes to take over the camp curriculum. Otherwise, those camp defenders who had run off would have been ratting on us.

Before us there were none.
While we are here there are no others,
After we are gone, there shall be no more.

Alpha and Omega Forever!

BLACK KNIGHT ALFA!

Blocking Position

To make the best of the developing situation, Battalion sent units to assist the two companies who had come in to help us, and they left a small unit to guard Charlie's jungle training center. They sent us to establish a blocking position along an excellent terrain feature that enabled us to command and dominate a critical ridge line and a narrow portion of the valley floor. Not only was the ridge line an important part of the Ho Chi Minh Trail, but it was also critical to Charlie because it offered cover and concealment and allowed speed of movement to the NVA and VC units.

Our mission was twofold. We would establish a good blocking position and deny Charlie the use of that ridge-line trail if he tried to send reinforcements south. From our blocking position, we would also prevent Charlie from using either the valley or the ridge-line trail as a northern escape route.

We monitored the battle even as we quickly moved to reach our new positions on that excellent terrain feature. Battalion was calling down a lot of shit on old Charlie, and he had to do something or face ruin. If you are wondering why Battalion did not have us slicked in, our objective was to get to the terrain feature and to hold it without Charlie knowing we were there.

The CO and I thought the battalion commander had given the job to Black Knight Alfa because he knew we would accomplish the task. Whether Charlie was traveling north or south, we would be there to make him pay the final toll in order to pass by us. Our mission was to send him straight to hell by the most direct route, but only after he paid his fee.

We were determined to reach our new positions before dark and to do it without Charlie even suspecting that we were in the area. This was going to be quite a challenge, considering that we were moving in broad daylight and at a rather quick pace, despite the few things that slowed us down a bit. We were still packing heavy because we had used very few of our supplies while taking over the jungle training camp. Also, S-2 had given us a Forward Air Control (FAC) team of air force personnel (an officer and two enlisted men), who clearly were not used to humping the bush. It was almost an impossible mission, but doing the impossible was our middle name. There was no doubt in anyone's mind; the Grand Company was ready to take on the challenge. It also helped that Blue Max was on station, serving as our guardian angel.

We practically ran all the way to that excellent terrain feature, and we reached it before dark, giving us enough time to do our thing. Everyone was dog-tired, strung-out, and drenched with sweat, but we did not become victims and the quality of our work did not suffer.

We did not overlook the fact that if that terrain feature was so damned good, it would also suit Charlie's needs. Therefore, before moving onto it, we lagered and sent two machine gun-heavy scout parties onto the position. When they signaled an okay, the entire company moved forward and occupied the terrain feature.

Before we moved any further toward our objective, Redleg planned our artillery supporting fires and concentrations, which included a protective "wall of steel" just in case Charlie came too close for comfort. Finally, we planned the usual "farewell thumbing of our noses to Charlie", whereupon our artillery fire would fall directly on top of our positions if we were in danger of being snuffed out by Charlie. In such a situation, we would not give Charlie the satisfaction of killing us.

We had the most faithful and accurate artillery fire support in the world. Those magnificent artillerymen shot for us anytime, anywhere, and under any condition. Their accuracy was legendary. Using anywhere from 105s to 175s, they could shoot from any distance and hit their target. Sometimes, it was a matter of life or death for us to walk their fire right upon us, and sweet Jesus, they always delivered. I can still hear them yelling into their mikes, "ON THE WAY!" or "SHOT OUT!"

From an old man and from Black Knight Alfa, we say "THANKS" to all of you guys still out there.

We were scheduled to receive the fires from two batteries of 175s, and they would be firing at maximum range, give or take a meter. Redleg locked us in tightly because our tired asses were out there all alone.

We went about getting into our new positions, and we did not stop until we were up tight and all right and as steady as the fabled Rock of Gibraltar. We were ready for Charles in record time and before total darkness came calling. It was not necessary to pass the word to dig in because our troopers knew exactly what to do. Digging in was simply a part of our continued good health and survival.

Our security and scout teams were already out, and we knew that Charlie was not nearby. Yet, we knew that he would be coming. The situation dictated that he would try to pass us without paying his toll.

The position that we held was a tactical dream, and it would definitely prove to be one of Charlie's worst nightmares. We were in a position to hurt him very badly if he tried to use the ridge or the narrow bottleneck portion of the valley floor that we were carefully guarding.

We put on old Charlie's racing slicks and looked at the situation from his point of view. Our other Cav units were eating up his ass, and he was trying to hold on until he could use the cover of darkness to slip away. Charlie was a master at knowing when it was time to pick up his marbles and run for the hills, and we were the masters at figuring out what he was planning to do. We knew he was coming our way, and he would be moving rapidly. We also knew that our guys would not be chasing him, even though they would certainly make Charlie believe they were dogging his ass.

We knew that Charlie was capable of doing anything under the cover of darkness, especially since he knew that darkness hindered our air support but not our artillery fire support. Once darkness fell, Charlie would be up to his old tricks, although we were already familiar with most of them. We were grand masters of deception, and we honed our own brand of deception to a fine point. It was like life insurance to us.

We determined when Charlie might break contact with the Cav units who were locked onto his ass, and we also estimated the time it would take him to reach us. We had a good plan in place, and we were there to catch him in the act, no matter what act he was planning.

Our security and scouting teams laid snaps and traps for Charlie. When they returned home from their outing, they showed us on our maps the exact locations of those snaps and traps. Consequently, if Charlie came near us and popped a claymore or set off a flare, we would know exactly where he was. He also had a tendency to scream bloody murder when he was loaded up with buckshot.

Let's face it. Old Charlie was not the superman that our news media and a certain person of distinction made him appear to be. He screamed just like anyone else when a claymore was popped on his ass.

In truth, Charlie, the NVA, and the Viet Cong did not have a monopoly on how to use the cover of darkness to their advantage. You were probably not told this in America, but we were just as good as, and in some cases a hell of a lot better than, Charlie could ever hope to be.

When our last listening post came home, they gave us an accurate report of what we were facing. Charlie was coming our way, but he was not moving as quickly as we had thought. He was dragging a lot of wounded with him, which told us that our other Cav units were chewing his ass quite well. Our team had also gotten a quick look at Charlie's lead unit, and they reported to the CO that the cautiously moving enemy had a small team forward and a connecting file. The majority of the enemy unit was some unknown distance behind, which was a wise move on Charlie's part.

This timely information was invaluable because it gave our commander some insight into the leadership of the enemy unit we were planning to hit. They were good soldiers, not just a mob like the VC. We knew when we hit them that we were going to have a real fight on our hands.

We had only minutes to prepare. Our fighting/defensive positions were rock solid. As always, we retained the flexibility to go with the tide, such as if we had to shift right or left.

If Charlie decided to send in fresh troops, they would most likely come south on the ridge-line trail. After viewing the narrow portion of the valley and noting that it did not offer the cover that the jungle canopy offered on the ridge line, we felt that Charlie would opt for the ridge line regardless of which direction he was traveling. Of course, there was always the chance that Charlie would lie dog and wait until around midnight or later to make his move. However, we were counting on him to run as far north as possible.

58

Our posted security teams said that Charlie was nearby and still proceeding north on the ridge-line trail, as we had assumed. Of course, the nearer he came to us, the better we could sense him. The CO and I shared a gut feeling that something unexpected was coming down.

"Top, have we overlooked something?" he asked.

Redleg, the FAC team, and I agreed that we had a good handle on the situation. I returned to my platoon.

Our security teams came home and slid into their assigned fighting positions. Once the last team was home, I received an "up" from all platoons. I informed the CO that we were all within our fighting/ defensive positions, which meant that we would light up anyone who approached our positions from the outside, even if he came dressed like the Pope.

The weather was quite decent. Darkness had brought a small amount of relief from the heat, and a slow breeze came through the valley, carrying the various odors of Charlie – odors of sweat, odors of various men and their most recent location, and odors of blood. No odors of fear were present.

That night there was a decent moon, and our night eyes were working perfectly. However, it was rather difficult to see Charlie clearly on the ridge line because it was covered with the edge of a canopy that cast shadows upon the majority of the trail. My M17 field glasses (compliments of my buddy Smitty) significantly improved my vision.

Previously, we had been able to predict old Charlie's actions, but on that night, we could not. As we lay in wait, watching him enter our kill zone, I used my field glasses to keep an eye on the lead element. As they approached, I had that same uncomfortable feeling that the CO also had, and what I then saw justified my feelings of uneasiness.

The lead element did not look dog-tired, as one would expect of a unit that had just had the piss kicked out of them. (Naturally, if the main unit was carrying wounded, they would be in the rear.) I noticed that the lead element were RPD[21]-heavy and that each man was wearing a pith helmet.[22] Something was out of line.

Except for the normal sounds of the jungle at night, all was quiet. We chose a section of the trail where the anticipated distance between Charlie and us would be within the maximum effective range of our M60 machine guns. We were well zeroed in on our kill zone. Our troopers had already laid snaps and traps along the trail, including claymores and flares. One set of flares was designated to start the action; its trip wires were positioned in an unavoidable place on the trail. Our initiating flare was not command-detonated because we were positioned too far away from the lead element and we did not want to position any of our men outside our perimeter when the fighting started.

Shortly before the lead man was due to trip the initiating flare, one Charlie wandered too far off the trail and tripped one of our back-up flares. Charlie was not exactly where we wanted him to be, but he was close enough within our kill zone for government work. After the flare was popped, the CO opened up and everyone who was designated to fire followed suit.

The ridge-line trail lit up like a Christmas tree. The silence of the night was broken as some of the claymores went off and some Charlies screamed in pain. The curtain had just gone up on our opening act.

The actions of the lead element reinforced my initial opinion of them. They were seasoned soldiers, and when that first flare went off, they took about the same actions that we would have taken in their shoes. There are some who say that when caught in such a situation, the best thing to do is to move quickly out of the light given off by the flare. This reasoning is based on the proposition that when the flare goes off, the person who set the flare and the person who tripped the flare will be temporarily blinded by it. This is obviously a myth because we were not temporarily blinded by anything.

Our first volley was successful. We took out over 90 per cent of the lead element, and not one of their RPDs (they had at least four) was used against our positions. Instead, those machine guns lay scattered on the trail, cold and silent, just like most of the men of the lead element.

Our mortars put two illumination rounds in the air, and when they popped, we could see that the trail was littered with the broken bodies of the dead and the dying. The canopy was playing hell with our mortar illumination rounds. One parachute had become entangled in the lower branches of the canopy on its way down. It hung there with its light casting an eerie glow over the trail of death, making the few Charlies who were still able to move look like broken puppets on a stage lit by a faltering candle.

All hell broke loose as the first salvos of our 175mm artillery supporting fires made the scene. That portion of the canopy became history, along with whoever was closest to the lead element. At that time, our only light was that provided by the exploding artillery salvos. Our mortar men were already saving illumination rounds. Normally, we did not carry too many, preferring to pack more high-explosive rounds because Charlie respected them the most. There was a fairly flat and grassy area between our terrain feature and the trail, and when our mortar men shot the next illumination round, we could not help but admire Charlie. The bastards were rushing our positions, coming en masse from farther down the trail.

Holy shit! Where in the hell were they coming from? It seemed as if an entire NVA company was heading directly toward us. If we had not been so well dug in, using the terrain and trees for protection, we might have been in a bind with our balls in the sand.

We still had our ducks in a line thanks to God, good planning, our top-of-the-line troopers, and Birth Control.[23]

Charlie's fanatical attack was a top-notch act. I often wondered if he had some of his news photographers and communist propaganda personnel present to document his good-looking attack. It sure would make General Giap happy, as well as one unmentionable Hollywood star. Yes, those two people (and many others) would jump for joy to see their boys looking so good. Charlie was rushing and yelling slogans and fixing to get his collective ass kicked. I say this with confidence because Redleg was prepared for Charlie. He and the CO had figured out that possible attack route while wearing Charlie's racing slicks.

Redleg called in the code words for Birth Control to fire another part of the mission. Their firing shattered Charlie's charge, and he fell back. Then Charlie realized that he might live longer if he could get really close to our positions and out of the hell that Birth Control was laying on him.

The chosen few who managed to reach our positions came at us near where my First Platoon and the Third Platoon overlapped. We locked up with Charlie like two crazed lovers going at it on the back seat of a Volkswagen Beetle that was on its way to hell. We embraced Charlie and gave him the sweet kiss of death. Two Charlies were practically on top of a command-detonated claymore, when our Second Platoon popped it. What a mess!

Our battle was over in less time than it took to relate.

It was getting darker, and we knew our guys were out of illumination rounds. Redleg shifted Birth Control's fires much farther down the trail because Charlie was heading for the valley escape route.

"Top, pass the word the FAC got two Fire Flies[24] for us, and they will be on station in zero five," the CO informed me.

By that time, we were not receiving any effective small arms fire, and Charlie's mortar fire was ineffective.

I cannot go on without exploding another damned media lie about all of the things Charlie could do that we could not. Have you heard some of those long-winded fables about what a great mortar man Charlie was? Well, those stories were all wolf tickets and bullshit. That night, when they shot at us, not one round hit us, but they did raise holy hell with the monkey population over in the next valley. Whenever our mortar men went up against theirs, we out shot their asses coming and going.

The FAC told the Fire Flies where to put their first two flares. They were on station in about zero three, and in zero five they lit up the valley like high noon on a bright, sunny day. After the Fire Flies lit up the valley and the ridge line, we adjusted our night vision and had our first real look at the size of the NVA unit in our presence. There were Charlies all over the side of the mountain, and they were descending to the valley floor toward what they expected to be a safer route north. It was not, of course, and our high-intensity flares caught what looked like a whole NVA regiment sliding down the side of the mountain. We also noticed some heavy machine guns with wheels and their crews.

We were still slapping Charlie first and finding out how big and bad he was after we slapped him.

It was obvious that Battalion had acquired some bad information. Those Charlies were not the ones who had been whipped by our other two companies. Our luck seemed to be holding out, though, because Battalion sent us Puff the Magic Dragon. By that time, our artillery could no longer shoot for us because the reasonably low-flying aircraft masked their high-angle fires. That was okay because Charlie no longer posed a threat to us. He was too busy trying to escape our Fire Flies and Puff.

The added awesome firepower of Puff the Magic Dragon was indeed a remarkable sight. The mournful refrains of the Gatlin, Chain, and miniguns[25] sounded rather sad, as old Puff walked their lines of fire at

6,000 rounds per minute, up and down that old valley like he owned every inch of it. At that time, old Death had to call down to hell for help to cart away the surplus of souls.

"Down in the valley, in the valley so low, hang your head over, hear the wind blow."

Our last view of the enemy showed them taking their only remaining, sane option – to scatter and run like rabbits. The hounds of hell were chasing and ripping Charlie's ass apart. Old Charlie was pulling for all he was worth to get somewhere else, anywhere that was far away from Puff.

When it was all over, the FAC team thanked our friends in support, and they flew away, satisfied with a job well done. Calmness came upon that little valley, and it was so quiet that we could "hear the wind blow".

Darkness came again to claim its rightful territory. We were certain that Charlie would not return. Those of our enemies who were still alive had left with a decisive finality. We had whipped them. We had kicked off on their asses, and they were going to run all the way to Hanoi while cussing the news media for telling them lies.

My sit-reps[26] began to come in over the radio. We had been hurt, but in comparison to the damage we had done to Charlie, our injury was a minor scratch. We did lose a few good men during that night's work, and I can tell you that they did not die all hopped up on drugs or trying to frag each other. Our men fought the common enemy like the superior fighting team that they truly were. Our buddies went to God as true men in the finest sense of the word. They went as true Americans and true soldiers. Let it be known that no one can ever take that fact away from them. May God bless those brave young men forever!

I cannot tell you how long we fought Charlie that night before Puff brought down the final curtain. After we hit the lead element on the trail, everything happened quickly and fiercely. Nobody, except perhaps old Death, kept track of time after that first flare was popped and we opened up.

The heat of the battle was upon us all. Even now, as I am telling you this story, I am remembering actions and events that took place while we were under siege, from our enemy on the battlefield and from the enemy within ourselves. During those fateful moments when we were locked up with Charlie, we fought him head to head, and we really whipped him. We whipped his ass all over the place, without artillery support and well before Puff arrived. We Skytroopers went hand to hand with Charlie, and we beat him.

I did not hear any of our troopers screaming in pain. Surely, some of them cussed at Charlie, saying bad things about his mother and yelling in frustration if they were hit. I could only see and hear those troops nearest to my position, and occasionally Pete told me about what was going on around the perimeter of our defensive positions. As always, we lagered into a strong, protective circle; in that case, however, our configuration was more oblong than circular.

The Second Platoon (our base platoon) sustained two direct head-on charges by Charlie, and they took a number of hits by Charlie's rocket-propelled grenades (RPGs). They were the only platoon to sustain KIAs. My sit-reps indicated that our wounded could hold on until first light.

Several of our wounded enemies called to us, pleading for help. We had already learned the hard way not to send or to allow one of our men to go outside our perimeter to help those who cried out. Sometimes Charlie rewarded those of us who tried to help with a bullet in the back. Therefore, we had to wait until first light, when our dust-off would arrive with help and Blue Max and the air force Phantom jets would be on station. It was very difficult to do nothing while a man was screaming in pain, begging for help, even when that screaming man was the enemy who had been hurt while trying to kill us. We had to lie there listening to those pitiful cries for the rest of the night, and you may wonder why we Vietnam combat veterans are the way we are.

As I remember, those wonderful personnel of the elite unit we respectfully called dust-off were there before first light. The engineer squad, whom Battalion had given us before we left the jungle training camp, were running their chainsaws at full speed, cutting a medical-evacuation LZ.

"Top, you keep your head down, and tell the guys I'm coming back in a few days," said one of my troopers from the Second Platoon.

He smiled at me as I helped to load him aboard a dust-off bird. One of his legs had been mangled, probably beyond repair.

Our CO was also wounded, but he refused to leave us as long as his injuries were not life-threatening and he could still get around. He was the only officer in our company. Although I did not want to see my CO in pain, neither did I want to see him sent out on a medevac because he was the best company commander in the Nam. Both of us helped to load our wounded men on the dust-off, and we made an effort to say something to and to touch each of those men before they were evacuated.

Our company medics worked tirelessly as they always did while tending to us. They were a great bunch of guys who kept us going, and most of the time, they did it without thinking of themselves. After taking care of us, our medics moved outside the perimeter and with one of our troopers acting as security, they applied their life-saving trade to Charlie.

First light brought more medical assistance, a unit of South Vietnamese Rangers, and our battalion commander. That was probably my first opportunity to get a good look around at the trail, the side of the mountain, and the valley floor below.

What I saw was like a scene from a horrible nightmare. Many broken and shattered bodies were scattered in every direction. The canopy that had covered the sections of the trail that were hit by our artillery and Puff no longer existed. Two sections of the trail were blown away in tribute to the accuracy of our Birth Control.

I was interested to learn why Charlie's mortars were so inaccurate. He was certainly not a terrible shot. I figured that maybe he tried to set up and fire conventionally because he was afraid to shoot through the canopy. The only terrain that was available for conventional shooting was out in the open, along the most sloping side of the mountain. Certainly, Charlie could have hit us by hip shooting, but he evidently could not hip shoot, or maybe it just seemed that he could not because we were more accurate hip shooters and quicker on the draw.

As soon as it was possible to count noses, I gave my sit-rep to the CO. Thank the dear Lord, our losses were minimal. Our troops hugged each other and shouted, "Black Knight Alfa! Alpha and Omega!"

The CO, Redleg, and I soon began our next planning stage, and we examined an area that would be an attractive place for Charlie to occupy because it represented his most direct route to our positions and offered good markers for guidance at night. We planned our course of action, assuming that Charlie would find and use the area. Redleg planned two concentrations on that possible route.

Charlie eventually found that area and tried to use it. We know that because he littered the route with some 20 bodies and equipment, including a heavy machine gun on skids. That served as mute testimony of the way our Grand Company worked. We called Charlie out, and he made the mistake of pulling on us when he should have simply diddy maued the area.

The surviving Charlies ran away and left nearly all their heavy equipment lying on the field, but we were not allowed to confiscate it for trading materials. The battalion commander said that the South Vietnamese Army Rangers (ARVNs) would take over and clean up.

On orders from Battalion, we were slicked out to another place, and as our birds flew away, I had the best possible view of our blocking position and the destruction, great loss, and pain that our position must have caused Charles.

I believe all of us shared this thought: God has been good to us, and we have been good to ourselves because we have been a team 25 hours a day. If you want to call it luck, that is okay, but our luck would only hold as long as we were a team.

Later, we were informed that one of the Cav units who had started the operation with us had caught some of the enemy personnel from the jungle training camp as they tried to escape north. Their catch produced solid information on the person who was teaching radio communications in the NVA training camp. She was a South Vietnamese civilian and a Viet Cong of officer rank. And get this – she was also on the payroll of the US Army, working at one of our major installations as an interpreter and communications instructor. On top of all that, she had worked in the Headquarters section. She was regularly on leave up north to visit her "ailing mother". (You know how close the Vietnamese are to their families.) As it turned out, her mother had been dead for three years.

Despite the hard-core behavior of that communications instructor, who refused to give herself up when she was busted, the South Vietnamese brought her down really hard.

The CO had been right in his guestimate of what we had faced. More than half an NVA regiment had occupied that area when we went in. Our presence had made their headquarters think we were the vanguard for a large operation, so that regiment was ordered back north so as not to lose their people. It was true that they were carrying some of the stragglers and the wounded from the fight with the other Cav units. Fortunately for them, a part of that regiment had already made it back north along the same trail. At that time, the NVA almost never moved an entire regiment together, unless they were under attack.

We had mauled that partial regiment, and it could no longer be referred to as a regiment.

After the Macabre Dance

With great care, combined with our respect for the living and the dead, we ventured out of our fighting positions and into the fields of death and destruction. As soon as our wounded and dead were lifted out, our medics and troopers went to see what we could do to help Charlie, our sworn enemy. All of the enemy soldiers we found needed medical attention. I swear to God that we gave medical assistance to our enemies. I observed our troops using their own issued bandages to help save the lives of wounded enemies.

Those compassionate acts were, in my humble opinion, another important part of what made the men of Black Knight Alfa, the Grand Company, the most outstanding soldiers in the world. You must understand that we were out there in the fields of death, trying to save the lives of enemy soldiers who only a short time before were trying like hell to take our lives. Our benevolent actions certainly proved that we stood head and shoulders above Charlie, and we will always retain that position.

Seeing all of the death and destruction caused me to weep again. I wept when our dust-off birds lifted our own dead and wounded comrades, and there I was weeping again for our enemies. The sight of our incoming medical personnel picking up the wounded enemy soldiers to transport them to our aid stations and hospitals soon relieved my sadness. Oh, where were the news media at that time? Where was a certain Hollywood star?

Oh, my God. My God. My God!

"Make you wanna holler, throw up both your hands."[27]

Ambush

AM-BUSH (am'boosh)   **n**   **1.**   A lying in wait to attack by surprise. **2.**   A surprise attack made from a concealed position. **3.**   Those in hiding to make such an attack. Et cetera.
ambushed, ambushing, ambushes
   From Middle English embushen, to ambush, from Old French embuschier, from Vulgar Latin imboscare.

The American Heritage Dictionary
New College Edition
1969–1976

OR   To wait for old Charlie and put his shit in the wind and on the fan.

Vietnam, the American GI Edition
1965–1975

When we slicked back into our battalion forward LZ, cold beer and soda were waiting for us, along with the many smiling faces of our battalion commander and his staff. We hoped that those big smiles meant that we had done well and had another successful mission under our belts.
   The senior squad leader of the First Platoon, Staff Sergeant Gonzalez, was back from his R & R in Hong Kong. He temporarily took over the platoon for me so that I could go to the Headquarters section.

As soon as our company was resituated into our fighting positions and I had an "all present", the CO, Redleg, and I hastily reported to the Battalion TOC, as we were instructed to do. There, the sergeant major greeted us with a bottle of the best rum in the world – Bacardi 151. We popped the cap and did the obvious, especially since he had cola and glasses waiting for us.

The battalion staff (minus the S-4) was there. An ARVN teota (major) from a Ranger battalion was also present. He was one of two people whom we had not seen before. The CO and I were quick to notice that the teota was proudly wearing an insignia of the Mobile Riverine Forces (MRF), and we wondered why he was so far from the Mekong Delta, especially so far north, all the way up in I Corps in the Quang Tri Province. Of course, we supposed his reasons for being there would eventually be disclosed to us if it became our business to know.

The other stranger in our presence was a distinguished-looking gentleman, Ivy League all the way, except he was not wearing his dark suit, white shirt, and carefully shined black shoes. Instead, he wore a jungle fatigue uniform like ours, but it was devoid of a unit identification and an insignia of rank. He was packing an almost new Stoner M63A1 system that I surely wished to have. The Stoner appeared to be in excellent condition and was well maintained. As I looked beyond its seemingly new appearance, however, I could see that the outstanding weapon system was as much a veteran as its owner. There was no need to wonder about this distinguished-looking man in his basic jungle fatigues. He was a Spook,[28] plain and simple.

The CO and I smiled at each other, a gesture that did not go without our battalion commander taking notice and nodding his head in the affirmative. Langley and SOG were written all over the Spook. By looking at his hands and into his blue-gray eyes, one could tell that he was more Langley than SOG. Knowing this made me want his Stoner even more. It looked as tight as Dick's hatband, and I would bet in that agent's hands that 63 would knock a single, long hair off the back of a fly at 800 meters or more.

The CO and I silently admired the agent's best friend. We were also probably thinking of the S-4's absence and the fact that when we had passed him earlier, he could have been going into our area to see our log men. We already knew that Black Knight Alfa would be resupplied and refitted.

You probably find it hard to believe me when I say that my CO and I were able to communicate without talking. Captain Harris was not as old as me and certainly did not have my years of experience. However, he was an infantry officer of the highest caliber, and I do believe that because he and I were so close to each and every man in Black Knight Alfa, it was only natural that we could sense each other's thoughts.

We also had mutual respect for each other, and we trusted each other's abilities. Captain Harris did not make the mistake of looking down on me because I was "just an NCO". Somewhere along the way, he had become aware of the crucial fact that the Non-commissioned Officer Corps is truly the backbone and the heart of the army. If he had checked my 201 file,[29] he would have known that I was teaching infantry officers at Fort Benning, Georgia, before he entered high school and that I had instructed infantry weapons and tactics at the French Military Academy (St Cyr), as well as at the British (Sandhurst) and Danish military academies. That period of my military experience began shortly after President Harry S. Truman stood up and corrected the US military system, and it lasted throughout the Eisenhower and Kennedy presidential administrations.

Thank God, Captain Harris knew that I was neither a gofer nor a virgin. He understood that I could command our company just as well as he could, if it ever came to that. After all, we had to be willing to walk through hell together, and that was exactly what we were doing. We entrusted our lives and the lives of the other brave young men of Black Knight Alfa into each other's hands, and we entrusted our souls into the most capable and eternal hands of God, the Father of all things. Frankly, I could not think of a better arrangement, all things considered.

Getting back to the Spook, he was an impressive figure. I admit that our impressions were slightly biased, based on our past experiences with other members of his elite fraternity, who had saved our butts on several occasions. We certainly looked up to those men; they were the best.

My CO and I had the feeling that Black Knight Alfa was about to embark on another hot one. Therefore, our stay on that LZ would be very limited. We sincerely hoped that our troopers were taking our advice and catching forty winks.

In typical fashion, the S-2 officer cleaned up the details of our last operation before introducing us to our new mission. Our S-3 officer gave us the complete operations order, including new maps and every detail possible at his command. The S-2 returned and gave us all of the new codes, call signs, and intelligence information that he had. Then, Mr X (the Spook) and the ARVN teota spoke briefly. (By the way, the Spook confirmed that there had been Russian, Chinese, and Cuban instructors at the jungle training camp.) Finally, we asked questions and received answers before returning to our positions with our troops.

Earlier, I said that the NVA unit we had hit on the ridge-line trail was only about half a regiment. After the body count was taken, the CO and I were given updated information on that operation, which claimed that the unit we hit had been a full regiment. We had caught the regiment as they were being recalled back to safety, and they had been unprepared for us.

On the way back to our positions, the CO, Redleg and I reflected on our last blocking-position mission, and we briefly discussed our mistakes and Charlie's. We were keenly aware that Puff the Magic Dragon had taken out that NVA regiment, and we were certainly remembering and learning from our mistakes.

Once we were back into our positions, we thoroughly reviewed our next mission and then arrived at a game plan. During that time, our supply personnel came to inform us that we had been completely resupplied, with emphasis on claymores, flares, starlight scopes, and LAWs. He told us that if we needed anything else, all we had to do was holler.

As soon as we had our ducks in a line, the CO told me to call all platoon sergeants to the CP to receive the new operations order. We always tried hard to get the word out to our troops as soon as possible because the final success of the mission depended on them.

Once everyone was there and in position, the CO issued the operations order, and Redleg informed us of his plans. Then we worked together to create Plans A, B, and C. The platoon sergeants returned to their positions to issue their orders and to ensure that every man in the company was fully aware of our mission and his role in it.

Once again, our instructions were to begin operations under the guise of a search-and-destroy mission, and that was to take place in a specific area. Once we were on the ground, we would move around seemingly in no specific direction, when in fact we would be heading in the direction of our real mission. As usual, there was a time factor involved, but it was governed by the need for absolute secrecy, and there was no doubt that if we slicked into or even near to our actual objective, Charlie would become aware of our presence. If Charlie knew we were there, our mission would fail even before it began. Therefore, to go near our real objective would be a stupid move of major proportions, and thank the dear Lord, such moves were not common to us.

We would be operating so far north that the only artillery fire that we might receive would be coming from the NVA and their artillery. We were given a priority code to receive TAC Air,[30] but we could not count on the Grand Lady of the Seven Seas to shoot for us. TAC Air was the only big stick available to us, and its size was greatly reduced by a time lapse factor, day and night situations, and the weather conditions.

On our second full day out, which was a full day north of Quang Tri Province, we had to use a rather nice jungle trail because of our close proximity to Charlie and those damned wait-a-minute vines. We discovered clear and recent evidence that Charlie was using the same trail, both backward and forward. We knew that it would be safer for us to meet Charlie on the trail than for us to go charging in and out of the bushes.

An American operation had been conducted south of that area within the last few days, which explains why it was not unusual for us to be there and probably why we did not run into more Charlies.

Our scouts found some traps and snaps, three beautifully constructed punji pits, and some other very wisely placed death-dealing snares and devices that would either take one's foot off or puncture holes in one's body. Were the traps compliments of the NVA? we wondered.

Strangely enough, the traps were different from those normally set by the NVA. We were certain they had been made and set by the Viet Cong, even though it was unusual for the "mob group" to be operating that far north. We mentally filed that bit of important information for future use.

There really was a distinct difference between the way the NVA and the Viet Cong made and placed traps, as well as the manner in which they positioned accompanying safety devices. We were concerned about those traps because they were designed and located to force the use of the trail upon unsuspecting travelers. We were very suspicious, especially since we believed that Charlie Cong was involved. Perhaps there was an ambush up that trail waiting to send us all to hell in a nice, red hand basket. We had already done enough to old Charlie for him to be really pissed off at us.

The CO called a halt, and we lagered and waited for our drop-off team to catch up to us. We were spread out to the max and in contact only by radio. We did not speak into the microphones. Instead, we used our very own "Alfa code", which was simply a series of clicks that we produced over the microphone by keying it (i.e., pressing and releasing the Press-to-Talk button). It was like our own personal Morse code, and it worked very well. Charlie could never break it, even if he figured it out, because we often changed our code words and we used words that Charlie would have difficulty pronouncing.

When the drop-off team reported in, they said that we did not have a tail. Because we were packing heavy in enemy territory, we knew better than to push our strength too much. We always had to maintain enough reserve to run like hell if that became necessary. The most important elements in our overall situation had been working for us, but we knew that could change with a drop of sweat. We were not rushed because our time factor was favorable.

We sent two teams forward to check the trail ahead of us. While they were out, we moved more slowly and in a configuration that allowed us to give them covering fire in case they hit some shit. When they reported back, they confirmed what we all thought and felt – the unit moving in front of us was Viet Cong. Their size was unknown to us because our teams were only able to get a drag view.

The CO said, "Top, I think we are going to find a good place to hold up, then go to ground. I know we can make a lot more klicks before dark, but I don't want to push it. We need to find the best place where we can defend if we're hit and also a good location with some high ground. What do you think of this place, which is only about a klick off that way?" He referenced a piece of terrain on the map as he spoke.

I agreed with the CO's suggestion, and he moved the company to a better position, where we could study the proposed location using our field glasses. After he examined the location and its surrounding area for a while, he passed his glasses to me. Then Redleg and he examined their maps before he decided to have me send a recon team to investigate the proposed location. Within minutes the Second Platoon had a team on the way. While we waited, the CO confided in Redleg and me.

"I know it's bothering you guys, too. What the hell is the Cong doing in this area? Their unit is too large for them to be just guides. Besides, the NVA normally doesn't require guides till they reach the foothills just before the flats. Is it possible that unit ahead of us is working on its own – a rebel force, a mob out for a piece of the action just for the fun of it?"

We had no objective answers to the CO's questions.

Meanwhile, our team found the newly inspected location to be clean. We moved on to our new position and set up our FOB for the night.

Our nighttime defensive/fighting positions were tightly locked in. "If" the Cong unit we were dogging knew we were there, they might come back around two or three in the morning and try to catch us napping, even though we never napped. We were ready for Charlie, but he did not come back. It was an uneventful night where the only forms of life that attacked us were leeches and skeeters.

The CO was clearly as befuddled as the rest of us as to why Charlie Cong was waltzing around in an area that was predominantly inhabited by his older brother, the NVA. Maybe the NVA was just using Charlie Cong for security missions while their real soldiers were doing the real fighting.

We were in good spirits the next morning, anticipating another day of pushing the bush all alone. According to our information, there were no other friendlies in the area. Once we were fully out of our FOB and moving along smoothly, we came across another trail that was overgrown in places, making excellent spots for ambushes (either the human kind or the snaps-and-traps kind). Both Charlie Cong and the NVA loved to place their traps beneath overgrown vegetation. Knowing this, we decided to examine the trail more carefully.

"Top, how do you feel about following the same trail?" the CO asked.

Following that trail offered good visibility and allowed us to spread way out and still have some amount of visible contact. Because of the trees, if our mortars had to shoot, it would be from the hip, and even that capability was sorely limited, although we could overcome the disadvantage.

Charlie used that trail because he could not be spotted from the air, and we used it because, according to the book, we should not use it. You see, Charlie read our tactical manuals and studied our tactics more than we did. Therefore, the last place he would expect for us to be was on one of his finer thoroughfares.

We moved carefully and quietly, with our lead platoon well forward. Our drag platoon followed the Weapons Platoon and served as our rear security. Our position allowed us to serve as the base of fire if our Second Platoon came under fire.

I was in the rear of the Headquarters section, slightly behind Redleg and his RTO. All of us in the Headquarters section agreed that we did not smell Charlie or feel that he was near. Still, we felt a heaviness in the air, a foreboding that made us all a bit jittery.

I asked the CO if I could call him "Six" because that was the way I liked to refer to him, especially when there was no time for formalities. He was Six, and I was Five. Anyway, because I had a strange feeling, I asked Six if I could move forward to be with the lead platoon.

He responded, "You know, Top, that's just what I was fixing to do. I'll feel a lot better if you are up there. Keep me informed, and don't let's get locked up in a fight with Charles. Remember the real reason that we are here."

I understood what Six meant, and it felt good to know that he wanted me up front. I moved behind the lead platoon sergeant, but not so close that I would interfere with his job. He also made me feel good because he looked back at me, smiled, and said, "Top, I'm glad you're here."

Pete was right there with me, tucking his short antenna back down. His thump gun was ready to shout. Sp4 Rodriguez (Rod) was on point. Like JoJo, he was a well-schooled, master point man.

We Skytroopers in Black Knight Alfa were ready to do our thing, and we moved along completely alert. Although old Fear was our constant companion, we had become accustomed to having him ride with us. I liked to think that we knew how to handle our fears and to make them work in our favor. This time, however, it was not fear that caused an unfamiliar uneasiness to descend upon us. It was something else.

I thought we were going to hit that Victor Charley[31] unit whom we had seen the day before.

We were approaching a bend in the trail that would make a perfect ambush point for Charlie. I looked back along the trail, and although I could not see any of my fellow troopers, I knew that most of them were spread out back along either side of the trail.

Rod halted and signaled for us to stop. Everyone sniffed the hot, humid air and smelled the sweet odor of old Death. We felt his warm, mind-numbing touch. No one had to say it, but he was very near.

We moved farther off the trail and searched the surrounding area, trying to note anything that was out of place. We caught a faint odor of Charlie Cong and the scent of a wood fire. A definite quietness and something else mingled with the natural jungle odors. The feel and taste of death floated gently on the otherwise pleasant mountain breeze. I knew that everyone had his safety off and was ready to pop caps. I am sure that some of us were thinking of the time when that young Charlie was dogging us, wearing a good coating of our bug juice.

Rod signaled that he wanted to move farther along the trail, alone. He touched the top of his helmet in a manner that said "Cover me." The platoon sergeant moved two men forward to form a connecting file so that we would not lose sight of Rod. However, well before those two men could move more than a few paces down the trail, Rod gave us the signal to proceed with caution. From where I stood, I could not decipher the expression on his face.

Only the lead platoon moved cautiously toward the place where Rod was standing and pointing. That way, if we hit some shit, only one platoon would be in contact, and the CO would still have a base-of-fire platoon and a maneuvering platoon, in addition to our mortars.

I still did not see what Rod was pointing at until I was close enough to comprehend the expression on his face. He was crying, almost uncontrollably.

Suspended above the trail, hanging 3 or 4 feet above the ground was a sight that nearly made us all flip out. I heard the painful intakes of breath from our troopers who got their first gut-wrenching sight of what hung above the jungle trail.

The man hanging above us was almost naked and strung up in spread-eagle fashion. His arms and legs were tied to the trees on both sides of him, and his body was positioned almost in the dead center of the trail. It was impossible for anyone to pass along the trail without seeing or smelling Charlie's handiwork. Most of the man's uniform had been burned away, and his personal belongings were strewn in a wide area around him. His mutilated body was mute evidence of the cruel, deliberate torture he had endured. There were several wounds on his body, including those from a gunshot and a bayonet or a knife. Leeches had been allowed to gorge on his body until they burst. The poor man either bled to death or died because of his other wounds. The horror of the experience was clearly etched on his face, particularly in his lifeless, staring eyes, which mirrored the merciless pain that Charlie had inflicted upon him.

Suddenly I heard someone screaming in pain and rage; the screams were so very close to the edge, like the screams of a madman. The pain in my throat told me that I was the madman. My comrades had to hold me back. I was blind with rage and ready to kill the cowardly bastards who were responsible for this insane act. I was so angry that I wanted to kill something, anything. I was certainly not alone; I think all of us suffered from a fit of total madness at that moment. However, I did not have the right to go crazy. I was Five, and all of those other young men surely needed me then, if ever at all. I struggled for control, and it was the sight of one of my troopers moving toward the dead man, intending to cut him down, that snapped me back to my duty.

"No!" I shouted, and the trooper stopped, suddenly realizing the danger of his intentions. Charlie most likely wanted us to retrieve the dead man.

Everyone at that terrible scene quickly managed to collect his wits and return to a state of full alertness. We were making a damned big mistake by standing around the dead man; it could cost us our lives.

Once again, I was angry at myself for my initial reactions. I felt that I was letting down my CO and my company. As the first sergeant, I was supposed to know better. There was no time for crying; the situation demanded that I remain alert and thinking. God forgive me for letting the human frailty of grief overcome me. It was neither the time nor the place to be human.

"Gonzalez, get everyone back at a safe distance, and be very careful! There may be snaps and traps. I don't want any more of our people to see this. Let's lager wide and tight. Get a machine gun-heavy team forward on the trail, and get JoJo and Doc up here on the double!" I barked out my instructions, and my wonderful troops responded.

"Pete, push up to Six and give him a first-hand view of what we have here, and ask what we should do. Oh, tell him that I want to take this guy down. We can't leave him here like this."

Again, I must thank God for quickly allowing me to return to the state of mind and action which I should never have left. There was a very good chance the body was booby-trapped; perhaps the whole area was zeroed in with Charlie's mortars and/or 120mm rockets. Maybe we were doing exactly what Charles intended; maybe the poor guy was

strung up on that trail as a trigger device that would snap a trap designed and calculated to send us all to hell.

My magnificent Skytroopers realized these potential dangers and acted accordingly. The machine gun-heavy security team was already out of sight and forward along the trail. Gonzalez had sent his radio with the team because Pete and I were with him. Everyone was fully alert and down behind whatever protection was available. We expected to be hit at any second. However, no mortar rounds or rockets crashed down on us. The security team reported that all was well on the trail.

"Top, Six is on his way. The company is well spread out. The drag platoon has a security team with a radio back down the trail. Right now we have all-around security, so Charles can't slip up on us. Oh, while I was trying to examine the body and the rigging that was holding it in place from a safe distance, Pete reported to me that Doc is coming with Six and Redleg."

Did you know that you can use a pair of field glasses to get an excellent close-up of a nearby object? That is exactly what I was doing. I was visually inspecting the body, the tie downs, the ground, and the surrounding area, searching for trip wires, devices, and explosive charges. I found it very hard to believe that there were no such devices, but the area and the body seemed to be free of booby traps and explosives.

All was quiet. The platoons reported to the CO, and Pete was doing his usual monitoring of the company net. He kept me posted on what was going down. In theory, Charlie was nowhere around, but we did not trust our lives to theories. Our troopers were out there actively ensuring that Charlie was not around so that we would remain alive.

"Top, no matter what happens, we are not going to leave him like that, you hear me!" the CO exclaimed with tears in his eyes. Then, he said thoughtfully, "You know, I'm so glad that you had the presence of mind to keep everyone back. I certainly didn't want any more of our troopers to see that horrible sight."

I was somewhat relieved to see that the CO and Redleg had almost the same reactions as I had when they first saw what those cowardly mothers did to that totally defenseless, unarmed man. Those bastards were all cowards in the truest sense of the word.

Six wanted to free the body from the trees, and Redleg offered to assist him. I talked them out of doing so because I could not guarantee that there was not a booby trap on or near the body. Doc B., JoJo, and

I agreed to get the body down from the trees. Other willing hands offered assistance, but we told them to stand back and pray really hard.

I asked the troopers at the scene not to pass the word around about what we had found. They understood and said they would keep quiet about it. We covered the body with a donated poncho liner while the CO requested dust-off. By that time, JoJo and my team of the best trackers and sign readers in the world were there. I told them what I wanted to know and then moved out of their way.

The CO confided in me. "Top, we are as lucky as hell there are no Charlies around for us to fight, at least not till our people regain control of themselves and their emotions. To tell the truth, if we were in contact with Charlie right now, there would be a massacre, and I am talking about a wholesale slaughter of major proportions. With or without us, Charlie would be taking the hellbound express on out of here."

We accepted the fact that dust-off would give our position away. In fact, we were looking forward to our next lock-up with Charlie. As we waited for dust-off, we solidified our positions, and we remained as spread out as the situation and the terrain would allow. Of course, the other platoons were wondering what the hold-up was, so the CO passed the word that we had found a dead body and we were planning to wait until dust-off arrived. He purposely avoided giving them any details about the body.

I assigned the lead platoon the job of hacking out an LZ. Fortunately, there was no jungle canopy, and they found an opening nearby and quickly put their machetes to work.

Meanwhile, our team of experts fanned the immediate vicinity, and in short order, gave us this evidence regarding the ABSOLUTE cowards who had tortured and killed one of our own:

1. It was a group of more than five but less than 12.
2. All except one wore racing slicks.
3. The one wearing boots was most likely a woman for two reasons. First of all, the boot impressions were much smaller than any of the racing slicks, which indicated the person wearing them was very lightweight. (She was also pigeon-toed.) Secondly, the boot impressions were near the only human dump site where toilet paper had been used, and that site was farther away than the others, which were marked by

racing slicks. (At least two other persons had a bad case of the GIs. Smile!)

4. The impressions left on the ground indicated that the group of enemy soldiers had at least two RPGs and two RPDs.
5. Everyone smoked, and there were three "tips" that were clearly marijuana.

It was the separate and collective verdict of three of our troopers that the murdering bastards who had tortured that young man were undoubtedly Viet Cong.

Whenever we came across Charlie Cong, we were going to bring him down so hard that his falling would shake the very gates of hell. Black Knight Alfa vowed to pay the Viet Cong back in spades for what those motherfuckers did to that poor, defenseless soldier.

The LZ was finished, and dust-off would arrive shortly. We moved the body to the LZ and waited. At that time, the most important thing in the entire world was to make sure our brother was returned to American hands. Our motto was "Brother, I'll die for you". It was our absolute but unspoken rule that if one of us bought the farm, his body would never be left behind, no matter what the dominant condition or situation. No power on Earth could or would change that fact.

Pete told me that dust-off was inbound, and a few minutes later we heard them. It was such a welcome sound to our ears. The aircraft commander (AC) called for us to pop smoke as "Goofy Grape". We were very happy to see that dust-off had gunslingers to escort him. Those gunships kept a watchful eye on the dust-off bird as it came toward us.

There were lumps in our throats as we sorrowfully watched Doc B. and some of the other troopers carry the body to the bird. Before they reached the waiting helicopter, one of our young troopers ran out to the body and placed his American flag into the folds of the poncho liner covering it. Most of us carried an American flag somewhere on ourselves, and most of our flags were small and dirty. Some were even handmade. Despite their ragged appearances, those little flags were extremely important to us. The young trooper's gesture said it all for us. "Dear God, please bless forever our dear brother and see him safely back home to those who love him. Thank you, God."

Within minutes, the dust-off bird and its escort were high and away. We quickly got our shit together and diddy maued the area. As a precaution, the CO decided to move in a direction that was contradictory to the direction of our real mission.

We moved as quickly as the situation allowed, and we avoided all trails. In fact, we ran for the highest ground available and did not stop until we were on top of the world. Once we reached the highest terrain on which we could navigate, and after some long, hard pulling, the CO called a halt. We lagered and took five.

I could still see the look in our dead buddy's eyes, and I am sure that the memory of it was also haunting the others who had seen him. I was very much relieved, though, that only a few of our troopers had seen his face before we cut him down and covered him with a poncho liner.

We had hot snake (chow), but I had no appetite after what I had seen. When chow time ended, we followed our routine of digging holes and burying our garbage. Of course, we left all of our fruitcakes for Charlie, and one hole was rigged to blow and send Charlie to hell with a surprised look on his face.

When we left our rest area, we traveled in the direction of our main mission. Battalion was planning to insert another company to cover our rear, so that we could move without the fear of Charlie crawling up our butts. The company would then follow us at a safe distance until we reached the stream where our planned "thrust line" ended. Once there, they would wait to be lifted out. We were also taking that precaution because it would force Charlie (if he decided to show up) to deal initially with our back-up company. After crossing the stream, we would be on our own again.

I was plagued with wondering why the Cong had mutilated one of our defenseless young soldiers. What could be the reason for such a cruel, cowardly act? My CO and I agreed that this was a new low, even for the VC.

I realize that you may have heard wild stories about American soldiers taking heads, ears, penises, scalps, and various other body parts from enemy soldiers. I will freely admit that some of those atrocities did occur, but they happened on both sides of the barbed wire. I also know that such vicious acts were the exceptions to the rule. I certainly cannot and will not speak for everyone. I do not dare to presume. However, I can and do speak for all of the units with which I had the honor of serving, and I can tell you with complete confidence that we never did those kinds of things. We regarded the NVA as soldiers like us, and we would never desecrate a soldier. We would rather die than to blatantly add disrespect to our profession, our army, and our great American people.

We were greatly relieved to learn that the cowards who had strung up our brother soldier were VC. We wondered if they had done it as a message or a warning to us or whether their foul act was merely an attempt to show off to anyone who found our brother. Why didn't they leave a calling card? Why didn't they leave some snaps and traps lying around?

Those unanswered questions rode our minds repeatedly, but we did not have the luxury of time to dwell on the whys of the situation when we were out there in the bush, where every breath and step that we took could be our last. Besides, our thoughts could not change the past. Our situation demanded our absolute attention to detail if we wanted to keep breathing and stepping.

Our company moved cautiously through the jungle highlands and avoided the trails, except where such travel was necessary. The CO and I took every opportunity to talk with our troops, and by that time, we knew without a doubt that everyone's mind was back where it was supposed to be – on our immediate mission. We were good to go.

There were no hot-headed individuals among us, no grand standees, no super heroes waiting for their turns to stop speeding bullets and to jump over tall trees in a single leap. Hell no! Our team feeling was in place and holding steady. Nonetheless, we never forgot what those bastards did to our poor brother. His great suffering and the way those cowards took his life made him live on in our memories forever.

When we came across Charlie Cong, we had no intentions of attacking him in a fit of mindless vengeance. Instead, we would call his cowardly ass out and hope that he would be foolish enough to pull on us. Then, in a calm, cool, professional manner we would do some real harm to him with absolute prejudice and malice. Charlie was going to fall, and we were going to take our good-old time and do a J.O.B. on him. Yes, Black Knight Alfa looked forward to meeting Charlie Cong in the flatlands or wherever.

As we pushed on, every man was on full alert. We were confident that our time would come according to the adage "What goes around comes around". It was late afternoon, and we still had not heard a peep from Charlie. We were way up in the highlands where the air was clean, if not cool. If Charlie came after us there, we would definitely know it. We would smell and feel him.

The CO came forward to walk beside me, and I knew it was time to look for a good FOB position. He pointed to a good-looking piece of high ground on his map and said, "Top, I was thinking about this position. It looks good on the map. We'll be coming to it in a few more minutes. Let's check it out."

"Yes, Sir," I said and began to decide which platoon I would direct to send in a recon and security team.

When we neared that high ground, which was to the right of our direction of travel, we took the same precautions that had saved our butts many times. On the CO's command, we quickly lagered and were ready to fight and defend in any direction. Our circle was flexible but also hard. Because the lead squad was the most familiar with the terrain between the high ground and us, they were assigned to give covering fire for the recon team I had sent from the Second Platoon in our formation.

The CO showed the recon team leader where to go, but it was not necessary for him to tell the leader why he was going or what he needed to look for. The leader already knew what he was doing because we performed that little operation every time we went on to an unknown position. (For your information, the recon and security team would verify that Charlie was not already in that position. If the area was clear, they would tell us to come ahead and provide us with security until we got there.) The recon team informed us that the position was clear and had not been used recently. We moved on to it, and the CO instructed each platoon where to go. Our troopers put out claymores, flares, and other little goodies that were designed to hurt and stop Charlie if he came calling.

Our experience was one hell of a teacher. From it, we had learned to post our security before putting out our claymores, flares, and other snaps and traps. We had also learned to use whatever protection was available and to dig all the way to China if time permitted.

We changed our method and pattern of putting out our claymores as often as possible. In some places we would back up a claymore with a dud[32] In another set-up, both claymores were live. This alternating method kept Charlie guessing. Imagine the jest of such an arrangement. If Charles tried to turn or disarm either the dud or the live claymore, one of them was surely going to blow up his ass. The only drawback was that the same person who installed the claymores had to pick them up again.

On the far side of the high ground terrain, there was a recently used trail that did not appear on our map. It did not lead to the high ground; instead, it came close to the base, making it necessary for us to ambush the trail.

No log bird would be coming in because it would give away our position. Therefore, we had to go over the mountain rather than around the base, which was very difficult because we were humping everything we needed for our mission – additional flares, LAWs, ammunition, and the other bare essentials for staying alive, such as water and chow.

Another night passed without incident, and the CO and I began to worry that Charles was being unusually quiet. We were not so stupid as to believe that Charlie was not around somewhere, neither did we have the illusion that we were so damned good that we could pass by him without being seen. In all, we were 88 men on the ground with an attached engineer squad. We did feel secure in the knowledge that if Charles knew we were in that area, he sure as hell did not know to the nearest 500 meters where we were. Even though we were "that" good, we never underestimated Charlie.

The next morning we policed our areas and were on our way early with the Third Platoon leading and two point men out front. One point man was experienced; the other was new. That is how we taught a new guy the fine art of being a point man. Here, it is noteworthy to mention that during my entire time with that unit, we never had to assign or order a man to the point position. It was an honored position of great responsibility, and there were always more than enough volunteers to fill it.

As we pulled out, I was standing in my usual position beside Doc B. He was popping malaria tablets into the mouths of the men as they passed by. When I saw that Sp4 Natkowski was the teacher and experienced man on point, I knew I had to talk to him. Nat did not like to wear his steel pot, even when he was on point. I thought of my dear friend Smitty as I ran up close to Nat. He was wearing a bandanna, with a sewn-on peace symbol, around his head Japanese-style.

When I cautioned him about wearing his steel pot, he grimaced and replied, "But, Top, that damn old steel pot is so uncomfortable."

"Nat, you get that damn pot on right now. I would rather you be uncomfortable from your pot than from the slug of an AK-47."

84

Nat gave in and put his steel pot on his head. Grinning all over, he said, "Why, Top, it's nice to know you worry about me." Then he ran back to his point position.

I had to smile because Nat was right. I cared about him, as I did every other man in Black Knight Alfa. I loved my troopers as if they were my sons, an inseparable part of me.

Our route for the rest of the day took us steadily downward. We were still in the highlands, enjoying the finer air. For days we did our best to make Charlie think we were the lead element of a much larger force who was looking for a soft spot to hit him in his part of the country. Of course, our primary objective area was a river on a much lower level, a river that Charlie was using too frequently to move his troops and vital supplies south. Old Charles had grown much too bold in his use of that river.

The term "river" may have been a misnomer, but the Vietnamese called it a river. Its sources included the Ben Hai and perhaps some of the waters from the Gulf of Tonkin and other tributaries. What I did know, based upon our pinpointed ground position, was that we were near that famous network of trails jointly known as the Ho Chi Minh Trail.

We pushed on and made good time. As the CO had planned, we reached our objective area shortly before dark, with enough daylight remaining for us to fully inspect our ambush site and to plan everything well. We approached the site from the densely wooded area, which allowed us to pass without making too much noise, although at the expense of slowing down. We used all available means of cover and concealment, and we moved the last few meters on our stomachs because to be seen at that stage of the game would spell D-I-S-A-S-T-E-R.

With the information provided to us by the Spook and the Vietnamese Ranger major, we were able to find the narrow point along the river exactly where they had indicated it would be on our maps. Although it was not book-perfect, it was an excellent ambush site, offering good protection and some concealment and providing plenty of opportunities for us to build upon.

That was my first time with the company where we were planning to ambush a river and bring down moving targets. It was going to be quite a challenge.

Redleg spent some time determining how fast the river water was flowing, which was vital information to us. We checked and secured the area on our side of the river, except for the cleared riverbanks where it was too light for us to break our cover. We inspected the riverbanks using our field glasses.

The CO and Redleg spread their maps on the ground and tried to positively identify our position. It was essential for us to be in the exact place that Battalion and the Spook had specified, especially since we were once again within the shooting realm of our long-range artillery. I do not mind admitting that we were very glad to have their firing support again. After all, we had just spent two days out there alone.

Redleg was a perfectionist, and he was outstanding with a map. Furthermore, he was fully capable of walking our artillery fire right up to the very brims of our steel pots. If we ever came to our Final Battle, he would bring it right down onto our heads rather than let us be captured alive or taken out by the NVA or the VC. For that ambush we would have long-range fire from those great 175mm guns, and the best crews who ever did the cannon cocker's hop.

Soon, Redleg and the CO looked up at me with big smiles. Black Knight Alfa was in the exact position.

Doing it Our Way, or Damn the Book!

There were times to "go by the book", and there were times to use the book only as a guide. There were also times to do a little of both. The Department of the Army had published manuals on how to set up an effective ambush. As we had learned when we brought down that jungle training camp, our enemy was a most enthusiastic reader of our training manuals, and he made it a point to teach our tactics to his troops. Therefore, Black Knight Alfa faithfully practiced "damn the book, let's do it our way", and this method was working because we were still around practicing our art.

It is interesting to note that my CO, Captain Harris, was the great-grandson many times over of a famous Confederate general and tactician. His famous namesake was also a cavalry officer. Although I am not saying that his ability was necessarily inherited, I am saying that my captain always knew what to do, when to do it, and how to do it.

He said, "Top, I think we are going to do it this way. To make the hit from the actual ambush site, I'm going to give you one platoon plus. I'll take the rest of the company up on this high ground to your rear. By organizing that critical high ground, we assure ourselves that Charlie will not be able to get around to either of our rears. That high ground will offer us a defendable, safe haven, and if we have to run for it, it will give us a better head start than having to run all the way up the hill to the ridge line."

Using his map, he indicated his plan of attack, and no such plan was written in any of our manuals. Thank God for that.

While the CO and I discussed the whos, whats, whens, and wheres, Redleg was busy planning our artillery fire support. He planned fire concentration directly in front of where our ambush positions would be facing the riverbank and the river. There would be fires all the way down the river, designed to isolate our kill zone, and there would be a wall of steel to hold the enemy at bay, just in case he managed to get too close to our positions. There were also fires planned to cover our withdrawal from the ambush site to where the remainder of the company would be set up on top of the hill. Redleg also planned fires from our own mortars, as backup. And as usual, there were supporting fires planned directly on top of our positions. If that was to be our Final Battle, we were going to take a lot of Charlies with us. Gratis, our final salute. Those fires were simply coded as Redleg Bravo, Charlie, and Delta. Sometimes we changed the code words, but we always kept them within the phonetic alphabet, such as Hotel, Indian, Tango (HIT). Notice that we avoided using "Alfa" because it was part of our call sign, and too many Alfas might cause a mix-up and possibly a delay. In our case, a minute's delay could be disastrous.

The CO took the rest of the company to the high ground and set up, paying special attention to our ambush site and verifying that there was a carefully planned and laid route for us to come home. For the CO and I to work that way was not at all unusual. Besides, the First Platoon was to be the ambush platoon with reinforcements from the Third Platoon, and when we worked the flatlands and fought Charlie Cong, I always stayed with the ambush platoon. I really appreciated hearing our troopers say that it was so good to have Top with them. To hear them say that meant a lot to me because I sure as hell was so proud to be with them, and time never diminished my pride.

As we went about preparing our fighting/defensive positions, we saw some grim reminders of how that same position had been used before as an ambush site by an American unit. The ground was still stained with their blood, and other evidence clearly showed that they had caught hell from Charlie. It hurts me to say this, but according to the Spook who had given us our briefing, that American unit had suffered a great number of casualties and KIAs. In fact, Charlie had overrun that ambush site and chewed up the American unit pretty badly.

Charlie was known to have American Browning .50 caliber machine guns mounted on his boats, and those Brownings had wreaked havoc on that American ambush. We could see where those .50 calibers had chewed up the ground, vegetation, trees, and the Americans. Let's face it. A Browning .50 caliber machine gun is still an awesome weapon today, and Black Knight Alfa fully respected that knowledge when we planned our ambush in that same position.

The Spook told us that Charlie had been using small boats and rafts during that earlier American ambush. He had also carried at least one recoilless rifle, which was one of our weapons. In a few words, the NVA units using that river were well prepared.

You might be wondering why the Americans did not just bomb the river, make air strikes, or put on a steel ambush to take out Charlie. After all, a steel ambush only required calling in a small team to adjust the artillery fire. Apparently, the other Americans had applied those tactics, but Charlie had continued to boldly move troops and supplies down the river. The reason that the South Vietnamese major had attended our briefing was because there had been a plan to move some of the American River Forces up to that river, that is, until the SOG figured it would be much better and more damning if an American unit could pull the plug on Charlie's little river operation. Why SOG was not doing the job, I guess I will never know. What I do know is that Black Knight Alfa was given the job of pulling the plug on Charlie, and we were going to pull that damned plug come hell or high water.

As a rule, we never ambushed from the same positions twice. We might ambush the same trail or location two or three times, but we would always be physically located in a different position each time. Then, why were we setting up in the same positions that the previous American unit had used to ambush that same point along the river, especially when that last unit had gotten their asses kicked so badly? Such a move was considered taboo by most American units.

Sometimes, long-standing rules are best broken, especially when the end results are calculated to fall in your favor. The most opportune time to do the unexpected is when you are expected to follow the rule and to do what everyone else does. The unit before us had hit Charlie slightly after the narrow part of the river, and we planned to hit him slightly before he came upon the minor bend that preceded that narrow portion of the river.

During our planning conference, the CO said to me, "Top, what do you think about us setting up right here, in the exact place along the river where that last unit set up and got murdered? Because it's the best place possible to hit Charlie. Also, you and I are not forgetting that Charlie has good intelligence, and although we sure do hope that he is unaware of our presence and that he hasn't identified our unit, both of us know better than to pin anything important on our hopes. Like you always say, let's make the obvious indistinct."

Again, I felt good because a great tactic does not depend on whether an officer or an NCO had already planned and used it successfully, but rather if that tactic actually worked.

Make no mistake, we planned everything we intended to do very well, leaving nothing to chance and letting nothing fall through the cracks. We even tried like hell to eliminate all potential cracks.

Please understand that I must re-emphasize an important fact now. Despite being the leader, the senior NCO, and the first sergeant, I always listened to what my junior NCO leaders and my troopers had to offer when we planned a mission, our defense, or any other task at hand. I listened to my Sp4s (specialists fourth class), Pfcs. (privates first class), and Pvts. (privates).

Some of our squad leaders were NCOs, or rather sergeants, but most of our squad leaders were Sp4s (some were Pfcs.). Each man's rank had nothing to do with his leadership ability. All of my men were the best available at that time and perhaps the best who have ever existed. When I directed where to put a machine gun, if the squad leader or gunner felt that the gun was better positioned a little more left or right, he said so immediately and I listened. Of course during times of emergency, when discussion was impossible, we did what we had to do. Mutual trust and teamwork were our game strategies, and we always played to win. Although our methods of playing the game were important, "winning was everything" because if we lost, old Death would not allow us to come back onto the battlefield, except maybe as ghosts or spirits.

As we were getting ready, I think all of our troopers saw one thing right away that our predecessors had missed. They had failed to really dig in so that they could get down below ground level and behind something. In the given situation, prone fighting positions did not hack it. In fact, none of the examples in the manual were designed to fit our situation. Nevertheless, the previous American unit had used the classic L-shaped ambush, and Charlie had simply come around the short end and hurt them.

If Charlie tried that tired old shit with us, we had something waiting for him. He would be denied an instant replay. He would learn once and for all not to fuck with Black Knight Alfa because we knew all that talk about Charlie being bad was just a bunch of bullshit. The only thing bad about Charles was his breath.

The CO wanted to get up the hill before it was completely dark, so he took the rest of the company and headed out. Once they were gone, we began to do in earnest what we did best. The platoon sergeant assigned two men to serve as guides for the company until they reached their set-up destination. Then, the two guides would return to our positions and serve as our guides when it was time for us to join the company. When they returned, they gave us the directions to the company in case one or both of them got hit during our journey. They also informed us of the special recognition signals that had been arranged to get us home safely without our troopers mistaking us for Charlie and lighting us up.

After our run-in with the jungle training camp, we were not foolish enough to use a book-recommended type of ambush. Those letter-shaped ambushes looked good on paper, but they probably would not be worth a damn on the ground in an actual tactical situation. We always planned for the unexpected. We designed our own style of ambush that suited our mission and the terrain. Our mission was to kill Charlie without losing any of our men, which was possible if we planned everything correctly. To accomplish that, we had to make the terrain and the environment work for us. We had to use the situation, weather conditions, and the cloak of night to our advantage and to do it in unison. All were prime factors in the establishment of our ambush site.

Our enemies would be just as determined as we were to live and to make victory theirs. They knew that river from start to finish, and we were told that they would have boats, rafts, and possibly smaller and speedier crafts. It was not known if they would be ferrying supplies and/or troops. The Spook said that they sent neither large nor long convoys, and they never sent more than one per night. He had also expressed his certainty that both NVA and Viet Cong soldiers would be involved.

We sent a team upstream against the river flow, and that team sent two men across the river to position two separate sets of flares about 60 to 70 meters apart on the far riverbank. Trip wires[33] were attached and anchored in two places – to each group of flares and back on our side around bushes and trees. One claymore was positioned as a distraction to our location.

Normally for ambush purposes, one set of flares and one trip wire across the river at the narrowest point were sufficient. The river was not very wide at its broadest points, but the lengths of wire we were forced to use made it almost impossible to keep the wire out of the water, prompting the dangerous possibility for any floating debris to snag the trip wire and set the flares off prematurely. By setting out two flare positions at least 50 meters apart, we were able to control them and not let them be dead-snare commanded.[34] After it grew completely dark, the wires would be invisible across the river. We could abort the popping of the flares on the far side of the river, and we had backup flares within our control on our side of the river.

Our ambush site was as deliberate as we could make it, but simplicity in arranging our fighting positions was the guide word. We knew in advance that the enemy had .50 caliber machine guns, and we planned accordingly. In particular, we positioned our troopers well down behind anything that might offer them protection against all flat trajectory weapons. As always, our fighting positions were designed to afford us with all-around protection and defense. We were formed into the design of a crude circle that enabled us to fight and defend in any direction.

Redleg planned two concentrations in the river where we planned to hit the lead boat. If we could catch them dead to right, the 175mm artillery barrages would work for us. Of course, we had to consider the likelihood that something would go wrong.

Unlike the previous American ambush unit, we posted two security teams along the riverbank, one upstream to our right and one downstream to our left. The team upstream was a little farther away than the normal 50 meters. Each team had a radio and a starlight scope. Our company was watching our rear, and because we would be receiving 175mm fire support, the bursting radius of the rounds would dictate how close we could bring them in to us.

We felt somewhat uncomfortable knowing that we were within the range of Charlie's artillery and that there was the chance that when we made our big hit, Charlie would get really pissed off and start shooting his artillery at us.

There were some disadvantages to having two security teams posted outside our ambush position. Having our own people detached from us reduced the amount of fire we could initially place on our target, thereby reducing our kill probability. Such an arrangement also greatly limited the use of our artillery fire support, including our own fires, because we could not fire into the areas where our people were. Also, if the enemy came too close to us, our security teams could not return to our positions, which is why they planned an alternate route up the hill to the majority of the company.

It was necessary to detect the early warning of the enemy's approach and to determine his approximate size, including the size of his boats and rafts. I had to weigh that important information against our initial amount of fire, our fire support, and the men outside our defensive/ fighting perimeter.

It was not easy to make decisions based upon these determinations because too many things could go wrong. When faced with that same dilemma, I could fully understand why the American unit before us had not posted security upstream and downstream. There was no time to dwell on whether I had made the right or wrong decision. The early warning/security teams were already out and in position. All I could do was wait and pray.

Soon it became dark enough for us to venture out along the riverbank to finish setting up and fortifying our positions, which were in the treeline some 50 to 60 meters back from the water's edge. Unfortunately, Charlie had done a job on that section of the wood line during his previous battle, and many broken trees lay scattered about.

Those trees would benefit us in their fallen positions by affording some protection and making it possible for us to be impolite. You see, we were going to "hit and run".

While we were setting up, our normal procedure was to have most of our troops establish positions so that we would have the best possible fire concentration in the planned kill zone. Additionally, we always placed some troopers in key security positions.

One of the main weapons we used in the scheme of our ambushes was the M18 A1 claymore anti-personnel device, which we simply called a claymore. The name of the device was derived from the ancient, large, double-edged sword formerly used by the Scottish Highlanders.

We used our claymores both as close-up defensive weapons and as far-reaching offensive weapons. I would like to think that we used them to their full potential and even beyond the role for which they were originally designed. Sometimes we spliced the wires together for added length, and we placed them in the trees, on the ground, and in other uncommon locations. We always tried to place them with their backs up against something that offered some stability and resistance to backward movement, such as the trunk of a big tree, a strong log, or a boulder.

I instructed our troopers to go down to the riverbanks and to set the claymores just above the waterline where they could do the most damage, backed up against the riverbank, which would serve as a solid backstop. Of course, the claymores and the wires leading back to our positions were covered and concealed. That way, when each claymore, containing 700 steel balls resembling buckshot, was popped, the balls would blow out in a fan-shaped pattern. We used our claymores to cover our kill zone, both forward and in close, as a last-ditch defense, just in case Charles made it across the open riverbank and tried to overrun us.

Our team upstream had the mission of warning us as soon as they sighted the enemy. There was always the distinct possibility that the enemy would put troops ashore and have them come along the riverbank in the areas where an ambush was most probable. If I were Charlie, that is what I would do, which is the reason why I sent that security team upstream. Many years before, some of the old Buffalo Soldiers had taught me about battlefield planning, and they had said, "Look at the terrain through the eyes of your enemy, and plan and think as if you were he. What would you do if you were in his shoes wanting to bring you down?"

The platoon sergeant who was paired with me was rather new in our unit, although he was not new in-country. That ambush allowed me to teach him, and he listened and learned.

We had a few things working in our favor, including the good, hard intelligence provided by SOG. We also received lots of valuable information from our LURP teams, and I was pleased to see that some of the information came from my former LURP team, Shaka. They had observed Charlie floating down that river, which was more like a big stream, but deep enough to allow some of those typically small Vietnamese boats to navigate its entire length. The SOG and LURP teams called artillery fire and air strikes; however, by the time either type of strike arrived, we had already taken care of Charlie.

We were hoping to hold Charlie in position long enough for help in the form of our 175s to get there and walk all over his butt. It was going to be ticklish because our ambush position was much closer to the river than we preferred. That is why the majority of the company was well up the hill on the high ground and out of the impact area. Once we stopped the river convoy and had all of our people with us, we would diddy mau the area and get up the hill as fast as possible. By that time, old Charlie would be onto us, but if he chased us, he would run into the fires of the CO and the rest of Black Knight Alfa.

I never doubted that the NVA and Cong units in Con Thien, Cam Lo, Dong Ha, and all the way down to the bottom of Quang Tri Province would feel the pinch of what we would do that night.

According to the SOG, the NVA had not used the river since that last ambush, and they felt certain that the NVA was coming that night. Even if the NVA decided to hold off for another night, we were prepared to wait until they made the first move. Then, we would make the second move.

Regardless of what Charlie did, we had to stay ahead of him. We waited with the sure knowledge that if we could kill his damned ass on that river, our strike that night would pay many dividends up front in saved American lives.

Darkness came silently in a grand rush. I could hear my wonderful Skytroopers still digging in and upgrading our positions. In between getting things in order, I was also digging my position. I never asked one of my troopers to dig a hole for me. I was well aware that my stripes did not cover my ass and that Charlie sure as hell did not care that I was the first sergeant. He would kill me just like anyone else.

I was a bit worried because it was my first time making a river strike, and I was thinking about what Charlie had done to the last unit who had hit him there. I knew that Charlie would be ready for anything other than for us to hit him from the same place where he had whipped the other American unit.

Our machine guns zeroed in on the entire kill zone, and our thump guns were set to hit the boats and the rafts. Our claymores along the banks were primed, and we had a good supply of LAWs. Both security teams reported that they were well dug in and waiting with their starlight scopes in working order. They had a great view up and down the river.

All was in order, and we settled in to wait. It was roughly after 2230 hours, and everything was very quiet. The CO called to check on us and to inform us that the rest of our company were all set up and waiting just as we were. His last words before signing off were, "Top, we got your rear covered". After that, there would be no radio communication until the hit occurred.

While we waited, I checked our first strike line and was happy to see that we had observed one of the fundamentals printed in the manual – KISS. We surely had "Kept It Simple, Stupid".

I moved around a little, observing our troopers and not finding one man who was worried about us getting hit like the previous American unit. My troopers were busy fixing something to eat, catching forty, changing their socks, and listening to their small portable radios and tape recorders. As I passed some of their positions, I heard many different songs and melodies, including the favorites of that time, such as "Those Were the Days", "She Came in through the Bathroom Window", "The Horse", and "Mercy Mercy Me". At one position, two troopers were busily making Jiffy Pop popcorn. When it was ready, the aluminum top swelled to resemble a big silver ball. They invited me to join them, but I declined and thanked them for the offer before continuing on my rounds.

In case you do not fully understand our situation, there we were, a reinforced infantry rifle platoon, sitting squarely in the same positions where an American company had sat before us and had suffered about 50 per cent casualties. We were close enough to North Vietnam that the

NVA could actually hit us with their artillery or their 122mm rockets. Although we were little more than a platoon, our troopers were not worried. They were going about their normal routine as if it were "just another day" that moved them closer to freedom-bird time. We were Cav, troopers of the 1st Air Cavalry Division. Sweet Jesus, that said it all. Black Knight Alfa. Alpha and Omega!

The time was 2352 hours, and our security team upstream broke squelch[35] two, then three times. That was our signal.

Charlie Was on His Way

We passed the word to the CO and to our troopers. Suddenly, Pete passed his radio handset to me. I took it and said, "This is Five, go."

My team leader upstream said, "Five, we got a problem. Charlie is being crafty. He has a small boat way out front, and if that boat trips our flares first, the big fish may get away. Talk to me. Over."

Before I could tell him what to do, the other trooper with him was already in the process of doing it, as if he had read my mind. He crawled down to the water's edge and quickly released the trip wire we had strung across the water, to prevent the lead boat from pulling the wires and popping our flares. That would have given away our intent and our positions before our target was within the boundaries of our kill zone.

Actions such as that demonstrated our brilliance and alertness. Once again, our teamwork was paying off. We expected the unexpected and properly dealt with it through good teamwork, which kept us alive. Each of our troopers was fully capable of thinking and acting on his own, in the absence of orders or instructions. If I were the first man hit, my troopers were fully capable of taking the mission to a victory. It was a matter of the American way versus the NVA way. Our way dictated that "The absence of one monkey doesn't stop the show".

We silently watched as Charlie's small boat slid by. Pete had alerted our team downstream of what was going down, and they were prepared either to hit or to allow the first boat to sail by and catch it on the rebound.

We were close enough to the small boat to count the men on deck. All eight of the NVA soldiers were in full battle gear and armed to the teeth. We were a bit disturbed to see radios, with long antennas attached and up, strapped to the backs of two soldiers. The small boat moved along the current in close proximity to our side of the river, and

I was worried that Charlie might see our claymores along the riverbank. Fortunately, he did not.

All of our troopers were waiting. They would fire only if I fired, because I was the initiator. If we hit Charlie, those men with the radios might be able to call their artillery down on us. Yet, if I allowed that lead boat to slide on by, it might be the one that could hurt us the most. I had to take those radios out before they could be used to call for help. However, if I hit the lead boat before the main part of the convoy was within our kill zone, we would not have a "clean kill" and we would be open to attack. That damned lead boat had to be taken out but in such a way that would allow us to make our hit and to haul ass if we had to. Let's face it, those radios meant that the lead boat had contact with the main body. Immediately I had to make an important decision and an effective change to our plans.

I could push up to the CO, tell him what we had, and await his instructions. However, that was not a good idea. First of all, I had no idea what other more sophisticated communications equipment our enemy might have on board. They might have locating equipment that would find us if we keyed our radios. Secondly, I was "the leader on the spot", and it was truly my call.

That call proved to be easier to make than I expected, because the main body of the enemy was far too close to its lead boat. Already we could hear the motors of the boats that followed the lead boat. That was Charlie's mistake, and I capitalized on it.

I quickly whispered my plan of attack to Redleg, and he agreed to call for our artillery fire the moment we shot at the lead boat. By that time, we could smell the exhaust fumes from all of the boats. The sounds of the boats' motors were distinctly different; those coming from the boats behind the lead boat were working under more stress.

If we did not act soon, our big red fish would get away. I passed the word to shoot on my signal. Then, I grabbed Pete and we moved as quickly and as silently as possible to a position where there were at least four LAWs. Redleg held his position, knowing exactly what to do. I prayed that I was doing the right thing. My plan hinged on whether or not the trooper at that position could see well enough in the dark to hit that lead boat, which by that time was already past the center of our kill zone, moving slowly downstream. I was going to ask that trooper to hit the rear of the wheelhouse with his first round. The boat was a moving target, but at that moment, it was almost directly opposite our position in the wood line.

The NVA soldiers with the radios were standing close to the rear wall of the boat's wheelhouse. I figured if we could hit them or the wheelhouse, we might silence their radios with one good shot.

"Top, I'm going to blow his ass away. Just you say when," my trooper said as he adjusted his position and verified that his back blast area was clear.

When he popped that LAW, the back blast would light up our positions like a Christmas tree. Of course, as soon as he fired the LAW, everyone on the kill line would open up because it would be show and tell time.

The little Vietnamese boat chugged along, unaware that we were planning to end its career. It was painted blue-and-pink, or some colors close to that.

Although I was pushing it, I waited because I did not want that boat to turn around and come back to haunt us. As I looked back, I could see the rest of the enemy convoy in its wake, slowly entering our kill zone. I let them come just a little farther into our web so that our sting would be more deadly.

The trooper who was set to fire whispered to me with a sense of urgency, "Top, I need to shoot now, or I can't promise you a hit 'cause he's entering a shadowed area."

"Shoot," I whispered, after observing with some satisfaction that the first boat of the convoy was well within our kill zone. It was HIT TIME!

I closed my eyes to preserve my night vision. WHAM! The trooper fired. BOOM! That beautiful LAW streaked straight and true. I think it hit one of the men with a radio. The boat's wheelhouse blew. Our second man in that fighting position already had another LAW extended and locked into firing position. He simply dropped the throwaway launcher, grabbed the second LAW, and fired. Both 66mm high-explosive, armor-piercing rockets slammed into the rear of the lead boat with deadly accuracy. The little boat was literally ripped apart when the second explosion occurred. There was no doubt that the NVA soldiers carrying those radios had no opportunity to contact anyone, except maybe the Hell Hotel to confirm their reservations.

All Hell Broke Loose

The serenade to almighty Death and to the Gods of War began in earnest. I heard the long-mournful stuttering of our machine guns and the thump-thumping of our thump guns, all carried on the rising crescendo of the stinging voices of our M16 rifles. The hit was on.

Even above the sounds of our weapons firing, I could plainly distinguish the screams of pain that were coming from our enemy. We were putting a lot of hurt onto old Charles.

It was time for the dead to start burying the dead.

As usual, we shot first and then popped flares. The river lit up like it was high noon. The boats caught in the harsh glare of our flares were just a little bit larger but still designed to operate in reasonably shallow water. I do not know anything about boats, but those boats seemed different from, for example, fishing boats, and they were much smaller than the ones I have seen off the coast of Maine.

Knowing that his shit was on the fan, Charlie sped up, trying to move quickly out of the danger zone. You should have heard the way he gunned his motors. It was all to no avail, though, because we were dropping the hammer on the lead boat in an effort to hold the convoy in position until our artillery could drop some shit on them.

We cut loose with all that we had, which was a lot, considering that our troopers were not just shooting for volume. They were aiming at and hitting selected targets. Our thump gunners were dropping their 40mm grenades right on top of any personnel who were within our shooting range.

You can bet that Charlie shot back. With his .50 caliber machine guns he tried to bring awesome firepower to bear on us. However, his fires were ineffective because he was busy ducking and dodging to try to save his ass. Black Knight Alfa was all over him like a very bad case of the Sin City Pox.

For those of you who are too young to know about such things as the Pox and Sin City, Sin City was a little village where all of the whores hung out and where one could get anything and everything for a small amount of P[36]. The Pox was an alias for a great number of social diseases that had a bad habit of refusing to go away.

Our flares lit up the area like the Astrodome for a night game, and we had the best seats in the house. From our vantage point we could see every move Charles made, and we could see the absolute terror on his face.

We observed some of the NVA soldiers as they jumped over the sides of their boats and rushed toward the nearest riverbank, which happened to be right down in front of us. The poor bastards were rushing headlong into our deadly accurate fire and our claymores that were embedded in the edge of the riverbank. Our Weapons Platoon began popping flares to keep some light on the stage so that we would not miss a single important, and perhaps impromptu, act.

Pete screamed in my ear, "Top, the marker round[37] for Redleg Bravo is shot out! Wait."

That meant our artillery supporting fire was on the way. Redleg had changed the first round to a marker round because of our proximity to the river and the enemy targets, as well as the bursting radius of the 175mm projos and the fact that we had the situation well in hand. There was no emergency or immediate threat to us. Redleg decided to test the water first by putting a single round on the target. From that round he could adjust our artillery fires to hit a dime and give you nine cents in change. Our Redleg and Birth Control (the 32nd) were that good. The marker round landed exactly where Redleg intended, and the 32nd was most obliging when that round hit one of the rafts being pulled by one of the onrushing boats. There was another boat just slightly ahead of the one pulling the raft. The two boats and the raft danced a crazy jig on the water before capsizing. The 175mm high-explosive round hit the corner of the raft. First we saw the raft, and then BOOM, it was gone.

Pete listened to Redleg's push on his speaker so that I could hear what was going on. Redleg confirmed the marker round, and Concentration Bravo was "Shot out!" in the air and on its way to us. By that time we could see that most of the boats were pulling unprotected rafts loaded with supplies and troops. Some of the troops were scrambling to hide behind the burlap bales and wooden boxes, but it was pointless.

Concentration Bravo arrived and pandemonium reigned supreme. We ducked to avoid the flying debris, water, and human body parts. As planned, the 32nd added into their delivery what we called "Killer Juniors". These were rounds with very special fuses, often called "proximity fuses", that caused the rounds to explode approximately 10 meters above the ground or the target. On top of all that, Battalion requested and received from Division 8-inch artillery fire. Redleg was already prepared to make the necessary adjustments for those 8 inchers to join the party.

It was all over. The only thing left for Charlie to do was to very quickly kiss his ass goodbye!

Payback for all that was due was in progress, payback for what they had done to that American unit before us and our poor brother whom they had strung up on that trail. What goes around …

I was lying on the ground beside a big tree, and Pete was down on his knees, leaning against the same tree. While he was switching back to our internal company frequency, something really big hit our tree. It felt as if the tree had been hit by a fast-moving Mack truck. The impact bowled Pete over, and his foot almost knocked my helmet off.

We were amazed to discover what had hit the tree. It was the better part of a Browning .50 caliber machine gun that was bent about midway. After hitting the tree, the barrel had stuck in the ground near Pete's outstretched foot. The bad news was knowing that the NVA really did have some of our .50 caliber machine guns and ammunition. The good news was that the bastards did not get the chance to use American-made weapons against us.

Birth Control was doing a bam-bam on Charlie. While that was in progress, our side fired only on targets of opportunity. The name of our game was to save ammunition. Experience had taught us well. Our location was no longer a secret, and Charlie was doing his best to return fire. However, by that time, old Charles was focusing his attention on a much more pressing problem. Birth Control was dumping a lot of hot steel on his butt, and old Death was having a field night with Charlie.

We received some illumination rounds so that we could see part of what was going on. We were already soaking wet because those 175s and 8-inch high-explosive projectiles had blown much of the muddy water out of the river and onto us. All kinds of shit was raining down with the muddy water. We were extremely glad for any protection our positions offered us. Once again, the wisdom of digging in and going way down below ground level was paying off.

Redleg suggested that we lift our excellent supporting fire, and I agreed. However, we did request illumination at an interval that gave us continued light on the stage. I told Pete to give the word to "Shift right." On that order, our M60 machine guns moved one position to their right, so that anyone who approached our ambush site would first be engaged by our thump guns and our M16s. The machine guns would fire only if it became necessary. That way we could hide our firepower from Charlie until it was too late for him. We remained down in our positions, silently waiting. I heard two of my troopers whispering about the dead fish in their hole; another position claimed there was enough water in his hole to go swimming.

The quietness was broken only by the pop of illumination rounds and the sounds coming from the broken and the dying. How I hated that time, and it always came to that time, when we made a hit and did not run immediately. No matter how hard you profess to be, to hear a man crying and begging for help, even if he was the enemy, was a horrible thing to endure. It was that sort of experience that still causes Vietnam veterans to wake up from their sleep screaming.

My sit-reps were coming in, and I could tell by the smile of relief on Pete's face that they were good ones. He gave me the thumbs-up signal. We had not lost a man and that included both of our security teams. However, we had hurt Charlie and the NVA most grievously.

I pushed up to the CO and briefly updated him on the information that I had just received. Happily, he told us to pull up stakes and come home as soon as our security teams returned.

I pushed up to our security team upstream and told them to come back to our ambush site. Because they held a much higher position along the riverbank, they could see the results of our destruction better than we could. They declared our mission a success. The team downstream had already received word to return to our positions, and they reported that the lead boat had exploded, leaving no obvious survivors.

I was talking to my team leader upstream when "it" happened.

If Something Can Go Wrong, Rest Assured it Will!

"Top, there are a lot of Charlies alive and well, and they are trying to come up on your position from behind!" my upstream security team reported in the open over their radio.

"Should we take them on or ...?" the team leader started to ask. Then he added, "Charlie had a boat running drag, and that boat was also hit by our artillery fire, but not before the NVA troops aboard were able to jump off and make it to the riverbanks. The boat was dead in the water, but the crew and most of the troops aboard were at that time moving up the side of the high ground, heading our way."

I told Pete to pass that information to the CO so they could be ready. It was necessary for me to implement Plan B, but before I could and because Charlie did not go far enough up the high ground, he ran into our upstream security team. Originally, I had planned to send only two men upstream, because sending two teams reduced the firepower left on the ambush site. However, I had thankfully followed my gut feeling and had sent four men.

Our security team had to shoot or be stumbled upon so they ambushed the enemy unit heading toward us. They had an M60 and two thump guns, in addition to their usual setup of carefully positioned claymores. Charlie was caught off guard by the ambush. He had known of our ambush position but had probably thought we were set up exactly like the unit before us, where everything was at a single ambush site. Charlie's incorrect thinking was a real killer to him. Our guys cut him a new asshole, and we could hear Charlie screaming "Foul!" from our positions.

I devoted most of Plan B's design to getting my security team safely back to our positions. I told them to come on home. While Charlie was adjusting to his new, unexpected threat, my troopers were running back to our positions and doing that under the covering fire that was coming mainly from our thump gunners.

Both teams safely rejoined our positions. They were intact and unhurt. We were scratched, bruised, and a bit out of breath, but those conditions were far better than being out of life. The CO asked if we needed some "sunshine".[38]

I felt that our best hold card was to keep the company's location under wraps, so I replied, "Negative on the sunshine."

I had no fear of the enemy surprising us. With both of my security teams back in position, I knew that anyone outside of our lager was the enemy and would be treated as such. The downside of that situation was that we could not fire in the direction of our company to our rear, and they could not fire in our direction. However, if we had to withdraw under enemy fire, they could give us accurate fire to cover our withdrawal up to their positions. Also, we had designed fires to prevent the enemy from getting between our positions.

We were going it alone and without panic. Using our starlight scopes, we could see the enemy very well, and we could accurately direct the fires of our thump guns. Unfortunately, we had no idea of how strong in number our enemy's forces were. Still, it was best to nullify him before we attempted to join the rest of our company on the high ground.

Because we did not know how many of the NVA troops we were up against and given the possibility that they might get between us, the CO suggested that I come home. The final decision was left open to me because I was the man on the spot. I based my final decision upon the unknown factors of how many Charlies were getting ready to hit us, how long it might be before they did, and the possibility that they might be strong enough to maneuver between our company and us. These unknown factors were clearly a disadvantage to us. Just as Charlie would do, I decided that a good run was far better than a bad stay.

I pushed back up to the CO and said, "Six, this is Five, over."

"Five, this is Six. Go."

"Six, I request permission to come home."

"Five, this is Six. That's most affirm. Come on home. Out."

We collected our stuff and moved out, going up the hill in an orderly manner while our thump gunners were shooting. I was the last man to pull out, right behind Pete. That way, no one would be left behind accidentally.

I know it was sneaky, but we were hoping that Charles would gather his troops and rush our vacated positions. Redleg was planning heavily on such an event. Come into our parlor.

We no sooner passed our first guide into the company positions when Charlie started hitting our vacated positions with a high volume of firepower. He also had at least one Type 63, 60mm mortar, but I guess he had only a few rounds of ammunition. Nevertheless, he kept hitting our hastily vacated positions.

We could clearly perceive the cracking and whumping sounds of the mortar rounds exploding, and we knew they were 60 millimeters. However, we also heard a much larger caliber, high-explosive ammunition hitting our old ambush site, although the larger rounds were hitting too far out and into the river.

Later it was confirmed that Charlie had indeed called in his artillery, so they must have zeroed in on that original ambush site even though they missed it by a good 100 meters and mostly hit the river. They were shooting the M46 130mm Gun-Howitzer at us. I think the gun's position and the mountain disoriented the gunners.

Charlie was also getting hit by some of his own artillery fire. To avoid being wiped out by his own men, he took his only option by rushing onto the target area that his gunners were trying to shoot but kept missing.

Then, Charlie made a crazy charge onto our old ambush site at approximately the same time our supporting fires arrived. As designed, those fires fell squarely on our ambush site, effectively bringing down the curtain on the final act of our night-time ambush of an NVA river supply convoy.

I say a heartfelt "thanks" to all of the wonderful artillery men who shot for us, especially to the men of Charlie Battery, the 2nd Battalion of (I think) the 32nd Artillery. If I got it wrong, I am sorry, but I sure as hell do thank you, whoever you were. We would never have pulled off our ambush without your help.

We prepared to move on at the first light of the coming day. We were very proud and happy to see a flight of F4 Phantom jets arrive on station. They were not there to shoot but rather to make sure that Charles would know that the unit on the ground who had kicked his ass the night before was no longer alone. Battalion requested a body count, so we moved down to accomplish that dreadful task. Our company medics rendered aid to those in need. I think most of us were awestruck by the complete devastation around us.

There was no way that Charles was going to use that river again any time soon. It was effectively plugged up with the debris of all the supplies he had lost, not to mention the blown-apart boats and rafts littering the water and banks. Some of the lighter debris floated on the slowly moving, downriver current. We placed some of our calling cards on the floating debris.

We tried hard not to be affected by the sight of the devastation, the body parts, and the bodies scattered as far as we could see. Although it was hot and we were sweating, our bodies were shaking with persistent cold chills. As always, I had no one but my old self and my mother to listen to my silent cries and screams of agony. I had to clench my lips tightly and grit my teeth together, often tasting my own blood. Maybe it was my imagination, but I do believe that I started turning gray there. I had not noticed any gray hair on my head before I went to Nam.

Upstream we found the battered hulk of the only boat we did not sink. One look at the boat was mute testimony to the accuracy of our fire and that of our artillery support. As we had suspected, that boat had contained some technologically good communications and locating equipment which, of course, were now junk. It looked like Charlie could have used it to call all the way to General Giap's headquarters in Hanoi. I wondered if he would continue to wave his fist and smile after he received the news of our strike. Anyway, it was sad to see that the equipment our enemy was using against us had been given to them by our friends, the Red Chinese and the Russians. Only God knew who else was supporting Charlie.

Two huge Johnson Seahorse outboard motors were attached to one big barge, and some of the other barges were powered by Russian-made motors. The rest were of unknown origin. I would guess that there were four large barges; three were manufactured and one seemed to be handmade. One of the manufactured barges had a .50 caliber machine gun on a pedestal mount, and another boat had one on its original tripod mount located atop the wheelhouse. Strewn all over the place were rice, racing slicks, canned fish, uniforms, all kinds of ammunition, medical supplies, some fresh vegetables, and chickens. We released those chickens that were still alive.

Pete gave me the word, "Birds inbound."

The battalion commander and the Vietnamese major were on the Charley-Charley bird, but we did not see the Spook. An officer and three enlisted men were there from the Brown Water Navy (a long way from the Mekong Delta), and they were anxious to inspect what was left. Our S-2 said he thought that Charlie's call to inform his headquarters about the ambush had been made from the boat with the radio equipment, but he did not think their call for artillery had come from that boat.

That night's operation had not cost us a single life, and none of our troopers had suffered a bullet wound. Our three men who went out on dust-off had been injured by falling debris. A few men had shrapnel wounds, and one man was being treated for a badly swollen bite wound.

We were relieved when the battalion commander released us from the task of body counting.

Sometime later, we were lifted out of that area to a more favorable LZ. Then, we moved back to a secure firebase/LZ.

After the Final Curtain

Our ambush went well not only because we were the best infantry Cav team fighting in Vietnam, but also because we always worked as a team, we planned well, and each of our troopers knew as much as we leaders knew. We always planned what to do when something went wrong, leaving nothing to chance. Notice that I did not say "if" something went wrong. We did it right the first time, every time. We viewed the mission and objective through the eyes and the minds of our enemies, and we listened to our troopers. Finally, we never underestimated the power of our enemies.

Am I ringing our own bell? Damn right I am, because most of the people who have written about "our" Vietnam experiences have told you about all of the bad things they said we did, but they never told you about the good things we actually did. They made it possible for you to hear the term "Vietnam vet" and immediately conjure up a negative image of us. You think of us as drug-heads and baby killers. You think of us fragging and killing each other, the Bloods against the Whites. You think of the Saigon Warriors – loud, drunk, and chasing girls. You think about My Lai and picture us smoking pot through the barrel of a shotgun. You probably think that we were all basically degenerates.

Well, I have news for you if you think that way. Our ambush was successful because we were good soldiers, and we went about our mission as professionals. Every man on our team knew his job and knew the success of our mission not only depended on him, but also on the man to his right and the one to his left, no matter what color that man was, how he prayed or whether he prayed. Let it be known that our American fighting men were outstanding soldiers in the purest sense of the word. We were the same type of soldiers that were sent to fight at Lexington and Concord, to become the Rock of the Marne, to fight at the Battle of the Bulge, Iwo Jima, Pork Chop, and Hamburger Hill. We were the salt of the Earth and certainly did not deserve the bum rap that the news media and a lot of others gave us. God bless us all!

Charlie and his supporters were out there with one purpose in mind, and that was to take our lives. They were Equal Opportunity Killers, and they did not give a damn what color we were or whether we were straight or gay. Therefore, we had to be the best and stay the best. That is why we lived and many of them died. We won and they lost. Victory was ours, but somehow you did not hear that our company took out an entire convoy of NVA soldiers including their boats, rafts, and all supplies given to them by our other enemies who included the Russians and the Chinese. We dumped it all into the river, along with Charlie. You were also not told that Charlie never again used that river to ship his troops and supplies. Somehow, you were never told about such actions on our part. Well, it happened that way, and that was just the beginning.

Black Knight Alfa. Alpha and Omega.

A Final Word

I am well aware of the fact that there are some things better left undisturbed and unsaid. However, I am moved to say these words regarding the practice of ambushing before I continue with the story of Black Knight Alfa.

Frankly, I do not know who introduced the ambush as a tactical maneuver. However, I will share with you my personal observations about the tactics of ambushing, based on the environment in which I grew up.

I remember going to the movies on Saturday mornings to watch my favorite cowboys in the white hats overcome the bad guys in the black hats. The good guys never shot a bad guy in the back, and they also never ambushed or bushwhacked a bad guy. Such tactics were simply unthinkable. It was also unlikely for the bad guys to shoot a good guy in the back. Of course, it was okay for either type of guy to cut off the other one at the pass, but bushwhacking did not happen.

At first, I found it almost too overwhelming to lie in ambush for the Viet Cong and even harder to do so for the NVA. For me that was something that went against the grain. Nevertheless, I became used to it after I saw what the Cong and the NVA did to some of our American units after they ambushed them. Charlie certainly used the ambush tactic against us. He poisoned us with his drugs, sold our soldiers Coca-Cola laced with battery acid, and set fiendish traps to mutilate and kill us whenever and wherever he could. I refuse to relate, however, what Charlie did to our guys after ambushing and killing them.

After having several opportunities to painfully observe and experience the inhuman methods employed by the NVA and the Cong,

I warmed up to the ambush tactic. I eventually began to look forward to ambushing the NVA and especially Charlie Cong.

Every man in Black Knight Alfa became hardened to the stark reality of the ambush, and we became extremely proficient in the matter. It was certainly a lot easier to hit and run, because you did not have to stick around and come face-to-face with what the dead did not bury. To lie there enduring the pitiful cries after a hit, however, was exceptionally difficult. And when it was all over, we acquired a legacy of painful nightmares that never went away.

Moving On

We had good days and bad days. During most of those days, either we chased Charlie or he chased us. We were not above hauling ass because it aided our survival. We understood the time-honored adage "There is a time to stand and fight, and there is a time to run away". Most of all, we knew exactly when to do which, and we knew the difference between bravery and stupidity.

We knew the fundamental rules of survival well, and we abided by them always in order to survive in hostile territory. Our ability to diddy mau had paid off for us many times. We were all willing to do whatever was necessary to realize our dream of getting on that freedom bird back home. Of course, it hurt us like hell to read in the newspapers and to hear on the radio that many Americans did not want us to come home alive. That knowledge hurt us more than anything that Charlie could ever have thrown at us.

On the other hand, not being wanted back home helped us to build a stronger brotherhood. Each day and night out there in the hot jungle brought us closer together as a team, a family, a close-knit unit, and a finely honed fighting machine.

More often than before, when Charlie was foolish enough to call us out and pull on us, we kicked his ass all the way up around his neck. When the NVA placed a large bounty on the heads of Black Knight Alfa, Charlie tried to collect it but soon realized that it was healthier to avoid decisive contact with our unit and to treat us as if we had the plague.

Late one miserably hot evening, just before we picked a FOB location, we received urgent orders from Battalion to go deeper into the jungle to rescue a downed American pilot who was presumed to be alive. An RF-4C Phantom had been hit over North Vietnam by a Russian SAM.[39] Although combat air/sea rescue teams quickly retrieved the weapons systems officer, they searched for the pilot for hours without finding him because he had crashed through a double jungle canopy some distance away from the weapons systems officer. If the pilot was still alive and conscious, his bleeper[10] must have been inoperative because it was not emitting a signal.

Among the rescue aircraft that flew over the area searching for the downed pilot were two Jolly Greens[41] and two A 1 Skyraiders. They tried everything, but they could not locate the pilot's exact position. However, they did have some idea of where he had gone through the canopy, but darkness and a low fuel supply hindered further search efforts from the air. Additionally, the rescue aircraft had to leave the area for fear of revealing the downed pilot's suspected location to Charlie. Upon learning that a Cav company was on the ground near where they believed the downed pilot was, they requested that we rescue him.

We had to hat up immediately and push hard to try to reach the pilot before Charlie did. Our new mission required us to move around in almost total darkness, which was a bit out of our line of experience. The moonlight was almost absent beneath the jungle canopy, except in places where there was a break or a tear in it. Fortunately, it was a clear night and the moon was slightly less than half full. We were under a single canopy at the time, but we knew that we might find ourselves facing a triple canopy before we located the pilot. Regardless of the conditions, we were going in, and we would not come out until we retrieved him – dead or alive.

I could not help but think about the fact that those rescue teams rarely gave up, even in times of extreme darkness and stormy weather. The pilot had to be in an area that was virtually inaccessible from the air.

"Top, make sure every man knows why we are moving and what our mission is," the CO instructed me.

We had just enough time to study our maps and apply the data we received from Rescue by way of Battalion. I called all of our platoon sergeants to the Headquarters position, and we decided on the best way to accomplish our mission. We would travel strictly by compass and magnetic azimuth because there were no prominent terrain features for us to use as guide markers. After converting the relevant data and information to a common thrust line under a magnetic azimuth, we prepared to move out.

We set up our compasses and the order of our march. After establishing our given formation, we were in motion. Once our eyes adjusted to the darkness, it became our friend and brought us some relief from the heat of the day. Meanwhile, we were on the move, balancing speed and silence on the scale of time.

Keep in mind that we are talking about a full Cav infantry rifle company moving with a full combat load through an unfamiliar jungle in conditions of very poor visibility. We were in Charlie's backyard, which was no big thing; however, we were almost running, engaged in a race with Charlie to find the pilot. For us, this was an uncommon and unfamiliar situation.

Under conditions of good visibility, we would probably have spread far apart and formed a wide column formation for flexibility and speed. In our given situation, however, we established a thinly spread column, spacing ourselves as far apart as the reduced visibility would allow. Because we required some form of contact, we used connecting files, with the lead platoon connected to the adjacent platoon by almost an entire squad.

The CO designated One-Six to lead out, and JoJo was on point with Nat from Three-Six. The CO, Redleg, and Doc B. pulled up behind One-Six, and I went forward to be close to JoJo and Nat. Even though JoJo was a long way from the Louisiana bayous and gator hunting, he was still part water moccasin or cottonmouth, and his heat-perceptive senses for detecting warm-blooded prey were in full bloom. If Charlie was near, JoJo would be the first to know it and to react.

Once again, we had to use those lousy, old French maps. We selected a good ridge line and headed for it, using a series of small trails until we found it. The ridge line ran in the same general direction we were going, so we decided to take "Route 66" because it was the best way to get to "LA."

Naturally, taking those trails presented many disadvantages to us, like making us candidates for an ambush. Therefore, we spread far apart to prevent Charlie from ambushing all of us at once. It also helped that our drag platoon was machine gun-heavy, and if we were hit, our base of fire would not be in the kill zone. Also in our favor was the fact that Charlie did not usually place snaps and traps on the trails that he used in the highlands and mountains.

Once we reached the ridge line, we discovered a good trail. While our company took five, the CO and I stood under a poncho with our light and studied the ridge-line trail on the map. We had been pushing hard for well over an hour. If we took the trail that went along the ridge line in the same general direction, we could get off at the point where the trail turned sharply to the right and then shoot an azimuth to our target. We would not have to travel very far before we reached the coordinates where the downed pilot was thought to be.

After deciding to take the trail, we determined the order of our march – One-Six, Headquarters, Two-Six, Weapons, and Three-Six running drag and machine gun-heavy. Our soon-to-be CO, Captain Brooks, accompanied us on that mission, and he was in the process of learning how we operated. This was his second tour in the Nam. He had spent his first tour with the 1st Infantry Division, and he had rightfully earned his way to Cav Country, where he would soon take over our company. During our initial discussion with him, he assured us that he would not change the way the present CO (Captain Harris) and I were running the company. We were off to a flying start.

In fact, we were almost flying along the trail as if we owned it. We were taking chances that we would not take under normal circumstances. It was possible that a man's life hung in the balance. The weapons systems officer reported that the pilot had been hit, but he did not know how badly. I know that every man in our company was praying in his own way that we would find the pilot alive. God knows we owed all the American pilots and their crews every effort we could muster, so everyone was pushing to the max. Our troopers were really humping a load. We were loaded for Charlie and had not yet had a firefight with him.

We came to the right turn in the trail, and Redleg shot the azimuth with his M2 artillery compass. Then, the CO and I shot ours, and we verified that JoJo's direction was accurate. We moved off the trail and knew it would be rough going for a while, but that was okay because we felt that we were on a mission of mercy.

Before long, JoJo stopped and sniffed the humid air. The distinct odor of old Charles floated on the slight breeze. We smelled him a lot sooner than we expected, and we knew that he was after the same prize.

113

The good news is that we reached our destination before Charlie did. Unfortunately, the area was rather wide. We set up security in the form of our typical lager and then had everyone move outward to widen the circle, as we maintained visual contact with the person on either side of us. Everyone searched the ground and the trees.

Within a few minutes, Pete said to me, "Top, the Second Platoon has found him. He's up in a tall tree."

As he spoke, we were already moving in that direction.

The pilot was tangled in his parachute lines and hanging very still at a crazy angle. His chute was torn and caught in the many branches that supported him. A bright ray of moonlight shone down on the pilot through a ragged hole indirectly above him in the jungle canopy.

Everyone who saw the moonlight shining on the still figure of the pilot noticed that the scene had an enchanting quality. The manner in which he hung made him look like a man on a Christian cross, and the angle of the moonlight perfectly illuminated his hanging figure, making him impossible to miss. It was as if God were showing us the way to the pilot, which was eerie to say the least. Some of the troopers and I crossed ourselves because we were experiencing a special moment.

Understand that I am not a very religious person. I do not go to church every Sunday, and I do not carry around a Bible quoting scriptures. However, I do believe in God. I was raised in the Mississippi Delta, and that alone should tell you something about my religious feelings.

It was time for action. Doc B. and a few other men formed a human ladder by holding hands with three men on the ground and bearing two men on their shoulders. In that way, they were quickly able to cut the pilot down.

Meanwhile, I shifted our company's defensive circle and formed it solidly around where we were working. We also posted security a little way outside our lager but within sight of the men on the red line. Although we were prepared to hip shoot our mortars, we did not feel that Charlie was near enough to make such an attack necessary. Nevertheless, it was always possible that our feelings might be off-center, so I positioned the drag platoon along the side of our lager on the red line where we figured Charlie might approach us. If he arrived early, we would be ready for him.

It was possible that Charlie had arrived at the scene first and was using the pilot as bait. However, we strongly believed our senses and intuition, which told us that Charlie was nowhere near to us yet.

With assistance from our two captains, our men very gently lowered the pilot to the waiting, outstretched arms of our troopers. Doc B. and one of our platoon medics immediately attended to the pilot. Some of the troopers fashioned a poncho liner into a hammock and attached it to a strong pole that they had cut. The hammock design allowed two men to place the pole across their shoulders and to carry the pilot suspended from it. That was how we (and also Charlie) carried our wounded. Plenty of volunteers offered to carry the pilot. We also transported his useable gear after we carefully buried the remaining, unimportant items so that Charlie would not find them.

JoJo whispered to me, "Top, I think Charles is heading right for us. We gotta get the hell outta here."

He was right. My alarm bells were ringing all over the place.

"Top, let's move it!" the CO yelled to me.

I knew he was feeling old Charlie as much as JoJo and I were. I responded, "Sir, JoJo and I feel that Charles is right behind us, and he is coming along about the same way we came. If we go back that way, we're going to run right into him."

"Okay, let's go east," the CO said.

Having overheard the CO, JoJo was already heading out. We were going to do the unexpected by making a beeline for the coast of the South China Sea, which was dead east. Our gut feelings told us to move quickly because old Charles was getting closer.

To go back the way we had come was not a smart option; however, Charlie would probably expect us to return that way because it was the best way to reach the closest American firebases and LZs. By going in that expected direction, we could reach Khe Sanh and arrive back in the range of our artillery support. In theory, it made very good sense for us to go south, but we went east because we wanted to confuse Charlie.

We were doing it our way – the unexpected way – and that became our hallmark. We moved east at a pretty good clip. We tried to reach Battalion but found that impossible. Then we tried to push up to Khe Sanh and found that a useless effort, too, even with our long antennas. We tried only three times because we did not want Charlie to get a fix on our location.

Pressing hard and strung out far too much, we ran for a long time and distance. We were definitely in unfamiliar territory. When the CO told us to slow down, we came to a halt and waited while a team swept our trail to ensure that we had not picked up a tail.

We caught the distinctive odors of JP-4[42] explosives, heated metal, and something burnt. These odors were alien to our jungle surroundings. After a hurried conference, the CO decided to take a few minutes to search for what we felt was the downed Phantom. The gaping hole in the jungle canopy indicated where we needed to look, and it took us a few minutes to locate the crash site.

We found the proud bird relatively intact, although the wings were gone and the tail section was blown away. Only one side appeared to have been hit, and there were a thousand shrapnel holes between the pilot's and the weapons systems officer's positions. The plane had probably not exploded and burned because the wings had been torn away before the fuselage came to rest.

"Top, someone has been here already. Maybe that old bird is booby-trapped. I don't think we should get any closer to it," JoJo warned, as he inspected the surrounding area. Despite the darkness, his keen senses told him that someone had been there.

Captain Brooks added, "There's a very good chance the air/sea rescue teams have already taken what they could from the wreckage and maybe set it to blow if anyone tampers with it. Charlie would love to get his hands on all of those useable parts, so if our guys were here, you can bet they didn't just leave it there for Charles to pick clean of all its goodies."

The CO agreed. There was one hell of a hole in the canopy, which gave us some moonlight to see by. From our vantage point we saw no evidence that someone had walked among the wreckage, which led us to believe that the rescue team had entered and exited the site on ropes.

The CO said, "You know, Top, Battalion did say the bird was hit over the north target, and the pilot was trying to get it home but couldn't. Maybe he was going south till he was sure he wasn't going to make it. Then he decided to ditch in the South China Sea and couldn't make it there either. That would explain why the bird is down facing east rather than south. Let's mark its location on our maps and move out smartly."

We did as the CO suggested.

"Top, I think there's a good chance that Charlie is onto us. After all, we haven't made it a secret which direction we're going," Pete said.

He spoke the truth. We had not made any good changes in our direction recently, and even Charles could pick up our trail. Normally, we would have doubled back on our own trail and bitten Charlie's butt.

However, we were in a different situation. We were not there to fight Charlie but to recover a downed pilot.

One of our effective methods to determine whether or not we were being followed by the NVA was to leave some little presents along our trail for Charlie while we were on the move. Naturally, we noted those places on our maps. That way, when old Charles popped one of our presents, we would know exactly where he was. I will admit that we designed our little presents to cause Charlie some severe pain. Who said war was supposed to be nice?

I noticed that we were dog-tired, so I addressed the CO: "Sir, I –"

He smiled and interrupted, "You don't have to say it, Top. I know it already. You remember that high ground we picked out, just in case we had to do this. Well, you tell JoJo to take us there by the most direct route. It's time we took a break."

I moved as fast as my tired, old legs and the situation would permit. Then I told JoJo and Nat what to do. As always, we sent a recon and security team to check out the position. When we got the all-clear signal, I moved the company onto the high ground. We were thankful that we had planned for that unexpected turn of events; otherwise, we would not have known where we were. Because of our planning, we knew exactly where we were and could give you the map coordinates right down to the nearest meter. We also had some prior knowledge of the terrain surrounding our positions so that we would know where the best positions were for our machine guns and also where the avenues of probable enemy approach were located.

I was surprised when the CO told me that we would spend the remaining hours of darkness there and that I should prepare the company to stay until help arrived if Charlie decided to hit us. Then I understood that the CO had selected that position as a rally/rendezvous point. I had mistakenly thought we would stay there only long enough to rest before continuing with our dash to the sea.

Once we had accounted for everyone, we quickly passed the phrase "You're home," which meant to stay put. We dug double fighting/defensive positions, placed claymores, and delivered mortar rounds to the mortar positions. We put all available cover and concealment to use. Very shortly, Black Knight Alfa would disappear. As I always said, old Charlie did not have a monopoly on "blending in" or "melting away". We could do the same thing but with much more class.

As soon as I received an "up" from all platoons, the CO said "50/50." This meant that one man in each double position could sleep while the other man stayed alert. We worked out the details of the arrangements among ourselves concerning the shift lengths and who would be the first to stand watch. Pete and I took turns digging our hole, and we split our shifts equally like everyone else did.

We decided to wait until daylight, when we would once again be in motion, before trying to reach Battalion. That proved to be a good decision because shortly before first light, Charlie found one of our little presents. We heard him screaming in the distance. That present had been attached to a flare, and we knew exactly where it was. We knew that a monkey had not set off our present because Charlie reacted by popping caps at the wind. He must have thought he was caught in an ambush because he seriously damaged the surrounding vegetation before he stopped firing.

Once the flare was popped, we went into full alert. We knew that Charlie had picked up our trail and was following us. The only thing we did not know was how many of him there were.

Everyone was ready, and the stillness was broken only by the night-time sounds of the creatures in the jungle. We got down as much as possible while maintaining good observation of our front and our area of responsibility. Then we waited.

I am not at all sure how long it was before we saw them. However, I do remember that even under the canopy, there was just enough light for us to get a good look at them. We could see them – a whole bunch of North Vietnamese Army soldiers – well, but they neither saw us nor suspected that we were watching their every move. One of Charlie's platoon-size units passed so close to our Third Platoon that our guys could almost touch the enemy soldiers. In fact, one Charlie stumbled over the branches used to conceal one of our claymores. Our nearest trooper had the safety on his M57 electrical firing device in firing position and was ready to pop the claymore into Charlie's face if he noticed it, but Charlie did not see it.

The style of walking and the attitude of the NVA soldiers told us they felt secure in their own backyard. Most of them were not paying much attention to their assigned tasks. Instead, they were talking back and forth and rattling their equipment. One soldier near us was smoking a foul-smelling cigarette. Charlie was underestimating us, and his negligence served us well.

The Third Platoon reported that the NVA unit who had recently passed them was carrying some type of fancy communications gear with extra-long antennas. This information reassured the CO that he had made the correct decision by not trying to repeatedly contact Battalion because the NVA's fancy radios might have picked us up. If those radios were what we thought they were, then there were at least two other such units looking for us. From all of the reports that we later received, those NVA units who had passed us were top-of-the-line, full-time NVA troops, and they outnumbered us by a very wide margin.

As soon as we thought it was advisable, we sent a team to dog the NVA troops for a measured distance, and we posted security in case there were others following the first group. When our dogging team returned and our security teams were in position, they gave us the all-clear signal. We were able to contact Battalion on the first push, and we relayed our latest information as quickly as possible. Soon thereafter, air/sea rescue teams were on their way to assist us.

When a flight of F4 Phantoms arrived on station, the rescue teams dropped us a jungle penetrator for the pilot. Once he was safely in their hands, we moved quickly to another area, where the canopy assisted us in quickly cutting an LZ. Then we were extracted.

Once again, we were proud of our successful mission, and everyone felt good when the pilot was lifted out. That we had found and saved him was further proof of our company saying "Brother, I'll die for you, and I'll never leave you out there".

Before and during the time we rescued the pilot, we worked the mountains and the highlands without losing a single trooper KIA. All the while, we had hurt the NVA in a most grievous manner, causing them to lose great amounts of supplies, equipment, and lives.

Did that amazing phenomenon result because someone up there was looking out for us? Was it just a stroke of good luck? Was it because we had played our hand right? Was it because we were always a first-class act who did it right the first time as a team without ever losing our cool? Was it a combination of all of the above or possibly none of the above? Were we, perhaps, the reigning champions because we could float like a butterfly and sting like a beautiful black-and-yellow krait?[43]

All indications claimed that we had indeed earned Charlie's respect. Otherwise, he would not be offering a sizeable reward for our heads. Had we not met him on the sacred fields of battle and thoroughly kicked his ass?

I do believe that old Charlie was having some misgivings about all of the bullshit the American media was printing about us not being capable soldiers. We were duly kicking off on his butt, which was not supposed to be happening. According to the news media, we were supposed to be too busy either running and hiding or smoking pot through the barrels of our shotguns. Instead, the only time smoke came out of our shotgun barrels was when we loaded Charlie's ass up with buckshot. As I have said before, that crap about the NVA and the Viet Cong being so tough and such great fighters was just a load of bullshit.

After rescuing the pilot, we were pulled back to our home LZ and positioned behind the green line, where our first order was to get some rest. During our time there, the unit of the pilot we had rescued gave us a special thanks. We also said goodbye to Captain Harris, our outgoing company commander and welcomed Captain Brooks, our new CO, as well as Captain Norris, our new redleg. Staff Sergeant Webb, our Weapons Platoon sergeant, also went to the rear in preparation to ride that freedom bird out of the Nam. We received some fucking new guys (FNGs), which brought us almost back up to our full personnel strength.

That was a big shake-up in our organization, and we were losing some outstanding people. I wondered whether we were also losing some of the magic that made Black Knight Alfa the best unit around.

As unfortunate as it was, the war would not wait for us to properly break in the FNGs. We considered ourselves lucky, though, that our old redleg was still with us and would have sufficient time to break his turtle[44] in right. That was indeed a good thing for all of us. Whenever possible, I always sent to the rear those men whose time in the bush was short. That way they could perform critical duties such as logistics without having to sweat out their last days in country smelling old Charlie's foul breath and ducking 122mm rockets.

I personally talked with all of our new enlisted personnel the night before we slicked out. I also spent some rewarding hours talking to Captain Brooks and Captain Norris. Everything was going to be all right.

We slicked out on a new mission, knowing that we needed to lock up with Charlie again in a fight to the death in order to find out if we still had our magical edge. As usual, we were packing heavy, and our new troopers were married up with seasoned troopers.

It was a beautiful morning, and as our birds rose up toward the sun, Pete played some Renegade music[45] on his radio speaker because he knew that I loved it. I heard one of my favorite songs over the whumping of the bird's rotating blade.

"Like a long, dusty road, I get weary from the load, moving on, moving on."[46]

Once again, we were inserted deep into the jungle, but we were not alone on our search-and-destroy mission. We were working with the other companies and attached units of our battalion. Both of our redleg captains were also there in the Headquarters group with us.

Normally, we were assigned the position of point company; however, because of our major personnel changes, Battalion appointed us as the second and right company. They wanted to give our new CO some break-in time with us and our methods of operation, which I am sure were very different from the Big Red One[47] mainly because we were Cav. It made me feel terrific to hear the battalion commander instruct our new CO to "Listen to Top Steen." He told me it was my responsibility to ensure a smooth transition between company commanders. The most important thing he said to me did not concern what I should do but rather that he smiled and added, "But then again, Top, I don't have to say anything that you already know because you're an old soldier. Excuse me."

Once we were on the ground and moving, I could feel our group's tension melting away and the alert efficiency of our Grand Company quickly returning. We were back in our element, back out there humping the bush as we looked for Charlie. I noticed how our troopers shifted into their familiar roles as absolute predators, which made our team so damned good.

We had been moving for a solid four hours and were all settled in when a team of those magnificent invisible warriors – our Cav LURPs – pushed up to us with a warning: "Charlie was ahead of us, and he was real strong and packing heavy."

Battalion and SOG issued similar warnings. Both the LURP team and SOG promised to be out of our way when the fighting started.

I had to smile when I recognized the voice of the LURP team leader on the radio. That team was so good they often raided Charlie's kitchens and took his hot, cooked rice and fish right off the fire. When they said it was going to rain, I put on my poncho.

According to the information that Division gave to Battalion, there was a large NVA unit coming down from the mountains and heading in the direction of Hill 484. Of course, it could be a diversion, with Con Thien, Cam Lo, or even Camp Carroll being the actual target. The Saigon River would be a major deterrent for the NVA in such an operation, but operations Hickory and Buffalo had proven without a doubt that Charlie was capable of such a major move. Because he had recently been very quiet, Division felt that it was time for Charlie to make a significant move, which was why they had sent us in to cut him off at the pass.

"CONTACT! CONTACT! We just got hit by an enemy unit of major proportions, and they seem ready to stay for the duration," our lead company informed Battalion in the clear.

We heard everything because we were monitoring the battalion net.

Momentarily, we were far enough away from our lead unit's firefight with Charlie. I was standing close to the CO, awaiting his instructions as he consulted his map.

"We could move forward and help Charlie Company, or … ," the CO said and paused.

I quickly responded, "Sir, the key words were, 'We just got HIT.' Now old Charlie will only hit you if he is sure he has the upper hand. So the fact that he has already hit our lead unit says that Charles is packing heavy with troops and weapons. He knows he outnumbers the unit he is in contact with now, though he is unaware that he has just hit a battalion, unless he is a division and doesn't give a damn. No matter what, Charles is sure he can take our lead unit out before our help arrives. Speaking of help, I'll bet Charlie is right up on our lead unit, so close that our artillery fire cannot be called in. Sir, I tell you truly, Charlie is coming our way in an attempt to get behind the lead unit, and I do believe that our best defense is to set up here on this terrain and do it like yesterday."

I ran my finger on his map along the terrain I was referencing. I had spoken as quickly as I could to give him my view in a manner that he might accept.

Because I could feel Charlie bearing down on us in an attempt to outflank our lead unit, I urgently added, "Sir, if you were the enemy commander, what would you do?"

The CO responded, "Okay, First Sergeant, let's do it."

The other two captains agreed.

Black Knight Alfa reached the terrain in record time, and we were almost set in rock-steady when our outguards reported, "There is a very large enemy force approaching our positions, and they don't seem to know we are here. Permission requested to come home."

Permission was granted, and our outguards and security came home. Show time was rapidly approaching!

Battalion called and said that we were to perform the same move and to set up as we had previously. He confirmed that we were already sitting on almost the same terrain they were telling us to hold. Redleg (our old one) looked at me and smiled, and I felt vindicated for helping to make the decision on the ground.

The First Platoon was the center and base platoon, the Second Platoon took the left, and the Third Platoon bent around to refuse our right flank.[48] Mortars were drawn up to the rear of the Second Platoon, and our Delta Company was watching our rear.

These Charlies were professionals who were coming toward us with caution and speed. Redleg said he could get Birth Control and fire support; however, the lead unit had priority at that time. Unfortunately, our positions were not free of an overhead canopy, and our mortars were useless in the standard configuration. Redleg was talking to Birth Control, and the CO was talking to Battalion. That was just about the same time that Three-Six opened up. They began their thump-gun serenade, and I knew Charlie was trying to crash our party.

"Top, I'm going to be with Three-Six. You stay here with One-Six, and 'Redleg' you come with me!" the CO ordered before he took off to the area where our Third Platoon was engaged in their firefight with Charlie.

I am not certain whether we caught Charles by surprise. However, when our center positions opened up, we took too many of them out for Charlie not to recognize our location. God, it was like an ambush hit; Charlie had to fall back or be totally slaughtered. Only our center and right platoons were engaged. That time old Charlie was not backing up or running away. We had a fight on our hands, but we were prepared.

We put it on him hard and heavy and shifted our right end ever so slightly so as not to be hit by the company to our rear. It was around high noon, and visibility was excellent. Charlie was relying on his nearness to our positions, the canopy, and his maneuvering capability to keep our air support and Birth Control off his ass.

I still think Charlie did not know he was up against a full Cav battalion. Through my field glasses, I caught a fleeting glimpse of our enemy. I know this will sound strange, but I was disturbed by the feeling that I had met those same enemy soldiers before, perhaps at the second Bong Son and at Hue.

When we heard the distinct sound of an 82mm mortar round exploding, we knew Charlie was trying to bring in his mortars. I was too far away to see what our new Weapons Platoon sergeant was doing. Pete read my mind because he was on the radio to our guys, and they were doing the same thing that Charlie was trying to do. The big difference was that we knew how to do it and got our rounds up through the canopy and down onto Charlie. However, Charlie was slowly comprehending our range. In our defense, one of our mortar men came to our position in the Third Platoon, and with his field glasses and radio, climbed a tree, located Charlie's mortar positions, and directed our fires on them. After a few well-placed rounds, the enemy mortar positions lessened substantially. Yet, Charlie seemed determined not to be denied. I think he knew he was working against time and that our help would arrive soon. Our mortars were running low on ammunition because of the number of rounds it took to punch a hole in the canopy.

Our young troopers had already stopped Charles twice, but he was still coming back for more. I had to hand it to those NVA troops for coming back around, and I had to hand it to our troops for continuing to dish it out.

Truthfully, I was scared, like always. Anyone who claims he was not scared was either lying or not engaged in eyeball-to-eyeball contact with Charlie.

The next time Charlie hit us, I heard claymores popping and knew that the enemy was about to penetrate our positions. The fighting was fast and fierce, but we did not intend to let those Red Star wearers get past us.

"Top, we are not going to let this be our Final Battle. We're going to get these bastards good and proper," Pete yelled to me in between shooting his thump gun. It was almost balls-to-the-wall time.

I moved around from position to position so that our troops and I could see each other. I could feel their resolute determination to hold what we had at all costs or to die trying. The expression on those young American faces told me everything. They showed absolutely no panic.

They were a bunch of real cool customers. Surely we were all thinking of our poor brother whom the Viet Cong had strung up on that trail. Retribution was ours!

Our whole company was under attack, as were all the other American companies in that area. It was turning out to be an all-day affair.

During our lock-up with Charlie, I discovered a badly wounded trooper from our Second Platoon and rushed to help him. He had not called for a medic but was instead trying to bandage his own wound. When he looked up and saw me coming, his face lit up with a big, happy smile. Dear God, I was so proud of the men of Black Knight Alfa, and it was indeed a once-in-a-lifetime honor to be their first sergeant. I was so proud to be one of them and to be an American.

Only the eternal kiss of old Death could prevent me from helping the wounded soldier. I smiled at him and told him to hold the bandage while I tied it. I screamed for a medic, and like magic, one was immediately at hand. I moved on to help wherever I could lend a hand and with a smile of confidence. I was doing my job as a first sergeant. I had been instructed by my mentors, the Buffalo Soldiers, a long time ago that a first sergeant must not be relegated to pushing a pencil and handling duty rosters. I was a graduate of the infantry school at Fort Benning, and I could lead that company just as well as any commissioned officer. Otherwise, I would not be worth my own salt.

Somewhere along the line, I found my new CO doing the same things that I was doing. Captain Brooks was going to be all right, and my company was going to be fine. There was no way in hell that we were going to let the NVA get the best of us.

Charlie's 82mm mortar rounds were falling on our positions; however, the density and size of the trees, along with the canopy, greatly reduced the effect that the rounds had on our personnel. Added to that, our troopers were pretty well dug in.

A slight depression ran partially across the front of the Third Platoon's positions, and Charlie was crawling along that depression, trying to get in position to rush us. If old Charlie got to us, he was going to pay dearly and in spades. One of our troopers saw what he was doing and pointed out the situation to some of our other troopers. Everyone in that section got ready for Charlie.

Our thump gunners began hitting Charlie within the depression, and he had to move or die lying down. Charlie chose to run away. One of our troopers yelled "Black Knight Alfa," and the rest of the company took up our battle cry. I can still hear them yelling it loudly and clearly.

"Top, Battalion says Charlie is pulling back, and we got F4s inbound. It's a little late, but help is on the way," Pete yelled to me. Then he put his mike on speaker.

The very British and proper voice of the flight leader intoned, "Black Knight Alfa Six, this is Night Hawk, your push. I understand you are in a bit of a fix and need some help. Over."

The CO responded, "Roger, Night Hawk. We have discouraged our visitors and think they may be leaving. But if they are getting ready to come back for another try, we could surely use some relief and encouragement to get them to go away. Over."

"Roger, Black Knight Six. That's what we are here for. You point the buggers out, and we'll take it from there. Come back."

"Top, pop smoke!" the CO yelled over to me.

Pete had one ready, and I nodded for him to throw it out to our left front as far as he could. He threw the M18 smoke grenade and got back down in position near me. It took a minute for the billowing plume of yellow smoke to penetrate upward through the now-ragged canopy.

"Black Knight Six, I see a bunch of bananas. Talk to me. Over." The flight leader identified the color of our smoke and requested the pertinent data that would give him the location of our positions on the ground in relation to the position of the smoke.

The CO provided the flight leader with the correct data as quickly as possible. Charlie had already ceased firing his mortars at us. He knew his shit was out.

The flight leader spoke as if he were giving a lecture at Oxford University. "Roger, Black Knight Six, I have a five-by-five copy. Hold on to your umbrella; we'll be right back. Wait, out."

I passed the word to duck!

They came back and let go on where we thought Charlie might be. The missiles were on line and short, almost on top of us! I think only the leader fired, giving us the opportunity to adjust, which was a very good idea. If the whole flight had shot, it would have been curtain time for us.

As the yellow smoke rose, some of the other smoke that was rising from our position joined it. The holes in the canopy had created a draft, and the combined smoke was drifting back toward our positions.

126

"Night Hawk, wave off, wave off, your pass was almost right in our laps!" yelled the CO.

"Sorry about that, old boy. Were any of your chaps hit?" the flight leader asked.

"No, I don't think so, but could you move your stuff a little farther out, about a hundred meters? Over," the CO responded.

"Roger, my friend, hold on. Out," the flight leader said.

When the flight of F4 Phantoms came back, they put a lot of ordnance on Charlie. A Loach spotter helicopter was now on station, and it took over directing the fires of the Phantoms. I felt rather sorry for old Charles because it turned out to be a bad day for him. They put his shit on the fan, and all because he had (for once) decided to stay and fight.

During that fight we lost some magnificent troopers, with the Third Platoon taking the brunt of the battle scars. Shrapnel had wounded more of our men than bullets. We lost one of our new men KIA; it was to be his first and last firefight.

Packages from Home

Division did not give us enough time behind the green line for a good night's sleep or even a break. They had other plans for us, and once again, we were operating on a mission with a much larger force. We were resupplied on the run, but the personnel we had lost during our last encounter were not replaced. Our new operation was going to be conducted in the mountain highlands and jungles, which were better places for us to operate than in the flatlands.

Around 1400 hours on our first day out, our lead unit hit an eight-man NVA patrol, and before I could get up front from my position in the drag platoon, it was all over. We collected eight AKs in decent condition, racing slicks, and several other trading materials. After updating Battalion on the event and its location, we marked the bodies to help Charlie find them, and then we pushed on.

The next day we did not hear a peep from Charlie until late in the evening. We popped some caps at him, and he popped some at us as he ran away. We did not chase after him because oftentimes when a small American unit chased Charlie, they were chewed up for being dumb enough to do what Charlie wanted them to do. Certainly, there were times when we chased him, but we knew how and when to do it.

Our AO was on the lower part of the DMZ. We were conducting our operation there because more "militarization" existed in that zone than anywhere else. I guess old Charles did not understand that he was not supposed to have a lot of troops in that area, especially ones who were packing heavy.

We were very near to the Laos border but still in Quang Tri Province. The push was in progress for five days, which was a long, steady haul for us grunts. Fortunately, our log bird came almost every evening just before we FOBed and provided us with fresh water, occasionally hot chow, and the ability to resupply. You would be surprised to see how the canister of an 81mm mortar round can get banged up after being humped through the bush all day.

Our log men also brought some of our mail, which we always looked forward to receiving. Of course, we could only receive letters and cards in the field because it was SOP to receive and store packages from home only in a secured area, like an LZ or a firebase.

During the evening of the fifth day, we received some new replacement personnel, including a medical aid man. This had not been my decision. I preferred to receive new guys while we were behind the green line rather than out on an operation, because I liked to have time to brief the new men and to have some eyeball-to-eyeball contact with them. Anyway, I assigned the new men to the platoons that most needed additional personnel, and I paired up each new guy with an old guy until the new guys got their combat legs. Usually, if a new guy lived through his first firefight, he would prove to be okay.

Our new medic was a different sort of guy, to say the least. He carried a pencil with him and drew peace signs on everything he could get his hands on. His motto was to make love not war, and he carried a battered ukulele with him which, as I later learned, he could play very well.

Unlike most of the men of Black Knight Alfa who kept a small American flag with them, our new medic possessed a flag that gave new meaning to the word. His state flag of California was as big as a beach towel. (Our native of San Francisco was very proud of his home state.) We began calling him "California", which he loved. He even wore a flowered bandanna around his head with peace signs drawn all over it. When the other medics warned him that I would make him wear his steel pot, he did not wait for me to tell him; instead, he began wearing it right away. I knew then that I was not going to have problems with him. He looked as if he had just walked out of a coffee house from that time period, and he was always singing "If you go to San Francisco, be sure to wear some flowers in your hair". Most importantly, however, was that California was one of the best medical aides we ever had.

Perhaps because of the size of our operation, our contact with Charlie seemed to be limited to small firefights. Most of the time, Charlie deliberately avoided locking up with us, which made good sense considering there were a large number of American units participating in that operation.

In our AO, most of the Charlies that we saw or hit were Viet Cong, with the exception of the eight-man patrol that we had iced during our first day out. Maybe it was just that particular area, which was more grassy than tree-filled. The existence of a few large trees, sparsely situated, made it seem as if long ago people had lived in that particular jungle area.

One night after we were set in and all was quiet, the CO, our two redlegs, and I discussed our AO. We shared the same general ideas about it. Considering the elevation level and the fact that many Charlie Congs were running around, it looked like we were operating in an enemy "staging area", where troops came and went either north or south. We figured the VC were mostly guides who had been assigned to lead the new NVA troops through that area. That would account for the large presence of VC.

During the first three days, we often encountered the enemy running away. However, we were able to identify Charlie's Russian and Chinese advisors. We could easily spot the Russians by their distinctive uniforms, their size, and their command presence. It was harder for us to identify the Chinese because they had a tendency to blend in. However, their overly eager attempts to kill us usually gave them away.

The VC whom we had taken out were probably guides. I cannot tell you what "guides" looked like, but that was the impression we got when we looked at them. It was just after we hit five or six of them that some others got away while we were looking around. Our browsing paid off, though, because our troopers found a large cache of rice, canned goods, some medical supplies, and a number of mimeographed copies of what appeared to be strip maps. We also found a graveyard containing both old and fresh graves.

The sergeant of the Second Platoon came over to me and said, "Top, we got another one, and we want you to see him."

I followed him to a place where some of our troopers were standing guard at the exposed entrance to a VC tunnel, and some of the tunnel rats were already coming out with grim expressions on their dirty faces.

They already had a Lima-Lima[49] running down through the hole. Telltale plumes of colored smoke were rising from another exit, the entrance, and various ventilation holes. The size of the underground complex was not nearly as large as the last bunker we had discovered.

The platoon sergeant said, "Top, this one isn't so big. It's mostly an underground bunker with a little sleeping space, an office, a kitchen, and an aid station. It's the aid station we want you to see. It's safe. Charlie diddy maued less than half an hour ago."

I squeezed my big frame down the entranceway. While I was underground, I could not stand upright. In most of the areas, I was either hunkered over or on my hands and knees. When old Charlie designed his tunnels, he definitely did not have folks like me in mind. I hated being down there. I was not suffering from claustrophobia; I was just plain SCARED.

I saw some uneaten cooked rice in the kitchen; a strongbox on the floor in the far corner of the office; an ancient, hand-operated mimeograph machine; and a few other odds and ends. Low-wattage electric light bulbs hung in key positions and received power through a small, bicycle-operated generator. There was also a radio connected to a hand-operated generator. The place was small and crudely built. It was shored up with small timbers, old wooden packing crates, and stones. However, there was some amount of efficiency to it.

I heard Doc B.'s voice and suddenly realized that he was in the aid station at the end of the passageway. "You guys move back so Top can see this, too," he said.

I squeezed part of my body into the main room. It was a lot bigger, but I still could not stand upright. Sweet Jesus! Before me was another sight that added to my overflowing cup of nightmares. Being fresh out of tears, my heart swelled with hatred for Charlie Cong.

One of our troopers was pedaling the bicycle so that we had electricity to see what I wished to my very soul that we did not have to see. A makeshift operating table stood on stakes near the center of the room. Above the table was another home-made apparatus – a boom with stones attached to one end for balance. On the other end, a Jeep headlight (powered by a Jeep battery) served as the operating light. Doc B. switched the light on for us to see everything better.

Neatly arranged and taking up the entire space on two walls were three-tiered, handmade bunk beds with the bottom bed sitting only inches off the earth and log floor. Along the third wall was a single bunk made of an old army stretcher attached to long stakes that had been driven into the floor. About half of the beds were occupied, and one of the occupants – a Viet Cong soldier – was still alive.

One of the less fortunate – an American soldier – was lying on the old army stretcher. He was much larger than the other patients and was tied to the stretcher and rack with strips of bandaging material. His body had been stripped naked, and there was a rubber surgical hose attached to a needle that was stuck into one of his main arteries. The other end of the surgical hose was attached to a hand-operated pump that had been used to suck out his blood. That crude, blood-sucking apparatus had Chinese characters on it, which clearly told us that it had been "Made in China".

The American soldier's blood had been taken from him and transferred into the veins of enemy soldiers so that the enemies might live to fight us another day. Certainly, the VC doctors of that time performed many emergency blood transfusions; however, we were certain that our American soldier had not been a willing donor. He apparently died because of his excessive "donations". I have often wondered what he must have thought about during his last hours.

In case you are thinking about the irony of the situation, try this on your mind and your heart. There were a number of packages on the floor, and one package lay open on the table near the violated American soldier. According to the letters, cards, and brief messages of hope that we found inside the packages, most of them were from the United States and addressed to the enemy. The letters, cards, and messages were either written or printed in American English and said such things as "To the freedom-loving people of North Vietnam" and "To aid you in your rightful struggle against the United States aggressors".

Most of the packages from home bore either American or Canadian postage stamps, but some of them did not have stamps. Inside them, we found both commercial and home-made bandage rolls, bandage strips, aspirin, alcohol, first-aid remedies, American cigarettes, candy, gum, and a variety of other American brand-name items. The price tags were still attached to some items.

Whoever sent the package from home that was open on the stand beside the American might have gotten his or her wish. That person's gift of bandages had been used by the enemy to tie the American soldier securely to the stretcher, which probably meant that the man was alive when the mad doctors began their task of siphoning all of his blood.

If you had been there, you would understand our feelings. That was the second American body we had to free and wrap in a poncho liner before calling for dust-off. Maybe now you can begin to understand why some of us Vietnam vets "lost it" and why Black Knight Alfa passionately hated the Viet Cong.

"I don't want any more of our troops than absolutely necessary to see what's in this room," I instructed those who were present.

Doc B. had already put the word on the Lima-Lima not to let any more people down in the tunnel. While he was trying to save the life of the VC soldier whom we had found underground, I told him to leave everything for Battalion to see.

"Top, I think this one will make it 'cause we got to him in time. I'm so sorry, but all the others are gone, including ...," Doc B. said as he tried to hide his sorrow.

That he could save the life of one of theirs, but not one of ours. "Make you wanna holler and throw up both your hands!"[50]

I squeezed out and above ground, and suddenly, my tears were flowing too much to hide. The CO was waiting to go down into the tunnel. Both redlegs were there, but only Captain Norris went down. Our old redleg had seen the poor guy the VC had hung out to dry on the trail, and I guess he had seen enough by now. I know that I surely had.

The CO just looked at me as he silently went underground.

We discovered that it was easier to dig the bodies out than to try to drag them out. We buried the enemy soldiers in a makeshift cemetery, and we sent our dear brother on the first leg of his long journey home. Doc B. found another enemy soldier who was still alive, and our medevac crews lifted him out. I do not know whether that Charlie survived, but I certainly hoped he did. Though I hated the VC, I would like to think I had not and never would stoop as low as they did.

"I'm so glad I done got over, I done got over at last."[51]

The rice and other foodstuff, as well as the contents of some of the packages from home, were taken from the underground bunker and given to the local needy villagers. Therefore, some of the American donations to the North Vietnamese really did serve a useful and peaceful purpose.

As for the locked strongbox that we had found in the underground office, it was empty.

Our troopers thoroughly checked the area but found nothing more of value. When some officers from Division came for a first-hand look at the evidence, they held a hush-hush discussion and then strongly advised us to keep quiet about the matter. I fully understood and agreed with their orders.

One of the doctors from the medevac birds complimented Doc B. on saving the two enemy soldiers, because they would not have survived much longer if we had not found them. He said that we had done the right thing by digging down into the bunker and extracting the dead and the living men.

The bunker's aid station, the painful sight of our dead brother, and the collection of those packages from home still haunt me. They serve as terrible reminders of one man's cruelty to another man and of what war did to all of us.

Through it all, though, we men of Black Knight Alfa never lost faith in ourselves and in the American people.

"LET HISTORY BE OUR JUDGE BECAUSE THERE ARE NO HUMAN BEINGS ALIVE WHO ARE IN A POSITION, OR WHO ARE WORTHY ENOUGH, TO JUDGE US."

Black Knight Alfa. Alpha and Omega.

Night Callers

We fought at the Bong Son Plains. Then we locked up with Charles in the battles of Jeb Stuart, Pershing II, Pegasus/Lamson, Delaware/Lamson, Hue, and the Que Son Valley – all of which led us deeply into the fabled A Shau Valley.

We found ourselves in our old stomping grounds of I Corps and Quang Tri. We were so far north that we could almost hear General Giap when he cried about things that were going wrong. Again, we were on the farthest firebase north, awaiting orders to slap the hell out of Charlie again.

By that time, I was almost skinny, in comparison with how big I had been when I initially unassed a hovering bird and locked up with Charlie. Every man in the company had a strange faraway look in his eyes, and all of us had a sidearm, loaded and ready. There was no fucking way that Charlie was going to capture us!

Our Grand Company fought in the relief operation for Khe Sanh after the 77-day siege during which General Giap threw the very best soldiers that he had at that marine base and discovered that his best just was not good enough. Those US Marines proved to the world that "a few good men", especially if they were US Marines, were a damned sight better than the whole North Vietnamese Army; their Viet Cong lackeys; and their Russian, Cuban, and Chinese advisors.

Given the possibility that we might be facing our upcoming Final Battle, we promised each other that if that time came, we would take as many of the NVA and Charlie Cong soldiers with us as possible. If we had to ride that hellbound train, it was going to be standing room only.

135

I hate to break your train of thought here, but I just have to say this. Maybe some good came out of all the bad press the news media heaped upon us. Perhaps General Giap and his staff of planners were reading the daily crap that the news media were always printing about us not being capable of a good fight and the NVA divisions being the cream of the crop. Perhaps those NVA bastards really believed all that bullshit and the media hype influenced Giap to hit Khe Sanh with his overrated divisions. After hitting Khe Sanh, though, Giap and the NVA discovered that fighting the American troops was not as easy as the news media had led them, and the world, to believe.

It is very sad that the faithful readers and listeners of the American media did not pause long enough to notice the important fact that Khe Sanh did not fall. The combined operation that went into effect to relieve that base, which was still holding on, proved another point. The combined power and tactical abilities of the US Forces in Vietnam and the rock-hard determination of our American fighting soldiers were enough to overcome the enemy. We could have gone all the way to Hanoi and cleaned house, once and for all, if only the fucking politicians and the armchair generals had let us finish the job that we had been sent over there to do.

There, I have said it and gotten it off my shoulders, at least temporarily.

While operating off that most distant firebase and during our daily missions in the almost unbearable heat of the dense jungles, we sometimes had daily close encounters of the first, and all the way up to the 21st, kind as we waltzed through the jungles with old two step and the NVA. They only fought us when they were sure they had the advantage. Otherwise, they pulled a disappearing act, which did not always work, because we often got a piece of them during their act. We always left our little calling cards – sort of like the old "Kilroy was here" graffiti – attached to the Charlies who were crazy enough to pull on us.

We were predators, born again and raised in that jungle combat environment. Every day I looked around at the faces of my outstanding troopers, and I was often saddened by some of their facial expressions, which told me that they had already seen too much death, too much killing. They had seen so much that they were becoming ACCLIMATIZED!

"Lord have mercy on such as we."[52]

We knew Charles well, and we never underestimated him. Actually, we felt that he was also reading the American newspapers and thought we were pushovers, that is, until he made the big mistake of calling us out. Then, he learned the truth right before we put his shit in the wind.

One day when we were pushing along a nice trail, the CO decided to stop for a "snake".[53] However, we did not just stop, sit down, and break out our rations. First, we lagered and posted security, and when we were prepared to fight, defend, or run like hell, we broke out our rations.

I was with the drag platoon that day, and shortly before we were about to move on, those of us in that platoon had the distinct feeling that we had a tail. Everyone was dog-tired, and we were feeling particularly bitchy that day. We were very unhappy that Charles was determined to fuck up our day, so we decided to act as if we did not know that he was on our tail. Of course, if he decided to pop caps on us, we would definitely ice him.

Our tail did not make any overt moves against us, so we continued to "ignore" him. After we finished our snake, we buried our trash. If our peeping Toms were watching, we would not do anything to give them away. I told the CO what we had and explained my plan to correct the situation. He gave me permission to proceed with my plan.

We played our cards close to our chest, and with our best poker faces, we made a neat pile of our fruitcakes. (We always donated our fruitcakes to Charlie because they were so bad. We figured he deserved to have them more than we did.) We buried the other stuff, with the topmost unopened cans of beans, spaghetti, and other good meals so that Charlie could see them. Under the cans we placed our special surprise dessert. We were surely hoping that Charlie would enjoy the sweets after his meal.

After moving a safe distance down the trail, we melted away to await the outcome of the little surprise dessert we had left for our unsuspecting enemies. We did not have to wait long at all.

Whump! Our surprise exploded with devastating effects. Charlie's blood-curdling screams hurt our ears and proved that the M26 had done its job well. (We knew the fruitcakes were bad, but we did not think they were that bad.)

Shortly after our grenade exploded, two NVA soldiers came running along the trail. I had no idea why they were following us instead of running in the opposite direction. Maybe they were in a blind state of panic. We promptly thumped them, and all was quiet again, except for some occasional loud moans and groans that we heard coming from farther down the trail where the grenade had gone off. By the time we retraced our steps to investigate, the moaning had stopped.

Doc B. could do nothing for the unfortunates. We liberated four AKs, racing slicks, and some other worthwhile trading materials. It appeared that our tail had been comprised of four Charlies – the two NVAs whom we had dropped on the trail and the two unfortunates whom our surprise had killed. We were not relying on our assumptions, though, and as we moved out, we sent two teams back to check our tail again, and we left a third team concealed along the trail.

Later that afternoon, we cut an LZ for extraction back to that distant firebase for the night. Hot chow and mail were waiting for us, and we were resupplied. My company clerk had a slew of backlogged paperwork, so I immediately began to process it in my orderly room by the dim light of my flashlight. I certainly hope that I did not accidentally sign my company clerk's promotion orders to the status of "General".

The CO and Redleg went to the Battalion TOC for a debriefing session. As soon as I caught up with my paperwork, I planned to read my mail and catch forty. However, wouldn't you know it, old Charlie came calling that night. Those bastards had no couth; they came calling without an invitation.

We knew that Charlie's visit was a serious one because he sent some 122mm rockets and some big bore mortar rounds in first. A rather large entourage of NVA soldiers was gathered around the base of the mountain. They made one hell of a racket, blowing all kinds of crazy notes out of their bugles. Because our enemies were interrupting our sleep, we wanted to do nothing except shove those bugles down their throats.

Captain Brooks quickly warned, "Top, those bastards are coming for this bunker, and we are almost right up on it."

Our company CP was not far from the main artillery ammunition bunker for the firebase, and Captain Brooks was referring to the largest of our bunkers, which was well dug in and covered with a lot of earth, logs, and PSP.[54] Sandbags were in place, along with everything else that was necessary to secure the bunker.

Captain Brooks spoke again: "Top, mark my words, they are after the ammo bunkers and not the guns."

We alerted the rest of the company that we might have to help man the red line.

"Get on the Lima-Lima and tell our guys to expect sappers, 'cause that's what's about to happen," Captain Brooks ordered.

We knew from experience that such an opening barrage meant that Charlie was very serious, and it also indicated that the sappers were already at the wire. The initial barrage was designed to create a diversion so the sappers could penetrate the wire and come in to blow up the ammo bunkers because they knew better than to depend on their rockets and mortars to do the job.

The firebase's TOC called to request that Captain Brooks come to them. Redleg and the two RTOs accompanied him.

Before leaving, Captain Brooks said, "Top, you got it till I get back." Then he asked, "You know what to do if or when the green star cluster goes off?"

I assured him that I knew what to do, and the four men quickly disappeared into the darkness.

Each firebase TOC had their own plan concerning what to do if enemies hit them or if sappers penetrated their perimeter. Everyone on the firebase was aware of such procedures. We were assigned additional positions on the red line where we would go if we were needed.

I was very concerned about Captain Brooks and Redleg running around while Charlie was throwing his big shit around. However, I knew that the barrage would be shifted once Charles knew his sappers were past the wire because he did not want to kill his own people.

With Charlie screaming, hollering, and playing all of his funky bugles as he made his way up the side of the mountain, I could not help but laugh out loud, which was an indication of how far around the bend I was. The situation was serious, but there I was laughing and thinking, "There goes the damned neighborhood."

I was laughing and telling Pete about my crazy thought when a flare went off at the base of the barbed wire, almost directly in front of our position. The sudden glare of bright light made it briefly appear to be broad daylight in the immediate area. The rockets and mortar rounds were no longer falling directly on critical targets. Instead, Charlie was hitting random places in an attempt to divert our attention away from the sappers who were penetrating our perimeter. Our troopers guarding the base were only able to drop a few sappers, and the rest of them made it past the red line. Those NVA sappers were very good.

One nervy little NVA bastard managed to get through the wire near Pete and me. We knew he was there because he popped one of our flares. However, we could not see him because he blended in so well with his surroundings, and he did not attempt to move out into the glaring light of the flare. Fortunately, Pete and I were so keenly familiar with our surroundings that we soon spotted him. At almost the same moment, the NVA sapper made his appearance in front of us. He was carrying two satchel charges and a toned-down Kalashnikov (AK), which he swung around toward us. Just as I began to fire, someone in the position to our left popped him. We watched as Charlie's AK sailed backward toward the wire. As the flare went out, darkness claimed the area again. I fired the remainder of my magazine at the spot where I had last seen the sapper fall. Experience had taught us well, and we knew better than to trust chance. Pete popped a flare as we went to confirm our kill, and we were extremely unhappy to discover that it was a false kill. The little bastard was nowhere in sight. He had moved away without his AK, but he was still dangerous because he had two satchel charges. If he could blow the bunker, it would take us all to hell.

I had to rise to look for the little sapper, and I heard Pete mutter, "Aw shit."

In a straight line, the sapper had crawled closer to our position. Suddenly, I could smell him. I could smell his sweat and blood because we had seriously wounded him. Knowing that his time was very short, he tried to ignite his charges so that he could unload on us and take us with him.

It was as eerie as hell because he was close enough for me to see the grin on his face. Pete had his thump gun loaded with shot, and he let it go dead in the face of the hunkered-over sapper who was rushing toward us.

For a few seconds, I thought it was all over for us too, because the rounds could easily have set off the satchel charges. We had seen such a thing happen before.

We were very grateful when the sapper's charges did not go off. I was also thankful that I had a change of shorts, because after that scare, I surely needed to change my underwear.

Meanwhile, some of the other NVA sappers had penetrated the wire and were already past the green line. Not one of them made it to the ammo bunkers because the Cav unit securing the base was instantly on top of Charlie. Also, Puff the Magic Dragon and Fire Fly were on station, leaving Charlie with no ounce of hope.

We could see some of the NVA soldiers hatting up for the shelter of the surrounding treeline past the cleared zone. I think old Charles was offended that we had not rolled out the welcome mat for him and invited him in for coffee.

Many of Charlie's buddies did not make the return trip across the cleared zone. We also had casualties, but theirs outnumbered ours by a very wide margin.

Once again, we had beaten Charlie at his own game. He had left in such a hurry that either he had forgotten to take his dead and wounded or he was just trying to get away with his own ass intact. All those little ropes and strings around the dead enemies' ankles and wrists[55] were going to waste.

"If you whip a man and turn him loose,
You may have to whip him again.
But, if you whip a man, and whip him till he break loose,
Then you won't have to whip him ever again."[56]

The next morning, the perimeter patrols found a lot of dead Charlies and many Bangalore torpedoes, satchel charges, smoke pots, and small blocks of C-4. It appeared as if the enemy soldiers had dropped most of the small stuff during their cowardly retreat. They had come prepared to stay, but they had been unprepared to get their butts whipped. We had forced many of them to stay, wrapped tightly in the arms of old Death.

Charley Alfa

An airborne combat assault, better known to our unit as a Charley Alfa,[57] was primarily the operation of flying our Skytroopers by helicopters to a designated LZ. A full-blown Charley Alfa was a major operation in which we had the support of artillery, fixed-wing aircraft, F4 Phantoms, and other air force combat aircraft, in addition to our own combat helicopters such as the Huey gunships and the Cobras. Sometimes even more support was provided for a major Charley Alfa.

Our Charley Alfa operation began when Battalion slicked us south to LZ Jane, which was far more secure than the last firebase we were on when our "night callers" tried to take over the neighborhood. After we were assigned positions on LZ Jane, which was still in I Corps (north) and Quang Tri Province, Captain Brooks flew to Camp Evans to attend a top-level briefing about a significant upcoming campaign.[58] Camp Evans was only about 21 klicks south of the DMZ, but it was all Cav Country in the purest sense.

While we were at LZ Jane, we were completely refitted. Our company received a new issue of jungle fatigues because the ones we were wearing were like rags from their regular exposure to the jungles, the highlands, and the wait-a-minute vines, and from simply being in the Nam. New boots were given to those of us who needed them. One of our 81s was taken in for repairs, and we were issued a reconditioned replacement. Our worn and damaged M16 magazines were replaced with new ones, our ammunition was totally resupplied, and all of our 81mm ammunition was exchanged for new stuff.

At LZ Jane, I greeted and briefed the FNGs and paired each one with an experienced guy in our company. With our new supplies and our new men, we would once again be packing heavy and back up to full fighting strength. This was a clear indication that we were getting ready to slap Charlie again.

There was time for us to be both happy and sad. We said "see you back in the world" to some of our best troopers who had survived hell and were completing their tour of pushing the bush. They were going to fly south, down to where they would board that great big old freedom bird back home. We were happy to see them go, and their departure reminded us that there was a good chance that we would someday also WALK OUT of the Nam. It was comforting to know that it was possible to live through the Nam experience and to go home still standing and moving.

Our food and accommodations at LZ Jane were first class, and the showers were so good that we kept going back for more. Of course, some of us (myself included) really needed several hot showers. We also found time to catch up on some details about the war going on back home and other events that were happening on the streets of America.

I was so happy to finally receive a package from home, though it saddened me to think of those other packages from home that we had recently seen in the enemy's underground aid station. My package contained photos of my two children (Doris and Thomas), some cookies, pre-sweetened Kool-Aid, and a replacement tape recorder for the one I had lost. There was also a tape recording of family voices and my very own copy of Marvin Gaye's "What's Going On". On my home-made tape, I had also recorded Joe Cocker, Hank Snow, Mary Hopkins, The Mamas and The Papas, B. B. King, and John Lee. Man, was I ever happy to hear some of my favorite songs.

When our CO returned from Evans, he brought a new and very young second lieutenant with him. Talk about not being dry behind the ears. Lt Zen, a Chinese-American from San Francisco, did not look like he was dry anywhere. The CO said the new lieutenant would be assigned to us as the Weapons Platoon leader because he had already gotten his Nam legs in another company and was ready for duty with our Weapons Platoon.

The addition of Lt Zen brought our officer strength up to three, which included our CO and Redleg, although I must explain that

Redleg was not assigned to us on our sidpers.[59] He was only "attached" to us for duty, rations, quarters, and administration. He was actually assigned to Division Artillery, or "Divarty" as we called them. I think his parent unit was the 1st Battalion of the 30th Artillery.

According to our S-2 officer, we were planning to go up against the 9th Battalion of the 18th NVA Regiment. Elements of the 7th and 9th NVA Battalions were dug in and fortified on a strategic piece of South Vietnamese terra firma, and Division wanted our battalion to go in and serve them an eviction notice. If Charlie did not agree to go peaceably, we were instructed to kick his ass off that hill with a lot of prejudice.

Black Knight Alfa's mission was to spearhead a major combat assault against that superbly entrenched enemy high-ground position. We would be the base company (the first company on the ground), and all of the other companies would follow us. After punching Charlie's ticket, we would move out smartly into the Valley of Death – the A Shau Valley.

Did I just get your undivided attention? Yes, I said the A Shau Valley. Now you can understand why the CO was called all the way to Evans. Well, the mission at hand simply called for us to lead a Charley Alfa against some dudes who were where they were not supposed to be. Our briefing was as thorough and complete as usual. We received supplements to our maps, and when we fully understood our mission and learned of all the help we would have, we went back to our positions. As soon as we determined our strategy for best accomplishing our mission, we called all of our leaders to the company CP and informed them of our plans. Then, they informed their troops straightaway.

One of the essential rules of "good leadership" is to always provide your troops with sound and timely information. Besides quelling rumors and uncertainties, that information kept our troops well informed and prepared for anything. If a leader went down during combat, the next leader in line would be able to continue our mission. In our Grand Company, this principal of operation remained true, right down to the last man standing in battle.

Our platoon sergeants always followed this good leadership essential and made sure that each trooper clearly knew and understood our mission, how we planned to accomplish it, and what we would do if something went wrong. Our lowest private was fully capable of continuing one of our missions and achieving the final results – VICTORY, always VICTORY.

Preparing for a Charley Alfa was always serious business, and we never took anything for granted because we never betted with our lives. As soon as we unassed our birds, we would be well beyond the point of no return. It was do or die, and we had no intentions of dying.

After we completed all of our preparations, our order of battle was simply to chill out. Some of our troops caught forty while others wrote letters to loved ones, cleaned their weapons, listened to music, brewed coffee, ate, or just fooled around. All such activities were possible on LZ Jane because we were inside the green line.

I think most of us got a good night's sleep that last night at LZ Jane with the help of a wonderful hot dinner. We ate steak and potatoes with gravy, green peas, home-made rolls, fresh salad, and apple pie. Each man received two cold beers or colas. I also remember that we had a large container of cherry Kool-Aid. I am not sure how they did it, but the Kool-Aid was cold.

At the prescribed time, I gave the wake-up call, and everyone ate breakfast. It was still dark, but we were acclimatized to the darkness. At first light, we were ready and waiting in our lift-out formation around the log pad. We were loaded for Charlie. Word had already been passed around that old Charlie was being obstinate. It seemed that another unit had already tried to serve an eviction notice to Charles, but he was downright rude and refused to budge. Therefore, we, the Cav, were being called in to put Charlie's shit on the fan.

"Top, we have birds inbound. The first lift will be popping over the trees shortly, and they already want us to pop smoke," Pete announced.

I ran out to pop smoke and remained in place to bring in the bird that would lead our attack.

We loaded only four men to a slick, and even then we were pushing it because of the distance that we had to travel and the load that we were packing. The lead bird of the attack formation was the last bird in. It was going to carry Pete, JoJo, Jones with his M60, and me. (SP4 Jones was my machine gunner extraordinaire. He and his "pig" could work wonders together; they were a class act and always impressed Charlie all the way to hell.) JoJo and Jones boarded on the left side behind the aircraft commander (AC),[60] and Pete and I entered on the right side. The rest of the company was already in the air, waiting for our bird to join the formation and take up the lead position.

One-Six was the lead platoon, which meant that Gonzalez and three of his troopers were riding in the second bird. Usually, we never put more than one leader on a bird, which explains why the CO and I never rode together. If our company had an executive officer or another "experienced" officer, perhaps that other officer would be on the lead bird of a Charley Alfa. The CO had decided that in the absence of an executive officer, I would always ride on the lead bird.

I agreed with his decision and felt it was appropriate for me, the first sergeant, to be the first person on the ground. Being such a leader gave one an awesome responsibility. While constantly facing death, you had to size up the situation in accordance with your time in the Nam and your experience fighting old Charles. Then, you had to let the commander know if the LZ was hot.[61] When it was hot, you had to determine whether your attacking element should either follow you in or wave off, pull up, and try again later. You also had to determine whether or not to abort the mission. Being the lead bird was not an easy assignment.

As our bird lifted out, I looked back at the log pad and LZ Jane. I thought of Smitty and wondered if I would ever see that LZ again.

"Thy will be done ..."

At my first opportunity, I studied our formation in the air. It was pure magnificence in motion and a sight of everlasting reverence. From my position, I could not see the entire formation because everyone was so well spread out that it seemed like we were stretched all the way to infinity. Our majestic birds were flying in perfect formation and climbing high up into the clear blue sky of early morning, going way up where the air was rare.

Our lift was on the bottom of the formation, a position that we shared with the two birds from Phy-Ops.[62] Their distinctive pairs of loudspeakers would soon be blasting Charlie's mind with the sound of music while we were blasting his butt with hot lead.

We remained in that formation for several minutes. Then, using a normal procedure, our formation changed directions for the first of three times. We enjoyed our great view of the lush green jungles and highlands passing slowly below us.

As usual, we sat on the floor of the birds, two on each side with our feet and legs hanging out of the doorway. Only the front doors to the

146

cockpit remained closed on our troop-carrying helicopters, to give the ACs some protection from enemy fire.

When I was on the lead bird during a Charley Alfa, I always sat near the door gunner because it was the best position for communicating with the AC. Because I could not speak to the AC directly, the door gunner served as our communications link. The door gunners wore mikes and headsets built into their helmets as part of the aircraft's internal communications system.

I looked across at Jones, who was always ready to pop caps in an instant with his M60. He was holding his machine gun in one hand with the barrel pointing out of the door, while leaning against the door-frame for support. He grinned at me and offered me a bite of his candy bar. I shook my head to indicate "Thanks, but maybe later."

JoJo took a bite of Jones's candy bar, and I had to smile because I was thinking about those popular slogans that appeared on many soldiers' steel helmet camouflage covers, proclaiming truths such as "GOD IS MY POINT MAN". I felt that this universal truth needed no advertisement. Nevertheless, I always felt a lot better when I knew that JoJo (aka Sp4 Johnny-Johnny LeCroix[63]) was out in front. I knew from experience that I could trust him and his judgment every day. We were two bloods out for a stroll right up past the very gates of hell.

During the next turn, I was able to see most of Black Knight Alfa in the formation, though I could not count all of the birds in flight. My heart swelled with pride at the sight. Blue Max were there, hovering high above us on both sides. It was impossible not to feel proud when you were in the presence of those majestic birds. Some units called them Snakes, after their official name of the king himself, the King Cobra. To us men of Black Knight Alfa, however, they were and shall always be Blue Max. They were truly awesome.

I sincerely wish that you could have been there to see us in our magnificent formation because it was so beautiful. All of our troop-carrying birds flew in the center, and we were surrounded by our supporters who represented gunslingers of all kinds, with the crowning glory being old Blue Max with their white teeth gleaming in the rays of the early morning sun.

No one doubted the cold, hard fact that Charlie had the utmost respect for Blue Max because those Snakes had one hell of a bite. If they got hold of Charlie, no snakebite kit in the world could save him.

Sitting there on the floor in the doorway, I had some time to think and to become organized. Also, I had some time to add another rainbow to those already in my pocket. That is, I tried my very best to have a few words with God. I did not wait until my ass was in a bind to call upon him. Instead, I thanked Him every day for letting me see the sunshine "one more time".

That morning I made a special request to God, asking for His help in making the right decision so that I could take good care of my wonderful Skytroopers. Then, I added, "And, dear God, if any of us have to fall, please Father, make it quick and allow us to come on home to You, standing up like men."

Then, I silently asked my mother to keep repeating my prayer to God, just in case there was some static on my line. I knew that if He did not hear me, He would surely hear her. I was counting on that.

After talking to God, I took a minute to adjust and to reach out for a rainbow. I was a dreamer, and I greatly believed in the American way, in Santa Claus, in the Golden Rules, in God, and in right and wrong. I experienced moments of enchantment as I sat in the doorway of our lead bird looking down at the lush green jungles.

The eerie quietness was punctuated only by the steady whumping of the whirling blades of our airborne helicopters. The dancing rays of the early morning sunbeams reflected off those whirling blades, forming colorful, kaleidoscopic patterns in the sky. When I gazed intently at them, they created hypnotic illusions.

The smell of the exhaust fumes mixed with heated cherry juice, the thundering of the rotors, and the roar and whine of the powerful engines contributed to the thrill of our hunt and the return to our primitive beginnings and instincts. It felt as if we were going backward in time, to the days when man brought down the woolly mammoth, the saber-toothed tiger, the mighty Tyrannosaurus rex, and the most cunning and challenging of all animals – our brother, man himself. Those were indeed times that caused great turmoil in our souls.

Soon, our entire formation turned toward our new and final destination. From previous experience, I knew that we were on our last turn because the morning sun was at our backs and our formation was slowing down a bit.

From our lead position, we had a bird's-eye view of our objective area in the distance. There was no mistaking that we were headed there because our artillery support had already begun their preparatory fires. They were lighting up our objective as if it were a Fourth of July celebration, and they were not skimping on the fireworks. Rolling Thunder[64] was the name of the game, and they were putting hot steel on their targets. We were very high up in the friendly skies, and I felt as if my nose were bleeding, which was normal for that altitude.

The marker rounds soon burst like bright yellow flowers among the plumes of black smoke. This signaled the final rounds of our artillery's introduction to hell for Charlie, and the yellow smoke ushered the second part of our opening act to the stage.

Two flights of F4 Phantom jets in full battle dress were already streaking down toward the target area, which was still billowing smoke and fire from the artillery barrage. The Phantoms were coming in out of the sun; their camouflage battle dress made them stand out against the blue sky. Those great birds of prey were laden with loads and loads of destruction – high-explosive rockets, bombs, and the awesome Whisky-Papa,[65] which some of us old grunts called "Willie Peter". They were not using napalm because we grunts would be down there in that hellhole in a very short time after their last pass.

We also called the white phosphorus rounds, canisters, and bombs "The Whispering Death" because when they exploded, the noise was not harsh. It was rather like a great "Whoosh!" when the white phosphorus burst into a giant white all-consuming cloud and sucked the oxygen out of the air. Somewhat like napalm, which had a big-ball-of-rolling-fire effect, the Willie Peter rolled, but its ball was like a ghostly gray-white cloud of instant death. Our Phantom pilots placed those devastating balls of Willie Peter at the bottom of the hill and rolled them like bowling balls up the side of the hill, where they consumed everything in their paths, all the way to the top. I think our Phantoms made two passes before occupying a position above us, higher than our Charley-Charley bird.[66] There, they remained on station until the next act was over.

That day, there were three Charley-Charley birds in the sky, so I guess Brigade and possibly Division were assisting with the eviction procedure. It was also possible that one of those C & C birds had been sent by one of our support organizations.

Suddenly, Blue Max dropped away from their positions beside us and headed down to get Charlie's attention. By that time, our objective was in flames, and the smoke was effectively obscuring the top of the hill. It was the Snakes' turn to strike, and they did. When they pulled away, they remained close to the ground in order to give us cover when we went in.

The stage was set, the curtain was up, and it was time for the real fighting to begin. It was time for US grunts to go down there and serve an eviction notice to Charlie. Whether he liked it or not, his ass would soon be out of there!

It was time to show old Charlie the hole in the wall that the carpenter had left. We afforded him every opportunity to get out, but all he did was run underground and hide. There was no doubt in our minds that as soon as the shit stopped falling on him, he would come above ground and it would be business as usual. Charlie was a stubborn little bastard, but we were even more stubborn.

The AC looked back at me and spoke into his mike to the door gunner. The door gunner hit me on the arm and pointed down at the flaming objective. At the same time, the AC nosed the bird down. That was our signal. It was party time, and we were going in.

Pete was on the company push, the AC was on the battalion push and his unit's push, and the CO was on the push with the Charley-Charley bird. I guess Battalion's Charley-Charley bird was on the push to Brigade, and I surely hoped that Division or somebody was on the push to God. I had the feeling that we were going to need a little help from our headquarters in the sky.

By that time, our company was well separated from the rest of the formation but still protected by Blue Max, who were hovering around us like big, camouflaged mother hens with gleaming white teeth.

The nose of our bird was pointed down toward the LZ, and we were gaining speed. I looked back at the Charley-Charley bird high above us, and I knew we were under the watchful eyes of our battalion commander.

I was terribly scared every time we reached that point in a Charley Alfa. I am speaking of the moment when fear suddenly wells up inside of you. It occurs soon after you are sure that you are "going in". Then, you feel a rush of the purest adrenaline that allows your fear to remain, but if you are "experienced", you can control it and convert it into strength that works in your favor.

The burning LZ, the smoke billowing up like that of a large campfire, and Blue Max going down with us to shake the earth – all of those sights affected our minds and completed the lines between the Gods of war and us.

Pete snapped me back from across the void when he screamed into my ear, "Top, we got the 'GO' from Six."

He gave me the thumbs-up signal, and I smiled and got myself in touch with the time, the place, and our mission.

The Phy-Ops birds moved into their positions to the right, left, and slightly above of us. They flew between Blue Max and us. They already had their speakers loudly but clearly blasting the marching band music of John Philip Sousa's "Stars and Stripes Forever".

Our hearts were pumping pure liquid steel. The hunt was on, the dogs of war were set loose, and it was far too late for Charlie to cry havoc. It was a time of exaltation, a time like no other. Our music blasted, our engines thundered, and our rotors whump-whumped. These sounds combined with the mournful chattering of the door gunners' machine guns as we came within range to hurt Charles.

We slid forward on our butts and stood up outside on the skids, using one hand to hold onto the door frame and the other to hold our weapons in place. We added our exuberant voices to the loud clamor and yelled as loudly as we could:

"BLACK KNIGHT ALFA. ALPHA AND OMEGA!"

As we rushed ever downward and closer to the LZ, we were able to see those Charlies who were still alive scurrying around on the ground, full of fight. Some of them turned to fire their weapons at us, as our two door gunners fired at them in a music-like rhythm of alternating long-short and short-long bursts. They orchestrated their firing with the same notes on the sheet music of the symphony of death.

I know it sounds as crazy as hell, but I remember during those times, even when we knew our bird was taking small arms hits, I never once saw one of our troopers duck to try to avoid being hit. We were not trying to be supermen; there was just no place for us to hide on the birds.

The closer we came, the more enemy soldiers we saw, and the more we knew that we had a "hot LZ coming right up". As we neared the ground, I directed the AC to my planned drop site by communicating the directions to the door gunner.

I had a good overview of our drop site, and I could plainly see many Charlies rushing to take their firing positions. We were certainly dropping many of our enemies. However, no matter how much ordnance our support put on an objective, in the final analysis, no battles were won until we grunts got there and physically locked up in some eyeball-to-eyeball contact with Charlie.

Without a doubt, that LZ was going to be red with Charlie's blood, even though there were still far too many healthy, living Charlies who were trying their very best to take our lives. The sound of the blades and the engine signaled that it was almost time. I looked for a good place to jump, because I knew the skids of our bird would never come closer than 4 feet to the ground. As I watched the door gunner for the signal to unass our bird, I tried to pop a Charlie who was trying to shoot me.

When the signal came, my team joined the firefight against Charlie, shooting all the while and staying alive.

Even before we hit the ground, the AC was turning the bird and giving it full pitch and throttle in order to get the hell out of there. Small bits of metal flew off our bird, and I saw many new holes in it. The beat of the blades rose to a thundering clamor, and the engine screamed loudly as our bird lifted off. The door gunners waved a sad farewell as they powered the bird hard and climbed away. I noticed that the AC was kicking it hard to his right so that he would not have to fly over the LZ and expose himself to more enemy fire.

I moved to a bomb crater and yelled to Pete, even though I already heard him repeating "RED!" I grabbed the mike and gave my assessment of the situation to the CO as the rest of our platoon was hitting the ground along a general line with us. Once I accounted for everybody, it was time for us to move forward and clear the drop-off site to make room for the rest of our company to come in.

Like Johnny Reb that afternoon of 3 July 1863, we were once again in our element on the ground and face-to-face with Charlie, our arch-enemy. Long ago, we had mastered the art of controlling our fears and making them serve us well, and we were caught up in the ancient emotions of the attack.

We were the absolute predators, and we shouted our battle cry as we rapidly formed into our attack formation and moved out smartly. We proceeded with our mission to put accurate covering fire on old Charlie, to allow the rest of our lift to get safely on the ground. As we moved forward, I proudly observed the perfect coordination of our Grand Company as it formed for the attack on Charlie.

The enemy soldiers spent more time shooting at us than at our incoming and outgoing birds. Sadly, our fire could only do so much damage because Charlie was well dug in, using earth and logs for protection. Some of his positions were very well constructed, and the fire from one of those positions scored a direct hit on one of our birds as it was lifting off after unloading its troopers.

I saw and smelled the hot cherry juice that sprayed out of the bird, as well as the smoke from the overheated engine. The wounded bird came directly over us, and it was much too low. The AC fought bravely to regain control of his badly hit bird, as black-and-gray smoke billowed out of it and trailed in its wake. Even over the din of our battle, I heard a muffled explosion on-board as the gallant bird tried in vain to pull up. The escaping cherry juice made it look as if the bird were losing its lifeblood. A little farther away and very close to the sloping high ground, the gallant metal warrior rolled over, and its straining blades dug into the earth.

It appeared that all of the bird's brave crew died in the ensuing great ball of fire. However, by the grace of Almighty God, we would make sure that those men continued to live in our hearts. Someone now sang:

"Mother, mother, there's too many of you crying.
Brother, brother, brother, there's far too many of you dying."[67]

Vengeance belonged to that magnificent bird and its crew, because they guaranteed that the NVA's machine-gun position and its crew who had taken them out would never again take out another bird or be a threat to us. Ironically, the NVA gun position near the top of the hill and the crew who had brought our bird down became victims of their own actions. The rotor blades of the downed bird broke free and flew out in an ever-widening path of destruction, cutting down small trees and bushes like a giant, sharp scythe in the capable hands of the Grim Reaper. A large section from one side of the bird's blades took out the NVA machine gun and then cleanly decapitated the entire NVA crew. A form of justice had been served.

By that time, we were on the ground in our company combat formation. There were Cav units on both sides of us and an airborne unit waiting in reserve to support our little eviction operation. Charlie put up a fight, but his best efforts were not good enough to stop our forward movement. I was still with the lead platoon, but the CO was the man in charge. Because we were the base platoon and the base company, everything depended on our direction and rate of movement. Therefore, the CO and I kept in constant contact with each other, and he told me when to move right or left. In such a large and combined operation, coordination was extremely important. Going too far left or slowing down too much could get somebody killed.

The LZ remained very hot. Charlie was jawed up tight and as mad as hell because we had already killed many of his men, blown out all of his windows, and fucked up his front lawn. He brought some 82mm mortars down on us, but old Blue Max quickly shut him up. Two of our men in the Second Platoon were hit, but they were able to wait until our dust-off birds came in.

By the time we reached the helicopter crash site (a few minutes after it went down), our situation had improved a bit. The Snakes got the mortars off our backs, and my right squad reported finding one of the door gunners still alive. We were all up on the company push, and this news brought loud cheers from all of our men. Either the door gunner had jumped or he had been thrown clear of the downed bird. No matter how it happened, he was alive!

Doc B. was with the door gunner, and I knew that he would pull another one of his miracles out of his heart and his hat.

We continued to push on up the side of the hill, kicking off on old Charles at every opportunity. Unfortunately, our lead platoon was now out in the open. Because we were the lead and base platoon of the entire formation, we had to continue on the same axis as we were told. If we drifted too far to either side, there would be problems.

We could see the top of the hill, and there were some fortifications and log bunkers still intact. It was from those positions that we were receiving the most accurate enemy fire, and we were too close to them for Blue Max to assist us, unless we pulled back and let the Snakes attack. The CO decided (and I agreed) that it was better for us to push on and maintain our forward momentum, since we were involved in a combined mission and had to consider the units on both sides of us.

Pete and I crouched near the remains of a tree, and I signaled to my left squad leader to have his squad move up more quickly. WHAM!

A bullet struck the tree between us, followed by two more rounds. We quickly became part of the earth around the base of the tree.

Thank God for all those times that Pete and I had danced the last waltz with Charles, because we knew right away what we had on our hands. It was a sniper, and according to the close pattern of those three rounds, he was either damned good or he had a scope on a Russian-made sniper rifle. We guessed that he had a Soviet Dragunov (SVD[68]) sniper rifle with a PSO-1 telescopic sight because we typically saw that kind in the field. WHAM! WHAM!! Two more rounds struck the tree in the same vicinity as the last rounds, and the pattern was just as tight. That son of a bitch was playing with us, and we did not intend to fall for his tired old shit.

We were on to that Charlie. What he wanted Pete and me to do was to run for a better place to hide, and then he would surely pop us. We did the unexpected and remained where we were, and we watched where he was hitting the tree. In doing that, we could determine where the bastard was holed up and ice his ass. Charlie the NVA was not skilled enough to play a game of cat and mouse with us.

Even though there was one hell of a fight going on around us, the sniper had picked out Pete and me as leaders. This was odd because Pete did not have a long antenna on his radio, which would have been a dead giveaway. Nevertheless, I had dropped the ball somewhere and was paying for my mistake now with the loss of time. We had to move out soon and catch up with our lead squad.

"Top, I got the bastard. I got his little ass!" Pete yelled jubilantly as he pointed out the sniper's position. "Top, let me thump the bastard. I know I can get him with the first round."

The sniper was in a spider hole on an extended portion of high ground in front of a large rock that offered him excellent overhead protection. Like most spider holes, his was almost invisible.

"Okay, Top, let's do it!" Pete yelled enthusiastically.

I threw a tree branch toward the spider hole to get Charlie's attention. He popped up instantly, and Pete put a 40mm grenade into the spider hole. WHAM! Charlie's body rose partly out of the hole, and his Russian-made sniper rifle flew down the hill toward us. We stood up and ran toward the fully iced sniper.

"Pete, I got to hand it to you. You and that old thump gun are the best. That was one hell of a shot," I said as we ran forward.

155

Grinning, Pete said, "No sweat. We aim to please. That'll show Charles not to play cat and mouse with us, 'cause we mice are bad enough to eat the cat's ass up!"

Pete and I caught up with our advancing troopers and were once again in our correct positions. I was happy to see Doc B., who told us that the door gunner was going to make it.

We passed through a rather large area that had been burned out by Willie Peter and napalm, and there were few if any places for us to seek cover. We were more or less out in the open and fair game for Charlie. Hitting the ground would be almost impossible because the area was still on fire. The best places to take cover were in the shell holes.

We were still right on Charlie's ass. It was not long before Pete and I had to jump into a nearby NVA fighting position to avoid being popped. We found ourselves in a sturdy, well-constructed fighting position, but we saw that it had been unable to withstand our preparation fires. The NVA's underground shelters in that position, where our enemies normally hid until after a shelling, had taken a direct round, which had obviously forced the hiding NVA soldiers to stay in their fighting positions. Pete and I found the bodies of six of these unlucky NVA soldiers. The Whispering Death had caught up to them.

Some sights merely boggle the mind, while others cause permanent damage to it. At that time, I believe that I was past the saturation point and well overdue to blow my top and slip off quietly to Never-Never Land. Let's just say that I would not be able to eat any barbecue for a really long time. The sights at that fighting position and at other more permanent positions that we crossed over as we neared the top of Charlie's well-fortified position were clearly sights to affect even our hardened exteriors. We found it hard to understand why Charles had refused to leave when he had the chance.

The first NVA bunker and fighting trenches that my lead group reached were mute testimony to the devastating effects of one of the missiles fired from only one of our Phantoms, or perhaps it was Blue Max. In any case, the strongly built bunker had taken a direct hit. It looked as if the missile had penetrated the bunker before it exploded, perhaps by entering through one of the firing slits. The walls of the bunker bulged outward, indicating that the explosion had occurred inside, catching an indeterminate number of NVA personnel.

Some of the trenches and fighting positions looked as if they had been dug up by a backhoe. The preparation fires, the fires delivered by the air force and Blue Max, and the Whispering Death had done a combined job on Charlie and greatly cut down on the number of enemy soldiers who were left to kill us. Of course, we of Black Knight Alfa had taken out more than our fair share of Charlies. The dirty work was always left to us grunts, and we cleaned out that shithouse on the side of the hill without the aid of chlorine bleach.

By now, we could clearly see the top of the hill and to the other side of our objective. The LZ was going to change hands very soon. Some of our guys were already shouting our battle cry, and everybody was caught up in the heat of the continuing battle. Some of my troopers were down, and I was hurting right down to my very soul for them.

On our left front, there was a rather sturdy-looking, covered fighting position, and inside of it were a few NVA soldiers hell-bent on getting the second award to their Red Stars. They were in a position to hurt us and to cause us a major delay. The CO went with the Third Platoon to try to find a blind side in order to shut down Charlie. My platoon was in the best position to be the base of fire, and we maneuvered in support of that role. Pete tried to find a good firing position to thump them, and I moved with him to add the firepower from my M16 to that of his thump gun. We broke cover and ran to a better position. Pete moved like a scalded dog, and I pulled for all I was worth to keep up with him.

Something wet, warm, and sloppy slapped me in the face and almost blinded me. My vision was extremely blurred, and I was terrified. Warm blood was in my eyes, nose, and mouth, and I reached up and slapped away what appeared to be a big, bloody piece of flesh. My legs gave out, and I fell to the ground, trying to wipe the blood and … away. I was shaking all over, and I tried to raise my left hand to see how badly I had been hit. When my blurred vision fell upon the big, bloody hunk of human meat lying on the burned grass, I almost lost it and the control of my hand, which suddenly seemed to be suffering from a bad case of Sydenham's chorea.[69]

I was hit! Fighting to control myself, I wanted to call out for a medic but could not. I spat out blood and somehow cleared my eyes and forced myself to look again at the piece of bloody meat. Then I realized that unless the color of my flesh had changed, that hunk of flesh was not from my body. It had come from an enemy soldier's body.

I cleaned my face with my sweat rag. I had not been hit! I was okay, if one could stretch the meaning of "okay" that far.

I giggled insanely and tossed my cookie called Luke.[70] Then, because I had to help Pete, I got up and started running again. I was still puking as I ran and dodged Charlie's bullets.

"Top, don't you scare me that way again, you hear me!" Pete hollered.

I tried to grin in between mumbling, "Credo in unum Deum."[71]

All of the companies involved in the assault up the side of the hill finally reached the last of the NVA stronghold of trenches, fighting positions, and bunkers. By the time Pete and I caught up with our company and established our shooting positions, we found Charlie to be well dug in, and there were times when we actually had to dig him out, but we were determined to win and we were better soldiers for our efforts. Our third squad convinced Charles to surrender by thumping his butt to a fare-thee-well. The few remaining defenders of the hill had the good common sense to realize that it was all over, and they ran away, defeated and demoralized. Some even threw down their weapons. Old Charles lost his contested hold on that piece of South Vietnamese real estate. He was officially EVICTED.

We swept over the top of the hill and down the back side to reorganize and consolidate our newly won objective. After clearing the back side and planning our artillery support, we pulled back and organized ourselves to repel any potential counter-attacks. However, the NVA did not intend to come back. They just wanted to get as far away from us as possible.

The NVA paid dearly for making us come to evict them. Their casualties were heavier than any I had seen in a long time. Judging from what we saw of their uniforms, equipment, and fighting techniques, they were first-line troops and did not have any gag-bag Viet Cong soldiers among them.

Redleg had our planned-and-ready artillery pop some marker rounds along our newly planned defensive positions. That was his way of telling Charlie, if Charlie were still listening, that he would be foolish to come back. After the marker and confirmation rounds were shot out, the strange mournful quietness that haunts every battlefield descended upon us all, both the living and the dead.

It was time for us to leave the mountain and return to the present time of men, machines, war, blood, guts, pain, tears, and death.

Truly, it was the right time for the dead to bury the dead.

The Silent Trumpet

Dust-off and medevac were the first birds in. Actually, our dust-off birds were flying in and out even before we won the battle. God bless those brave and gallant pilots, crews, and medical personnel. Even in the heat of battle, they were always right there – flying in and out and saving lives on the ground, in the air, and at various base hospital facilities.

I know that our fallen brothers were receiving prompt medical attention and the best available care at that time. Some of them would be going all the way home to those who loved them, but they were surely leaving men who loved and respected them, which certainly included me, their first sergeant.

I moved among my troopers, talking to them and offering words of encouragement and condolence to those in need of such words. Even after such a major battle, the spirits were still very high among the proud men of Black Knight Alfa. Sometimes I stopped to put my arm around a trooper, and I let each one know that we had accomplished a mighty mission. There were also places where I stopped and cried along with my men, sharing the pain of a lost brother-in-arms. We also mourned the crew of that magnificent bird that crashed shortly after dropping some of us off. Sometimes no words were necessary, and my troopers and I merely looked at each other in silence with a shared understanding. Sometimes the silent trumpet was so loud that everybody could hear it.

We of Black Knight Alfa were of one heart, one mind, and one soul, which were the essence of our being the *Grand Company*. We were always together as one.

The CO asked me if I had been hit because I looked like hell and did not smell much better. Then we chose an NVA bunker that suited our needs and identified it as our company CP. It was located near the center of our positions.

After I received all of my sit-reps, I briefed the CO on the status of our personnel and equipment. I told him the names of the three men we had lost KIA, as well as the names of those who would not be returning to us and of those who might be returning. I do not know how many casualties and KIAs the other units suffered, other than the men who had perished in the downed helicopter.

"Top, I hear that you are a praying man, so I want you to thank God for us all, and I'm going to do some praying too," the CO said to me after we confirmed the miracle of only losing three men during the day's major lock-up with the NVA.

I must say that losing three men was still three too many.

Once the CO had our sit-reps and other essentials, he hatted up to Battalion. Meanwhile, our troopers were clearing an area for us to spend the night. When the CO returned and gave us the body count of the losses that the NVA suffered, it was hard on us, too. I could not help but feel sorry for them because they were good soldiers. However, just because I say this, do not think that I ever turned soft where Charlie was concerned. None of us in Black Knight Alfa ever considered honoring Charlie, and we certainly never addressed him as "Sir Charles".

We spent the night within Charlie's former positions. He did not come back to haul off his mountains of dead soldiers, and he did not try to reclaim the hill from us. However, around 0300 hours, Charlie shot in two 122mm rockets, but they did not strike near our positions. I have often wondered why Charlie only fired two 122s that night.

The next day, we turned the bloody hill over to another unit, and we humped out of the area in the direction of Con Thien. We headed toward an old, safe LZ area that was already cleared. From that LZ, we waited to be picked up and slicked out to our next rendezvous, the Valley of Death.

We were going into the *A Shau Valley*!

Into the Valley of Death

Introduction

Someone once said or wrote, "A Shau Valley was the single least hospitable region in all of South Vietnam." I might be so uncouth as to add "especially to US Americans."

The A Shau Valley sits close to the Laotian border in the Thua Thien Province. There had already been several major operations conducted in "The Valley" (as I will hereafter refer to it). These operations included:

<u>Operation Delaware</u>   Conducted around 19 April 1968. This operation encountered heavy anti-aircraft fire but not much ground combat. The NVA decided not to come out and fight. Units of the 1st Air Cavalry Division and ARVN participated in the operation with very little tactical advancement.

<u>Operation Somerset Plain</u>   Conducted in August of 1968. This operation saw units of the 101st Airborne Division go in and come out with results similar to those encountered during Operation Delaware.

<u>Apache Snow</u>   Conducted in May of 1969 and involved units of the 101st Airborne, the 9th Marines, and the 3rd ARVN Regiment. Earlier in 1969, SOG reported to MACV that there was a very large amount of renewed NVA activity in the A Shau Valley, and in March, the 101st began their fourth incursion into The Valley. Two months later, the operation code-named Apache Snow began. The NVA did the unexpected and stayed to fight. For 10 whole days, the NVA held onto the Ap Bia Mountain, which is more popularly referred to as Hamburger Hill.

As I have said before, doing the unexpected was definitely the winning tactic in the Nam, and Black Knight Alfa had it down to an exact science. That is why old Charlie could never get his greasy little shit hooks into us and why we kicked his grubby little ass every time he was foolish enough to lock up with us. There were no exceptions, which is why we survived and I am still here to tell you our story.

Day One

Battalion resupplied us on our last objective, right there on that bloody hill. They brought us ammunition, water, medical supplies, bug juice, new machetes, heating tabs, claymores, and a special supply of LURP rations. We would also be packing Thermid grenades, C-4, and extra batteries for our PRC-25 radios. Everything was replaced except for our three lost brothers, and God knows they were irreplaceable. A little part of me went with each of them. May God bless them always.

We were completely refitted well before darkness came to cover us. If Charlie were to come back to protest his eviction, we would be ready, willing, and able to kick his ass out again. In addition to our material supplies, we had all the intestinal fortitude that we could give ourselves. No power on Earth could take it away from us, and we were greatly comforted by that resolute fact.

The CO and I knew that we were going to be inserted deep into the A Shau Valley on the following day. Battalion usually gave us time to rest somewhere behind the green line, but the time factor of our new mission prevented us from getting any stand-down time. We were going straight into The Valley.

As a single Cav rifle company, we of Black Knight Alfa went into the A Shau Valley bound and determined to play Russian roulette with old Death and the very best of General Giap's North Vietnamese Army. We would be skating on really thin ice all the way, but that is what made us the best soldiers. We were like Olympic-class skaters and swimmers, not to mention that we had more than once "broken the minute mile".

Our goal was to thumb our collective nose at Giap and his army, who were in complete control of The Valley at that time. We were going to make Giap react to our bolder-than-brass incursion, to make him "try" to eliminate us or throw us out. We would call his hand and make him play a card that he had not expected to play. We would make him think.

It was certainly unthinkable that the American military would insert a single rifle company into The Valley, hoping to stir the pot or perhaps even to achieve what a big operation that put entire battalions into The Valley had not achieved. It was sheer madness, UNTHINKABLE, UNEXPECTED, but our Grand Company would pull it off with style and class.

Although I would like to think that we were the only company in the Cav capable of pulling off such a bold plan, there were certainly other Cav companies who could do it. We simply got there first.

The CO said that we were going to fly directly to our drop-off point and jump off in broad daylight, acting as if we owned The Valley. We were going to jump and then disappear. There would be no false insertions, no snooping around, and no hiding. We knew that Charlie would see us; we were counting on that. He would find it hard to believe the Americans were sending a lone rifle company to do what many divisions had failed to do. It made no sense at all, and that was the beauty of the plan.

The kicker was that old Charlie was going to lose a lot of sleep trying to figure out why the Americans would do such a thing. It did not make sense, at least not to Charlie or to his boss, the little general.

During the short hump to our pickup point and the subsequent wait for our lift birds, I took the opportunity to read the faces and to feel the thoughts of my troops. I could detect apprehension and the wonder of what would come next. We had just fought some of the best soldiers the NVA had to offer, and we had come away clean, losing only three men. We were on our way to twitch the noses of another group of some of General Giap's best men, and we would be doing it right in the enemies' living room.

We met them on the sacred battlefields, and each time we were victorious. We kicked off on them like they were stepchildren, and we dared them to holler. Our casualties were minimal in comparison to Charlie's losses. We always terminated them during our lock-ups with extreme prejudice. We did unto them before they could do unto us. During our last encounter, we had hurt Charles most grievously by assisting our other units as they did a major job on portions of the7th and the 9th Battalions of the 18th NVA Regiment and other elite NVA regiments.

Frankly, we wondered if our time would soon come. Would our going into the A Shau Valley signal the end of our run of good luck, or whatever you could call it? Were we going into the end of our longevity? Were we heading to our Final Battle? Would Charles finally "win one for the Giap"? Would the A Shau Valley turn into our Waterloo? Would Charles finally get his revenge for all of the suffering and loss of face that we had heaped upon his pointy head? Would he finally get his revenge against us for always showing him up and for not believing the crap the news media published about his being so good? We had always said that Charlie was "overrated, overstated, and overstretched". All these thoughts ran through the corridors of our minds, and we concluded that luck had nothing to do with it. We were Black Knight Alfa, the reigning champions.

Our thoughts did not distract us from carrying on with our normal activities. While we were in place and waiting, my troopers played around, throwing an old half-inflated football. They joked and told lies about their last night in Sin City, about their last down on Tu Dor in the Gon.[72] They also laughed about the night a big old mama monkey dropped down on me in my fighting position. It had scared the hell out of "old Top" so much that he became monkey-shy for a very long time. Yes, I had freely given up my hard-dug hole to a mama monkey who insisted on my eviction.

My troopers also brewed coffee, smoked, munched on candy bars, and listened to their small portable radios and tape recorders. From all around I heard the mixed sounds of the music of those days – Mary Hopkins, Joe Cocker, Hank Locklin, Johnny Cash, Don Gibson, Smokey Robinson, Jimi Hendrix, and Marvin Gaye. Hearing all of that different, wonderful music simultaneously was like hearing a grand symphony, except somehow the music blended into a beautiful, soul-stirring melody in the steady, rhythmical beat of true brotherhood.

I was always so proud of every man in our Grand Company, but that day was special, and I was prouder than ever of my troopers. Thank the dear Lord I was old enough to know that I was experiencing a once-in-a-lifetime moment. It was a bright, shining rainbow that I put into my pocket and saved, along with the others. Not one of those wonderful young American soldiers was sitting around crying in his coffee out of fear that the mission we were about to begin might be our last. It was quite impossible to walk in shit and not get some on your boots. However, Black Knight Alfa could walk on water and jump over the

164

entire NVA in a single bound. Otherwise, we would not be there, waiting for our meeting with old Death in The Valley.

The A Shau Valley was a 30-mile-long, natural funnel that was located south of the Ho Chi Minh Trail, and it served as a major NVA and Viet Cong infiltration route. The Vietnamese called it Dong Ap Bia, but some American GIs had aptly named it the "Valley of Death".

The Valley consisted mostly of rolling terrain covered by almost 8-foot-high elephant grass. In it, we found description-defying species of living things that were unrecognizable to Mother Nature. The Valley was a natural fortress in the grand tradition of the Great Wall of China and the terrible Russian winters that had successfully repelled the invading armies of Napoleon and Hitler.

The Valley was protected on all sides by a formidable rim of triple-canopied hills. Hill 937, also known as Hamburger Hill, was among the hills that protected The Valley. Throughout its entire length, The Valley was as rugged as hell and densely forested with high peaks that were covered with lush green vegetation and all kinds of painfully spiked bamboo.

I remembered The Valley from experience and how it seemed to come alive and could literally eat you alive. That had certainly been a memorable time in my life. Sweet Jesus, I was going back in there.

With all those memories and facts chasing through my mind and heart, I walked among my waiting troops, talking to them, laughing and joking and drawing into my body some of their undeniable strength. To them it was just another day and another seemingly impossible mission that would become possible by the presence of Black Knight Alfa. I felt good because I knew with certainty that if any Cav company could pull off the mission, it just had to be the US

"Top, we have birds inbound, and they are asking us to pop smoke!" Pete hollered as he hurriedly replaced his long antenna with the short one.

I moved to my planned position, pulled the pin, and threw out my M18 smoke grenade. Once the smoke billowed out and started to rise, I recalled this portion of the 23rd Psalm of David:

"Even though I walk through the valley of the shadow of death,
I fear no evil; for Thou art with me.
Thy rod and Thy staff, they comfort me."

As we shouldered our great loads and moved into our assigned positions to board our lift of slicks, we began to chant our own version of the 23rd Psalm:

"Yea though I walk through The Valley of the shadow of death,
I will fear no evil, or Charlie
'Cause we're the meanest motherfuckers in the whole damn Valley."

Black Knight Alfa. Alpha and Omega!

Everyone in the company joined in the chant, and our voices rose to a climax to challenge the louder whumping sounds of the rotor blades of our very large lift of Huey helicopters as they came in to pick us up.

As usual, we were loaded and on our way in record time, and we were headed directly to our walk "through The Valley of the shadow of death". Along the way our very dear friends Blue Max joined us, and we shifted into a classic Charley Alfa formation. It was good to see those beautiful Snakes hovering around us with their full battle dress of camouflage and their gleaming white teeth.

Shortly before we reached our insertion point, a flight of perfectly synchronized Phantoms showed up and remained on station with us. We were supposed to look as if we were the lead element of another combined force that was coming to kick off on Charlie, as had occurred with Apache Snow and some of the other large-scale American operations in the Nam.

While Charlie was running in fear of a major attack to his underground hideout, we unassed our birds without popping a round. Because Charlie was too busy hiding instead of watching, we quickly moved out of our insertion area and pulled a neat disappearing act. We went to ground, lagered, and broke out our maps and compasses to get our bearings, starting at an old LZ that was cut by one of the last units to leave The Valley after Apache Snow. The elephant grass was fully grown now, but most importantly, the canopy was not. It contained a hole that was large enough for our birds to enter and exit.

Shortly after our lifts were on their way home, we heard some firing in the distance. Blue Max reported having caught an NVA unit crossing a stream where there was very little canopy, so the Snakes decided to join in the fun. Because they had no reason to carry all of their ordnance back to their bases, they unloaded it on poor Charles. They radioed to us that our enemies liked the water so much that most of them would be staying in it. Of course, we could not answer their call because we were on radio silence. Once their traffic ceased, all we heard were the new sounds of The Valley.

What initially affected us the most was the heat. Man oh man, it was a physical force with which we had to contend. There was barely any breeze, and it felt like we were in a very big sauna where the air was moist. Perhaps it would be better described as being inside a giant pressure cooker.

Once we were tightly locked in, every man lay dog and began to acclimate himself to his new environment – to the sights, sounds, smells, feelings, and tastes. As always, our survival depended on our five God-given senses. Using our senses had been advantageous for us in the past, and there was no earthly reason for them to let us down now.

In The Valley, the damned leeches were as big as Oscar Mayer hot dogs. While we lay dog, the leeches must have thought we were a combined Republican and Democratic convention because we could see each of them making a competitive effort to get there first. I even saw two or three of them with white napkins already fastened around their necks and one big, fat leech with a battery-operated caloric counter.

The skeeters in The Valley were as big as hummingbirds, and there were sticks that moved and others that screamed "Fuck You!" if you stepped on them. Needless to say, our experiences in The Valley mercilessly assaulted our minds and our souls. We were truly in another world, like something out of a science fiction movie where we were battling the environment in addition to the enemy soldiers. Objects around us were constantly nipping at our asses. If we grabbed a stalk of green vegetation, it burned like hell.

Everything required some adjustment time, but we did not have much time because we expected Charles to come investigating soon, and it was to our distinct advantage not to be there when he did.

As the CO saddled up, he said, "Let's move them out, Top. I want to put as much distance as possible between us and this LZ before dark, so that we can find the best possible place to lager. Remember, it is possible we might have to fight the night away."

We had already planned our order of march and our formations that we would use until Charlie fired at us. However, we changed our direction of travel from our original plan, and after about an hour, we shot another azimuth and headed for some promising high ground.

We pushed on for another two hours. Then we lagered, waited, and listened. We checked our maps again to ensure that our compass headings agreed with one another and that we were still in good shape. Our checks indicated that we were A-okay.

It was well over four hours before we found a suitable place to lager for the night. We had to stop before dark because when night falls under a triple canopy, it is literally a black darkness.

We found a place to set up and defend where it would be difficult for Charlie to attack us. A large stand of elephant grass stood squarely in the way of one possible avenue of approach. The jungle to our rear was full of wait-a-minute vines that even a snake would have trouble coming through. There were also spiked bamboo and a lot of hot electric grass nearby, and we had learned long ago that those things hurt Charlie as much as they did us.

While our troopers were locking us in tightly, the CO, Redleg, Lt Zen, and I closely studied our maps. However, in a location such as the A Shau Valley, it was like being in a double jungle, and a map was mostly good for heating your rations or wiping your butt.

In that area it was plain suicide to wipe your butt with a handful of grass. If you did, you would experience something unforgettable. Imagine rubbing salt into an open wound, and you would come close to an experience that often made grown men cry like babies, and you would not be able to sit for days. Actually, the best thing to do was to hold your waste until your eyes crossed, your vision went, your ears rang, and your breath ...

Anyway, in The Valley a map was often just something else you had to hump. Sometimes there were terrain features that appeared on the map, like the hills that helped to form the rim of The Valley. Although our maps were not too helpful in The Valley, we were fortunate to find certain valuable markers that the American units who were operating there before us had left. They had also left behind some ammunition and supply caches. As a result, we had at least two nice stockpiles very well hidden ... just in case.

I am not trying to say that we did not know where we were, because we did. It was a matter of our good health to know within the nearest 10 meters where we were at any given time. We were in The Valley without artillery fire support, and we had only our mortars and what 81mm mortar ammunition we could carry with us. However, we did have TAC Air "on call", but they could not reach us quickly because of the weather conditions, the level of visibility, and the jungle canopy.

Our arrangements were that we could call for help at any time. The 469th Tactical Fighter Squadron in Da Nang usually had birds in the sky, sometimes going and sometimes coming from having rattled General Giap's false teeth. They always had a few rounds up their sleeves and would not hesitate to go a little out of their way to put those few rounds on Charlie for us. If they had to make a special trip for us, they would. At that time, they were using the F-4B and the E models. The distance from Da Nang to the A Shau was greatly reduced because the F-4Bs could haul ass at about 1,485 miles per hour with their GE J79-8B afterburning turbojet engines pushing them. It was always a good feeling to see their camouflage battle dress and gleaming white sharks' teeth, which assured us that we had the best with the most there to protect us. Canopy or no canopy, they would shoot for us.

As we moved, Captain Norris – our redleg and acting forward air controller – kept a running and accurate account of our location on the ground and on the map. He was a wizard with a map. We could usually ask him where we were, and he could put his finger on our location on the map and give us the map coordinates down to the nearest 10 meters. His map-reading abilities made him even more valuable as our artillery forward observer. We were all skilled map readers, but Captain Norris seemed to have an edge.

Our platoons reported that they were in rock-solid positions. There were several things that I did not ask them because it would have been considered insulting. For instance, I did not ask if they were well dug in, if their claymores and flares were already out, and if any of their men were outside their perimeter. If they were not prepared, they would have told me. I reported to the CO that we were locked in solid for the night, and he smiled his acceptance of our position for that first night right there on old Charlie's back porch.

We were absolutely certain that Charles was aware of our presence, but he did not know exactly where we were.

Before I go on with my story, I need to clear up an important point about our communications. Our radios were regular ANPRC-25s. Their range did not reach outside The Valley, and it was greatly reduced by the mountains around us, the thick jungle foliage, the jungle canopy, and a host of other variables. If we needed TAC Air, we had to go through our battalion. There would always be one company from our battalion operating near The Valley, so we would go through them to Battalion, and Battalion would contact the 469th, unless of course the 469th had birds in the air or on station above us. In that case, we could push up and talk directly to the squadron leader. Frankly, we sometimes had absolutely no radio communications with Battalion or the "outside world". The good news was that our radios worked well on our company net, and we were able to talk to each other, which was essential. We were truly in The Valley alone, and if we got our asses in a crack, it was really up to us to pull ourselves out. I guess that is why Battalion gave us the ball.

We spent the night in total quietness with no harassment from Charles. I still believed that the enemy had no idea where we were. Both the CO and I thought that Charles was waiting to see what additional American support would come to join us. Charles was probably thinking that there had to be one hell of an act following ours. Little did he yet know that we were the only act on the stage.

Morning came slowly for us because it took some time for the light to filter down through the canopy. We were thankful for that night because it had given us the opportunity to fully get our A Shau Valley legs under us. That morning we performed our normal activities of making sure we did not have visitors, brewing coffee, and preparing to move out.

It was always best to get our heads together and plan our movements to avoid leaving anything to old Chance. We verified our location by orienting our maps with the prominent terrain features, good trails, streams, and hills. (There were no main highways or villages in the area.) In addition, the commanders of the units who had previously operated in The Valley since the time of Operation Delaware had already identified various areas and locations. The CO had received much of that essential information while he was at Evans, and it proved to be highly valuable to our continued survival.

Many more trails and secondary roads existed on the ground than on our maps. Therefore, to get from one point to the next, we had to depend on our trusty compass for the exact direction and upon our gut feelings and experiences for everything else.

The CO gave all platoon sergeants a detailed briefing of what we planned to do that day, and he outlined what we would do if we were hit. Our current position was named as our first rallying point if we were hit some distance after we left it. After that, we had to decide on some other unknown places as rallying points. After the CO finished speaking to us, I sent the platoon sergeants back to their platoons and allowed them enough time to pass the information to their troops.

"Top, let's saddle up and get the hell out of here. I have the feeling we've been here too long," the CO said.

I told Pete to pass the word that we were planning to move. Within minutes, I received an "up" from everyone, and I informed the CO that we were ready to go.

Three-Six was leading with Nat on point. Then came Headquarters, One-Six, Weapons, and Two-Six. When we left the FOB, we were in a staggered column with connecting files between platoons, using radio and connecting-file contact instead of visual platoon contact. That way if we were hit, only one part of our company would be affected. Our formation was also supportive of our new surroundings, which had greatly reduced our ability to rely upon our survival senses. All of us agreed that we were not as familiar with our surroundings as we typically were. We were experiencing new odors, different vegetation, and unfamiliar jungle sounds that made us unsure of whether or not we would be able to smell Charlie as well as we usually did. Those of us who had been to The Valley before noticed that the temperature was definitely different – more moist than dry – and we had to become accustomed to it.

It was almost impossible to move using stealth and speed without using a trail. The tall grass and the wait-a-minute vines were everywhere. When we avoided the trails by going through the woods, we often encountered many birds. Our presence spooked them, and they flew away as noisily as if we had announced our presence with a marching band.

"Top, this is just not going to work. Sure, there are areas where we can avoid the trails, but I think we have to accept the fact that there are areas where the only way is by trail." The CO spoke honestly.

"Well, sir," I replied. "If I were Charles, I wouldn't expect us to be using the trails."

We decided to use the trails whenever and wherever possible. While we were on a trail and approaching a position that appeared to be a good enemy ambush site, we left the trail and found another way to travel. Sometimes we even doubled back on our own trail and then went off in an entirely different direction.

We pushed along in the general direction that Battalion had told us to move, and all the while we did not see Charlie. Frankly, we were happy about that because we did not want to lock up with him during our first day out. The going was very hard because we were packing heavy and carrying more water than usual. The CO found a good place for us to take a break. We did not pull in closely to lager together; instead, we allowed each platoon to lager in three strong points with Headquarters and Weapons in the middle.

Everyone was already tired, so it would not pay for us to push it. If Charles located us, it would be very hard on us to have to run. At that point, we were on the side of a good hill and along the military crest, which meant that Charlie could not sneak up on us.

"Top, let's take a good break here, 'cause I don't see another area as good as this one. Let's have chow before we push on," the CO said.

I put the word out.

We were very well concealed above a decent trail that showed some recent use (which is why we were avoiding it). Only one of my 2-quart canteens was full, and it was only our first day out. I had a nasty cut on my left arm that hurt like hell when my sweat rolled into it. Doc B. eased my misery by giving me some salves.

During our break I carefully studied our environment. To say that it was hostile was putting it mildly. We could not see the sky because of the canopy, which told me that we would not soon receive any supplies or water. If we needed dust-off, a jungle penetrator would be required. Our hostile environment also had an over-abundance of beautiful but deadly black-and-yellow kraits. I remembered reading that there were more than 130 species of snakes in the Vietnamese jungles, and about 98 per cent of them were poisonous.

Judging from the number of snakes that we had seen, I think the A Shau Valley was a mecca for them. During our break the First Platoon

172

came across a stubborn, mean krait that refused to move out of our way. When JoJo tried to push him out of the way, the krait struck at him three separate times. Our men did not kill the snake because JoJo said that it would not be right since the snake had been there first. During the previous night the Weapons Platoon said they had to run off old two step. Most of the two steps were bright green and not as pretty as the black-and-yellow kraits. However, both snakes were equally deadly.

In that hostile environment we also encountered many large, bloodsucking leeches, huge red ants that set you on fire when they bit you, and skeeters that were slightly smaller than F4 Phantom jets but just as fast. There were also trench foot, the heat, exhaustion, jungle rot, and all kinds of flying, crawling, and just plain old being-there things that all teamed up to make our lives perfectly miserable. That was just for starters. Then, there were punji pits, spider holes, bamboo whips, and, of course, Charlie.

With such dangers lurking about, it was a risk to even take a dump. You might squat too low to the ground and have your butt wiped by a bamboo viper. Or, you might be bitten by a giant skeeter, burned by electric grass, or shot for being in the wrong place at the wrong time. We were also exposed to something that could sneak up on you and make you break out everywhere with a lot of gigantic bumps, even on the bottoms of your feet. Now that is hostile!

During our long break we spent some time getting accustomed to our surroundings, and I am pleased to say that we were starting to feel as one with our new environment.

The CO surprised me by quietly saying, "I don't want to go near the Ap Bia if we can help it. Top, I got me a real bad feeling about that area, so let's avoid it, okay?"

Naturally, I replied, "Okay, Sir."

We learned long ago to go with our feelings, because they had saved our butts more times than we could remember. Going against our feelings would only result in self-inflicted wounds.

I put the word out to bury everything, to leave no trace that we had occupied the area. Two Six took the lead out, and I did not see who was on point. After Two-Six came Headquarters, Three-Six, Weapons, and One-Six.

Because no one had appeared on the trail below us during our long break, we decided to use it. After all, it was a perfectly good trail, and it offered us speed and stealth of movement in the general direction that we wanted to travel.

Tran was with my platoon, and he requested to go up front with the point man when we reached a place along the trail that gave us "that feeling". Tran was well versed in the methods of the NVA and the VC, so we agreed that it would be best for him to go up front.

About 45 minutes later, Tran's presence up front paid off. We came upon a large punji pit that was filled with numerous spiked bamboo stakes that were long and sharp enough to go cleanly through a man. The pit was placed in an offbeat area, which was not the VC's style, and near the pit were three more snaps and traps than the VC customarily used.

As we examined the pit, our company remained in a well-spread-out defensive/fighting position. Each of our platoons had given me an all-clear signal beforehand, so I knew that it would be impossible for anyone to sneak up on us.

Tran said the punji pit and traps were there as silent sentries to guard a valuable cache, which would be somewhere nearby. He also informed us that the punji pit and all the traps were the work of a school-trained specialist who was so proud of his work that he had left his signature on it. That specialist was an engineer/sapper of the highest order.

The traps were fiendishly clever, and the backups were as perfect as we had ever seen. They were not, however, invincible if you knew where to look and what to do. Tran, of course, knew exactly where to look and what to do.

The CO took the mike from his RTO and spoke to all platoons: "This is Six Alfa. I don't want anyone to move around till he first checks the area. We are in snap-and-trap heaven, so be very careful. The trap setter was an expert. Hold your security in close, and if you find any traps, don't try to deactivate them. Some of them are explosive devices, and if they go, it will give our position away. Do you copy? Six out."

The replies came back immediately.

"One-Six, Roger."

"Two-Six, Roger."

"Three-Six, Roger."

"Four-Six, Roger."

The CO spoke as he and Redleg pointed out and traced their ideas on a map for me: "Top, you know of course that pit and those traps are in illogical positions, and we came upon them mainly 'cause we are where we are not supposed to be. Neither the road nor the trail is showing on our maps, and to top that off, our present position is in an area where no Americans have been for a long time. However, if you look closely at the map, it's a very good route off this portion of the Ho Chi Minh Trail, and the canopy is perfect. Charlie could move a division of tanks down this road in relative safety, even during daylight hours."

The road the CO was referring to was a new road close to the trail we were following. We had been very careful to avoid it because it was constructed well enough to allow for vehicle traffic, even though we had not seen any yet.

While we were discussing the possibilities, Tran was busy deactivating the snaps and traps. It was an easy task for him because he knew where to look for the safety/deactivating devices, which were hidden exactly where the NVA instructors taught their students to hide them. Here is an example of how being "perfect" has its drawbacks. That "perfect" engineer did his job according to the book, but his being "perfect" was ultimately his undoing. In a reasonably short time, Tran found and deactivated all of the traps, and the platoons reported that they could find no others.

Because we did not want to be sitting ducks or to get caught ripping Charlie off, we felt it was best to post security a little farther out and to make sure our lager was tight. It did not take Tran long to locate the cache; he simply followed the typical NVA markers and went directly to it. Actually, the cache was right there before us. Once Tran pointed out the signs, even I could follow them. He showed us how to deactivate the traps around the cache, and when he determined it was safe, we sent in some men with entrenching tools to dig up what we thought would be rice or ammunition.

The cache was something else.

"Top, we just hit something!" a trooper called out, and we moved closer to see what they had turned up.

As they hurriedly cleared away the loose earth, something long and tubular-shaped appeared, covered with grease- or oil-soaked protective materials. Redleg seemed to recognize the shape, and he called for caution, just in case the object was booby-trapped. Very carefully, they checked it again and found no booby traps. Redleg used his K-bar knife to remove the protective materials, which exposed the distinctive muzzle brake on the end of the long barrel of an M-46 130mm Gun-Howitzer.[73] It was a Chinese copy of the original Soviet M-46 that was developed from a naval gun and adapted for field use.

The importance of our discovery was slowly dawning on us as we rapidly uncovered the gun. At the same time, we removed some of the greasy rags and, where possible, the special protective materials that had preserved the almost new NVA field piece. All of the OVM[74] equipment, including the sight, was packed with the weapon. Even the fully inflated tires were floating on skids and covered so that the earth packed around them would not come into contact with the rubber.

While we quickly uncovered the M-46, Tran said he thought there would be ammunition for the weapon somewhere nearby. (The NVA instructors told their students to bury or conceal the ammunition within a certain radius of the buried weapon. Of course, certain conditions had to be met if the ammunition was to be stored for an extended length of time.) Everyone agreed that the M-46 had not been there for a long time, but we could not agree on an exact time frame.

We easily found the ammunition approximately 50 or 60 meters away on higher ground. There was quite a haul of boxes of 130mm ammunition. The markings on the gun were all in Chinese; however, the markings on the ammunition boxes were in several languages – Russian, Chinese, and German. The Russian ammunition bore the oldest packing dates; the Chinese, the most recent.

Altogether, it was quite a haul and just another gift to General Giap and the NVA from our friends in the People's Republic of China and the Soviet Union. Just another gift from those governments whose express purpose was to kill US American soldiers. With friends like Russia and China, our cups were running over with kindness. Unfortunately, it was the sort of kindness that was killing the US.

We realized that our great find presented us with a rather large problem, which was what to do with it. Our options were sorely limited because of our situation and our time factor. We had already spent too much time in one location, and the longer we spent there, the more likely we were to be discovered. Although we were there to shoot at

Charlie and to make him react to our presence, we planned to conduct our little operation when we, and not Charlie, chose to do so.

As we went to check the ammunition, we became conscious of the fact that we might find another cache or two of ammunition in the area. However, the CO told us not to look for any. At that point, we could either push up to Battalion and ask what to do or call in an air strike on that position after we were safely away from it. We did not take the first option because it might give away our location. The second option was not safe either, because even if we gave the pilots the exact coordinates, the jungle canopy would make such a strike a less positive way to take the gun out. We also had a third option, which was to get the hell out of the area and to forget we had ever seen the gun. Of course, this option did not sit well with any of us. There was no way we could take the damned thing with us, and we would not just walk away and leave it. We had to think fast because Charlie might be on to us by now.

"If I can have about 10 minutes on the gun and a few more at the ammo, I can solve the problem by blowing it all to hell and in place. I think we got enough C-4. There's no need to try to destroy the gun, only to render it unserviceable, and I think I can do that." Captain Norris said this because he was an artilleryman and would know what system to destroy to render the gun useless.

"Top, let's get some of that C-4 up here on the double so our redleg can do his thing," the CO ordered.

I was already on the radio and shortly thereafter, Captain Norris had his requested amount of C-4. I helped him to place the charges, and we used the cap from a claymore and an M-57 firing device to set it off. We packed the sight tightly with the charges, and then we performed the same operation on the pile of ammunition, only we used det cord.[75] We stood back and let our demolitions expert, Sp4 Worthington, do his thing. As I remember it, Worthington could blow the hairs off a fly's leg without breaking it. He was happy about being called upon to do the job, and he put a time fuse on his explosive train that would be a safe-cracker's delight.

The CO told Worthington to cut his time fuse long enough to allow us to get a safe distance away. When it was ready, Worthington bubbled over with pride and could hardly wait to light the fuse.

177

Sfc. Tuzo had the mortar platoon, and he offered one of his Thermid grenades that the Weapons Platoon always carried to destroy our mortars if it looked as if they might fall into enemy hands. On the strength of its intense heat, the Thermid grenade could melt steel and would be used to fuse together the breech mechanism, thereby ensuring that the M-46 would never kill another American soldier.

The CO agreed to let us use the Thermid grenade as a backup to the C-4, which would do a job on the sight but was only capable of blowing away or bending the recoil and traversing mechanisms. The company moved out, but Captain Norris, Worthington, Pete, and I stayed back until the drag platoon was almost out of sight. We had already popped the Thermid grenade because it gave off very little smoke.[76] We sent Worthington to fire his time fuse when we popped the C-4.

"Fire in the hole!" said Captain Norris into Pete's radio mike, and he pushed the lever of the M-57.

The C-4 blew while the Thermid already had the breech smoking and turning red. We ran like hell. Worthington was already way ahead of us.

Charlie would have to know that we were responsible for the explosion. Besides, we left our calling card attached to a tree where he could not miss it. The explosion shook the jungle quietness and upset most of the jungle creatures. Complete rounds of 130mm ammunition flew everywhere.

"Well, there goes the neighborhood!"

We were in The Valley for only a short time, and already we had depreciated its property value.

There was no doubt in my mind that Charlie would be jawed up tight when he saw his M-46 and all of that ammo blown all over the area, not to mention our Cav calling card on the tree.

The fat was in the fire; the cat was out of the bag. The next move was truly up to old Charlie.

Everyone had a big, mischievous grin on his face as we diddy maued the area. I was tired and puffing like hell, but our efforts were worthwhile when we thought of how Charlie would feel when he saw the mess we had made.

It was rather difficult to find, but shortly before darkness set in, we found a place where the canopy was thin, giving us a good chance of popping smoke through it. The terrain allowed us to spread way out and to have decent fields of fire if we were hit. Digging in was a little more difficult, but we knew that we could do it. It took a little longer than normal, but in good time, we had our defensive/fighting positions arranged so that we had 360-degree firing zones and very good security. However, the terrain did not allow for physical security any farther out than approximately 60 meters, and the situation would be worse if we were hit before our security came home. Therefore, we put our flares out and did not have physical security outside our perimeter. Once we were locked in, anyone found outside our perimeter would be dog meat.

After our meeting, the platoon sergeants returned to their platoons, and no one moved about much because it was dark. We had an area to take care of business, and it was possible to heat water for coffee and our LURP rations there. I ate chili that night, which was not one of my favorite LURPS. For me, it did not get any better than the beef and rice.

We had to be very careful concerning odors and lights because they might give away our location. The odor of our cooking, cigarette smoke, and the small light given off by a tiny square of C-4 or a cigarette could spell disaster for us. The CO, Redleg, and I were not smokers, so we did not have that problem, and those in the company who did smoke knew the rules of the game.

It was almost impossible to sleep. We were bothered by the fact that we did not feel Charlie's presence. In fact, we had been in the A Shau Valley for one full day and night, and we had not yet seen Charlie. Was he in hiding, or was he watching us to see what kind of fools we might be? Most of us thought that Charlie was waiting to see if we were the beginning of a major operation, and once he discovered that we were alone, it would be "time for Katie to bar the door"[77] because old Charles would try to eat us up.

We had to apply bug juice or suffer the extreme consequences. The hoary host of jungle predators promptly moved in with us and would not be denied. The ants seemed especially hungry. (I have since wondered why the dictionary labels the ant as "a small, social insect" because the ants in The Valley were not very pleasant companions, and they sure as hell were not very "social".) The leeches came running, and the skeeters seemed a bit put out because we had an ample supply of bug juice.

The CO decided it was okay for us to 50/50. I dug in as close to a big tree as its roots would permit, and I put my claymore where it would do the most good in case Charlie came calling. Maybe he was waiting until after we had survived our first full day in his sanctuary before making his move. I, like the CO and Pete, did not feel that our old enemy was anywhere near our positions.

While I ate the last of my chili, I observed Pete having it out with a tough root, and I overheard a heated discussion between two big skeeters trying to decide what to do with me.

The smaller of the two skeeters said, "Let's eat his ass right here and now!"

The larger one replied, "Now don't you be no fool, there's no need to eat in a hurry. Let's take him with us, and then we can take our time eating him."

A third angry voice chimed in. (It was a gigantic leech.) "Like hell you will. I saw him first, and he's all mine!"

Day Two

First light was a most welcome sight to our troops as we started taking stock of what was left of our weary bodies after the social, indigenous occupants went home to sleep off their feasting on us. The damage that they inflicted upon us was clear and in sight everywhere.

"Look, Mama, a big old leech was sleeping in my bed, and he's still on me now!"

Our medics were already up and doing the best they could for us, attending to our non-battle "casualties". The CO decided that we would stay put for breakfast. Our positions were as secure as possible, and we were relatively familiar with the surrounding area. Besides, it was good for our morale. We left our FOB position a little later than usual.

The heat was already like an oven that had been left on overnight. We humped along at a steady pace for nearly two hours. The wait-a-minute vines forced us to use a trail, and from my position in the Headquarters section behind the lead platoon, I could see a rather wide break in the woods and the trail up ahead.

I knew Rod was on point, and I was greatly relieved when I saw him signal his platoon to hold up until he checked the wide clearing. I was standing on the high side of the trail behind a tree, and I could see ahead and observe Rod as he moved forward cautiously. However, Rod disappeared from my view when he reached a slight bend in the trail, where the tall grass obscured him after his first few steps. When he started popping caps, I knew that we had finally hit some shit. Everyone took cover, and our thump-gun serenade began immediately.

"CONTACT, CONTACT! Christ almighty, it looks as if we hit the whole damn NVA!" the Second Platoon sergeant yelled into his mike. I overheard him on Pete's radio.

Damn it to hell, I thought angrily. There we were, practically nose-to-nose with Charlie, and I had not felt his presence. Was I losing my survival senses?

Our lead platoon was creaming Charlie. It was "Slaughter on 10th Avenue" revisited. They were hitting Charles with all their might and their will. They were machine gun-heavy, or as we often called it "pig-heavy". Their machine guns played the sad refrains of old Charlie's swansong. They were working fully and had dropped so many of the NVA soldiers on the trail that when I pulled up near their right and high gun, the gunner was having trouble shooting over the stack of bodies on the trail.

From the high side of the trail, I took a quick look down the trail to my rear and once again felt so damned proud of my company. Not one of my troopers was lying on the trail. Black Knight Alfa had disappeared, except for the platoon in contact. I was lying right beside their right machine gun, and I could not see half of the platoon.

Our Grand Company was preparing to do a job on old Charles, and I believe that even Charlie knew he was going to get his ass whipped. I also believe that Charles figured out where he had dropped the ball. There he was, overconfident on his own turf, on his own trail in the A Shau Valley, and now he was being popped for taking too much for granted. Once again, we had caught Charles with his pants down by doing the unexpected.

Our initial formation was beautiful and correct. We were spread way out, and we maintained all-around security. We hit Charlie as soon as we had contact. The CO did not have to say anything to us; I went forward as the lead platoon formed a base of fire. The Weapons Platoon had already popped a round down the trail to Charlie's rear, and they would work their rounds up on us, as long as the base of fire did not move forward. The CO moved behind the second rifle platoon in our formation, and they became the maneuvering element when we made our hit. The drag platoon then formed to cover our ass.

In the meantime, just a little over 100 American Cav soldiers had melted into the jungle in a much better fashion than Charles ever had. Until that time, no transmissions, other than those by the lead platoon sergeant, had been spoken over our radios on the company net. All the while, we were in contact with the enemy. The trail to our front was piled high with their dead and dying. Our mortars were shooting, our thump guns were thumping away, and the lead platoon's riflemen were firing at the visible enemy.

We called our successful method of working together "fire discipline or control". Only the thump gunners fired at targets they could not see. We never just popped away at the wind; we made every round count and tried like hell, as a rule, to equate one round to one dead enemy soldier. We could hump only so much ammunition and to fire it all at where we "thought" the enemy was would be a stupid move. To run out of ammunition would be just like committing suicide, or as we called it "committing sideways".

Of course, our method of fire control prevented the enemy from knowing our size, strength, and locations. It was also a good method for our commander to have a good idea of what the enemy was doing. If, for instance, our left security or drag unit suddenly started popping caps, the CO knew the enemy was hitting us from the left and/or the rear.

Getting back to the fight at hand, the trail on the enemy side seemed more restricted than on our side. Our company had lagered with the base-of-fire platoon, and our Weapons Platoon was somewhere within our defensive circle. We were prepared to fight and defend in any direction. At that time, however, it seemed that our only threat was mainly on the trail facing us, and we had already hurt them badly. Charlie had not expected to lock up with an American Cav infantry rifle company and to lose control of that portion of The Valley and the Ho Chi Minh Trail. What we were doing was downright mean and unheard of. The NVA would probably lodge a long-winded complaint with someone.

We guessed that the unit we hit had outnumbered us by at least 3:1. Yet, judging from the evidence that was scattered all over the trail, we had greatly reduced those odds.

"Five, this is Six Alfa, over."

"Six Alfa, this is Five Alfa, go," Pete replied for our first radio transmission of the contact.

"Five, this is Six. Are you where you're supposed to be, and what's going on?"

The CO came on the radio and asked if I was with the lead and contact platoon and requested my view of the situation. Then he said, "Five, you hold your position and cover me. I'm to your left and moving to get a better shot."

From the sound of the CO's voice, I could tell that he and his RTO were running, and I knew they would swing wide and left to maneuver and catch the enemy in a deadly crossfire.

All of our platoons heard the CO's transmission and knew what to do. In an effort to conserve ammunition, our mortars were not firing. They would fire again only if the enemy threatened us or brought up his mortars, or if we had to break contact and run like hell.

I cannot say how long it was before we heard our maneuvering platoon opening up on the enemy, who had begun to react in a more positive manner to our sudden onslaught. The lead platoon and the left portion of our lager were taking small-arms fire. Charlie had moved up his RPD light machine guns, and there were the definite sounds of SKS Simonov carbines and AKs. They were using at least three Type 63 mortars. The small 60mm rounds were not hurting us because we were down low enough, and Charlie was only certain of the lead platoon's positions.

Once the CO and his maneuvering platoon lit in on the enemy's right side from a position on the high ground, Charlie probably thought he was being hit by two large American units, or perhaps by an entire battalion.

From the CO's position, they brought the enemy mortar crews, who were trying to set up 82mm mortars, under accurate fire. We could hear the NVA soldiers screaming in pain, anger, and frustration just before the CO and his platoon were all over them.

I do not know how our troopers spotted a group of enemy soldiers moving closely together; however, I witnessed one of our guys shooting a LAW directly into them. Sweet Jesus! What a mess!

It was past the time for the dead to bury the dead.

One of the hallmarks of the American soldier was that our troopers were always thinking for themselves, and they did not require constant supervision. When they saw something that needed to be done, they did it with full knowledge. On the other hand, Charlie required someone to pull his chain. By the time he got accustomed to the feeling of "this can't be happening to us", it was too late for his ass.

The enemies' leaders ran around shouting orders (and probably cussing in Vietnamese and Chinese). Charlie fought back, and unfortunately for us, there were far too many of him. There were so many bodies on the flat ground in front of us that our fires were losing their punch, and our ammunition supply was low.

The CO said, "Five, this is Six. We did it again. Charlie is a giant, and it's time for us to diddy mau. Do you copy? Over."

It was time for us to fight in reverse.

"Alfa Five, Alfa Six, over," the CO called.

"Alfa Six, this is Five, go," I said after taking Pete's mike.

"Five, this is Six, CABOOSE. I say again CABOOSE. Do you copy? Over."

"Six, I copy caboose, over."

"Five, Six, NOW, out."

The CO wanted it done yesterday. The sergeant of the platoon in contact was there with me. I heard an "up" from all of the other platoons, which meant the word was out.

"Caboose" was our code word instructing all units in front of the drag platoon to pull back[78] through the drag platoon's positions, as the drag platoon reverted to the base-of-fire platoon.

We fought as we moved to our rear, and we did so without Charlie noticing our change in formation. I knew the drag platoon behind me would be ready. They had stopped firing their M16s, and I had seen a few of them shooting only with their thump guns as they moved past our left flank. We had to stay in position until the Weapons Platoon was pulled back and could hip shoot for us so that we could break contact. Pete and I heard Sfc. Tuzo say that Four-Six was "all present", which was my signal to pull back.

Sergeant Webb and two of his pigs moved back one squad. They covered us as we pulled back. We went through that procedure one more time before we were safely home within the drag platoon's positions.

If we had remained another two minutes in our positions, we would have been in serious trouble. Old Charlie had finally got his 82mm mortars into the game, and they hit our old positions in short order.

Although Sfc. Tuzo fudged a bit while breaking down his last mortar, the Weapons Platoon sent one last round way up the trail to Charlie's rear. I waited for them, and Tuzo grinned and gave me a thumbs up. I did not know what he was trying to say because I was trying to get everyone moving. The drag platoon were already in their defensive positions and had the most ammunition. They remained the drag and base-of-fire platoon to cover the company as we pulled through them. It became my position to remain with the drag platoon, and the CO took the lead platoon as we got the hell out of there.

I believe that Tuzo's last round hit pay dirt. He took a chance to hit Charlie's positions after realizing that the enemy would have to do the same thing that he was doing and shoot from a position directly on the trail because there were too many overhead branches to shoot from within the trees. That trail was on the map, so Tuzo estimated the range and shot one last round to hit where he thought the enemy mortar positions would be. Maybe that round did not hit them, but there were multiple explosions some distance behind the enemy positions, and their 82mm rounds that were falling on us began to slack off.

Before I left my last position in that firefight, I could swear that I saw two bicycles lying on the trail in the midst of the NVA bodies. It was certainly strange, but I figured that maybe there had been two NVA soldiers just diddy bopping along before our battle began with their brother Charlie. Later, Gonzalez told me that he had seen the bicycles, too, so I was not hallucinating.

Our entire company was on the run, and each platoon reported in over the company net.

"Alfa Five, this is One-Six, Sixty-nine. Do you copy? Over."

Pete came right back, "One-Six, this is Five Alfa. Roger, out."

The code word "Sixty-nine" meant that everyone was present. Soon I received that code word from all platoons. We were very fortunate that we had not lost a single man to Charlie during our most recent firefight. Of course, we were still in shit, but it was reassuring to know that we were all still in it together, as a team.

The CO moved a safe distance back down the trail until he found some nice high ground with some desirable features. Deciding that the high ground was the best we could find, the CO ordered the company to set up and lager. When he pushed up to us and told us to come home, we broke contact. I took the drag platoon, and we quickly and efficiently pulled back into our new positions.

The CO hurriedly told the platoon sergeant where to place his platoon. Then, he smiled and said to me, "Top, we got to cut this shit out. I have some very good reasons to believe that once again we managed to hit a whole damned NVA battalion – plus! Top, I saw them stretching all the way back down the trail as far as I could see, and that was using Redleg's field glasses. Now how's that for our luck?"

"Well, sir, Captain, there's something else you oughta know," I responded. "There's a whole lot of Charlies right on our asses, and in minutes they are going to be all over our boiler room floor."

"We got everybody?" he asked.

"Yes, sir. I was the last man of the drag platoon to come into the position."

"Then, anyone outside our lager is fair game. How's our ammo holding up?"

"Well, sir, the pigs who were with the lead platoon are more than half-empty, plus I would think that whole platoon is in about the same shape," I replied.

I turned to Pete and told him to tell the company to "praise the Lord".[79]

Sergeant Webb and I were almost last in the drag platoon as we moved away from Charlie. We both felt the bastards were following us, despite the fact that we had just torn the NVA a new one. Charlie was doing the unexpected by coming after us with the knowledge that he had the edge in strength.

Naturally, we were a bit unsettled by the fact that Charlie had discovered that we were alone and a hell of a lot smaller than he was. He probably also knew that we had neither artillery support nor air support. We wondered whether Charlie was throwing caution to the wind and going to charge in to get revenge for all of the NVA soldiers that we had killed. If he was hopping mad, then he probably would not be thinking too clearly, which would be to our advantage.

Our speculations about Charlie were correct. Before I stopped talking with the CO, several NVA soldiers charged up the hill, screaming and yelling. We rewarded them with buckshots from our claymores. We brought all of them down, but while doing it, we gave away our location.

"First Sergeant, let's get the hell out of here. We definitely do not need a lock-up," the CO ordered.

There was a distinct lull in the sporadic fire that we had been receiving from the base of our hilltop location. We could no longer see the trail, but everyone felt that Charlie was massing for an assault.

"Top, are you thinking what I'm thinking?" Redleg asked.

"Yes," I replied.

I was having the same thoughts. Three-Six was nearest to the back side of the hill, where they had physical security posted with a radio.

Sfc. McKinnon (Mac) had the Third Platoon, but he was too far away for me to physically get to him in time. I could only push up to him in the clear, so I did.

"Three-Six, this is Five. Let's diddy mau the area, now! Down the hill in the direction you and your security are facing. You are leading. MOVE! MOVE!"

"Roger, Five, we are moving," Mac said.

Again in the clear, I said, "Order of march: Three, Two, Four, and One dragging. Let's move!"

The CO, Redleg, Doc B., the RTOs, and I ran like hell trying to get into position near the front of Two-Six. It was unnecessary for me to announce the formation we would use because we were moving through a thickly wooded area where the enemy could be anywhere. Therefore, we used our own version of the column, with the lead platoon in a rough diamond and well spread out behind the point man.

Two-Six, Weapons, and the drag platoon were in a rough column – well spread out and with all-around security. Before the drag platoon reached the bottom of the back side of the hill, the first of the enemies' mortar rounds hit the bottom of the front side of the hill.

Damn! We would have to hit an NVA unit that had a good mortar section. Those rounds were dead on top of where we had just been. It did not take a tactical genius to figure out where the next rounds would land. They would either hit on the back side of the hill or dead on top of the hill. If they hit on top or their rounds hit on line and over, we were up against a very good mortar section. It was definitely time for us to quicken our pace.

Charlie's mortars came right up front and hit the top of the hill on their second try. That hill took one hell of a beating, but better the hill than us. I did not have time to stop and admire the shooting skills of the enemy mortars. We were sorry that we did not have the time and the ammunition to stop for a shoot-out with them. I knew that we could have beaten them.

Our movements were cool, controlled, and well calculated. Our driving forces were our will and our absolute determination to survive at all costs. We were not out there to die. We would meet Charlie again on the flip side and at a place and time of our choosing. It was far better for us to run away now so that we could fight another day.

However, if our CO had ordered us to turn around and fight Charlie at that time, we would have done so and won. However, in the absence of such an order, we kept getting up, with the desire to put as much distance as possible between the NVA and us.

After a long run we slowed down to a fast walk in an effort to conserve our flagging strength. Boy oh boy, if you could have seen me that day, even my mama would have had trouble recognizing me. I was dirty to the max and as ragged as a can of sauerkraut or a nickel mop.

Our company pushed on, heading deeper into the jungle, and we were once again under a very thick canopy. We had no real objective way of knowing whether it was a single or a triple canopy, and we continued along until the sunlight was greatly reduced. Then, we halted to catch our breath.

We were all strung-out and hurting, but we were still alive. I really felt sorry for our mortar men, even though the 81mm mortar M-I is broken down into three parts – the base plate, the tube, and the bipod assembly. There is also the optical sight, but it is light and carried in a small, strong metal carrying case with a shoulder strap. No matter how you look at it, even when broken down, each of the three major components is heavy and hard to carry while walking, let alone while running. Almost every man in the company carried a minimum of one 81mm mortar round. By that time, we had fired some, but we still had a decent supply.

The weight of one round of high-explosive 81mm ammunition was approximately 3.3 kg; the white phosphorus, about 5 kg; and the illuminating round, about 4.6 kg. We also had the M-10 plotting board, but it was plastic and not at all heavy. Needless to say, I was close to passing out because we were running with a huge load, which also included our claymores, C4, M-18 smoke grenades, loaded M-16 magazines, ammunition for the machine guns, and all the water we could carry.

Even though we were tired, we were never too tired to set up our defenses or to put out our claymores. We were in a good, strong lager, using a piece of terrain that would enable us to defend against or fight Charlie.

The CO, Redleg, and I used our maps to try to determine our location. We were lost to the max! However, that was a small thing, because we were certainly not virgins when it came to being lost.

Once again, I had the utmost confidence in my survival senses, which were almost up to par and told me that Charlie was not close at hand. As I related my instinctive feeling to the CO, we received a call.

"Five Alfa, this is Alfa Four. Over."

"Alfa Four, Five Alfa. Go," Pete answered.

"Five Alfa, can Alfa Five come right away to my 10-10?[80] Over."

I took the mike and replied, "Alfa Four, Alfa Five, on the way. Out."

Pete and I were instantly in motion. Something was wrong!

When we arrived at the place where the Weapons Platoon was situated within our company's defensive position, we found Sfc. Tuzo and his platoon medic bending over a soldier lying on the ground. I was saddened to see that one of our young mortar men had been hit very badly.

That brave young lad was Pfc. Roberts, and he was another example of the reason that I can tell you and the whole world that I loved and respected every man in my company. There were no greater, finer soldiers in the world. Pfc. Roberts had taken a round in our last firefight with Charlie, and he had not said a word about being hit. He had not called for a medic but had attended to himself. During our long getaway run from Charlie, the wounded Roberts had kept up with us, running all the way without a complaint. He was carrying an 81mm mortar tube and ammunition. Sweet Jesus, I felt so humble and privileged to be there with men like him because he was one hell of a man. If only you could have seen Pfc. Roberts and his wound, you would know that the Grand Company was full of men like him.

I was so angry with myself for not knowing that one of my troopers was hurting. I raised my voice and scolded him, "Roberts, why didn't you let your aid man know you were hit?"

I was immediately sorry I had raised my voice at him.

"Well, Top, it ain't so bad. It just kinda looks worse than it is," said Roberts with a smile. His lips were trembling painfully from his efforts to speak. "I knew we hit some big-time shit, and I didn't want to hold us back because someone else might have been hit, too."

The color of Roberts's skin and lips indicated that he was bordering on shock. Doc B. had already given him a hit of happy juice, and his blue-gray eyes were growing dull.

I apologized for raising my voice at him, and I had to stop speaking because of the big lump that had formed in my throat.

"That's okay, Top. I know you got us all to look out for ..."

All of our troopers who heard him said aloud and in unison, "Brother, I'll die for you!"

I clearly saw the look of concern on Doc B.'s face, and his expression told me that Roberts needed more help than Doc B. could provide.

I did not want to use the radio any more than was necessary, so after Pete and I moved back to let the medics work in peace, I went back to the CP and told the CO about Roberts. I could see that he was also pained by the news. Pete and I decided to make our rounds of all platoons to see if any other troopers were hiding wounds as Pfc. Roberts had done.

Certainly, there were some differences in Black Knight Alfa since Captain Brooks had replaced Captain Harris as our CO. However, the heart, mind, and soul of Black Knight Alfa had not changed. We ate, slept, laughed, cried, fought, and died together, and there we were walking through the Valley of Death TOGETHER. If we were on our way to hell, we would go together. There were no finer men on this Earth who could accompany me there.

Black Knight Alfa. Alpha and Omega!

The CO and I looked at each other. Old Charlie would soon be on our asses, and we had to move quickly out of the area.

Pete whispered to me, "Top, Doc told me that Roberts isn't up to another long run, even if we carry him."

Pete was echoing what I already knew. We needed dust-off!

If we called dust-off, however, we would have to pop smoke and that would pinpoint our location to the more-than-full NVA battalion who were after our butts. To pull Roberts out would require a jungle penetrator,[81] which would make the process slower and give Charlie an advantage over us.

The CO looked intently at me and then around at the faces of everyone standing there. The life of one man versus the lives of all the men in our company – a ratio slightly higher than 100:1. Nevertheless, that one man was an intrinsic part of our team.

We knew that calling dust-off would endanger our company and our mission, but one of our troopers was down, and he needed dust-off to survive.

Our decision was plain and simple. We called dust-off.

It was not necessary to inform the company of the CO's decision. All around our perimeter our fine troopers were digging in, positioning claymores, and getting ready to fight Charlie to the death if required. Redleg was fixing our position, and Sp4 Danzig (the CO's RTO) simply passed the mike to the CO with the long antenna already attached. No words were spoken among us; instead, we communicated through our united hearts and minds, and our method of communication became our greatest asset.

We were lucky that the CO got through to Battalion on the first boot, and the push was completed via our way stations. Dust-off was on the way. God was blessing us because there was a mission not far from our location in The Valley, and dust-off was on station in record time.

"Thanks, guys. You were indeed our very own angels of mercy and right there when we needed you. If they gave gold medals or some kind of award to people who went the extra mile, all of you wonderful personnel of medevac/dust-off surely deserve to be at the front of the line. You were always risking your lives to save ours. We will always be grateful to you. May God bless you always."

– From Top Steen and the men of Black Knight Alfa.

Shortly, dust-off pushed down to us, and we heard the welcome sounds of their birds as soon as we gained radio contact. Our security informed us that old Charlie was coming at us again. The bastards knew we had dust-off and, therefore, wounded, and the fools thought they had hurt us badly. That was the only reason they were getting ready to make a run on us. They thought they had us this time, but it was the other way around.

Our lager was as rock-steady as always, and we were determined to beat Charlie, even if he had the whole damned NVA with him with

General Giap in the lead. (If that were true, the General would be the first to go down.)

"Black Knight Alfa, this is Caduceus three leader on your push. Pop smoke so I can find your 10-10. Over."

"Caduceus leader, this is Black Knight Six. Smoke popped. Come on back with the flavor. Over."

"Black Knight Six, Caduceus leader. Wait. Out."

Popping smoke under a jungle canopy was a bit tricky, to say the least. The smoke had to travel upward and penetrate the canopy. Often the canopy would filter the smoke to the point it would exit the canopy some distance away from where you desired it to show your location. (Remember, we had problems with that factor before.) If there was a breeze, it was necessary to determine how much and which way the wind was blowing, which we accomplished by holding a handful of dried leaves or grass high enough so that it would float on the breeze for a while before hitting the ground.

We had already gone through that procedure and popped our smoke. Fortunately, the canopy was close, the trees were not too tall, and the breeze was practically non-existent, so the smoke did not have much space to drift and give a false location.

My survival senses were screaming madly, and I knew that Charlie was near. The birds hovering above were definitely not helping us, but we had no alternative way of saving our trooper.

"Five, this is One-Six. We got company!" the First Platoon warned.

I grabbed Pete's mike and said, "One-Six, Five, DO IT! Out."

The distinct chattering sounds of some angry AK-47s told us that those NVA bastards had chosen a bad time to come calling. One-Six began their thump gun serenade.

An RPG whistled over our heads, indicating to Pete and me that old Charlie had come prepared to stay. Of course, Black Knight Alfa was prepared to be very hospitable and planned to make Charlie's stay as permanent as possible. The whistling RPG seriously damaged a tree and blew shrapnel and tree splinters everywhere. Those RPGs were certainly not very environmentally friendly and neither were they friendly to us.

Some distance away, I saw an NVA machine-gun team attempting to get into position, but they fell over screaming after one of our troopers put a high-explosive 40mm thump grenade on them. Next!

"Top, you take care of getting Roberts out, and I'll take care of keeping our unwelcome guests off our backs!" the CO yelled to me as he ran toward the area of our perimeter that was under heavy fire from the NVA.

"Black Knight Alfa, this is Caduceus leader. I see your smoke and identify it as Goofy Grape. Do you copy? Over."

"Caduceus leader, Black Knight Alfa Five. Six is busy entertaining unwelcome guests. Goofy Grape is correct. Can you drop your penetrator slightly SOUTH of Goofy Grape. One to come up. Over."

"Alfa Five, Caduccus leader. That's most affirm. Heads up. It's coming right down. Wait."

After a few anxious moments we saw the jungle penetrator slowly descending through the canopy, but the damned thing was coming down at least 20 meters outside our perimeter. There was no time for them to try again, so we were forced to go to the penetrator.

The NVA paused in their attack because they were unsure of whether Blue Max or some other gunslinger gunships were up there with the dust-off bird. We took full advantage of their moments of indecision. The CO quickly adjusted our perimeter by moving a platoon to where their positions would encompass the slowly descending jungle penetrator. Leaving Pete to give directions to the dust-off flight leader, I went with Doc B. and the troopers who were carrying Roberts toward the penetrator.

Because of the happy juice, our wounded comrade was not feeling any pain and was resting peaceably on cloud nine. He was properly tagged with all pertinent information regarding his identification, his wound, and the medication he had received. We used his poncho liner and some of his webbing to secure him to the penetrator. Doc B. gave the OK signal to Pete, who told the dust-off bird to haul away. We stood clear as the wounded trooper began his ascent to the medevac team.

As our wounded trooper was lifted out, Charlie threw caution to the wind and came after us again. Perhaps he had figured out what was really happening. Out of the corner of my left eye, I saw a lone enemy soldier rush forward and pause briefly to fire his RPG upward at our wounded soldier. The cowardly NVA soldier chose a helpless target, which pissed a lot of us off to the max.

Our troopers who witnessed that incident reacted quickly and riddled the body of the NVA soldier with a high volume of rifle and machine-gun fire, but not before Charlie was able to shoot his RPG. His grenade just missed its helpless target and punched a hole in the canopy, encountering enough resistance to explode. Shrapnel and foliage rained down, leaving a small, ragged hole in the canopy.

I guess it was a time for cowardly NVA acts, because no sooner had the RPG shooter bought the farm than another fool appeared and repeatedly fired an RPD at the jungle penetrator. With his pig, Jones blew that Charlie's chest apart. In a single, long burst, the pig's 7.62mm slugs ripped the bastard's guts out. His innards flew in all directions, just as the slugs from his machine gun were doing. His lifeless finger still held the trigger of his RPD, and the weapon fired continually until it either jammed or ran out of ammo.

It was clear to everyone who saw those cowardly acts that the NVA was trying to shoot our brother on the penetrator. All of us started firing without bothering to wait until we saw a target. We just cut loose to protect our brother until the penetrator cleared the canopy and was out of sight.

Pete yelled into his mike, "It's okay, it's okay. He made it safely!"

The loud firing made it impossible for me to hear the dust-off bird's exit. We were involved in a major encounter with Charles, and he apparently thought he had us. It was time for us to do some major ass-kicking. No matter how many NVA soldiers were out there trying to take our lives, we did not intend to roll over.

The CO sent a sit-rep to Battalion. There was no longer a need for radio silence because, by that time, even General Giap knew of our presence and our identity. Our fight with those foolish Charlies who tried to surround us was a fierce one.

I think the NVA still had some reservations about us. The fact that we could have dust-off must have told them that we could also get Blue Max or the Phantoms on their asses. Their only current advantage was the jungle canopy, which greatly restricted the accuracy of our mortars and of any fire support that might come to help us. Of course, the canopy negatively affected Charlie's mortars, too.

I heard the distinctive, harsh chattering of at least one of the enemy's heavy machine guns, and I told myself that it was time for us to show Charles a ghost because our ammunition was getting low.

Years before in the Mississippi Delta, my grandpa had told me, "Sonny, always remember, there's a time to stand up, and there's a time to shut up; a time to stand and fight, and a time to run like hell. Now son, the most important time of all is to know what time to do which."

I guess the CO must have been thinking along those lines because he yelled to me, "Top, saddle the company up, and let's get the hell out of here while we still can. Let's diddy mau the same line-up as when we came. Let's move!"

He pointed in the only direction left open to us.

I took the mike from my RTO and began issuing orders in the clear as Pete and I ran to get into our positions in the formation. My platoon sergeants talked back to me as we faded away. Only half of our perimeter was under pressure so we were able to slip to the left, break contact, and run away. Charlie believed we were staying in the area and interpreted our slipping left as a means to reinforce our perimeter under his pressure. The dense jungle helped us to fade away. We made our move with class, and our whole company of over 100 men outsmarted Charles. He was still shooting at us, but we were no longer there to shoot back at him. Once again, we accomplished the impossible, and running away from Charlie did not bother us at all.

We hauled ass as fast as the wait-a-minute vines would permit. We effectively put some high ground between Charlie and us. As soon as we found a trail going in the appropriate direction, we took it and stretched way out, running as fast as we could for as long as possible. We took most of the necessary survival precautions by changing directions at least twice and doubling back on our trail once.

When we were far enough away, we slowed down to catch our second (or third) breath, and the drag platoon reported that our tail was clear. If Charles followed us, we were going to ambush his ass.

We found a safe location and strongpointed it with three positions. The Headquarters section and our mortars were positioned within the Third Platoon's lager. We pulled out our maps, our compasses, and our good luck to try to determine where the hell we were.

While we rested and studied our maps, Pete took my sit-reps. We had wounded, but no one was seriously hurt. Our wounded refused to leave on medevac. Showing their pride and determination, they elected to stay with the company. Besides, up to that point, we were thumbing our noses at the entire NVA and getting away with it. It was too good to be true, and everyone wanted to stick around because none of us had experienced so much fun since coming to the Nam.

Black Knight Alfa. Alpha and Omega!

Our sit-reps provided us with the following information: (1) Our ammunition supply was low, except the 81mm kind, and we did not have enough to sustain us in another firefight. We had humped into The Valley with our normal load of 18-to-20 full magazines of 5.56mm M-16 ammunition. However, our run-ins with Charlie had greatly depleted that supply. We had consumed most of our fire keeping Charlie pinned down while dust-off lifted Roberts out. (2) Our high-explosive thump gun ammunition was almost gone. Each gunner had only two or three rounds left. Although they had enough shot rounds, we did not plan to let Charles get close enough for us to use shot. Because of the size of the 40mm grenades,[82] it was hard to carry enough for a long turn against the enemy. Our thump gun ammunition was very important to us, as were our methods of employing our thump guns. In fact, we often used our thump guns in place of our mortars when we fired at close range. (3) Our wounded would be fine with the aid of our medics. (4) Our drinking water supply was low, and we had not yet passed a stream with drinkable water. The only creek we had seen was a mud hole that even Charlie would not touch.

"Top, we have to reach our stash, and we must do it before nightfall. I didn't plan on going near it till tomorrow evening, but our sit-reps dictate otherwise. According to what Redleg and I have come up with, we are about here," the CO said while pointing to his map. "Our stash is over here." Again, he indicated the relevant location on his map. "If we go through the jungles, we will never make it before 0100 hours tomorrow. First Sergeant, we have to reach our stash today, or we have to go to our emergency pickup point and request extraction, which will mean our mission in The Valley is a failure. We do have the option to request a supply drop. If we can reach Battalion, we can do that from here, but if we are hit before or during that drop, it could cost us a lot of lives. Plus, we would have to cut an LZ or take the drop through the canopy, and we know how hard that is on 81mm ammo. Well, First Sergeant, what do you think?"

That was certainly a long speech for the CO, and I understood the gravity of our situation while knowing that every trooper in Black Knight Alfa wanted to accomplish our mission. We were Cav, and that's what it was all about.

"Sir, let's make the run for our stash," I said, and everyone else agreed.

Stash

We were clearly skating on the edge. For us to reach our stash in time, we had to break all of the old rules of land warfare. Also, darkness was not available to mask our movement. It was sheer madness, bordering on absolute stupidity, which may account for why our plan worked so well. Our enemy would never think to look for us running along one of their trails because it was unthinkable. Even if they saw us, they would never believe their eyes. In that way, we would pass unseen.

JoJo was on point, and his Louisiana Cajun senses were perked up to the task at hand. Rod was the second point, and Nat was the third point and the leading man of the three-man connecting file. A thump gun-heavy rifle squad followed them, and behind the squad there were two more machine gun-heavy rifle squads who brought up the rear of the First Platoon. One-Six was moving in a well-spread-out, staggered column formation that was designed for speed.

I positioned Pete and myself behind and close to Sfc. Gonzalez and his RTO. Two-Six followed us in the same formation. The CO, Redleg, and Doc B. were with Two-Six in a position where they could maneuver the Second, Third, and Weapons Platoons. The Weapons Platoon was behind the Second Platoon and the Headquarters section with their mortars in the very rear of their formation, ready to shoot standard from the trail or to shoot from the hip. Three-Six was running drag and would post right and left outguards/security when and if the CO instructed. That was our running formation as well as I can remember it, and that formation had always been good to us. We used it in the highlands and also in the flatlands, naturally with some variation. That particular formation provided us primarily with speed of movement, all-around security, and total control. We were well enough spread out and staggered to make it rather impossible for everyone to be caught in an ambush. If we hit some shit, the CO was in the best position to control the outcome.

Now I would like to tell you about our stash and how it came to be. As I may have mentioned already, Charlie and the VC were not the only Nam combatants who stored and used hidden caches, or "stashes" as we called them. Neither did the enemy hold a monopoly on clever methods of hiding stashes. Our stash consisted mainly of ammunition, but we also hid water, medical supplies, a small amount of LURP rations, batteries for our radios, bug juice, claymores, and flares – the essential items for our survival.

Unfortunately, we did not have a sufficient stash of water because we had counted on finding some drinking water along the way. Most of us were down to our "iron ration" of water.

Battalion had previously arranged for SOG to position our ammunition stash. The CO had the map coordinates to locate the stash and the proper sequences to disable the booby traps used to safeguard it. We simply had to find the location and remove our necessary supplies. We elected to get there during daylight hours so we could set up around the site and secure it before we went to retrieve our stash.

JoJo set an easy pace that depended heavily on a set rhythm. We moved along in almost the same rhythmical pace as that used by the legendary Zulu warriors of King Shaka's mighty army.

I was the oldest man in the company, and when I had joined them, I had worn large-size trousers. By that time, I had to tie up my trousers because of the A Shau Valley reducing plan.

As soon as I got my second wind, I was running cool. We moved as fast as we could under the circumstances, and we made some noise as we traveled. That time was very stressful because we could come under enemy fire in an instant or run headlong into an enemy unit using the same trail. That had already happened to us once. If it occurred again, we were counting heavily on our survival senses to give us enough early warning to react effectively. Luckily, Charlie was nowhere near, and we kept using the trails and steadily getting up.

When we stopped for a breather on the trail, we cleared it and lay in hiding. If you had the occasion to pass by on that same trail, I would bet my life that you would have walked right past us without seeing one man or anything out of place, when there were well over 100 of the best damned soldiers in the entire United States Army in the area.

When we started moving again, we fell into a good rhythm and like those mighty Zulu warriors, we set a pace that literally ate up the klicks. I was tired, but there was no damned way I was going to fall back. I was the first sergeant of those mighty American warriors, and I would rather run until I dropped dead or until my heart burst wide open than call a halt just because I was tired.

I prayed to God that our wounded were not suffering too much and that they would be able to keep up. I glanced back once or twice, and my heart swelled with pride when I saw some of our troopers carrying the loads of the wounded. One trooper was practically carrying his wounded buddy, too. God, I loved them so much that if I were to fall down and be unable to get up, I swore that I would just take my .38 and blow my damned brains out.

JoJo was like a homing pigeon. No one had to tell him which way to go unless there was a distinct change in our original instructions. In fact, old JoJo was a hell of a lot smarter than a homing pigeon because a pigeon could only "return" to a place where he had been, whereas JoJo could locate a place where he had never been. Now he was heading straight to our stash.

The CO pushed up to me, "Five, this is Six. Tell that Cajun to pull up somewhere. I need five. Out."

I had to smile because old JoJo had run the CO into bad health, too. I was certainly happy to stop. We lagered in an area where the elephant grass reached my shoulders and the stands of bamboo were as strong as steel tubing.

We hacked off some young tender stalks of bamboo and sucked the moisture with our parched lips. In some cases, the stalks provided almost a full swallow of sweet water. This helped us to conserve our water supply, even though I do not think anyone was down to his last drop of canteen water. We were much better soldiers than to allow that to happen.

We stayed in the elephant grass long enough to catch a few breaths. Then we pushed out again. I thought of changing our formation line-up, but the CO told us to leave it alone because we were working well that way. JoJo did not want to be relieved, and he refused Rod's offer to replace him up front.

We pushed on out and found another trail; then we kept on getting up. Approximately two hours later, the CO moved up beside me and said in a wheezing voice, "Top, we made it. See that high ground and the treeline to the left rear. That's where our stash is located. Tell JoJo to pass it by and hang a hard left on my signal."

Shortly thereafter, the CO gave me the signal, which I passed on to JoJo, and he acted accordingly. We pulled into the jungle (well off the trail) and lay dog. If we had a tail, we would soon know it. However, no one was dogging us, so we moved back to the area where our stash was located and formed a secured perimeter around it. We waited again and observed in a full 361 degrees. (The purpose of the extra degree was to verify the other 360 degrees.)

Once the CO was sure we were alone, he went to the stash location. After he rendered the devices safe, he called me forward and showed me where everything was. Then he went to take care of a big blister on his foot.

SOG had done a great job of hiding the stash. (Thanks, guys!) Everything was neatly in place. Charlie could certainly have learned some lessons from our SOG on how to bury, hide, and booby-trap a cache properly. I had the sergeant of each platoon come to me with a carrying party, and I distributed the supplies as equally as possible.

The water was hot but sweet, and we now had all of the other necessities to help sustain us during our waltz through the NVA's private sanctuary. Once again, we were packing heavy with enough thump-gun ammo to take on the entire NVA at once. We also had plenty of ammo for our hungry pigs, including Thermid grenades, C-4 and caps, det cord, and the works. We buried our garbage and moved to a piece of high ground that better accommodated our company lager instead of having to use strongpoints.

"Top, I can't go on any more, so let's just FOB here and get a good night's rest. I think our troopers have earned that much. And Doc is already checking on our wounded. Let me know how we stand ASAP," the CO ordered.

I passed the word that we would be spending the night there, and my troopers responded with big sighs of relief.

We took care of business and had a rock-steady FOB position. If Charles had the extreme misfortune to come upon us, he would regret it until his dying day, which would likely be that same night.

Once again, we were under a canopy. We had chosen our FOB position with lots of natural barriers. Even a leech would have a tough time sneaking up on us there, which said a lot because there was a vast marsh nearby, where I think a leech convention was being held. Actually, I think every creature in the jungle came to our position that night. They were probably attracted to our fine LURP rations, which we were able to enjoy, along with our coffee, before the darkness engulfed us.

The skeeters in our FOB area were so big they had numbers painted on their tails. The ants were almost as large as Shetland ponies. There were literally thousands of species of hell-spawned Vietnamese creatures in that jungle area. At first they did not seem to bother me, probably because my body odor was so awful. Or, maybe I was just too tired to notice them on me. It was not long, though, before I discovered two big leeches on my leg, and when I tried to get them off, one of the big bastards pulled a switchblade on me. I still carry the scars to prove it. At that time, I also swear I saw a skeeter wearing a gas mask.

There was a seldom-used trail to the left of our positions, and it seemed to be the only way anyone could approach us without making one hell of a racket. The CO assured us that we could deal with this one downside to our security during our FOB stay. We located our company CP close to that trail. A small portion of our FOB was obvious during the daylight hours, but it was fortunately the farthest away from the trail.

As soon as it was really quiet and everyone had their night eyes and ears tuned for our environment, we began to have some reservations about that trail. Would you believe that an enemy patrol who was out looking for us passed us right by? It was a good thing that we had placed command-controlled flares on that trail instead of trip flares.

There was a sufficient amount of light for us to see the enemy patrol, and we counted eight men and one radio. We did not try to hit them because doing so would have given away our position to the entire NVA. Taking out eight Charlies was not worth such a consequence.

Within a short time, another patrol followed closely on the heels of the first one. They were just like soldiers all over the world – tired, hungry, and pissed off that they were out looking for us. They were diddy bopping along the trail and complaining. We heard them much sooner than we saw them.

Fortunately for us, they were a bad bunch of soldiers who were out there because someone said they had to be there. Man oh man, were they ever bitching. It was obvious to us because bitching is plainly bitching in any language. The second group stopped to smoke very close to our position, and some of them hauled it out to take a piss. We could hear everything they were saying, and Tran was right there with us in the Headquarters section to interpret every word.

We learned several important pieces of information from that group's bitch session. They said that there was a price on our heads, but they did not mention how much. We also learned that we had destroyed the unit's M-46 130mm Gun-Howitzer and its ammunition, and the unit knew that Black Knight Alfa was responsible because we had left our calling cards. The NVA soldier who mentioned our name made it sound more like "Blok

Knife Alfe". The bitchers also mentioned that the unit whom we had met head-on (on the trail earlier that day) had received several awards because of their Valley fighting performance against the 101st Airborne, the 9th Marines, and the 3rd ARVN. Apparently, the unit's commander had a swelled head from his success, that is, until we hit them on the trail. Of course, after we got through with them, his head was swollen, but not from internal boasting. We learned that every NVA unit who was sent to look for us had been told not to come back unless they found and destroyed us. And, every available unit was indeed looking for us.

The soldier in the group who had talked the most had lost a brother-in-law on the trail that day, and he swore to do us a job when he caught up to us. That defeated unit had been due to move south, but we had gone through them like a whole box of Ex-Lax and cut them up so badly that their move was postponed indefinitely.

Before the bitch session ended and the unit moved on, Tran heard them mention that they were the last unit scheduled to come that way for the night.

"Goddamn it, Top, we're really hurting them bad," whispered the CO.

Aside from Tran, Captain Brooks and Captain Norris also spoke Vietnamese fairly well. I am sorry to say that my knowledge of Namese was limited to words like "Ba-muey-Ba" and "Chow-co-dep".[83] (Smile.)

The CO spoke. "So far, our mission has been successful, and we've only been here in The Valley a couple of days. That's not too bad when you consider how bad we hurt the NVA, and we have no KIAs. Top, that's unbelievable. Oh, I didn't have time to tell you till now, but put the word out that Roberts is going to be okay. He won't be coming back to us, though. He's going back home to the States. Let's put him in for an award. Matter of fact, I don't want to leave anyone out who deserves some kind of recognition."

I agreed wholeheartedly and responded, "Sir, this whole company deserves some form of recognition. I wish I could tell the whol world about their bravery and the fact that they are the finest soldiers in the world."

Well, all of you magnificent troopers of the Grand Company, of Black Knight Alfa, here I am trying to keep my word. I am just sorry that it took me so long.

Throughout the night my greatest fear was that my troopers would fall asleep from pure exhaustion. I deliberately did not tell the company all of what Tran had said. In particular, I left out the part about the NVA patrol being the last one scheduled for the night because I did not want anyone to think it was okay to cop a few Zs.

We reeked and had to take a bath in bug juice because we could no longer stand our own smell. Unfortunately, I think those hungry jungle creatures became acclimatized to our stench. Either that, or they went home to retrieve their gas masks. That night they descended on us with a vengeance, and it was pure hell on all of us. I do not think that anyone fell asleep. (Maybe the hungry insects were a blessing in disguise.)

I could not help thinking that we had already achieved some measure of distinction if the NVA was actually offering a reward for our heads. I guess that M-46 had meant a lot to them, and they were pissed off to the max when we came along and fucked it up. Therefore, it was prudent for us to sleep with one eye open; otherwise, we might never wake up again.

Somewhere around 0100 hours, I felt vindicated for not telling my troops about the "last" NVA patrol of the night. One of our security posts reported that another NVA patrol of about eight or nine men was approaching our position along the nearby trail. That part of the trail seemed to be turning into Times Square.

I held a whispered conversation with our security post over my radio.

One of our security guys said, "Top, those bastards are heading straight for our perimeter. Of course, they don't know we're here. What should we do?"

"Wait," I told him and then shook the CO to let him know we were going to have guests.

"So far, they can see only eight or nine men. Is that right?" asked the CO.

I asked the security patrol to verify this information using their starlight scope.

They reported, "That's most affirm. We can make out nine and no more. It looks like another patrol."

"Okay, Top, let's do it this way," the CO began as he took the mike and issued instructions to our security post and the rest of the company. "Let them walk right on into our positions. Don't pop caps. We have to take them out without a sound. If we hit them, it will only bring the rest of them down on us. Top and I are on the way to your positions. Out."

Everyone was fully alert, and our defensive circle was ready for anything. The CO decided to leave our security posts out because he believed that the group approaching our positions was just another small patrol.

The patrol was a lot quieter than the previous one, and they were all on the trail where we could see them without the aid of a starlight scope. The CO and I had the feeling that the enemy soldiers planned to walk right into our positions. Maybe they planned to take a break, and our positions looked like a good place to do it.

As they approached us, the word was passed along to everyone. "Let them walk right on in. Then we will take them all down without making a sound. Remember, don't pop caps."

I could feel the unified heartbeat of our magnificent fighting team as we sensed our impending kill. As anticipated, the enemy patrol came directly toward where we were lying in wait. We could not determine which man was the leader; however, we could see one man carrying an RPD, another carrying a radio, and a third carrying what appeared to be a map case. The platoon sergeant and I concluded that the man with the case was the leader. He was behind the man with the RPD, who was the only person moving with any caution.

Come into our parlor, I thought.

They walked right into our FOB. It became obvious that they were moving off the trail to take a break where they would not be seen. Each man was looking around for a tree. One man leaned his AK against a tree and squatted to take a dump. Another man said something to the squatting man as he moved away from him. The cautious carrier of the RPD did not come directly in; instead, he stood aside and allowed the others to pass by him, as if he was counting noses. Perhaps he was the leader. The entire patrol did not come into our perimeter. From my flat position on the ground, I could tell they were too spread out, and some of the men had gotten between our security and us. Damn! Damn it to hell! They were going to be difficult. We held our breath and dared ourselves not to move a muscle or to make a sound.

The squatter finished his dump and reached for a handful of grass to wipe his butt. Instead, he grabbed a handful of one of our troopers. Our trooper latched onto the startled and speechless soldier and struck him with his entrenching tool.[84] The man grunted and sat down in his own shit, where he died.

Our troopers were forced to go out and get half of the patrol as silently as possible. The man with the RPD proved to be the hardest to kill. He managed to fire his weapon, but the muzzle on it was jammed into the soft earth, which muffled its single burst. Someone did a job on the gunner, and it was once again time for the dead to bury the dead.

Scratch one NVA patrol off the list, minus one man. He was an older soldier who possessed the ability to think for himself. He felt it was in his best interests to throw down his AK and to raise his hands in surrender. None of us wanted to kill him. Even in the heat of battle and the throes of completion, none of us could kill the little man who begged for his life.

Let's just call him Hahn. He sat down with his hands atop his head and looked around at what we had done to his comrades. His eyes pleaded for us to spare him.

We did not harm Hahn. Doc B. kept an eye on him as we cleaned up our mess. We got back into position in case there was another NVA patrol coming along the same trail, which was turning into an LA freeway.

After everything was back to normal, except for the stack of dead bodies that we had covered with branches and whatever else we could find, we took Hahn back to the CP, where Tran had a very serious conversation with him. We learned from him that the dude with the RPD had been the patrol leader. Hahn delivered bad news and good news. The high command of the NVA wanted us badly, and there was a reward on our heads. It was true that lots of patrols were looking for us, although most of them were concentrating their efforts on preventing us from reaching Khe Sanh. Fortunately for us, the high command was unsure of whether we were trying to go north to Khe Sanh or south to Phu Bai. Hanoi also had no idea why we were there. They thought that we might be a quartering party with a big push in progress. They also considered the fact that we might just be as crazy as hell. In any case, we had the NVA worried, and they removed a few commanders from their ranks (one because of our destruction of the M-46). The NVA was also halting troop movements in preparation for another invasion of The Valley (after Apache Snow had failed to clear it). General Giap's headquarters thought that if the Americans were coming back again, it would be a major push. They figured that after the Ap Bia affair, the Americans wanted to try to save some face.

The bottom line was that Hanoi was worried, and the NVA was doing things they had not planned to do. The commanding general issued the order himself to stop us at all costs or their unit commanders' heads would roll down the entire 30-mile-long funnel of the A Shau Valley.

Our little walk through the Valley of Death was already a success.

Day Three

When it was light enough to safely move around, we decided to get as far away from that stack of NVA bodies as possible. It would not be long before they were missed. Before we left we made sure that the NVA would be able to find their dead soldiers. Charlie would surely be moved to the point of violence when he found the mess we had left for him to clean up at our most recent FOB.

We moved out of our FOB when I received an "up" from all platoons. Like a company of ghosts, we moved deeper into the jungles and away from the trails. After moving for a little more than three hours, we found a position that we were sure we could defend and hold until help arrived from Da Nang. We moved onto that position and set it up as quickly as possible because we had to get our wounded evacuated. It was not that their wounds were critical, but under our existing conditions, we feared that our men's wounds would get infected. The CO said that they must be evacuated, along with our prisoner, whom we wanted to give to school-trained personnel for further interrogation.

Our newly chosen position was the best high-terrain feature in the area. There was no canopy, and the trees were small enough to enable us to hack out an LZ very swiftly. From that position we were able to see down the hill in all directions. Charles would not be able to sneak up on us, but he could put a lot of mortar fire on us (if he had his mortars with him).

Because of our elevated position, we were able to link up with Battalion on the first try. The CO gave them an updated sit-rep, and he requested medevac, water, and some small items. When he told them about Hahn, our NVA prisoner, they replied that they would be right out. The S-2 was so excited about the news that he was coming to personally pick up Hahn and also to bring us more water.

We were set up around the hastily cut LZ with our mortars in their standard firing position. Our troops heated what water they still had to make coffee.

When Pete gave me the word that our birds were inbound, we did not pop smoke. We brought our birds in using our radios. Blue Max came with them and buzzed around looking for Charlie. Our wounded were lifted out, and the dust-off birds flew away swiftly. The S-2 brought some disposable blister bags of water, but there was not enough to fill all of our canteens. He also brought some other essentials that were not in our stash. All the while, Charlie did not make a nuisance of himself.

The S-2 announced that the NVA was rattled by all of our hellraising. They knew we were Cav and Black Knight Alfa. Apparently, General Giap had put the word out to his men to lay low because we were either fools or we were carrying one hell of a big stick. Then, the S-2 discussed some particulars with our battalion commander. Finally, he bid us farewell and took old Hahn, who smiled until he was forced to get on the helicopter, where he started praying.

Our battalion commander asked if we felt up to the task of spending another day walking on the wild side. He said that our high-ranking general officers were keenly watching our little stroll through the Valley of Death and were already overjoyed with our accomplishments. He assured us there were very good reasons to warrant our staying another day, although he was not at liberty to mention what they were. He said the S-2 would give us a complete packet of instructions and a new pickup point, along with his promise that we would have some real stand-down time when we came out of The Valley.

Before the S-2 was out of sight, we were moving and simultaneously cutting up the plastic blister bags that contained our new water supply. We did not bother to stop to bury anything because we wanted to get the hell away from that hill. Blue Max remained on station until we diddy maued the hilltop. They pushed down to inform us that they were leaving and to wish us a good hunt.

About an hour later, Doc B. discovered that the water the S-2 had brought us was too overly chlorinated to drink. When he tried to drink it, it burned his mouth like flaming pepper chili. He asked me to pass the word to our troopers to dump their water.

We pulled up and stopped because of our sudden water crisis. The CO, Redleg, Lt Zen, and I huddled around our maps. There was a stream, creek, or river somewhere near our line of travel, and no matter how small it might be, we had to investigate it. We could not bear the risk of calling in a water bird. We were also under a canopy again, which compounded the difficulty of our situation. The only helpful factor was that the terrain leading to the water source was ridge-lined, which made our journey relatively fast and easy.

We did not carry our ponchos even though it was the rainy season. They were just another load that we did not need to hump. When it rained, we just got wet, which was not often a problem because the sun usually came out and dried us off. Naturally, if we had carried our ponchos, we could have used them to catch some rainwater. However, that would not have solved our water supply problem because the rain that fell through the canopy was more often than not accompanied by a host of unwanted jiggly things. The simple sight of some of them was enough to gag a maggot.

I have mentioned the rain because while we were making a run for the water source, it began to rain so hard that we had to pull up and wait it out. The rain dislodged all kinds of hellish creatures, both living and dead, from the canopy. One could safely say that it was raining monkeys, lizards, snakes, leaves, branches, and things that defied description. It was not raining cats and dogs, though, because they were not indigenous to that region.

When the rain let up, we pushed on. The humidity was so high that you could almost swim in it or surf on it. Pure misery prevailed when the sun came out. The very hounds of hell were riding on our backs.

We passed through an area where a major fight must have taken place (perhaps during Apache Snow or another similar operation). There were a lot of deep ruts and shell craters that were full of fresh rainwater. We got down on our stomachs and drank that water, ignoring any little jiggly things in our desperate attempts to quench our thirst.

When we moved on, some of our troops began to drop in their tracks from sheer exhaustion, but a buddy's welcome hand was never far away to help them up and along. By the grace of God Almighty, we refused to lie down and roll over.

The CO and I knew we could not keep up our pace for much longer. We had to stop and rest to regain our strength, to fight the wolves that were surely on our tails by then. Each minute that we continued on was an assault to our minds, and we tried hard to hold onto what little sanity we had left in order to keep our minds and bodies together.

"I fear no evil; for Thou art with me. Thy rod and Thy staff, they comfort me". (Psalm 23)

We pushed on because we felt that Charlie was near. Later that afternoon we came out of the deep jungle to a place where there was no canopy. Sweet Jesus, it was so good to look up and see the sky.

We could breathe the sweet, cooler air as we traveled across a reasonably flat area with lots of trees and grass that was not too high. The ground sloped upward to our right, but we easily moved along it. Thankfully, the feeling of Charlie's presence was subsiding.

I gave the signal to spread out more because of the relative flatness of the terrain. As I turned around, the men nearest to me and I heard the distinct "ping" that was made by a safety lever leaving an M26 hand grenade. Everyone suddenly realized that one of our grenades had just been armed.

Someone shouted, "Grenade!"

We hurriedly unassed our loads and hit the dirt.

WHAM!

One pile of gear exploded. Miraculously, none of us were injured. The gear must have been lying on top of the armed grenade, which had somehow protected us from the deadly little fragments of the explosion.

That event was a familiar old story. The trooper who was responsible for the explosion had been carrying an M26 fragmentation hand grenade affixed to his webbing. As he passed one of those wait-a-minute vines, the vine had gotten tangled in the safety ring of the grenade and had pulled its pin.

Before putting our gear back on, everyone paid particular attention to the ends of the safety pins on their grenades, making sure that they were properly bent backward with the rings tucked away. Then we continued moving toward the water source.

We found the stream to be wide, yet we were easily able to wade to the other side. We decided to cross the stream because there was a far better route of high ground on the other side for us to travel. The CO had us pull up into a very tight lager as we studied the stream and the surrounding area. We sent some security teams out, and they returned with an all-clear report. This method caused us some delay, but it was necessary for our safety.

We lay there waiting and watching, and all the while we tuned our survival senses to the task at hand. We did not sense Charlie's presence, and when we were satisfied that our way was clear, we sent one rifle squad reinforced with a machine gun, two thump guns, and two LAWs across the stream. The rest of the platoon stayed behind to watch the squad's back.

We used that same procedure with each platoon, but we would cross at different places. As each platoon crossed the stream, their first squads would serve as security and set up a base of fire in case the rest of their platoon were hit while crossing the stream. The main body of the company held a lager position on the near side and did nothing until they received an "all clear" from the far side.

The First Platoon was the center platoon, and they sent one mortar across with their first squad. The Second Platoon went upstream, and the Third Platoon went downstream. The Headquarters and Weapons Platoons followed the First Platoon across in the center.

We sent a mortar squad across with the lead rifle squad from the First Platoon, so that it could assist the base of fire squad if they hit some shit on the far side. Also, once in position on the far side, that mortar could cover the remainder of the platoons coming across. We set up our other mortars, who were with the main part of the company, to protect the main body and the lead squads as they crossed the stream. They were the last to break down and cross.

We always used that basic procedure, with variations as dictated by the situation, and it always worked well for us. It was not by the book, but when the book was written, the authors were not aware of "the Vietnam experience". We were.

While crossing the stream, the tactical situation dictated that we choose positions that would prevent our being in sight of each platoon. Therefore, we only had radio contact between us. Each lead squad carried a radio. (This was always true whenever we sent out a scouting party or a security element.)

Here, I must interject with a note about crossing bodies of water. We always chose the more difficult, or the least likely, place to cross. Charlie was known to booby-trap easy crossing locations. Most of the time, he placed trip wires well below the water level in locations where you were bound to hit one of them as you waded across. It was certainly a dirty trick, which is why we played even dirtier tricks on Charlie whenever we had the opportunity.

After each platoon received an "all clear", we were coordinated so the main body would cross at the same time. When the CO gave the word, we moved cautiously to the gently flowing stream.

The water was clear and cool. To us, it was the legendary Fountain of Youth. The cool, gentle touch of the slowly moving water engulfed our tired and worn bodies. The water felt so invigorating to our bodies and our minds that it lifted our spirits. We could not resist taking turns to completely submerge our bodies in the stream. Of course, we held our weapons above the waterline and maintained security for each other.

When I neared the middle of the stream, the water level was almost up to my chin. (I am 6' 2".) I held my M16 high above my head with my right hand and used my left hand to fill my canteens. At the same time, I stooped slightly, enough to bring my mouth down to the water level, and I sucked up my fill of that sweet, cool, crystal water. I took on water like an old steam engine.

Meanwhile, Pete was receiving a call and moving toward me as he put his speaker on. After saying into the mike, "This is Five Alfa, go," he offered me the handset.

"Alfa Five, this is Alfa Two. Are you drinking water? Come back."

I responded, "Alfa Two, Alfa Five. That's most affirm. Over."

"Alfa Five, be advised there are about eight to ten ripe and popping NVA bodies in the same water that you are drinking. Do you copy? Out."

Everyone in the company was monitoring the net and clearly heard what the Second Platoon sergeant had said. When I returned the mike to Pete, he was already turning a little green. I moved away from him because I thought he was fixing to call Luke all over me.

The Third Platoon got into the act, and we recognized Mac's jovial voice as he spoke into the mike, "Alfa Two, this is Alfa Three. Are there any girls among them? Come back."

"All Alfa stations. Get off the push! Out," the CO commanded.

I was not feeling well either, as I recalled several memories of overripe and popping dead bodies, memories of la Drang Valley, the second Bong Son, Thien Province, A Shau Valley, Que Son Valley, and Hue. Truthfully, I was giving some thought to calling old Luke, too.

Then I reasoned and came to the logical conclusion that there was no reason for me to get sick. Hell, I was already about to pop from drinking so much of that cool stream water. To throw it up or to worry about it was pointless. All I could do was grin and bear it.

As soon as I reached the other side, I passed the word for everyone to add water purification tablets to their water. Doc B. agreed that this was the only precaution we could take. He said that as long as the water was flowing and Two-Six did not disturb the bodies in their location, there was a good chance that the water was safe to drink. He also assured us not to worry because we were already receiving antibiotic tablets along with our daily dosages of quinine tablets.

The sergeant of the Second Platoon did not disturb the bodies, and he reported that it was a clear case of Blue Max catching Charles crossing the stream and doing a job on him. They had found shell casings and other positive evidence to prove that fact.

We made it across the stream without further incident. Then we pushed on. It began to rain again, which brought us some relief from the mind-bending heat.

Later that evening, while we were searching for a good FOB position, we discovered a most excellent and well-used trail covered by a canopy. The trail was not on our map, because the NVA had recently constructed it as their version of the Dan Ryan Expressway. It ran from the Ho Chi Minh Trail straight into South Vietnam. I know Uncle Ho would have been proud of the trail builders, as well as those who were using the trail.

The CO interrupted my thoughts when he said, "Top, let's get as far away from this damn trail as we can before dark."

Then, he looked silently at our new discovery.

I saw the gleam in his cold, hard eyes, and I said to myself, "Aw shit!"

I knew what he was thinking. That trail gave us a golden chance to really kick off on old Charlie's collective butt and to do it on our chosen terms, ground, and location.

The CO said, "On second thoughts, First Sergeant, let's just get up on that high ground over there and plan a kill zone just a little farther down that way, where some sunshine is falling on the trail, 'cause tonight there will be some moonlight in the same place. So if our dear friends, the NVA, come diddy bopping down this trail going north or south, we got their butts. What do you think about that, huh?"

"Right on, sir," I replied.

"Redleg, are we still out of Birth Control's fan?" asked the CO.

"Sir, Battalion has arranged with Division to get us some help from our most distant firebase, packing 175 and 8 inches. Where we are now, I can only get the 175s, but I gotta tell you, we would be stretching their maximum range to the max. Remember I told you a ways back we were back within the fan? Are you sure you want to do this?"

"Yeah, we are going to do it, and now I remember you telling me we had Birth Control. Sorry that it slipped my mind. Soon as we find a good location, I want you to lock us in tight enough that we can hold on till Da Nang can send us something, okay?"

The CO smiled and turned his attention to me.

"Top, I want you to move the company to that high ground over there," he said, pointing to where he wanted to put the company. "Let's 'box' tonight with our heavy side to this trail and machine gun-heavy. Tell Tuzo and Zen I want to hit that trail in any way possible. You move the company. Redleg and I need to check out that bend. Then, I'll be right there."

Using our proven survival methods of operation, I put the company on the high ground as instructed, while the CO and Redleg studied their maps and determined how to get Birth Control all the way out to us effectively.

I put the company in position and assigned sectors of fire. The troops did the rest, and within minutes, we were rock-steady and ready. They were digging in and prepared to stay for the duration. I did not have to tell them that it might indeed be our Final Battle. Hell no! They already knew that. If that were to happen, we would all go to hell together.

While the company was setting up, the CO and Redleg came and asked me where I put the CP. I directed them to it, and they pored over their maps, trying to come up with a good, solid plan before darkness arrived.

When he was ready, the CO told me to get our leaders to the CP. Once they were all present, we got right down to the nitty-gritty. It was time for some serious planning.

Because the CO was sure the NVA would use the trail that night, he was also sure of their direction of travel. He wanted to ensure that when we hit them, we would make a positive kill and take out all NVA soldiers who were caught in our kill zone. I set up our positions in support of our mission, making sure that we, the ambushers, did not become the ambushees.

To achieve a positive kill at night was a major undertaking, and we had to follow our customary habit of designing our ambush in accordance with the terrain, the tactical situation, and our strength.

We decided to set up our positions similar to those we had used during our recent night-time river kill. We would hit Charlie with a reinforced rifle platoon and lots of machine guns and thump guns. That platoon would be as close to the trail as the situation would permit. The remainder of the company would be organized on the high ground immediately to the ambush platoon's rear, which was where I had already set the company in. Of course, that portion of the company would be home, and they would provide the ambush platoon with positive backup and right and left security. They would also cover our rear. Artillery was planned to cover and protect our entire company, and if it came down to it, the CO, Redleg, or I would call that fire right down on our own heads.

I asked to go with the ambush platoon, and Sfc. Gonzalez asked if that platoon could be One-Six so that I could be there. The CO granted us permission. That is when the new lieutenant asked if he could go with the ambush platoon. Sergeant Tuzo could handle the mortars without him, so the CO said okay, but he stressed that the lieutenant was only there as an observer – to look, listen, and learn.

As we got our shit together, Captain Norris pushed up to Birth Control and arranged for a "steel ambush" to hit the junction of the trail farther south. As I said earlier, the trail ran from the north to the south, and we were in an excellent position on the east side of the trail, facing west. Our two captains discovered the trail junction when they went to reconnoiter the north and south sides of the trail. We did not know from which direction the enemy would approach or even if he would be using the trail. Everything was based on our CO's gut feelings, and he believed the enemy would be traveling south.

Captain Norris served as our forward artillery observer par excellence, and he planned our artillery support, placing concentrations on both sides of the trail to maintain a steel box around us in case Charlie became rambunctious. We also employed all of our normal defensive tactics.

When we were ready, the First Platoon reinforced. Lt Zen and I moved very silently down the trail. Darkness cloaked our movements, but it did not restrict our preparations. By that time, we were very much like all of the other jungle creatures, because the great outdoors had long since become our natural habitat. Most of us had not seen a bed in six to eight months, and we had not been inside a real house, used a flushing toilet, or lived like a normal human being in many other ways. We were supreme jungle predators who could hunt and bring down our prey in darkness or in daylight. We had long ago learned how to use the cloak of darkness as our friend, and we could see well enough to do anything that was necessary for our survival.

Our company addressed every possible contingency, including the little things that could cost a life if overlooked. We used command-controlled flares and positioned them on the opposite side of the trail. When we popped them, the enemy would be lit up like puppets on a stage between the flares and us. We certainly did not want to miss Charlie's last act. We positioned our "mighty swords of destruction" (i.e., our claymores) on our side of the trail and aimed them so their deadly fans of fire overlapped to cover our kill zone. We also appropriately placed some backup claymores in case Charlie did not fall on the trail.

We positioned some of our flares to blind him while causing him to stand out in great detail so that we could easily pop him. We knew from experience that positioning our flares in that manner caused our enemies to naturally react to them by moving into our direct line of deadly fire.

We positioned a pair of two-man security teams slightly down the trail on both sides of our ambush position. Each team had a radio, and they planned to give us early warning of any sighted enemies. However, they would not take the enemy under fire. Instead, they would contact me and on my command, they would move to our position. I decided on that plan because we had no idea what size unit we were planning to hit.

We settled in to wait after I received an "up" from all of our squad leaders.

I chose the best position from which I could see most of our kill zone, especially that portion that would tell me when to start the action. I was the "trigger man", and no one would fire until I popped the first cap.

In a short while, we noticed that moonlight was beginning to shine down on some areas of the trail. I hoped that if the enemy came, he would be moving south as the CO suspected. On the strength of his gut feelings, I put the only starlight scope we still had working with the security team to the north of the trail.

The witching hour came and went, and the increased amount of moonlight gave us an excellent view of our kill zone. It was a perfect night, time, and position to go bushwhacking.

Everything seemed to be too perfect, which made me suspicious. However, I was very tired, and the load on my heart was heavy from having the lives of our wonderful American soldiers in my hands. Such times really tried my soul and turned my hair gray. I am sorry to say that I was almost nodding, almost asleep, when Pete shook my arm.

"Top, Charlie is on his way, just like the CO said, and they are traveling south. Now how about that?"

Suddenly I was wide awake and pleased to see Sfc. Gonzalez telling our guys to get on it. I told Pete to bring our security teams home and to inform the CO that we were getting ready to have company. My squad leaders would let me know as soon as both teams were safely within our position.

We were on radio silence the whole time, and we communicated with each other by keying the mike using our special code of clicks.

Both of our teams safely returned to us and took up their firing positions.

I could feel Charlie's presence, as well as something else that was not quite right.

Gonzalez whispered to me, "Top, we are ready. The security team said ..." He stopped whispering because we could see the lead NVA soldier approaching.

The lieutenant squeezed in between us and whispered a little too loudly, "Are they really coming, and can I stay here with you all?"

I responded that he could and instructed him to follow Pete if we had to diddy mau.

I could not shake the gut feeling that something was radically wrong. I wondered if I had goofed and let something important slip through the cracks. Because I was so tired, I had tried to be overly cautious. I knew there was a possibility that we might not be able to push up to Birth Control when we needed them. Because I was also an old cannoneer and chief of smoke, I had spent more long hours

216

shooting than I can remember. With our supporting fires at their maximum distance and range, there was a good chance of variations that could adversely affect us. However, I knew that Battery C (the 2nd Battalion of the 32nd) was the best. If anyone could handle the situation, it was they. They could strike an apple on a person's head and do it accurately every time.

Well, the time for worrying was past. It was time for action, not self-recrimination.

The lead NVA soldier strutted boldly into view, looking straight ahead and acting as if he were participating in a formal May Day dress parade. Another NVA soldier in full combat gear accompanied him, along with a Viet Cong, who was probably their guide. They were not snooping and pooping or showing any signs of caution. Still, something was definitely wrong!

The darkness made it impossible for me to see the expression on the lead man's face. Nevertheless, I could feel his expression. The little bastard was radiating CONFIDENCE.

That was what bothered me. My Mississippi Delta survival senses screamed out to me, "Don't shoot! Don't shoot!"

My body was shaking, and cold chills were running rampant through my mind and body, even though it was hot lying there in the Vietnamese jungle. Many questions raced through my mind. My dear God, what's wrong with me? Am I just suffering from battle fatigue? Am I just being gun shy? Have I been shot? Am I going around the bend? Lord, have mercy on me. I had already seen too much death and destruction. Was that why I was about to flip out? The CO and my company were counting on me to stay with them. My thoughts began to collide.

Closely behind the three lead soldiers came a large unit, walking with two files on each side of the trail. What I guessed to be their officers were walking right down the middle of the trail.

Charlie's odor was overpowering, and my skin felt like I was being devoured by an army of red ants. "Don't shoot!" my senses continued to yell.

I smelled cosmoline and heard the enemies' equipment rattling. They were packing heavy, and there were far too many of them to count. They did not seem worried about a possible ambush because they were walking fairly close together. If we hit them, it would be like shooting ourselves in the feet, only worse.

217

Their body language told me not to shoot. They were a very large, well-equipped combat unit. Old Charles appeared to have the upper hand, and he was confident that he had enough shit to come out on top if any crazy Americans had the gall to shoot at him.

The first three enemy soldiers were already past the left extent of our kill zone and into our final take-out area. Our kill zone was filled with NVA soldiers, and it was the proper moment to shoot! I knew that all of the wires set to pop our flares were pulled tautly, just awaiting my signal. All I had to do was pull the trigger of my M16. Everyone on my ambush sight had their fingers on their triggers.

I stuck with my gut feeling and made the firm decision not to shoot. My mind reeled with the extreme pressure of that single decision. I did not know whether I was right or wrong to make such a call. Would my decision not to shoot cause the men of my Grand Company to look at me with disgust as if I was a coward? If they did, I would no longer be the first sergeant of the finest Cav infantry company in the universe.

I was nauseated, and my head and chest ached. I mentally commanded my troopers on the ambush site, "Don't shoot. Don't pop your claymores or flares!"

It was certainly possible that they might think something had happened at my location and shoot anyway, even though none of us was being threatened. Thank the dear Lord that the grand men of Black Knight Alfa heard my silent screams. They held their fire, and not one round, flare, or claymore was popped.

Keep in mind that all of this happened within a matter of minutes. However, that chain of events was extremely important.

The lieutenant grabbed and shook my arm and said much too loudly, "Top, what's wrong? You are letting them get away. Do you want me to shoot?"

Pete grabbed the lieutenant by his web gear and pulled him off my arm. "Sir, lieutenant, keep your voice down. Top knows what he's doing. He's brought the company this far … Now, lieutenant, you just be real cool." Pete spoke slowly to avoid a misunderstanding.

Somehow, some way, I knew in my very soul that if we had popped caps on old Charlie, it would have been our Final Battle.

Pete held the mike to my ear because the CO was clicking to find out what was happening. I ignored him until his voice replaced his clicking signals.

"Top, do you see what I'm seeing?" Pete asked with a huge, proud smile on his dirty face.

"Yeah, I see them, too. Push up to the CO and let him know what we got going on down here, and tell Redleg to definitely avoid shooting the steel ambush. I think old SOG got our situation well in hand."

As I said those words to Pete, I was certain that the SOG team had something to do with my recent premonitions of disaster.

I watched the SOG team intently, and my mind raced with the possibilities of what could go wrong. While Pete whispered into his mike, my blood ran cold. One of the guys on the SOG had suddenly frozen in his position and was looking directly where we were dug in. Oh God, I had a sudden sinking feeling that he had spotted one of us. I did not think he would pop caps on us, but it was still a volatile situation. I was not sure how he or my troopers might react, although I came to an instant conclusion of what I would do if I had to.

The young man stood motionless, looking in our direction. Then, after a long, drawn-out moment, he moved forward again.

I believe the young man knew we were there and also that we were those Americans the NVA was so intently seeking. I could not see his face, but I knew he smiled before continuing on his mission. Later, when I talked with the men who were on the ambush site with me, they all agreed that he probably knew we were there.

That was my first experience observing an SOG team at work. To this day, however, I am not quite sure whether they were all SOG or if some of them were CIA, CCN from I Corps, or part of the Phoenix program. No matter where they were from, I thought they were the greatest bunch of men. They were pure poetry in motion, just gliding along, blending into the shadows and disappearing when it was necessary. They were absolutely beautiful as they operated under the wary eyes of the enemy's rearguard. I was very proud of them and wished that a certain anti-Vietnam-War-famous lady could have seen them in action.

Although I did not get to observe the SOG team for very long, I think I picked out their leader, based on my runs as a LURP team leader. He was tall and slender with blondish hair, and he wore a dark bandanna tied on his head like a skull cap. He carried a Stoner 63A 1 for silent running, with a fringed peace band on his shoulder strap. If I had not known any better, I would have thought he was a California surfer the way he just floated along like he was fixing to catch a big wave and hug its tunnel all the way to the break.

The SOG team was traveling lightly. The man behind the "leader" carried one of those new, special, long-range radios, which told me that the NVA regiment was not going to get away and that Pentagon East knew exactly where they were located and would take them out if and when they wanted.

My friend, if you by some strange quirk of fate may someday read this account of your movements that night, you will surely know it was you whom I saw. You reminded me of some photos I had seen of General Custer. You and your team gave us Cav Skytroopers a strong jolt of pride that has lasted forever. Hang in there, man!

Our company stayed in place for the rest of the night, in case we got a second chance to pop Charlie. When morning came, I went to the CP and tried to explain to the CO why I had not fired.

"First Sergeant, what I told you already still stands. You were right. Our ambush was not coordinated with Battalion, so I did not know Charles had an SOG team on him. Top, you saved the night. I went up with Redleg and saw what we almost hit. Had I been in your place, I would have made the same decision. There is one thing I would like to know. How did you know before they got there?"

I had no answer, but I said, "Sir, I'll die for you."

Day Four

Just before first light, the CO pushed up to Battalion through our relay station and made a full report, paying particular attention to the early morning ambush hit that we had almost made. He reported the time we first saw the lead men, how long it had taken them to pass our positions, the direction they were going, and the fact that SOG was dead on their asses. Lastly, he stated our shackled/coded positions.

Battalion instructed us to wait and promised to respond on the final outcome of the NVA regiment that we had to let waltz past us. After some time, the battalion commander came up on the push and ordered us to come home. He said our mission in the Valley of Death had been "very well done".

Next, the S-3 came on the push, but we began to have trouble with our communications. He was not coming in loud and clear, or as we called it "five by five". All of us knew that old Charlie was jamming our transmissions, so we had to shut down or lead him straight to our positions. The last information we received from the S-3 was shackled, so we had three people on the receiving end take down the same message to reduce the chance of misunderstanding it.

The shackled message contained a thrust line from our known location to another distant location, where we would find a mountain containing an LZ that we could use for extraction. Because that LZ had already been mentioned to us as a possible lift-out location, we had a good idea of where to find it. The damned thing was directly on top of a mountain that was way up in the clouds. It had been cut out by the men of the 101st Airborne Division and was first used during Operation Massachusetts and last used after Apache Snow. Elements of the 101st, the 9th Marines, and the 3rd ARVNs had already used the LZ.

Division thought it was the best possible location for our extraction because it was surrounded by reasonably flat terrain, defensive positions had already been cut, and it was large enough to accommodate more than one slick simultaneously. Division was planning to position one of our favorite artillery units there to support us with some heavy shit.

When it was light enough, we deactivated and safely removed all of our snaps and traps in a hurry. We had no time for coffee or to fill in our positions like we did when time permitted. We had to diddy mau that area as soon as possible, if not sooner. It was common knowledge that old Charlie would soon be on to us with a vengeance.

We leaders passed down to every trooper in the company all of the latest information and complete instructions regarding how to get to our pickup point. That way, if we were caught in a fight with the NVA and all of our leaders went down, the last men (or man) would know where to go and how to get out. Unfortunately, we had to get to that LZ in time to meet the birds that were scheduled to be there for us, and that time factor was being rubbed the wrong way by the weather, which was turning nasty. The only good thing about the weather was that it was a bit cooler.

We set our compasses on the same azimuth, as dictated by the thrust line, to intersect the high mountain where the LZ awaited us. Of course, we knew it was best to avoid the trails when we could. We did not underestimate the NVA. They were out there beating the bush for us, and The Valley was their territory, not to mention that they outnumbered us by about 75:1. Common sense dictated that it would not be very long before they would run into or corner us.

We moved out in our running-and-fighting formation. The Third Platoon took the lead, followed by Headquarters, the First Platoon, and Weapons. The Second Platoon was running drag. We had two point men well forward, a connecting file of two men with a radio, followed by a machine gun-heavy and thump gun-heavy squad. Avoiding the trails, we headed for all available high ground and ridge lines. That was our best means of travel, and we tried to stay just below the crest but not so far down that we had a blind side.

The high grounds were about the only place where we could maintain radio contact with our relay station. At one point shortly after we gained some altitude, Battalion pushed up to us, and we stopped, lagered, and waited while the CO talked with them. It was a very good location, so the CO decided that we should have breakfast there.

Battalion informed us that General Giap's office in North Vietnam had issued a direct order for the NVA to pull out all the stops to get us. Our lone Cav infantry company had raised more hell than all of the major operations in the A Shau Valley had accomplished, considering the time factor. We had chewed royally on Charlie's ass.

Heads were rolling down the valleys of the chain of command for those in charge throughout the A Shau Valley. The last word from Hanoi was that more heads were going to roll if we were not caught soon. They wanted us dead, period. An NVA colonel was reamed to the point that he would not be able to sit down for a month, and when he spoke, he squeaked like a mouse.

The battalion commander's parting words were, "Black Knight Alfa has added new dimensions to the GI's proverb, which says in part: 'Cause I'm the meanest son of a bitch in the whole damn Valley.' Truly, Commander, you and your magnificent unit are the personification of that GI's proverb in its entirety."

The fact that Battalion was pulling us out was a clear statement that we had accomplished our mission. We had killed a lot of the NVA, including some Red Star-wearing, fancy pants, officer hero. We had flipped the great, big black-and-gold bird at General Giap and his damned army. Our accomplishments aside, Battalion knew that we were living on borrowed time with Charlie, which was no longer in our favor.

It did not take a college professor to figure out that old Charles was jawed up to the max, and he desperately wanted our heads, which was a big incentive for us to hurry to our pickup point. We were also very careful to clean up our breakfast area, leaving no trace that we had stopped there.

We were not yet running because we had calculated our time and were using it efficiently. Caution was the name of the game, and speed represented the high stakes. Our lives were the hold card, and the deuces were certainly wild.

Again, in our running-and-fighting combat formation, we moved out but headed in a completely different direction from the way we intended to go. At no time would we let our guard down.

After about an hour of traveling, we pulled one of our unique tactical maneuvers of which no other unit could lay claim. To explain it, I will use an example. Let's say we were moving south. Then, on a signal from the CO, the lead platoon stops and forms the first portion of a circle facing our direction of travel. The second rifle platoon forms the left portion with the left end of their left squad visible to the drag platoon so the drag platoon can complete the third and last part of our lager. The Weapons Platoon and Headquarters were (as always) located some place within our lager.

We could perform that maneuver even in darkness, and after having done it many times, it had become second nature to us. Using our special maneuver, we formed into a good defensive circle, ready to fight and defend in any direction. In that particular case, our intentions were to kill anyone who might be following us. After waiting a measured amount of time, we formed again into our running formation and headed toward the mountain to our pickup point.

There was a long furrow along the jungle floor that appeared on our maps and was similar to a trail. Like our thrust line, the furrow pointed in the direction of our mountain destination. We used that particular terrain feature to guide on, and we made good time after finding it.

We pushed steady but not hard, taking occasional breaks to conserve our strength. We were still packing heavy, and our water supply was again decreasing significantly. Our troops were feeling good, especially knowing that we would soon be getting out of that hellhole known as the A Shau Valley.

When we were far beyond our recent FOB position, we found a decent place to lager, have chow, rest, and catch five. We stopped only briefly, because we were anxious to continue our long journey to the top of the mountain.

Later, while trying to skirt an open area to our left, I noticed a treeline on some high ground to our right. Frankly, when I looked at those trees and the shape of the treeline, in addition to our direction of travel, I said to myself, "Now I would use that high ground and treeline to ambush us if I were Charlie."

No sooner did I finish my thought, when my Charlie alarm went off. I could not smell him, but I damned sure could feel his presence. My old Mississippi Delta survival senses were screaming out a warning that Charlie was waiting in ambush to take our lives, just as soon as we entered his kill zone.

YES! The bastards had to be in the treeline because it was the perfect ambush location. I once again heard the words of my infantry tactics instructor at Fort Benning, Georgia, who had often said, "You have to think like your enemy, put his boots on, and do some backward planning from his point of view."

Pete eased up close to me and said, "Top, I think we are fixing to hit some shit. Do you feel it, too?"

"Yeah, I feel it, and I know where they are. Keep near me and get Six on the horn, NOW!" I replied without looking his way. I knew we were being watched.

There was a hot breeze from the direction of the treeline, and it brought the definite stink of the NVA to Pete and me. We both knew that we were looking right into the eyes of old Death. The feeling was tangible, and I knew that all of Black Knight Alfa were aware that we were in great danger. Charlie was preparing to drop a dime on us.

We were well spread out and staggered, with the Third Platoon leading, Nat on point, and our regular connecting file. I think that our well-organized running-and-fighting formation was causing our enemy to wait. Charlie was probably trying to decide what portion of us to take out first, because he knew damned well that he was not going to catch us all in his kill zone.

The CO was in front with Mac so that he could guide Nat along the correct azimuth. The Second Platoon was next in line, followed by the Weapons Platoon. The First Platoon ran drag. I was all the way to the rear with Gonzalez.

I told Gonzalez what was going down and instructed him to pass the word to the others not to make any Mickey Mouse moves that would let Charlie know we were aware of his presence. Meanwhile, Pete gave me his mike.

I had to break radio silence; there was no other way that I could quickly pass the word to everyone. We were about to walk into an enemy ambush.

"Alfa Six, Alfa Five. Come back."

"Five, this is Six. Go."

"Six, be advised we are walking into an ambush near the treeline to our right."

I was on the company push, so everyone heard my warning. The CO did not have to tell the company to act naturally. That was not the first time that Charlie had caught us cold and probably would not be the last time. Each of our troopers knew what to do, and they waited for the CO to tell them when to act.

"Five, this is Six. Give us your umbrella. Out."

Thankfully, the CO did not waste time asking me how I knew that. He simply went into action.

All of us in Black Knight Alfa were locked and cocked and aware of our life-threatening situation, but we did not panic.

The CO and the Third Platoon moved in unison. Their machine guns stuttered, their thump guns thumped, and before the 40mm high-explosive grenades reached the treeline, the 7.62mm slugs from our pigs tore into the treeline and Charlie.

Charlie was forced to shoot; he had no other recourse.

Upon the first "thump", Black Knight Alfa scattered to the four winds, and Charlie watched as we melted away into the environment. We received "a little help from our friends" (i.e., our enemies), because Charlie opened up with his machine guns, which told us exactly where his shit was positioned. Our thump gunners thumped Charlie's heavy firepower. We put such a strong amount of accurate firepower on his automatic weapons that we rendered them ineffective, allowing the CO and Three-Six to maneuver under our umbrella. I saw one LAW hit an enemy machine-gun position, and one Charlie was thrown out into the open, screaming because one of his arms had been blown off.

Everything happened at once, and some of the actions were nothing but blurred motions. Our mortars fell back to a more protected position and had two HE rounds in the air as quickly as possible. The second round hit its target, and the third round shot out was Willie Pete. They lit Charlie's ass up, big time.

I screamed in anger and frustration, with a lot of pain in my heart, because I had allowed my company to walk into an enemy ambush. I should have sensed Charlie well before we had come close to the ambush site.

In my heart's eye, I could see the Third Platoon lying on the ground dead. I could see Nat lying out in the open, with his body all shot to hell. He was bleeding and dying, or perhaps he was already dead. The mere thought of such a disaster made me sick to my stomach. I was soon awakened from my daymare by the sound of the CO's voice coming through Pete's PRC-25 speaker: "Pull back, pull back!"

The CO yelled, "Alfa Two, look out for their hit squads."

Maybe old Charlie did not know it, but we were on to his Russian-, Chinese-, and Cuban-taught ambush tactics. One of the most well-known tactics of the NVA and VC ambush was to have our lead man hit a mine, booby trap, or any explosive device that would initiate their ambush. Once they figured they had us, they would seal the deal by sending between one and four maneuvering units to attack us from various directions. We called that tired old tactic "hit squads". We had already "peeped" at Charlie and positioned units accordingly.

The First Platoon reacted just like Alfa One was supposed to react, and they lagered without instructions while their squad leaders determined the most likely avenues of approach of the enemy hit squads. Their defensive line was as hard as steel; their perimeter was complete and adjustable. They would automatically refuse our rear and flanks. If Charlie attempted a run on our company's rear, the First Platoon would have something special waiting for him. Their thump gunners were already hitting the area to our rear to discourage a hit squad from coming up behind us. It was dog-eat-dog time.

Old Charles thought he had us, and it certainly might have appeared that way. However, we were as slippery as a greased pig, and in a split second, our positions were reversed. It was time for us to teach Charlie some respect and that it was a no-no to pull on Black Knight Alfa, especially when he did not have his shit in order. It was our time to make him pay the piper.

So far, the NVA were running true to the teachings of their Chinese, Cuban, and Russian instructors. The far right of their ambush site actually signaled the nearness of their hit squads by shifting their fire to allow freedom of movement of those hit squads who were already moving on us to deliver "the coup de grace". Were they ever in for the surprise of their lives, which were rapidly approaching an end.

We had some very favorable circumstances. First of all, we were not afraid of the NVA, and we were confident about bringing them down. It was also broad daylight, and Charlie did not have the skirt of darkness to hide behind. We had caught on to his act before he could spring his ambush. The terrain prevented him from attacking us from our left side, so his offensive actions were restricted to one side. Finally, the dirty little bastard had underestimated our will to survive and our heartfelt desire to send his little ass straight to hell. We fully intended to give him the opportunity to die for his country.

Once again, we did the unexpected and confused our enemy. Charlie fully expected us to start running amidst a lot of screaming and hollering. Instead, we simply hit the ground and returned fire – accurate fire. We had no intentions of running, and we lit into Charlie's butt like a mad dog. Some of our troopers were yelling our battle cry. Clearly, we were not at all like the media and our other detractors had told him.

Gonzalez and I did not feel that our enemy had the time to get behind us, but we still took positive steps and were ready for anything because we could not underestimate our enemy. By that time, the Second Platoon was our base of fire, and the Third Platoon was in motion. The First Platoon served as our home platoon and rearguard.

From our positions, both the Second and the First Platoons could place highly accurate fire on the NVA's main ambush site in the treeline. Sfc. Tuzo and our mortars were hitting Charlie's hip pocket. Charlie had begun to use his Type 63 mortars against us, and I was hoping that his gunners were not as good as ours. Our gunners were already settled into some serious shooting.

The first of Charlie's unknown number of hit squads made the ultimate mistake of moving on Black Knight Alfa. They charged out of the bush at us, and all of those fools quickly died. Their second and third hit squads suffered similar fates. The third enemy squad of four NVA soldiers ran right into Sp4 Jones's favorite girl, and she chewed them up.

All three NVA hit squads were down and out, never to return. Their little maneuver cost them dearly and whoever was in charge of their side was forced to change his plans. We were no longer the ones being ambushed. Because I had no idea where the CO and Three-Six were, we had to concentrate all of our firepower on the treeline. A lot of smoke was coming from the enemy position, but I did not know why. The grass was too damp to be burning.

Charlie was shooting RPGs at us, but the trees limited their effectiveness, and they exploded before hitting our positions. Fortunately, our LAW-shooting men were not having that problem; they were hitting the enemy's main positions with a very high degree of accuracy. Although Charlie was hitting our positions, our troopers were using all available cover and concealment, which seemed to be helping us.

Clearly, we were hurting old Charles. However, I could not help feeling that he was just trying to hold us in place until his big brother arrived. There had to be a time factor involved in their ambush.

A good, experienced Eleven-Charlie (11-C) mortar man, especially one from the golden days of the Brown Shoe Army, knew how important it was to have an exact knowledge of "counter-mortar fire procedures". Basically, no self-respecting mortar man should leave home without them. Those procedures include some set rules and methods that, when applied, can enable an astute, well-trained observer to look at incoming enemy fire and to ascertain with great accuracy the correct millimeter of the mortar rounds, the direction from which they were fired, and the approximate location of the enemy mortar positions. Such a mortar man could work all of that magic in a moment's time so that the friendly mortars could place accurate counter-mortar fire rounds on the enemy mortar positions.

That is exactly what Sfc. Tuzo was doing. He knew that the rounds landing on and near our positions were 60mm, which suggested that the mortars being fired at us were Chicom Type 63 with a maximum range of 1,530 meters. From his position he could see the treeline, and he knew the enemy mortars were somewhere behind it. When they brought in their 82mm mortars, Sfc. Tuzo followed the same procedures, and he was able to silence their mortars with ours in a brief period of time.

"Alfa Five, Alfa Six, hold your fire 'cause we are now in a position to clean house. Do you copy? Over."

"Alfa Six, Alfa Five. I have a good copy. Out."

Lt Zen and I moved two machine guns to a better position to cover the enemy ambush site as Six and the Third Platoon maneuvered to finish bringing Charlie all the way down. We heard them firing and yelling our battle cry as they hit and kicked Charlie's ass.

The fight was over almost before it began. Although we had broken Charlie's back, some of our enemies ran farther back into the jungle. Those who stayed behind would never run again. The CO called to tell me not to pop caps because they were coming home.

It was all over. He told me to get the rest of the company on the road because he felt that troops were on the way to help the NVA. If we were caught lollygagging, we could wind up just like the Charlies we had just chilled. As usual, we did not stop to count the dead. That was the Grim Reaper's job.

Understand that Battalion always asked us for an enemy body count after we won a fight. In order to satisfy them, we would pull a number out of the air and give it to them to get them off our backs. We of Black Knight Alfa thought it was most undignified to go around actually counting the dead bodies that we had iced. We saw this job as a point of honor to the dead and to old Death himself. After all, old Death had been counting the dead since time began, and he was still doing a good job of it, so we did not dare to presume.

Anyway, I had the rest of the company saddled up and ready to go. Our mortars were the last to break down, and at the same time, our men carrying 81mm ammo dropped it off with the mortars to replace the ammo fired during our fight with Charlie. Sfc. Tuzo pushed up to tell me he was ready to move, and as soon as he got off the push, the CO came right back on it. He had changed his mind and told me to bring the company to him on the enemy ambush site, so we hauled ass to where he was waiting.

Our luckless enemy bushwhackers actually had a Goryunov 7.62mm machine gun but did not use it because the damned thing was tightly jammed. I quickly kicked the feed cover catch forward and took out the feed carrier. That was all it took to ensure that it would not be used against us. We took what we could with us and got the hell out of there.

We moved smoothly into our running-and-fighting formation. Once we were stretched out enough with One-Six leading, we gracefully slipped into our rhythmical, easy-going pace.

As we trotted along beside each other, the CO said to me, "First Sergeant, I'm so damned proud of our magnificent company, Black Knight Alfa. I can hardly believe what we can do. You should have been there with me and Three-Six. I told Mac to tell them … Oh, I did not see anyone being carried. Does that mean that we …?"

"That's right, sir. We have some slightly wounded guys but no KIAs. Don't you remember, sir? I gave you our sit-rep as soon as I got the last report from Sergeant McKinnon."

"Yeah, now I remember. Guess I had too much on my mind," he answered with a smile.

JoJo was again on point with a new man just slightly to his rear, learning while covering JoJo's butt. The CO wanted to run up with the lead squad, which definitely was not the best position in our formation for him. I advised him against it, but he did not listen. Redleg and he had discovered a more direct route to our mountain pickup site, and he wanted to be in a position to better control the directions of the point men.

I dropped back with Sergeant Webb and the Second Platoon. We ran to the first available high ground in our line of travel. I told Webb to send a two-man left security team to the ridge line, and we got on down.

The CO adjusted the pace so that our wounded men could keep up. My last look back at the smoking ambush site, strewn with dead bodies, was as usual quite a jolt, and I tried in vain to wipe the sight out of my mind and my heart.

I was greatly relieved to see Nat and to know that he had not received a scratch from our recent firefight with Charlie. Old Nat had come out of the fight smelling like a … I started to say "rose", but that would have been an abusive use of the word because all of us reeked. We smelled like a large shithouse in motion. My skin was broken out all over as if I had some kind of pox, and in some places, my skin was raw and bleeding. I did not need any bug juice at that time because no self-respecting skeeter or fly dared to come near me.

We pushed on for a little more than an hour. The hot breath of the steaming jungle was an overwhelming stench that made us, by comparison, smell like a French whorehouse. I feared that we were going to witness another group of decomposing human bodies, which always smell worse than any other dead creature. Soon, however, I began to notice a distinct chemical matrix to the offensive odor that increased in strength with each step that we took in our direction of travel. I could feel that the CO was giving some thought to changing our direction; however, the terrain would no longer be in our favor. We continued in our current direction because we had no desire to have another run-in with Charlie so soon and also because we did not have the luxury of time to change our course.

A little later, JoJo stopped and looked back for instructions. The CO went forward and said something to the platoon sergeant as he passed him. Then he said something to JoJo, and I saw another man run forward to join JoJo in the point position.

The CO pushed on the company net and ordered us to "Spread out, be more alert, and be prepared to cross an open area." He also told us that the lead platoon would cross first and that I would bring the rest of our company across on his signal. I acknowledged the CO's instructions as Pete and I moved forward. Then we saw it – a wide area of destruction that looked like the set of a Hollywood science fiction movie. It seemed as if we had entered the Twilight Zone and were on another planet. Reality no longer played a role in our situation, and we saw something that took our minds out and played with them like yo-yos on a string.

I stood still, staring at a vast area where everything was dead. It looked as if there had been a chemical or a nuclear attack upon the environment, which turned out to be partially true. The trees that remained standing were stripped naked; others were bent over as if kneeling in prayer or in mourning. What was left of the naturally tall grass and other vegetation was completely burnt, withered to ground level, and discolored, and it emitted a foul stench that burned our eyes and our noses. We could see the bloated, decomposing bodies of many different species of Nature's creatures whose habitat had been willfully invaded and destroyed. Everything there that had once lived had been a victim of Operation Ranch Hand, a chemical defoliation mission that was later named Agent Orange.

When we received the CO's promised signal, I quickly moved the remainder of the company across the wide area. A long, ragged hole in the jungle canopy allowed the sun and rain to fall directly on the affected area. We passed the bodies of dead animals, and I could not help but notice the body of a tree monkey. In his little hand, he seemed to be clutching the remains of one of the leaflets that our military had dropped earlier to warn the Vietnamese of its intention to defoliate the area. There was also a colored smoke canister lying very close to the monkey's body, which called our attention to the silent, yet screaming victim.

My eyes overflowed with tears, and it was not a result of the chemicals burning the air.

I urged my troopers to move quickly without stopping or pausing, and I cautioned them to walk with care so as not to slip and fall because of the mushy and slimly substances that made walking difficult in places. I especially wanted to cross the area quickly because if we were hit, we would have to experience further contact with all of the awful debris on the ground. Of course, at that time, we had no idea that Agent Orange was harmful to humans. It had surely played hell with that poor monkey, though.

In the dry areas, the dead vegetation crumbled into a fine, ash-like powder, which made its way onto our clothing and did a nasty job on our skin. Later, the affected skin on my body cracked open, particularly in the areas between my toes, under my arms, and between my legs. It became excruciatingly painful to walk.

As we moved deeper into the pus-filled, open wound of the earth, it started to rain. We used the rain to wash our clothes and our bodies. I had the uneasy feeling that the falling rain was a by-product of Mother Nature's tears, as she cried in great sorrow for the damage that had been done to her formerly beautiful, natural jungle. I prayed to God and to Mother Nature, asking them to take that little monkey along with the rest of the dead jungle creatures into their home in Heaven.

I believe that rain was a blessing. Who knows what could have happened to us if we had not quickly washed the Agent Orange off our bodies.

We pushed on even harder than before, though we kept our strength and limitations in mind. We were running low on all supplies, although the rain had replenished our dwindling water supply a bit.

Doc B. spent a lot of time attending to our wounded, and he said to me, "Top, I don't know how much longer I can keep them going at this pace. We must slow down, or we're going to lose some good men." His expression was serious, concerned, and haggard.

I immediately conveyed Doc B.'s concern to the CO, who instantly slowed our pace. In order for us to improve our speed, we might now have to use the trails.

Our trek took us through another brief encounter with our bolder enemy, the NVA. It was clear that they were getting even more desperate to collect the bounty on our heads. They were after us like a pack of wild, hungry dogs trying to bring down a wounded buck. They seemed to know that we had wounded. Perhaps they could smell the blood.

I shall always believe that the only thing that kept the NVA at bay and away from our throats at that time was plain old FEAR. After all, we had proven to them that we were no easy kill, that they had to bring ass to get ass, and that if they locked up with us, they were sure as hell going to die.

The NVA that we encountered then was another eight-man patrol with a radio. When they boldly began to dog us, we selected a team of three men to do a job on them. That team simply moved slower than the rest of the company so as to steal some distance between themselves and the rear of our drag platoon. When the time was right, our team positioned their claymores and waited. When the enemy patrol reached the desired position, BOOM! We took all of them out in one smooth motion. Charlie ended up all over the trail because we popped the claymore close to his face.

I do not know if the claymore explosion caused more NVA soldiers to arrive or whether the eight Charlies had radioed for help before they died. The new group of soldiers shot at us from a distance and then ran. Charlie had the honor of a buzzard, the balls of a female fly, and no guts. The bastards did not have the stomachs to stand and fight us, and their lack of intestinal fortitude was once again working in our favor. They were trying to wear us down before moving in for their kill, but we kept on getting up and striking back.

The CO and Redleg plotted our route with the hope that the NVA would believe we were running to Khe Sanh or across the border into Laos. Actually, we were going to continue toward our desti-nation in the Ap Bia mountain range. All things considered, we were freshly out of options and in dire need of pulling a rabbit out of a hat, any hat.

By that time, the long run was beginning to tell on all of us, especially with old Charles constantly nipping at our heels. Our wounded were obviously suffering the most. I was carrying part of the load of one of my wounded troopers, and other men were either almost carrying or carrying some of our wounded men. And to think that we still had to climb to the top of that damned mountain.

Whenever Charlie hit us, we hit him back and refused to let him know how bad off we were. It was impossible for us to get dust-off down to us, and if we stopped, it would almost guarantee our death. More and more Charlies were on our tail, and they grew more persistent as their numbers grew. It was simply a matter of time before one of their commanders decided that they outnumbered us by a wide-enough margin to call an attack.

We continued to push on.

As we moved along the terrain, it gradually climbed upward, and we knew our pickup point was growing steadily closer. The weather was getting progressively worse, and the overcast sky was creeping in and preparing to dump rain on us again.

Everyone was already completely soaked from a mixture of sweat and the previous heavy rain that we had encountered. I moved among the Skytroopers in the platoon nearest to me, and we shared some easy-going conversation and wisecracks to pass the time as we pushed onward. I saw only smiles on the troopers' faces, and I heard comments such as "Top, did you hear about Sergeant McKinnon and Rizzo bringing that Charlie down?" and "What I wouldn't do for a great big cheeseburger, fries, and a cold Budweiser." One man said to me, "Top, let's face it. Even without stopping on purpose, we are really hurting Charlie to death. I'll bet he wishes that we would just go away."

The troopers' faces were dirty and tired, but their smiles were bright and cheerful. Maybe those smiles were in remembrance of their last date back home in Kansas, Florida, or somewhere in the big sky country where they had spent a lovely evening with "Kathy Smith", the pretty girl from next door or across town. They certainly had not lost their sense of humor, their will to survive, their purpose for being in the Valley of Death, and their belief that all of the damned NVA, Russians, Chinese, and Cubans did not stand a snowball's chance in hell of stopping us now.

Just before we reached the bottom of the mountain, another group of NVA, who were willing to die for Uncle Ho and Giap, pulled on us.

We blew them away while we remained intact. If ever we were pumping iron, it was at that time.

When I saw that old mountain looming almost up to the sky, I thought, moaning long and low, dear God, it looks like Mount Everest. Oh my God, I'll never make it.

I swear it looked every bit of 29,028 feet.

When we reached the foot of the mountain, I was sure I was not going to make it. My crotch and underarms were raw, and my feet and legs felt as if they belonged to someone else. By that time, I was carrying a mortar tube. As we started upward, I heard someone say, "Black Knight Alfa. Alpha and Omega!" The rest of the platoon immediately took up the call.

Before we started up the side of the mountain, the platoons rotated the lead until the First Platoon was leading again with JoJo on point. Gonzalez tried to put another man up front, but old JoJo begged to stay where he was. Rod asked if he could go up front and cover JoJo's butt, and I approved because they were the best team of point men in the Nam, and God knows that we really needed the best we had up front at that time.

We did not dare to use the main trail to the top. It was just too good-looking and inviting. Instead, we went straight up the side through the trees and underbrush. We used a well-spread-out, diamond-on-diamond formation. This meant that each platoon in the company was in a diamond formation, with the Weapons Platoon drawn up behind, but not too close to, the lead and center platoons. The CO and Headquarters were behind the lead platoon, and I was back with Sfc. Tuzo and the Weapons Platoon. The going was rough, and the branches and wait-a-minute vines were ripping our already tattered jungle fatigues off our bodies in various places.

I wondered if Charlie was waiting for us at our destination LZ. To catch us on the side of the mountain and shoot down on us would give him one hell of an advantage. We realized that Charlie was probably aware of our roughed-up condition and that he had a good opportunity to move on us while we were exhausted and not in tip-top shape. However, like the coward that he was, he would wait to catch us with our backs to the mountainside. I kept expecting to hear caps popping at our backs, but I did not. It was unusual for old Charles not to strike us when he must surely know that we were heading for the old 101st Landing Zone.

The climb was taking the very last of our reserves of strength, but we steadfastly persisted. I was huffing and puffing like the old wolf trying to blow the three little pigs' house down. I am very sad to say that I was having trouble keeping up with the pace, and I had fallen back quite a distance. I was experiencing terrible pains all over, and every step that I took brought on new pains. My fatigue trousers were bloody between the legs. However, there was no way that I would let myself stop, not with some of the men of my Grand Company struggling there along with me. I was their first sergeant, so I could not fall. I silently pleaded with God for strength. My physical pain was greater than any I had ever known, and I made up my mind and heart that I was going to push on until I dropped, and then I would crawl. No power on Earth, short of old Death, was going to stop me. I had made it out of the cotton fields of the Delta, and I would make it to the top of the mountain.

Somewhere along the way, the load of the mortar tube became too much for me. My head swam and I fell down. I struggled on the ground, but my body no longer seemed to be functioning. My mind was certainly willing, but the rest of my systems were offline. I gave a mighty effort, but I slipped right back down, flat on my face. God was not hearing my prayers, and I was crying out of sheer frustration. I heard Sis's voice in my ear, telling me, "Sonny, falling down ain't no crime. The crime is when you don't try to get back up. Staying down is the crime, and getting back up is the man."

I dragged a dirty hand across my eyes and gave it another try. Two weary, concerned voices seeped through the cobwebs of my mind. One of them said, "Top, give me your hand. Let me help you up." The other voice asked to take part of my load, and I saw another pair of hands pick up the mortar tube. I thanked them and said that I could make it by myself. However, I could not, so I started to crawl and cussed at myself, spitting out a lot of really dirty names.

"First Sergeant! You always have your heart and your hand out to help us. Now you give me your hand 'cause damn it all to hell, I ain't moving till you do!" The trooper holding out his hand spoke slowly, and I could tell that he meant every word.

I humbly, and with much gratitude and respect, extended my hand. The trooper helped me to my feet. Someone else tried to take my rucksack, but I refused to let it go. I no longer felt ashamed and disgraced. Instead, I felt a great surge of pride, love, and strength flow through my tired body. Sweet Jesus, I loved all of my troopers so much back then, as I still do now, and I still thank God today for the privilege of having been the first sergeant of the great men of Black Knight Alfa.

My troopers refused to give me back the mortar tube, and when I tried to carry a base plate, one of my troopers said flatly, "No way!"

If I went down again and could not get back up by myself, I was going to stick the muzzle of my little black Bessie (my M16 rifle) in my mouth and blow my damned brains out. I refused to go down again.

We reached the prearranged location on the mountain where the CO was supposed to make his first call to our relay station. I do not know if our birds were already in the air, but I knew that there was a fuel/distance situation, which was like the Maxwell House coffee logo – calculated down to the last drop.

At that coordinating point, we took a breather before attacking the last leg up to the LZ. Our wounded were really hurting, and two of them had passed out and had to be carried all the way. And there I was falling down just carrying an 81mm mortar tube. I found the young trooper who had taken the tube from me, and I stubbornly took it back. Our drag platoon reported that there were no Charlies in sight, but Mac said he felt Charlie's ominous presence and believed that there were "a whole lot of them"!

All of us shared Mac's gut feeling. It was unusual that Charlie was not crawling up the side of the mountain behind us, especially after he had dogged us and popped caps on us all the way to the foot of the mountain. The bastards must have something up their sleeves besides their arms. We knew that the NVA would certainly have to try to make a final run on us. They could not let us simply waltz into "their valley", bust up and kill a lot of them, and then waltz out again.

The CO made his call to the relay and received his confirmation. Dust-off would be coming in with the slicks to lift us off. While we were taking our little breather, Sp4 Danzig suddenly held up his hand for silence. He listened intently to his handset and then switched the incoming radio transmission to his speaker for everyone to hear the message. The batteries in our radios were weak, and we had used our reserves. When the CO pushed up to our relay station, the transmissions were weak and distorted, and the bad weather was interfering as well. However, the transmission that we were currently receiving was five-by-five. Our phantom caller identified himself as the "Gray Ghost". He took and held our attention because he had the correct push, and when Danzig challenged him with our code instructions for that day, he came back quickly with the correct responses and even gave Danzig the emergency codes that only the CO, SOG, and Battalion were supposed to know. The Gray Ghost was the real thing – a Langley-level Spook – so we listened to him very attentively.

The Spook told us to move our asses because the better part of the whole North Vietnamese Army was heading to our mountain, almost running and packing heavy. Their orders were to bring us down once and for all. Charlie was approaching our mountain from at least three different directions, and all would converge on the mountain and the LZ. They knew about the old LZ and what we were planning to do. The Spook also said that the NVA was smoking mad because they had found the stack of bodies of their men who had walked into our perimeter. We were no longer wanted dead or alive, just dead. The orders from Hanoi were "Do it or don't bother to come back!"

We were rather daunted when the Gray Ghost congratulated us on the way we had turned the tables on Charlie when he had tried to ambush us. He said we were smooth operators and that our mission was so successful that we had clearly worn out our welcome in the A Shau Valley. General Giap had actually declared us to be persona non grata.

The Gray Ghost's final words to us were: "Your birds are on the way. I suggest you move from your coordinating point ASAP because your enemy will be at the foot of the mountain shortly, plus you have another enemy. The weather is also closing in on you. Move to the LZ now! Out."

The Gray Ghost had spoken quickly, distinctly, and with absolute authority. We knew it was not necessary to push up to Battalion to check him out. The date, letter series, and Zulu time code he had given us were sufficient verification points. The Gray Ghost was the fabled Phoenix bird that had risen from the ashes into the Shadow World.

"You heard the man, Top. Let's move on up to the top of this ant hill. I certainly don't want Charles to catch us here. Besides, we have our orders," said the CO.

I hurriedly got our troops moving. We kept our formation and guided on what looked like a main trail all the way to the top of the mountain. Following the relevant SOP, we stopped short of the reasonably flat area that marked the summit and sent two machine gun-heavy squads forward to check it out. When we received their okay, I moved the company onto and around the LZ.

Our intelligence was correct. It was a beautiful LZ that had been cut very high near the sky by the men of the 101st Airborne Division. It was well planned. The trees had been cut so the birds could almost fly straight in and out the other side, similar to the glide path of fixed-wing aircraft. There was enough room for three slicks, but the weather conditions were rapidly growing worse and some of the trees in the path of approach had become bushy enough to create a hazard. Perhaps two birds would be safer than three on the LZ.

Existing fighting positions surrounded the LZ, and I quickly moved the company into them because they formed a good perimeter. We placed the last of our claymores in the most likely avenues of enemy approach, and I positioned our wounded so they would be the first to be lifted out. Specifically, the men waiting for dust-off birds with qualified medical personnel would go first, followed by those who did not require immediate medical attention. Doc B. and our other platoon medics prepared for the dust-off birds.

The platoon sergeants had already taken the added precaution of placing physical security and listening posts down the side of the mountain. Anyone coming up would be seen; therefore, Charlie could not surprise us.

I was particularly unhappy to discover that we had almost no ammunition left. Most of us were down to one or two magazines for our M16s, and our machine gun ammo supply was just as low. Our troopers were already redistributing what ammunition we had left. Over half of our thump gunners were down to only one round of HE. They still had some shot, which I hoped they would not need. If they had to use shot, it would mean that Charlie was too damned close. We certainly did not want to lock up with him because we had no mortar ammunition.

We accounted for everyone in their positions. I had already given the lift-out order, and the fighting positions were manned. Although it was unnecessary, I reminded our troopers to make each shot count. One shot fired must equal one dead Charlie.

"Top, are we ready to fight for and hold this LZ 'cause it may come to the point of balls to the wall? Look at the sky. It's almost black, and the clouds are moving in like they are at the Indy 500. We may have to hold this LZ all night." The CO spoke grimly, and I did not have the heart to tell him that we had almost no ammunition left.

From what the Gray Ghost had told us, I knew that old Charles was going to have us for supper if we did not get the hell out of there.

As we waited, the weather and visibility continued to deteriorate. The height of the mountain was clearly starting to work against us, and the low ceiling was also beginning to adversely affect us. What had been a perfect LZ was quickly turning sour.

The lift commander of our inbound birds pushed up to the CO to inform him that because of the bad weather, they were having trouble finding us. Their visibility was almost nil, and they asked if we could hold off for one more night.

"Negative, negative, Fox Trot Lima Five. Be advised that we are about to be overrun. If you turn around and leave us, you are dooming my whole company of men to NVA history. Do you copy? Over!" yelled the CO into his mike.

"Black Knight Six, this is flight leader Five. I have a hard copy. We won't let you down, but be advised that we can't see very well. Pop smoke NOW 'cause I can't find you. Over."

"Top, pop smoke!" the CO ordered. Then, he added, "I hope we have birds inbound."

I immediately set off our first M18 smoke grenade. Its colored band identified the smoke color as violet.

The CO tried to mask his growing concern, remembering that most of The Valley all around us was covered by a thick canopy. He knew how it must have appeared to the flight leader of our lift of slicks. That portion of The Valley when viewed from above was mostly a sea of green with no visible landmarks. The cool rain falling on the warm jungle canopy was creating a blanket of fog that almost obscured the sea of green. The pilots were flying only on instruments. From our position on the mountain, we could no longer see very far below.

The thick blanket of fog rolled in at an alarming speed. Soon, our beautiful LZ on top of the mountain would be completely obscured. With the whole NVA around the base of the mountain, we had nowhere to go except to hell.

"Black Knight, Black Knight, did you pop smoke? Over."

"Fox Trot Lima Five, Black Knight Six, yes we did. Can't you see it? Over."

We could hear the faint beat of the rotors in the distance and were happy when that wonderful sound grew progressively louder.

"Negative, Black Knight Six. I ... wait! Yes, I see your Goofy Grape. I'm turning and will be there, toot sweet. Wait."

Louder and louder came the sound of the familiar whump-whumping of the rotors, heading straight toward our LZ. Then we saw the lead bird slide to the left and hover, allowing the medevac dust-off birds to come in first.

"Black Knight Alfa, this is Caduceus Five. Get your wounded ready 'cause we're coming in first. Don't look now, but I think you are fixing to have unwanted guests, and it's not us. Talk to me. Over."

Danzig began to guide the lead dust-off bird in. I stood on the LZ to actually bring the lead bird in as soon as the AC could see me through the pouring rain. Pete was directly to my rear, and he turned up the volume on his speaker so I could hear our security as they reported, "Holy shit, the NVA are coming right at us. It's party time! Permission to come home?"

We responded in the affirmative because we did not want any of our friends to be stuck between Charlie and us.

Boom! Our first non-command-detonated claymore blew. Boom! Boom! Additional claymores exploded from various widespread locations on the side of the mountain. The NVA had arrived, and they were coming at us from all sides. Show time was upon us, the curtain was going up, and the first act was on the stage.

The popped claymores gave us an indication of the NVA's proximity to us. The loud screams of anguish told us our claymores were doing their jobs.

I heard the distinct firing of an M16, which was soon answered by the chattering of a Chicom RPD light machine gun. Charlie had come prepared to stay for a while. I hoped that the active M16 was one of our security teams popping caps at Charlie in order to confuse him about where we were deployed.

Meanwhile, our dust-off birds were in and out. They had come in so close together that I thought their rotors were going to smash into each other. Many tree leaves and branches flew through the air as the blades of the dust-off birds made their approach to the LZ even wider.

"Top, all our wounded are away," Doc B. reported.

The LZ was being socked in so quickly that our birds had to come in one at a time or risk crashing into each other. We loaded as planned, with five troopers to a bird (two men on each side and one in the middle). The bad weather and poor visibility caused a slight delay in the typical time that it took for us to slick out.

Charlie attacked our perimeter as he simultaneously tried to take down our life-saving birds. Our door gunners could not fire for fear of hitting our own troopers. The amount of enemy fire told us that we were being hit by Charlie's lead element, so we had a precious few moments before the bulk of our attackers were in place to rush us. Fortunately, we were covering the main trails to the LZ with our machine guns. I borrowed some ammunition from the door gunners and quickly passed it on to our machine guns that were still on the ground.

Up to that point, our troops were holding the enemy at bay, but our numbers were rapidly growing smaller as our troopers ran to the birds and flew out.

Because some of the NVA soldiers were coming up the side of the mountain where our birds were taking off, our pilots had to force the birds straight up and power off in a banking right turn, rather than going straight out as they had done during their first lift-off.

The 101st had chosen that LZ well and had prepared great defensive positions. There were actually three separate perimeters, and we had already been forced to fall back to the third and last perimeter immediately surrounding the LZ. From those positions, I could see all of our troopers who were still on the ground.

Things were getting really tight for us. The fog had rolled in and covered the LZ. We were out of smoke, and the pilots could no longer see the LZ. Therefore, we lit anything and everything that would burn, which was not easy, considering that everything was soaked.

To help light the way for our birds to come in and take us out, our troopers hauled out their small supplies of C-4 that we had used to heat water for coffee and a few cans of sterno.

One bird remained on the LZ, and our last bird was waiting to come in. I knew those two birds would be able to take the rest of our company, and I called the last of our defenders to me so that we could lager right there on the LZ.

"Top, you get on this bird, and I'll get on the last one waiting to come in," yelled the CO.

I was surprised to see the CO because I thought he had left on the first bird out.

I expressed my confusion, and he replied, "No, that was Captain Norris. I sent him out first."

"Sir," I said, "that last bird is mine. You go on and I'll cover for you."

As I said those words, a Charlie ran out of the bush and shot at us. The CO dropped him as I turned and ran to where I could see an NVA squad rushing toward the bird to stop it from taking off.

The CO yelled something and started to follow me. Then he realized that he had to get on that bird. "SHIT!" he yelled and then jumped on the bird.

"Pete, tell the door gunners to open fire, only try not to hit us!" I yelled.

The door gunners followed Pete's command and opened fire on the onrushing NVA squad. After shooting every last man in the squad, the bird powered out and turned so that the door gunner on the inside of the turn was able to hit two additional NVA soldiers who were aiming RPGs at the bird. The slugs from the door gunner's M60 tore into the two Charlies, and the impact of the hits caused them to fire their grenade launchers. One RPG struck one of the Charlies in his midsection, and the other sailed off into the fog.

Our bird then completed its turn and disappeared into the fog.

Visibility was reduced to only a few feet, and we were totally socked in.

Five troopers and I remained on that barren LZ, aside from the large number of Charlies who were still scrambling up the side of the mountain. Aside from me and my M16, there were Sp4 Jones with his M60, Sp4 LeCroix (JoJo) and his M16, Sp4 Natkowski and his M16, Pfc. Walker and his thump gun, and Sp4 Peterson and his thump gun and radio.

Somehow we had one man too many. The pilot of the last bird was on the radio saying that he could no longer see our LZ, and he was low on fuel. He had just finished his second unsuccessful pass as Pete desperately tried to talk him in.

We were lying on the center of the LZ in a tight circle, with five men facing outward and Pete in the middle with his radio. Our ammunition supply was gone, and everyone was down to his last magazine or round. Jones had about half of a 100-round belt left. It was truly pucker time.

I instructed Pete to tell the door gunners to come in firing heavily. I was no longer worried about being hit by them. Better to die from their fire than from the NVA's.

We could hear the NVA moving around in the underbrush and the voices of their leaders. They did not know that we were almost out of ammunition, and I do not think they could see us through the fog.

"Black Knight Alfa Five. Please be advised. I have enough juice to make one more pass. If I miss you, I'm real sorry. I'm not sure we have enough juice to get out of here. I am so sorry. I'm flying totally blind. Talk to me. Over."

Despite the noise around us, we heard the sadness and finality in the pilot's soft Southern drawl. We heard the helicopter but could not see it. The pilot circled and came back toward us on his final run.

"Well, Top, this surely does look like it's going to be our Final Battle, and I'm happy that we are going together 'cause I'm so proud of you," JoJo yelled to me as he dropped a Charlie.

The NVA moved slowly because they knew the bird was making another run, and they wanted to hit it as well as us. Jones put a well-calculated burst into the middle of a group of Charlies and was rewarded by their curses and cries of pain.

Pete was talking the bird in strictly by the sound of its rotor blades. The air blast driven by the whirling blades washed over us and blew some of the fog away. We saw the rotating light and watched as the loudly popping blades sliced off the tops of some trees like a giant power mower.

Sweet Jesus, the sight of that single bird was indescribably beautiful. As the pilot gently lowered the bird, Pete coaxed him away from the trees that were big enough to break a blade. All the while, the door gunners' M60s were singing a death song for Charlie.

"Move, move!" I yelled as we scrambled onto the bird. Jones and Walker were totally out of ammo, so they sat on the floor in the middle. Pete and I sat on the right with JoJo and Nat on the left.

"GO!" I commanded the door gunner.

Of course my order was unnecessary because the pilot was already giving the bird its maximum power.

As we struggled upward, a high-ranking NVA officer broke into the clearing and headed straight for us, firing his pistol wildly. Pete unloaded his remaining thump-gun round directly into the officer's face, and we watched as his head exploded.

When we were high enough, the pilot dropped his bird's nose so we could see the LZ. It was covered with NVA troops all shooting upward at us. Our bird took some hits and our door gunners continued to fire back as we left our journey through the Valley of Death behind.

We feared no evil or the NVA because we were the meanest motherfuckers in The Valley.

Postscript

I am so very proud that I had the honor of walking the entire length of the A Shau Valley, the Valley of Death, with the magnificent men of Black Knight Alfa, the Grand Company.

We kicked off on the asses of the NVA every time we were able to get them to stop running and fight back. We went boldly during broad daylight into the sanctuary of the overrated North Vietnamese Army, right into the nerve center of the fabled Ho Chi Minh Trail. From there we whipped the NVA like stepchildren, and we did it without losing one man KIA.

I know that it may be hard to believe that Black Knight Alfa lost so few men in comparison to our enemies in the Vietnam War. However, it is the truth. We did lose men, but if you compared our losses with Charlie's, the ratio was always about four or six of them to one of us, and that estimation is at the bottom of the curve.

Did you know that during the first 10 days of February 1968, the 2nd Brigade of the 1st Air Cavalry Division[85] was under constant enemy attack in which the 2nd Brigade killed 381 enemy NVA soldiers, and the whole 2nd Brigade lost only 4 of its own men in the process? That is a recorded historical fact.

I hope that you will better understand now that when I say we put Charlie's shit in the wind without losing a man, I am not just whistling Dixie. The NVA and Charlie Cong were greatly overrated, and all of the bullshit the American media fed the public about our enemies being such great, invincible fighters was just that – bullshit!

It is interesting to note that General Giap was told that we were a specially trained American Special Forces unit who represented years of training by the CIA.

Did you know the Russians suggested that we were trained by a rogue Spetnatz captain who was Jewish and defected to the United States? The Red Chinese told a similar story, but in their version, our trainers were Black Dragons.

Well, General Giap, those are all lies. I have news for you. We were not trained by any special person, group, or forces. We were not even part of the Special Operations Group or Special Forces. We were just Cav, and that says it all.

Oh, by the way, General, you and I both know that you did not win the Vietnam War. You did not earn a victory; it was given to you on a silver platter by the assholes on our side.

Some time after our fateful stroll through the Valley of Death, we were finally told that some very valuable information had been acquired by our high command as a direct result of our Valley campaign. That information was processed at Pentagon East and then forwarded to the main Pentagon. Details included how certain NVA field commanders reacted to our bold incursion, what units were moved, and what units were held back because of us.

The enemy was forced to react to our actions and to admit that a lone American infantry Cav rifle company had left a string of dead NVA soldiers across The Valley that no one could deny. Their admission caused a reaction that forced the enemy to come looking for us and to watch his left hand while our right hand was killing him.

Our stirring the pot enabled the Gray Ghost to gain free access to some very important enemy secret plans, and the information that he acquired saved American lives, perhaps even ours.

The SOG Team Cobra, who had so expertly dogged the NVA unit moving south, continued to report that unit's every move. Then, they arranged a steel ambush on the unit that reduced it to almost nothing. The remaining soldiers of that NVA unit were pressed into service with the Viet Cong.

As for those NVA units who had chased us to the mountain LZ, they were reduced to rabble by hot American steel in the form of thousands of rounds of high-explosive projectiles that rained down on them and that mountain as soon as our last bird was safely away. At least three of our firebases participated in that time-on-target (TOT) attack. Some say the mountain was much shorter after the attack, and a whole NVA unit was forced to case its colors because no one was left to carry them.

The forward observer who had directed and adjusted the American artillery barrages continued to be known only as the "Gray Ghost".

Standing Down

We experienced a long but worthwhile journey down to the flatlands and to LZ Hard Core. The old, dilapidated Vietnamese buildings were the first hard structures we had seen in a long time. When we had the opportunity to sleep inside a building, no matter how much in ruin that structure was, we felt as if we had moved into a fancy hotel on the main strip of Las Vegas. Only the slot machines and the girls were missing.

Once we settled in, we showered our weary, filthy bodies more than once, indulging in the luxury of real soap and hot water. Our supply personnel provided us with fresh uniforms, complete with socks and jungle boots for those of us who needed new ones. Doc B. gave me some antibiotic shots, some soothing salves, and some red stuff that set my ass on fire. We also had two excellent barbers at the LZ, so I finally had my hair cut.

When the CO and I had first gone into The Valley, he had worn medium-size trousers, and I had worn large-size. However, when we came out, each of us had dropped a full size and had to exchange our trousers. The NVA and the A Shau Valley certainly ran one hell of a reducing salon, although I would not recommend it to those without very strong hearts.

The chow at LZ Hard Core was terrific. They offered huge steaks that were cooked to order, potatoes, vegetables, and a wide variety of other items. They also served many flavors of ice cream, including pistachio nut, and there was cold beer to drink. It took us a while to get used to the coldness of the beer because we had gotten accustomed to drinking our beer almost as hot as our coffee.

We were allowed to eat as much and as often as we wanted. The cooks kept the dining facilities open 24 hours a day. It was food heaven. One of the cooks was from Mississippi, and he served us such specialties as hot fist biscuits, sausages, and home-made Mississippi Delta syrup. To our surprise, he had his own supply of chicory coffee, and do not tell anyone, but he also had the makings for Delta White Lightning. Let's just say that we completely enjoyed a little bit of "down home".

Although I have thanked them many times before in person, I would like to repeat myself in print. My special thanks go to all personnel who managed LZ Hotel Charlie: your dedicated work made our stay so wonderful. To the dedicated mess personnel and to "Bubber": your biscuits were great and your White Lightning was as smooth as they used to make it down around midnight. Some of the cooks even worked during their off-duty time. Thanks to all of you, including the personnel who kept the water hot at the shower-head. Thanks to all of you from Black Knight Alfa.

I would also like to thank the wonderful American companies who went out of their way to send us free supplies of cigarettes, tobacco, candy, gum, writing utensils and paper, fresh fruit, vegetables, beer, soda, and many other well-appreciated consumer goods. It was always nice to know that there were Americans who cared about our well-being during the Nam.

Our log personnel brought our mail and packages from home. I also received a mountain of backlogged paperwork from my company clerks, Anderson and Winestein, who came to LZ Hard Core the day after we arrived. The documents required the CO's and my immediate attention. I asked my two clerks to bring out our company guidon and to get a large American flag for me. I posted both of them outside the building where the CO and I were staying, and it became our instant orderly room. We were not afraid to show our colors, and we proudly displayed them for all eyes to see. God help the unfortunate bastard who attempted to desecrate them, because we would be all over that person's ass.

Our first night was rather sleepless. I sat outside in front of my orderly room and observed about 80 per cent of my company lying down but not really sleeping. It was very hard for us to adjust to dozing without having one eye open and one finger on the trigger. It was equally as hard for us to adjust to the toilet facilities, which were the outhouse drum type.

We were completely refitted and resupplied with everything we required, including our starlight scopes. Our ammunition resupply was complete, and we spent some time loading our magazines. We only put 18 rounds in the 20-round magazines (to avoid some problems we had experienced with full magazines). We had a good supply of the 30-round magazines, but for a grunt, the 30-round ones had some drawbacks because of their extended length. There are some times when a grunt has to get real close to the ground and shoot from that position. I requested a good supply of C-4 to replace the supply we had used to bring in our lift of birds on the mountaintop LZ. We also received new claymores and LAWs.

The old Vietnamese structures that we lived in were the first hard billets I had occupied since An Khe. There were no beds, so we slept on earthen floors. A few holes in the walls served as windows. Of course, sleeping within walls and roofs was a whole lot better than sleeping in a mud hole or your own shit.

During our third morning at Hotel Charlie, we went out on a "Mini-Cav" that was not very long, and no one was hurt. After the operation, we received a personal visit from our sergeant major and colonel. They came to congratulate us on our mission in The Valley and to tell us the fate of our wounded personnel. We plainly saw that even our own leaders found it very hard to believe that we had spent over four days in the A Shau Valley, walking almost its entire length while kicking off on the ass of several of the NVA's best troops, and we had not lost a man KIA. They acknowledged that we had set a record of some kind.

Our wounded personnel who had gone dust-off were still alive. Some were at Phu Bai waiting to ship out to Japan, some were already in Japan, and some were back home in the good old US of A. There was a very good chance that those men at Phu Bai and those on the USS *Repose* would be rejoining us shortly, maybe even before we left our stand-down status.

The sergeant major and colonel brought us some FNGs. One was a private just out of AIT, and the other was a staff sergeant on the list for sergeant first class. He would be taking over the First Platoon because Gonzalez was so short he did not have time to smoke half a cigarette.

The new staff sergeant, Preston Long Claw, was on the promotion list. My first and lasting impression of him was favorable. Long Claw was from the Land of the Sky Blue Waters. He was proud and unbending, and my years of experience in dealing with people told me that we were fortunate to have another good leader. He seemed to be a good NCO and leader, and I welcomed him as such to join the eternal fraternity of Black Knight Alfa.

The sergeant major told me that he had personally arranged for me to get Long Claw because I was losing a good man in Gonzalez. He also stated that he knew that LC (his nickname for Long Claw) and I would get along.

When the sergeant major introduced me to LC, we shook hands and looked into each other's eyes. LC said he had already heard of the Grand Company and was proud to be with us. After the sergeant major left, I took LC to meet his new company commander. I could immediately tell that Captain Brooks was also impressed by LC. I left them alone for a few minutes, and then we went to have some chow.

While we sat eating and talking, I took the opportunity to look closely at Preston Long Claw and to do it in the time-honored manner that my old Buffalo Soldier mentors had taught me. As I listened to what he was saying, I read his facial expressions and his body language. I did this to get past his public face – the one that we often present to the world as we play our part on the world's stage.

LC told us that he was married and the father of two pretty little girls. His wife's name was Netti, and his father was the medicine man of his tribe. LC was a career soldier and would someday be the chief of his people (a tribe of Chiricahua Apache Indians).

I wished that I could have introduced LC to the company in the proud tradition of the old army, but our situation at LZ Hard Core did not permit it. Instead, I took him around to each platoon and finally to Gonzalez and the fine men of the First Platoon. Gonzalez introduced LC to the squad leaders and the other men of One-Six.

I knew the men of the First Platoon would take LC under their wings and teach him to fly, as they had taught me. Before I left him in the capable hands of One-Six, I told him that if he listened well, he would live to tell his grandchildren about his Vietnam experiences.

During our free time, I found it nice to just kick back and read the latest editions of *Stars and Stripes*. The news from home was not good. There were photos of people protesting in the streets against the Vietnam War, social injustice, and just about anything you could imagine. The students were protesting, while many of the flowers of

American manhood were burning their draft cards and running off to foreign lands. There was one particular photo of an individual who had sewn the American flag to the seat of his trousers so that he could place his ass on our beloved symbol of freedom whenever he sat down. And there we were, trying to carry our small American flags as close to our hearts as possible because we loved our country and were prepared to die for it.

There were also photos from Selma and Montgomery, Alabama, and I thought of that poor soul, our dear brother whom the Viet Cong had strung up and crucified on that lonely jungle trail. Then, I had to put the newspaper away because smoke was forming in my eyes.

I sat there for a while, thinking back across the years, until I remembered something I had read while I was still attending Smith Robertson Elementary School in Jackson, Mississippi:

> "Sir, I disapprove of what you say. But, I will defend unto death, your right to say it!"

These were Voltaire's words; however, they seemed so germane to the subject and the situation in which we of Black Knight Alfa found ourselves. For were we not in an actual situation where we were offering and sometimes giving or losing our lives for the rights of all Americans, including those protesters, draft-card burners, hate-mongers, and those of even worse character, to exercise their beliefs? That was indeed one of the foundations of our great country – the American way – which was bought and partially paid for by guys like us. We were just over there to make installments on the loan, so that all living Americans could continue to exercise their rights under the best system of government in the world.

I went to talk with my troops, and I made sure that I spent a few minutes with each man. I listened to everything they said and then offered suggestions and told them what I thought. I reminded them that they were the greatest soldiers in the world, and I promised them that I would someday tell their story to the world if I could just get people to listen.

During our four days of stand-down time, some of my troopers engaged in games of checkers, chess, and cards. We also had the opportunity to see two movies, and the Doughnut Dollies came to bring us a little bit of home. To all of those wonderful pretty ladies: thank you from Black Knight Alfa. It may seem hard to believe, but we were already growing restless and ready to go back to our natural environment, to get back to the hunt. The easy life was not so easy for us.

Some of my troopers expressed their restlessness by saying, "Top, we know that we have worked hard to earn an edge, but we feel that if we stay here too long, we are going to lose that edge, and to lose our edge is to put all of our lives at risk. Look at it this way: we've kicked Charlie's ass coming and going. We just walked all the way through the Valley of Death and came out without losing one man, and that says it all."

His opinion was certainly valid.

As usual, our medics did a wonderful job of getting us back into shape. I was almost back in full operating order, thanks to the shots, pills, and salves that Doc B. had given me. The worst places were still below my belt, but the medicine and a daily shower were healing me.

We went on a cordon-and-search mission with the ARVNs to a village that was a suspected VC hideout. When we arrived, we were told the common response that the VC were long gone. Of course, this was a self-protective lie. The village chief had recently died with a little help from the VC, and the villagers were scared to speak to us or anyone else. When we tried to talk to them, they said nothing, but their lips quivered and their eyes watered.

We knew that the VC were among those villagers at the time, but we could not prove it. It was common for the VC to murder the village chief and his family if the chief did not go along with the VC's game of strict obedience to the orders of the Cong. Sometimes, the VC killed women and children to emphasize their power among the villagers.

It is so interesting that our detractors failed to tell you about those horrible actions of the VC, yet they never failed to tell you about all of those babies that we supposedly killed. They certainly failed to give the VC "equal time". If they had, then you might have seen behind the mask and the curtain of lies that were so well formulated to keep you watching the US while the VC got away clean with taking out entire villages. Think about it.

The VC made any lies that I have ever told look like a Sunday school picnic. They did not hesitate to blow up those little blue buses loaded with innocent civilians and animals. Then there were the sweet little boys and girls whom the VC pressed into service to sell American soldiers cola laced with battery acid.

The Russians and Chinese – the communist puppet masters of the NVA and VC – literally flooded the drug market with tons of pure heroin and opium, directing most of it to the American soldiers in South Vietnam.

Can you even begin to imagine what happened when a junkie who was used to shooting heroin that was only about 50 per cent pure suddenly absorbs heroin that is 90–95 per cent pure white death? I think such a malicious and cowardly deed goes way beyond such common excuses as "After all, it was war" and "The death or destruction of a junkie who overdosed simply meant one less junkie".

Using such tactics was the lowest form of cowardice. My Lai paled considerably in comparison with the tons of heroin, the battery acid-laced cola, the blowing up of those little blue buses, Hue, Tet, and the whores who dedicated themselves to spreading a social disease that was anything but social.

Think about what I have said for a while, and wonder why those truths never made the big, bold American news headlines during the Vietnam War.

I certainly agree that My Lai should never have happened, and I am personally very sorry for what may have happened there. My heart went out to those villagers, as it did for all of the poor, innocent people who have suffered scars from the Vietnam War.

Getting back to our stand-down, the CO slicked out to a high-level briefing and was gone during most of our last day on LZ Hard Core. I told our platoon sergeants that they should be ready to move lock, stock, and barrel in five minutes, and they were, just like always.

When the CO returned, the battalion commander accompanied him in the Charley-Charley bird. As the battalion commander flew away, the CO smiled and said, "Top, get our platoon sergeants, Captain Norris, and Lt Zen to the orderly room. We're going to the flatlands!"

The Flatlands

They took great care of us at LZ Hotel Charlie, doing everything possible to provide us with a good stand-down period. Our log personnel made sure that we received everything we needed. There was a crew from Ordnance who checked and repaired our weapons and recalibrated some of our sights. They also checked and repaired our radios. Some newer-model rucksacks were issued, and the soldier who had lost his stuff to his own grenade received replacements for everything, except for his personal items.

A nice thing happened to us the day before we left Hotel Charlie. We were escorting a supply convoy, and one of the trucks was loaded with pallets of beer and soda. We asked the driver of the truck if we could have some of his beverages. He was very friendly and nice. His face split into a big grin as he said, "Sure, you guys can have all you want." He pulled his truck next to a tree, bounced out of his cab, found the length of rope he needed, and tied it to a full pallet of beer and soda. He jumped back into his truck, said goodbye, and drove away. The rope anchored to the tree held onto the pallet, and as the lowboy trailer moved away, the rope dragged the pallet off the trailer and onto the ground.

To the driver of that truck, I want to say "thank you" again from all of us. Your kindness was warm and heartfelt, and you made many of us grunts very happy.

Our new AO was located in I Corps, but we were going to be operating in the flatlands in areas where there were villages and people. We were obviously going up against the Viet Cong mob group who terrorized the civilian population and operated mainly under the cover of darkness. The I Corps AO consisted mainly of Quang Tri, Thua Thien, Quang Nam, and Quang Tin provinces. Therefore, we would be able to operate in the flats as far south as Quang Tin Province.

One advantage that we had with our upcoming assignment was that the Cong in those areas were more predictable than the Cong in the areas further south, especially around the larger cities like Saigon. In those built-up areas, it seemed that the Cong were mainly washed-up petty crooks, cowboys, and sickies who were all drunk with the full power of their Russian- and Chinese-made AK-47s.

The fact that we were going back to fight the VC did not make us happy. Although we were not afraid of the VC, we had absolutely no respect for them and their fighting methods. We felt it was better to be bitten by a snake than to be shot by a VC, because the snake was more honorable and more humane. Of course, we were soldiers, and we would do our jobs to the best of our abilities until it came time for us to catch that freedom bird home.

As I have said many times before, we never underestimated the VC's ability to take our lives. Even a tree monkey can kill you with an AK-47 if someone aimed the weapon for him. We knew them for what they were, and we had to adjust our thinking down to their level and fight them by "their rules". Of course, we had to modify their rules in order to bring them all the way down permanently. To do that, we had to think like the VC, and in that way, we could get ahead of them in thought and behind them in reality.

When we learned about our mission in the flats, we began our single-minded, ruthless trip, much in the same order as one Nguyen Ai Quoc,[86] who later became known to the world as "the one who enlightens". However, we had no intention of letting the ideas of a ship's cook, who had sacrificed thousands of lives, to become a martyr in his teachings of twisted Marxist politics, intimidate or control us. We also never entertained the idea of letting his horde of minions take our lives. No! We were going to survive at all costs.

Each of our new men was married up with an old hand, and when we moved back out into the full combat zone, our company was once again up to its best fighting weight. We were packing heavy, carrying as many 81mm mortar rounds as we could, because we had to depend on ourselves completely. Often in the flatlands, Birth Control came under the control of province, and we could not count on their supporting fires.

We paid particular attention to our grenadiers, those men armed with the M79 grenade launcher (or thump gun). Most of them had the unauthorized 40mm grenade-carrying vests with multiple pockets for carrying ammunition. Across his shoulders, every grenadier carried one or two canvas satchels filled to capacity with 40mm grenades. In the flatlands we also carried smoke rounds, flares, air burst projectiles, and some of those special-purpose 40mm grenades, such as the Flechette rounds that contained 45 little steel darts. Unfortunately, the air burst rounds were always in short-to-no supply. We always carried more high-explosive rounds than we did anything else.

Our grenadiers were proficient in using their knowledge and experience in conjunction with the 400-meter maximum range of the M79 grenade launcher, the 30-meter arming safety distance, and the 5-meter kill radius. When they used their thump guns, they did so with maximum effectiveness for whatever round they were firing, and they never missed. When operating in the flatlands, our grenadiers had an even more important role than they did in the highlands, jungles, and mountains. Because of our previous experiences in the flatlands, I put the word out to make doubly sure our grenadiers and mortars were all up to par.

Our first full day in our new AO was very critical to our mission. We were well aware that the VC knew we were the new guys on the block, and they would undoubtedly be peeping at us. It was important for us not to show fear or indecision, so we strutted to our new AO like we owned the damned place. Of course, we knew the VC would surely test us, and when they did, we were going to kick off on their asses like they were less than stepchildren. Our new AO was a known VC stronghold, and our mission was to seek them out and bring them down.

Two other Cav companies were operating nearby, but not close enough for us to worry about friendly-fire accidents.

We pushed the bush for two whole days before the VC were dumb enough to pop caps at us. They thought they had us figured out, but they did not. When they pulled on us, we were ready, willing, and able. We killed five of them flat, without preliminaries. Two were busted up bigtime, and we allowed the unhappy survivors to drag them off. Then, we continued along our way as if nothing had happened.

We knew we were being watched during our first brief encounter. The only thing we left behind besides the five belly-up VC soldiers were our calling cards. We wanted the survivors to run and say to Papa Ho or whoever was in charge: "Don't fuck with those guys, 'cause if you do, you got an ass-whipping coming."

We expected them to hit us again right away, which they did before we had gone another 150 meters.

The second hit was a tired old Red Chinese tactic designed to confuse us into doing something unintentional, in the name of fear. It was supposed to be a complete surprise and more ferocious than the first one, but it was not.

Two heavily armed VC squads wearing black pajamas hit us while trying to make us think they were bigger and tougher than they actually were. We literally flew into them with a calm, controlled vengeance. Our reactions were well calculated to achieve the same results. The VC chose a second place to hit us that was near the outskirts of a village where they knew we could not obtain air or artillery support. However, they failed to realize that we did not need the extra support.

The VC's guts, brains, and hair were all over the place after they made the same fatal mistake as the first squad – they jumped us. Their other mistakes included firing their Type 63 mortars from an obvious location and using the wrong range when they shot at us.

They had chosen to shoot at us from an old rice storage hut, thinking that we would be afraid to shoot back for fear of hitting civilians. To us, though, the VC were civilians only until they began shooting at us. We could also identify the VC as enemies by their typical garments – black pajamas, flat conical peasant hats, and typical vest-type arrangements for their AK magazines. Sometimes, they even wore short shorts. Because these particular VC were shooting at us, we flew into them and hit that little rice storage hut.

Sfc. Tuzo and his crews made an incredible shot by dropping a single 81mm high-explosive mortar round down through the thatched roof of the little hut. It was a beautiful, short-range, line-of-sight shot, made at an impossibly high angle and so accurate as to seem even more impossible, but true. That shot destroyed the three or four VC soldiers inside the hut.

During that brief firefight, the Third Platoon figured out the most probable location of the observer, and Mac spotted him up in a tree.

The Third Platoon lit his ass, and he fell from the tree like the sack of shit that he was. He must have been taking notes because his little notepad, pencil, and leather pouch fell with him. He howled in pain as he hit the ground very hard. He was still moving, and his keepers immediately went to him and dragged him away. That action suggested that he was an advisor. Otherwise, they would not have been in such a hurry to get his tired ass out of there.

The Third Platoon checked where the observer had fallen, and they found his leather pouch, his pencil, and his small notebook. To our satisfaction, a rather large blood trail led slightly away from the village. We believed that it deliberately led away from the village, when in fact the wounded man had been taken to the village in a roundabout way. Doc B. said the size of the blood trail indicated that the bleeder would not have much blood left when they took him to a doctor.

It is very important for you to understand that the observer had taken his notes in Spanish, particularly Cuban Spanish. Sp4 Sanchez, one of our mortar men, was Cuban. He was born, raised, and briefly schooled in Camaguey, Cuba, before his family escaped to Florida. (These events occurred before Fidel came to power.) Sanchez and some of the men of the Third Platoon agreed that the observer was too big to be Vietnamese, and he was neither Chinese nor Russian. Sanchez was easily able to read the observer's notes.

He said to me, "Top, I'm positive the man we knocked out of the tree is Cuban, and everything we have here strongly points to his nationality as Cuban."

We knew it would be a waste of time and very unwise for us to chase the VC. After all, they were probably hoping that we would chase them, and they were probably waiting to ambush us. We decided to move back into our original route and act as if nothing had happened.

The CO pushed up to Battalion to inform them of our contact with the enemy and to say that approximately 12 VCs would not be returning to their kennel for supper.

We avoided the village because going there would have been another sucker play, and we were fresh out of suckers. Battalion arranged for the ARVNs to investigate the village later. We left our calling card with the dead VC soldiers, who were waiting to be dragged away.

We surely hoped that our first and second firefights with the VC had formed a lasting impression on them. When they came at us later, they would be better prepared. Moreover, just like any human being, they would be out for revenge for the noticeable dent that we had put in their numbers. However, the next time we would not fight them in the same manner.

Our presence in that area, coupled with the fact that we were not afraid to fight the VC and had already been pulling on their chains, was certainly not welcome news to the local Cong commander. We were a direct threat to his reign of terror and power, so he had to either put up or shut up.

After all, we had flown into his little test hit and kicked his ass, right there in plain sight of a village, probably one of his choosing where the local VC commander could show the villagers his power and that of his local Cong units. Instead of running around screaming and getting ourselves killed, like our media and theirs said we would, we did just the opposite. We killed at least 12 VC soldiers in the plain sight of the villagers. Clearly, we were a major problem for the local VC commander, especially because we had iced his black pajama troops without losing any of our men. Then, we had strolled off into the sunset as if nothing had happened.

It had been a set-up by the VC to try to make us look really bad in the eyes of the villagers, but we had ignored our parts in the VC's script, and for that, someone was surely jawed up really tight and out for our blood.

Along our way, we encountered some booby traps, but not nearly as many as we had expected. All of the snaps and traps we discovered could be made safe, if you knew where to look and how to apply the safety devices. Because we did not have time to deactivate them, we simply avoided them.

We chose a FOB position far from the villages and local settlements and one that offered us as many tactical advantages as possible. However, we did not initially occupy that position. Instead, we chose a dummy FOB position, and moved onto it slightly before dark. When complete darkness had settled fully upon us, we slid over to our real FOB position. It was more of an ambush site than a night-time resting position. We lagered into a reasonably tight circle, with our mortars set up in standard fashion, ready to shoot in any direction. Our outer ring of flares and claymores was trip-activated, and our inner ring was command-controlled. If the VC came, we would not be caught short.

Once we were tightly locked in and I had given my sit-rep to the CO, we discussed our situation and the day's activities. We always did this because it helped to unite our efforts, and it brought to light any mistakes we had made that day, which we learned from and never made again. I believed our talks helped us to focus our minds and our efforts, which contributed to making us the fine fighting team that we were.

The VC had purposely called us out that day. However, they had not expected us to blow them away. The VC commander could not afford a repeat performance, so we expected him to come at us that night, most likely after 0300 hours. That was when our news media and most of our detractors said we would surely be caught sleeping or too high on drugs to put up a fight. Such false reports actually helped our situation.

Once it was quiet, I had time to think personally about the day's activities, especially about some things that pulled me down. Mainly, it bothered me that we had to kill human beings. We knew that each of those men in black pajamas whom we had killed had people who loved them, just as we did. However, we were in a situation of kill or be killed, and I am not at all ashamed to say that I encouraged my troops to be first – no shucking or jiving, shoot to kill.

If my thoughts and feelings were wrong, then I am guilty of trying my very best to make sure that your husband, son, boyfriend, father, family member, loved one, and anyone else that you cared about in the Nam returned to you safely. That was my job and my profession, and I did it to the best of my ability. I have asked God many times to forgive me for my sins, and I certainly felt remorse for all of those soldiers who we had killed. Those thoughts haunted me then as they still do now.

On our fourth morning out, we moved along the tactical portion of a low ridge line and followed the many signs that told us the VC had recently used that route. There were some obvious blood trails, and we found a place where the VC had spent the night, as evidenced by the cooking fires and the banana leaves and strings used to carry cooked rice. There was also the unmistakable pure odor of the VC and of nuc mam.[87]

To our left we could see the valley floor, and that is why we were following the ridge line. It provided us with cover and concealment to our right. We also had teams moving along higher up, and they had a good view down the right side of the ridge line.

The Third Platoon was leading, and Nat and a new man were on point. Next were Headquarters, the First Platoon, Weapons, and the

Second Platoon. I was with Headquarters, and I was thinking that it was time for me to drop back with the drag platoon.

The CO interrupted my thoughts when he said, "First Sergeant, do you feel anything new?"

"Yes, sir, I was just fixing to drop back to drag. I have that old, familiar feeling the VC is somewhere near. Because of the ridge line to our right, the VC must be somewhere to our left."

"Top, sometime, you've got to tell me how you do that, although I must admit I have the same feelings. You stay up here with me for a while longer, and let's see how long it takes us to find the VC," advised the CO.

We moved a little more slowly and cautiously. We had gone only 15 or 20 minutes longer, when Nat gave the signal to halt and take cover. We did so, and the CO, Redleg, and I moved forward. Nat and the new trooper were pointing down to the valley floor and in the direction of the trees that the CO had indicated earlier while talking to me.

A lone bird broke cover and flew toward us, which alerted us that the VC might be coming our way. Then, there was a very slight movement in the brush. We glued our eyes to our field glasses and soon spied some black pajamas. Those VC soldiers were hard hats, and some of them wore less conventional uniforms, except for their racing slicks. All of them were carrying weapons, mostly AK-47s. The others carried weapons of a different age, design, caliber, and make. They even had some American M16s. They also had some RPD light machine guns. Altogether, they were well armed and spread out so well that we could not determine their numbers. We were able to pick out their leaders, though. They wore pith helmets with Red Stars, as well as issue boots, and they carried map pouches and side arms.

The VC seemed in high spirits, and they were moving well spread out and observing the rules of snooping and pooping. They did not appear to be carried away with all of those great powers and fighting skills the American news media kept reporting that they possessed. They had a good formation and seemed to know what they were doing. If they had appeared self-righteous and indestructible, we would have known it was a trap, and we would have changed our strategy.

According to our maps, if the VC and we continued heading in our original directions, our trails would cross in about 800 to 1,000 meters. The VC were moving slowly and cautiously, as if they were expecting to hit some shit. Maybe they had heard about how we had chewed up those small units who had hit us, and they were not taking any chances. If that was the case, our reputation was preceding us, and the VC knew the new kids on the block were not going to take any shit from them.

After observing the CO as he studied his map and calculated the distance and speed in his mind, I knew what was about to happen. He looked around at Redleg and me, smiling and looking like a cat that was about to catch and eat a mouse. Then he stabbed his finger at a point on his map and said, "According to my map, this two-hill terrain feature forms a crude saddle, right there at the mouth of this little valley. Now those Victor Charlies are down on the valley floor and are heading toward those two hills. If they don't decide to go up to the ridge line, they will come out about here." He pointed to where he thought the enemy would exit the valley.

Then, he said, "First Sergeant, do you think we can reach the end of this valley before those VC who already have a slight lead on us do? Or do you think it would be better for us to come up behind them and wipe their butts?"

I answered, "Sir, if we start now, and if we can use these trails, we can beat them to the two hills, no sweat. We'll have to hump it hard, but we can do it."

I pointed to a trail on my map that was on the other side of the ridge line. Taking that trail would put the ridge line between the enemy and us, and we would not be able to keep them in sight. On the other hand, the ridge line would serve as a buffer and keep any noise that we might make from reaching our enemies' ears. I would send a three-man security element with a radio to the ridge line and they would prevent the enemy from sneaking up on us.

Upon hearing my plan, the CO said, "Okay, Top, let's do it!"

Then, he moved up front to a position where he could see Nat.

Because Long Claw was still getting his "Vietnam legs", I moved to be near him and the First Platoon. We moved out as rapidly as the overall tactical situation would permit. Once the terrain allowed it, we stretched way out in our running-and-fighting formation. It was difficult to pick up the rhythm because we were negotiating the bush.

It was impossible not to be proud of my magnificent infantry company. I am talking about a full rifle company of American soldiers: three full rifle platoons, a full Weapons Platoon, and the Headquarters section – well over 100 men, loaded down with weapons, ammunition, and equipment. Yet, they were so quiet that I could hardly hear them.

We were well strung out, and I could see only the few men nearest to my position. Had you been observing Black Knight Alfa moving, you too, would have been proud of us, because never at one point in time would you have been able to see our entire company. When the signal to halt was given, you would not be able to see anyone.

I could only see the connecting file from the Headquarters section. Pete and I followed Long Claw, and once during our run, Lt Zen moved forward to our position to talk to me.

Fortunately, the leaves were not dry, and the grassy areas were soft. The trees were large and comfortably spaced, which allowed us to make excellent time. I knew that we were well ahead of the VC, unless they had drastically changed their pace and were now running. I was a bit worried about the CO being so close to the front of the company in our formation.

We covered the distance in record time, and I was surprised when the halt was called. Pete said the CO was ordering the company to lager and he wanted me forward. When Pete and I reached the position where the CO and Redleg were waiting, two machine gun-heavy security teams with the mission to reconnoiter and report were already approaching the nearest of the two hills. After completing their mission, they reported that our objective was clean.

"Top, send two men with a radio back to locate the VC so we will not be surprised," the CO ordered.

I passed the word for the drag platoon to take care of that mission. Two of our fastest troopers were stripped down to the bare necessities, and they went back along the valley floor in search of Victor Charlie. They found him and then moved to a safe position to keep an eye on his every move, which they reported to the CO.

The CO took the lead part of the company first, and I stayed with the Weapons Platoon and the drag platoon, until we received the signal to join the rest of the company. There was no time to get cute. The key word was KISS, and we did just that.

Together the terrain and our mission dictated that we form the company into a box-shaped fighting perimeter rather than our regular circular perimeter. I passed the word to dig in.

Our two-man security team which was watching the enemy reported that the VC were heading straight toward our positions, and they were moving fast as if they were nearing their destination or expecting to meet up with someone. Of course, the latter possibility was a bit disturbing, but in our case, in for a half pint, in for a fifth or a liter.

Our box was designed with our heavy side facing the enemy. We set up in ambush fashion because that was what we planned to do, and the whole company would be present on the ambush site. Because those twin hills were the highest pieces of terrain in the immediate vicinity, we were going to bushwhack the bushwhackers with a lot more class than they were capable of showing. Regardless of what the news media said, we had our ambushes down to an exact science. In the flatlands we did not have the problems that we had when we were operating under a jungle canopy. Sometimes we had trees to worry about, but that was a minor issue that we did not sweat.

Sfc. Tuzo found a good protective position and set up our mortars there. Then he sent an observer to a good observation position very near the heavy side of our box. (The CO was with the heavy side, along with Redleg and Doc B.) Within minutes our box was as solid as the word and as hard as the times were in 1932.

Our two-man observation team came home and personally reported to the CO that old Victor Charlie was still heading directly toward the hard side of our box and if he did not change his direction, he would walk right into our kill zone. We were pleased with that news, but some bad news came along with it. The unit we had spotted and were waiting to bushwhack was definitely a company-size Viet Cong unit consisting mostly of hard hats. At least two advisors were with them, and one was a short, stocky, brown-haired Caucasian.

"Sir, we were close enough, just before coming home, to hear one of the advisors, the Caucasian, chew one of the VC soldiers out for making a mistake. And, well, we are not sure about what we are thinking, but ... well, sir. We both overheard that guy, and, sir, he was speaking American English. He ..."

The second man added, "Sir, they have their shit together. We didn't see all of them from the ridge 'cause they were so well spread out. There are NVA cadres with them, and they are packing heavy. They have a lot of RPDs and RPGs, plus they have mortars along with them, but for some reason their mortars are near the lead."

Although our security told us that the enemy was heading straight for our positions, we figured that they would pass us by. That was not true. They were actually heading directly toward the same piece of terrain that we occupied. So, the VC were doing something unexpected for once.

We had to remain as flexible as ever to adjust to this unexpected situation, and we had to move a few things.

We wanted the enemy to pass by our ambush site so that we could get a side shot at them. However, the die was cast differently, and it was far too late for us to pick up our marbles and go home or to call the game because of rain. Instead, we called our security teams home.

When an enemy unit came directly toward you, which was less than desirable, you could only play hell with the lead element. Unfortunately, that gave the elements following the lead plenty of time to move, even if you shot the entire lead element. To complicate matters, you had to shoot over the dead bodies of the lead men, which presented an obstacle to you and an advantage to the enemy.

Adding to our discomfort was the fact that Birth Control did not recognize our push or call sign. Redleg pushed up to Battalion. When he reached them, he learned that we would not receive artillery support. Something was wrong somewhere, and Battalion told us to wait.

There we sat, directly in the path of an advancing, company-size, VC unit, who were apparently very well trained and packing heavy, not to mention that an American-speaking advisor accompanied them. Our situation was quite clear; we were going to have to shit or get off the pot.

Our security teams were home and in position, and anyone outside our box became fair game. Rules were rules.

We lay dog and waited for them to come straight to us. The CO would pop the first cap. He was on line and by that time had his intended target lined up.

The lead man was upon us, but the VC did not detect our presence. When the CO hit him, we could see puffs of dust fly from his black pajamas as the small but powerful 5.56mm projectiles tore into him. The force and shock of the small projectiles literally blew him apart. He had been wearing the traditional web harness with three long magazine pouches across his chest. Those pouches exploded as some of the rounds struck his AK-47 and sang a song of finality as they ricocheted in another direction.

The entire lead element of the VC unit fell dead. Our mortar rounds were falling on what we hoped would be the rear of their formation, which was reputedly very good. Our machine guns and thump guns worked the line, along with our M16s. We were cutting our sworn enemy to ribbons. Carnage was the name of our game, and we did not cut the VC any slack. Payback was a motherfucker.

On 41st Street, this saying was once popular: "Do unto others before they do unto you". In the light of that old proverbial south-side saying, we did unto the Viet Cong.

We performed nicely until the piles of dead VC soldiers in front of the heavy side of our box made it impossible for us to see our remaining enemies. They were probably getting away.

"Damn it, Top, I want that brown-haired, American-speaking advisor!" yelled the CO.

I had the feeling that he would escape our meat grinder. As expected, some of the VC were running away while the remaining hard-core men attempted to draw our fire, but we were not falling for that old shit. Fire discipline and ammunition control were two of the hallmarks of our Grand Company. Much like the men of General Lee's Army of Northern Virginia, our troops knew how to make each shot count for one VC and to use their sharpshooting skills just as Johnny Reb had done. When the VC moved and showed themselves, our troopers became Johnny Reb on the spot and popped them dead. Our mortars had already stopped shooting to conserve ammunition. There were no set rules on how long we might have to hold our positions.

The CO ordered us to hold our fire, and we knew to do so unless we were threatened. Everyone remained still so as not to give away our positions. The VC had trained snipers, and they were good, so we had to be wary of the tall treetops.

We had learned our lessons well in the Ia Drang Valley, the Bong Son Plains, A Shau, Hue, and Khe Sanh, to name just a few of the places where we had learned to stay alive. Because of our experience we certainly knew how to apply ourselves in threatening situations.

The VC tried to flank us, thinking that our ambush was an L-shaped one. The far side of our box was just as strong, and the VC found to their great and painful dismay that we did not operate by the book. No matter which way they came at us, they met a solid wall of coordinated, accurate fire.

I moved up beside my CO and reported that we were good all around and that we had no serious casualties. Lt Zen had received a flesh wound while helping to hump ammo from the Second Platoon's position, but he was coming along very well. He was a fast learner and a good man.

"What do you think, Top? We surely do have a large body count, but for some reason, I …" Zen's voice trailed off. He did not have to say anything because I felt it, too.

I was experiencing the same uneasy feeling that something was definitely wrong! I could tell from the expressions on my troopers' faces that they were feeling the same uneasiness.

This feeling was gut-wrenching and heart-and-mind-bending, and it always struck us after a kill. We had plainly slaughtered the VC's lead element, and there was the gore of blood and guts all over the place. None of us felt like cheering. Sweet Jesus, they had walked right up on us, and we had simply shot them down. We could still hear their grunts and screams in our minds. Oh God, oh Jesus! I wondered how much more killing and how much more pressure my mind would be able to bear before I went all the way around the bend.

Have you ever seen a man with his guts blown out?

"Make you wanna holler, throw up both your hands."[88]

I knew deep down that it was not over. The VC would be back. My sweet Lord, I was burdened to the ground, carrying the lives of Your sons and loved ones on my shoulders. I just knew that I would not be able to carry such a great load for much longer. My days were numbered. "Make me feel like my time ain't long".[89]

Those VC had killed many American soldiers before they were unfortunate enough to walk in on Black Knight Alfa. I wondered when our turn would come, when we would be on the receiving end of this awful violence.

I told Pete to stay where he was, and I moved over to a lone tree where I got down on my knees and prayed like I had never prayed before that time. I also cried. Several of my tears dropped onto my hands, but I could not feel what should have been their warm saltiness. Oh my God, was I losing my ability to feel? Was I becoming used to and starting to accept the cold-handed touch of old Death? Was I helping the dead to bury the dead? I could now see myself among them.

After I finished my prayer, I went back to tell the CO that I felt the VC were going to make a second run on us. We had taken out too many of them, including a lot of experienced hard hats, and the VC would be forced to make a second mistake, but it was a matter of honor and saving face.

Thank goodness for our presence of mind and our SOP, which had us hold our defensive positions after a successful hit. We had also decided earlier to shift left, so the enemy would not know where our machine guns were located.

The first salvo of 82mm enemy mortar rounds fell short and blew away some of the piled-up bodies in front of the heavy side of our box. The resulting explosions caused it to truly rain Viet Cong body parts. The VC mortar men must have believed their first salvo was on target, because they let go again and at the same range. They were raising hell with their own dead soldiers and missing our positions by a wide enough margin that we had time, by using our counter mortars, to get a good make on their positions. Our mortar men shot back with devastating results. Unfortunately, we did not have enough ammunition to take out all of the VC mortar positions.

We heard their leaders shouting orders as they tried to get up the steam to make a run on us.

Are you ready for a strange quirk of fate? Our luck of biting off more than we could chew was holding steady, but we were not aware of this fact until after our battle. We had once again hit an enemy battalion. Specifically, we had hit the lead company of K-5 Battalion. We had locked up with our old nemesis, K-5, many times before, and it is still a mystery to me why we always seemed to be drawn together. They were like bad pennies coming back to haunt us, because we sure as hell reduced their numbers by an alarming rate each time we ran into them.

They pulled on us as if they knew who we were and they were seeking revenge for the fact that we had literally wiped them out twice before. Now they were going for thirds, thinking that their daunting numbers would make us an easy kill. However, their first mistake was pulling on us, and their second mistake was lifting their mortar fire. They were in the process of making their third mistake, as they rushed our rock-steady fighting positions.

Their commander made the decision to make a run on us before we could get artillery support or gunslingers in to help us. Maybe he figured

271

that since we had not put any real shit on his ass that he was in the clear to bring us down. The VC commander thought he had the edge; otherwise, he never would have made a run on us in broad daylight.

They came in a wave, screaming their heads off. We distinctly caught the words "American Black Knight, you die now!" So the bastards knew who we were. At that time, we did not know who they were. Nevertheless, we would still try to blow their heads off.

It was rock and roll time.

We held our fire until we were sure of first-round kills. The CO held back until we could smell shit. Then he popped the first cap. While trying to attack us from all sides, the enemy fell like newly mown wheat. Our box was steady, and our troopers were well dug in and using all available cover. Our combined accurate fire was like the super-sharp scythe in the hands of old Death. Once again, we reduced the number of personnel in the enemies' K-5 Battalion. Finally showing some good sense, they pulled back to hide. One thing was certain: they stuck out their arm and drew back a nub.

Victor Charlie opened up again with his mortars, but it was too late for him. Redleg had solid communication with Birth Control, and help was already in the air. The 1st Battalion of the 77th was shooting for us – those wonderful cannoneers of the En Garde, or the Golden Yellows. I think it was Bravo Battery 1st Battalion. With Redleg's assistance, they dropped their 105mm Howitzer projectiles, each at 38 pounds of high explosives, dead onto the VC's asses. After that hit, the more sensible VC soldiers tucked their tails between their legs and melted away.

Black Knight Alfa knew it was all over and that the VC would not be coming back any time soon. It stood to reason, however, that we would have to fight them all over again later, but even with their Russian, Cuban, and Chinese advisors, we went through them like a whole box of Ex-Lax. Those who survived ran for the hills to catch up to their advisors, who were well in the lead.

We had gunslingers on station and dust-off was prompt. Our log personnel was also prompt, and we were resupplied right there on position. S-2 was checking and counting the VC bodies.

Our new supplies included everything we needed, even fresh water. An ARVN officer was with the battalion commander, and our S-2 was giving the officer some of the stuff he had collected from K-5.

As we received our supplies, I told the platoon sergeants to send the new men to me. Because it had been their first firelight with Black Knight Alfa, I took them to the killing ground so they could see up close the true face of old Death and the faces of their sworn enemies.

They had stood up well under the pressure of their first contact and firelight with Charlie. They knew that we had taken out a most determined and well-trained enemy, and I made sure they fully understood that we had won because we were better trained, we fought as a team, and we were more determined to live. I also made sure they understood that it was impossible to tell just by looking at the Vietnamese whether they were from North or South Vietnam. Additionally, I explained that the Viet Cong, Charlie Cong, and Victor Charlie were all one and the same enemy. The news media preferred to use the first name, we preferred the second (as well as several unmentionable names), and the people who held the VC in higher esteem than the news media preferred the third.

I told the new men that the Cong was a "feeling" and often one that could not be seen until it was too late, which was the reason we always had to keep our guard up. We had to be wary of the VC's indirect operations and refuse to accept soda from pretty little girls and to not trust any little boys who rode water buffaloes near our positions. I told the men about a similar situation when Tran had stopped and searched a Viet Cong boy. The kid was carrying an accurate drawing of our positions and the locations of our machine guns. If we had not been suspicious of the boy, we might have lost our lives.

Whenever the situation permitted, I always gave my new men such a briefing. I showed them the leech bites on the VC's bodies because the media said that leeches did not bite the NVA or the VC. It was too bad that the media did not tell that lie to the leeches. I showed the men the drag cords around the lifeless wrists and ankles of the dead men and explained their purpose.

Some of our new men wanted to collect souvenirs, and I explained to them why they should never rob any personal items from the bodies of the dead. Doing so would be sacrilegious and way beneath our dignity. After all, we were Christian soldiers. Of course, we sometimes took pith helmets with Red Stars, steel pots, racing slicks, and AKs, but those were not personal items, and besides, they made excellent trading materials.

On the other hand, the VC often stole from us. Not only did they take our weapons, but they also stripped our dead soldiers of personal belongings. We often discovered VC soldiers who carried American wallets, photos, Zippo lighters, and other possessions taken from our dead soldiers.

I pointed out the differences between a VC officer, an NCO, and a common trooper. They studied the Chinese-made boot worn by the officers and the racing slicks of the common troopers. Finally, I told them to get a good whiff of the VC's body odor, their equipment, and their blood and shit.

During my macabre period of instruction, I hoped to gain and hold their attention as I taught them ways to survive out in the bush while fighting our deadly enemies. I most certainly gave them every important bit of survival information that I could in the given time that I had. Now you might think it was overkill, giving instruction on a battlefield littered with dead enemy soldiers, but what better place was there to talk about life and death? My job, my sworn duty to you, was to bring them back alive, and there were no ends to which I would not go to do what I was sworn to do. I wanted all of the soldiers in my company to live, and I wanted them to walk out of Vietnam just as they had walked in.

In the aftermath of our fight with K-5, we noted that they were much better equipped than the last time we had met them. Their black uniforms were much better constructed, and their "Made in China" web gear was almost new. The M1940 Tokarev and the SKS Carbine Soviet-made rifles had been largely replaced by AK-47 Kalashnikov assault rifles. They were carrying a lot more RPD light machine guns and RPGs. They also had a few of our M16 rifles.

We spent the night in the area where we had fought K-5. Of course, we did not stay in the same positions. Despite what the news media believed and falsely reported, the VC never came back to use those drag cords on the bodies of their dead soldiers.

During our talk that night, the CO and I had to admit that in comparison with the last group of VC soldiers we had fought, the new breed was much more cunning, better trained, better equipped, and better armed. They also did not run away until they were bloody enough to know that their ass had been badly whipped. They had been very well organized when they hit us, and in that way, the VC were more dangerous than they had been in the past.

We never found the brown-haired Caucasian who spoke such good American English. That was a terrible shame because we wanted his ass very badly.

The Master of Ceremonies

After cutting up K-5, we worked our area for a number of days before we saw any black pajama-clad individuals who were armed. However, they did not pop caps at us. When we found the VC stronghold, old Victor Charlie showed us a ghost. In other words, the VC had simply moved somewhere else and had gone a little deeper underground.

In the meantime, whenever we met the VC and they had the balls to stand and fight, we kicked off on their butts. One of those times, we cornered three of them loaded down with rice taken from a village. We gave them the chance to give up, but their leader miscalculated the difference between shutting up and giving up, so we had to bring them down.

We returned the rice to the village, and while we were there, Doc B. cured a sick child and put some drops into the eyes of an old lady suffering from cataracts. Maybe that rice still found its way into the stomachs of the VC soldiers, but I think we proved to those villagers that we were not the ogres that the VC had told them we were.

One night we set up our FOB at the junction of a trail leading down from the mountains. Actually, it was more of an ambush site than a FOB. We did not have any contact with nor did we see the VC for three days, so we decided to stir the pot a little by surprising anyone who came down the trail heading for the junction.

Soon after our ambush site was ready, along came a well-armed party carrying a lot of stuff down from the mountain. We dropped them cleanly. Because of the time and the terrain, we simply shifted our positions after the hit and dug in a little deeper. We spent the rest of the night in the same positions. Naturally, we had a Plan B and alternative positions to fall back on, if the VC came back for more.

That night, the VC surprised us by actually coming back. However, they did not mount an attack. We knew they were out there, and they knew we were nearby. We expected a mortar of rockets because Redleg received that information during his push with Birth Control.

We did not call for illumination. Instead, the CO decided to wait and call old Victor Charlie's bluff. We waited and watched. Although we could hear the VC moving around, they did not move toward us, nor did it appear that they were trying to find us.

Then, old Victor Charlie popped another surprise on us. He probably did this because we had not called Rolling Thunder down on him and had not even popped a flare or a cap on his ass. Maybe he "assumed" that we did not have artillery support. Evidently, the VC commander was unaware of the old saying that "Assumption is the mother of all fuck-ups" because we did, in fact, have all of the fire support we needed. We were just trying an all-day (or an all-night) sucker trick on the VC.

The VC's surprise for us came from the sky in the form of a loud, clear voice that spoke English (although it was not an American dialect). Everyone could hear and understand what the voice was saying through some type of megaphone.

The "master of ceremonies" began by extolling the many virtues of the People's Army of the Viet Cong. Then he moved smoothly into such rhetoric as telling our black soldiers that they should rise up and rebel against their white officers and "masters" and that they should shoot and frag their leaders and come over to the side of the victorious People's Viet Cong. He promised that if they did, the VC would welcome them with open arms and would treat them like men.

The master of ceremonies went so far as to call the CO and me by our correct names – Captain Brooks and First Sergeant Steen. He had some very unkind and uncomplimentary things to say about us. As long as he did not say anything nasty about our mothers, everything was cool. However, what was not cool was the fact that the master of ceremonies knew our names. Could he be the brown-haired white man from K-5? Our surveillance and security team, who had heard that man's voice before, said that it was not the same man.

277

The person who used the megaphone (or whatever it was) to amplify his voice ranted and raved until he started to become a definite bore. I noted that when he said Black Knight Alfa, he screwed up the Knight and the Alfa in the traditional Vietnamese fashion, so the master of ceremonies was either Vietnamese or Chinese. He was certainly not aware that his little tirade was not working and that it was all lost on us men of Black Knight Alfa. We bloods still carried the image of our butchered brother who was bled and smoked like a pig and then hung out to dry on that trail. If "that" was an example of how the VC treated a black man like a man, well …

I knew without a doubt in my mind and heart that our troops had already peeped in on the master of ceremonies, and all of his efforts were going to waste. Sure, I will stand right up and say that I wished I had been able to get a shot at the mother or had the opportunity to jam his megaphone all the way up his ass. However, we were aware that the VC might be using that tired, old rabble-rouser trick to provoke us into shooting at them, which would tell them exactly where we were located. It was an old VC trick, tried and tried again on Black Knight Alfa, but it did not work.

I was thinking about that when I heard two distinct explosions, one right on the heels of the other. WHAM! WHAM! The explosions were definitely caused by exploding fragmentation hand grenades, and I honestly believe that those hand grenades were American-made M26s.

Some very loud shrieks of pain, loud moaning, and much cursing in Vietnamese followed the two explosions. Then, there was a sudden outbreak of automatic weapons fire. The VC were shooting at the wind.

The master of ceremonies was suddenly very quiet.

Both the CO and I noted with great satisfaction that not one round was popped on our side. Mum was the word, although I heard some quiet snickering from our men.

The badly hurt VC soldiers screamed with rage, and the VC seemed to be firing at least two full 30-round magazines from their AK-47s before they got control of what was left of them. Then it became extremely quiet, except for an occasional low moan coming from their side.

During that quiet time, I overheard part of a hurried conversation between Pete and the guys in the hole next to ours. Pete was grinning from ear to ear. Then there was a most distinct cheer over our company net. Something was afoot.

The VC fired off some additional rounds to cover their hasty withdrawal, and for the first time, they were dragging off their dead. I hoped that one of those being dragged off was the asshole we had nicknamed the master of ceremonies.

After that little Marxist, wooden-nickel opera, which was undoubtedly taken from the scripts of the now-defunct Communist Manifesto (1848), the rest of the night was quiet and peaceful.

When first light crept in and pushed the darkness away, I went to the positions of the platoons that were most directly in line with the sound of the voice of last night's master of ceremonies and the resulting two hand-grenade explosions. I knew something had gone down, and I had the feeling that Black Knight Alfa was somehow responsible for the sudden demise of our late-night master of ceremonies.

I knew that I was on to something when I found JoJo and Nat in the same fighting position, which was not a lock-up position from their two platoons. With a little friendly persuasion from me, JoJo and Nat agreed to come clean.

They told me they had volunteered to take out the master of ceremonies because he had royally pissed off the men of Black Knight Alfa. The VC made the grievous error of trying to sow seeds of racial hatred and ignorance among the men of the Grand Company. All of US knew the bastard was lying through his betelenut-stained teeth. He had also made the mistake of failing to realize that we were a team with a resolute determination to stick together, especially against stupid bastards like him and his Russian and Chinese puppet masters.

With the help of others in the company, JoJo and Nat had stripped off some of their gear and slipped silently out of our perimeter to go hunting. Born and raised near the Louisiana swamps, JoJo had grown up hunting snakes and alligators for fun. He was in his element. Nat, however, had a baby face and looked rather like an altar boy. Of course, the nature of his countenance changed when it was time to kill. Then he turned into a personified version of the Grim Reaper. That master of ceremonies did not have a chance against the wrath of JoJo and Nat. JoJo could follow the sound of a cottonmouth slithering through the water or two mosquitoes making love on a leaf in the pale moonlight. Therefore, it had been child's play for him to zero in on the sounds of the bastard's ranting voice and to quickly locate the master of ceremonies.

On the way to their pitiful target, JoJo and Nat had encountered two VC soldiers and had silently taken them down. They had found the man with the megaphone squatting down behind a tree, surrounded by an unknown number of VC protectors. Although JoJo and Nat had been unable to see the speaker's shoes, they had surmised from his clean uniform and manner that he was an NVA officer.

After pulling the pins of their grenades and quietly allowing the firing mechanisms to activate, JoJo and Nat had waited until the time train functioned to their desired time. Then they had thrown the M26 fragmentation hand grenades right into the middle of the little VC group. Nat said that the master of ceremonies had surely gone to hell wearing his megaphone jammed through his mouth and out the back of his head.

Once their job was finished, JoJo and Nat had safely returned to our positions. Their return trip had been easier because the VC had made a lot of noise while venting their anger and frustration at the loss of their high-ranking political officer.

Upon hearing of JoJo and Nat's amazing accomplishment, I had to "slap" the two commandos on the wrist and invent a good lie for the CO. Well, sir, now I am telling the truth. I am sorry that I had to lie to you, but somehow I think you already knew the truth of the matter.

The trails of spilled blood and guts told the story. A lot of dead VC bodies were dragged away that night, except for the two soldiers that JoJo and Nat had taken out on their way to bring down the distinguished master of ceremonies.

By the way, we never did find out how the master of ceremonies knew our names.

The Sniper

SNIP-ER (sni'per) 1. Military. A skilled rifleman detailed to spot and pick off enemy soldiers from a concealed place. 2. One who shoots at other people from a concealed place.

The American Heritage Dictionary
New College Edition
1969–1976

Our campaigns in the flatlands were very taxing and required detailed planning, precise execution, and the frequent need to hold ourselves in check. The stress factors were enormous. We did not want another My Lai (September 1969), not just because of the notoriety and the wrongful actions on anyone's part, but because we did not want in any way to harm or kill innocent people. We were not the mindless, drug-headed murderers of the innocent and each other that our many detractors have always accused us of being.

On the contrary, Black Knight Alfa never at any time, with intent of malice or disregard for the innocent, fired our weapons in anger, hate, or under the influence of drugs. We never killed innocent civilians. When we brought our enemies down, they were armed and usually shooting at us. We were soldiers and Americans who conducted ourselves in accordance with the proud traditions of our great country. Our heritage and those many wonderful professional attributes made us who we were and who we shall always be.

Here is a case in point: our mission was to assist an ARVN Ranger unit in the search for an unknown VC command center that the cowardly bastards had established within a "pacified" village. The VC were known to hide behind old people, the skirts of women, and the shitty diapers of babies. Our part of the mission was to move under the cover of darkness to our blocking positions that would surround the entire village and to be there before dawn. We referred to such a mission as "cordon and search". In our case, we were not supposed to do the searching; the Vietnamese Rangers would carry that out. We were the "cordon" part of the mission. Once we surrounded the village, we were not supposed to let anyone in or out.

To this day, I believe that we moved to that village under the cover of darkness, and we assumed our positions without anyone in the village knowing of our presence. That was quite a feat, considering the terrain, the size of the village, and the fact that the VC had guards posted on the side of the village closest to the treeline.

Even the VC guards did not see or hear us as we moved into position. The only living creature from the village that knew we were there was a skinny, old dog that ran out and barked once. Then he wagged his scrawny tail and became our friend.

I think that poor, old fellow probably had only one bark left in him, because he was so skinny that his ribs looked like railroad ties. He seemed confused and uncertain as to what he had to do next. Sp4 Caldwell responded by whispering soothing words and then beckoning the dog to his side. The dog wagged his tail and rushed to nuzzle Caldwell. It was a relief to see that we would not have to subdue the old fellow. He was just a friendly, old mutt in the wrong place at the wrong time. None of us had the heart to hurt him.

Instead, we fed him a big breakfast of C-rations and after that, the mutt refused to go away. He made himself at home, staying close to Caldwell, who gave him the name "Blue Max". The dog seemed to like his new name and responded to it immediately.

When first light came, the ARVNs were not there. Within minutes, the villagers knew that we had them cordoned off. Before long, our new friend bit one of the male villagers who had kicked him. When the man pulled a knife and went after Blue Max, the dog ran to Caldwell for protection. We noticed that the man's knife was identical to those typically issued to our Special Forces units, and we were suspicious of where the man had gotten it.

When the angry villager cornered Blue Max, Caldwell intervened and stuck the muzzle of his M16 in the man's face. The language barrier did not interfere with the obvious message of what would happen next if the man hurt Blue Max. The villager was a very strong young man in abnormally good physical condition, a detail that made us even more suspicious. Seeing the cold look in Caldwell's blue eyes, the man backed off. However, he did not keep quiet. He shot off his big mouth, speaking in Vietnamese, of course.

Tran was too far away to hear what the man was saying; however, Redleg's RTO, Sp4 Li Ping, clearly heard what the man said. Li-Ping had completed the Vietnamese language course with outstanding grades. He was Chinese-American and spoke several foreign languages. He called Tran and told him what the villager said to get corroboration on the translation. Tran told the CO while we detained the angry villager. What he had said got him into serious trouble. He had lost his head and yelled that he was a sergeant in the Viet Cong, as well as a hard hat. The ARVNs were certainly going to be very happy to get their hands on that loud-mouthed bragger.

Our kindness to the skinny, old dog paid off. I think that old dog was protecting Caldwell when he bit the VC who had posed as a villager. The dog's owner came forward to say that the loud-mouthed VC was always kicking the old dog around, but that this was the first time the dog had fought back. Then, the dog's owner whispered to Tran where he could find the VC sergeant's uniforms and equipment. Big Mouth had three uniforms – one black and two of the other NVA and VC colors. He had a good-looking AK-47 and three automatic handguns. We gathered a lot of other useful information from the VC's living space. Tran and some of our troopers brought the stuff outside and secured it until the ARVNs arrived.

The Cong trapped inside the village were forced to put their Plan B into operation, and many things began to occur when it was clear that we were not letting anyone out. The VC forced the old people and the women with babies and children to come out of their homes and to stand closely together so that the VC could hide behind a human shield of innocent people.

Now if that was not a pure act of cowardice, I would surely like to know what is.

The stinking bastards were crouching down behind the skirts of the old women and some bare-assed babies because they knew we would not fire upon the innocent villagers. I was most happy to note that some of those cowards were already bloodied and wearing bandages over various parts of their bodies. We knew they had run afoul with Black Knight Alfa and were carrying the lumps and scars to prove it.

The terrified villagers stood facing us. One old man, who prayed to his God, reminded me of my grandfather back in the Mississippi Delta. Sweet Jesus, there was no way I could shoot. Neither could anyone else, for that matter.

So there we stood after walking through the Valley of Death without a scratch, after locking up with Charlie at the Ia Drang, Bong Son, Khe Sanh, and Hue. We had taken on entire regiments and kicked K-5's ass. Yet, there we were, facing a few assholes who could shoot us, but we had no sane way to drop them. Where in the hell were the ARVN Rangers?

There were only four VC soldiers, and each was armed with an AK. Our troops had a hard lock on the village, and there was no way the VC was going to get by us.

I was afraid if the VC took us out, the remainder of our company would take out the VC and the victimized villagers, and all of those prime ingredients would add up to another My Lai.

I heard the CO on his radio ordering our troopers, "No matter what happens to us, DON'T SHOOT. DON'T POP CAPS! Hold on, the ARVNs will be here shortly."

I believed that all of us were thinking about our families back in the States when we looked at the helpless villagers. No, we could not shoot. I kept telling myself that repeatedly. We were not the heartless hopheads that the news media portrayed us to be. While thinking about that, I knew that none of our troopers would fire. We were soldiers in the truest sense, and we were Black Knight Alfa, the Grand Company.

Where in the hell were the ARVN Rangers? They were supposed to be there on the ground at first light.

BLAM! A single shot rang out, and I thought it was all over for us.

Most of the villagers hit the ground, and the four VC with weapons tried to run, but they fell over their human shields. That provided us with the opportunity to bring them down and without firing a shot.

"Medic! Medic!" came the voice of one of our troopers.

I saw California running toward where one of my troopers lay face-down and motionless.

"Top, we got us a sniper. He shot Wilson in the back, but California says he will be okay. He is okay!"

I could hardly hear or recognize Mac's voice on the radio. I started to get angry and to lose my temper. I wanted to kill the VC bastard nearest to me. One of my troopers was down, shot in the back by some bastard Victor Coward who was hiding and taking potshots at us.

Blam! Blam! Two more shots rang out, and another of my men fell forward.

The shots were not coming from the distant trees, so the sniper had to be inside the village. Only one tall structure existed in the village from where a sniper could shoot down at us, and it stood high above the other houses in the village. It appeared to be some kind of special house built on stilts, and it had curved eaves and dragonheads painted red, black, and gold.

Blam! The sniper fired again. He had a Russian-made sniper's rifle, which probably had a very good scope. However, his last shot did not hit anyone.

With two of our troopers down, I felt as if I had been hit, too. I certainly wanted to shoot back at him, but there was a very good chance that innocent people might be in that house, maybe even a monk or some other holy man. I came close to losing my cool. The load was so heavy that I wanted to blow that damned house and the sniper away no matter who the hell was inside. I knew that if I gave the word, my troopers would shoot.

"It's okay, Top. We'll get the bastard. All the guys know why we can't blow that damn place away. I think most of the villagers are on our side. Top, Wilson is not dead. His rucksack saved his life. We got wounded but no KIAs. We will get that dirty bastard!"

Pete's voice came from far away. What helped me the most was when he said that our two wounded troopers were very much alive. I whispered a special thanks to God for saving the lives of my fine soldiers and for saving my career.

Blam! Blam! Two more shots rang out, and I heard someone scream in pain. Those shots were too close together for a bolt-action rifle. Judging from the blast signature, I guessed that the sniper was using a Dragunov 7.62 rim fire, and if my memory served me correctly, he had a box magazine that could hold 10 cartridges.

I pointed to the sniper's location and yelled for everyone to get down and stay down.

All of us hid behind something sturdy.

By that time, I had pushed aside my anger and was thinking objectively again. Clearly, the sniper was inexperienced. Otherwise, he would have taken out our CO first and then me. His hitting Wilson's rucksack told me that he had been firing at the center of mass, a method that usually guaranteed a hit. An expert sniper using the short range with the Russian PSO-1 4x power scope would have taken a head shot. The sniper had to be an amateur, and that likelihood presented us with an advantage.

"Alfa Five, Alfa Two. Come on back!" called Sergeant E-5 Tashida, the leader of the Second Platoon.

Pete handed me the mike.

"Two, this is Five. Go," I responded.

"Five, we know positively where the sniper is located. He is under the roof closest to your side, and we can take him out positively. Over."

"Negative, Two!" the CO pushed in. "We will wait for the ARVNs. Don't anybody do anything but keep down and wait. Six OUT!"

Now that was the way that Captain Brooks issued an order. You had better believe that everyone understood it. I was willing to bet there was not a man among us who did not want to personally take the sniper down, but we followed the CO's instructions and waited, although a bit impatiently.

That is when old Fate decided to play his card, and the sniper made a huge mistake. Perhaps the Victor Coward was shooting at one of us, but he hit a villager. It was even worse that the victim was a woman holding a baby. The woman had been seeking cover when the 7.62mm slug hit her. The striking energy lifted the woman off her feet and threw her face-down onto the hard-packed earth. The baby flew from her arms and tumbled head over heels backward. One of our troopers tried to catch the baby but missed. The baby screamed in shock, fear, panic, and sudden pain.

Doc B. was already moving toward the downed woman and her baby. The cowardly sniper shot at him but missed, which was a blessing for us. The CO yelled for Doc B. to get back to cover, but Doc B. did not listen. He was also a doctor at heart.

The CO was now majorly pissed off. His eyes turned cold and hard like steel as he snatched the mike from Danzig and began to issue some slightly different orders.

"Alfa Two. This is Six. Can you get that bastard without getting anyone else killed? Over!"

"Six, Alfa Two. That's most affirm. Now we know for sure where that motherfucker is holed up. Over."

The CO ordered, "Then you go and get his ass. Take the bastard down. Take his ass down. NOW! Out."

Mac keyed the mike and then yelled, "Go get him, Two!"

The troopers closest to the woman and her baby moved quickly to protect them and Doc B. The woman lay still and silent, but the baby screamed from the top of its lungs, which appeared to be a good sign.

Once again, Black Knight Alfa served as true soldiers and good men. They shielded the Vietnamese woman and her baby with their bodies. That is exactly how most of our American soldiers acted. They were not hopheaded, mad dogs who killed each other and innocent Vietnamese civilians, as the media and our detractors wanted everyone back home to believe.

Some of the villagers saw our troopers' actions, and they pointed toward the roof of the tall house and screamed curses at the sniper.

Pete said, "Top, we have birds inbound. The ARVNs are coming. The Third Platoon is popping smoke, and the CO said his last orders still stand."

The Second Platoon was in the process of taking the sniper down. Meanwhile, Tran talked to the villagers and kept them away from the possible line of fire. The villagers who had seen the woman shot were well aware of who their real enemies were, and a small group of them attacked and spat on the four VC that we were holding captive.

Elements from the Second Platoon had the house surrounded, and a squad was already inside and moving on the sniper. He had no place to go except hell, unless he was planning to sprout wings and fly away.

The squad from the Second Platoon radioed that they were within sight of the sniper. We could hear them yelling through Pete's speaker.

"Put it down NOW!"

"Drop it, you bastard, drop it I say!"

A single shot rang out from the Dragunov, followed by an undetermined number of shots from our M16s. A long, deafening silence followed.

Somewhere among the innocent villagers, a baby was crying.

Our troops cornered the bastard who was trying to eject a magazine. Evidently, the sniper did not know that on the Drag, you must pull the magazine down. There was still a round in the chamber, and the sniper used it to try to take out one of our troopers. Having lost their patience, our men popped the bastard.

By that time, the ARVNs were there, and the CO quickly briefed their officer in charge, who then sent some of his Rangers to help. It was not necessary, though, because it was all over for the sniper. Our troops backed off and let the ARVN Rangers handle the mess.

The Rangers brought the sniper's body out to the main village street and contemptuously dumped it on the ground for the villagers to see. The sniper was a woman! Even some of the villagers were surprised.

The ARVN Rangers also brought out the sniper's cache of weapons and equipment, which had been hidden under the roof of the sacred house. The female sniper had possessed a radio (which had been turned on), two AK-47s, a pistol, grenades, and plenty of ammunition. As I had figured, her weapon was a Russian-made Dragunov with a PSO-1 scope.

After the villagers saw who the sniper was and because she had shot a woman with a baby, they turned state's witness and rolled over on the VC. They revealed to the Rangers all of the known secret hiding places of the VC, including those underground.

The ARVN Rangers found the VC perpetrators cowering behind sacks of rice, under dirty clothes, and in caves under the village. One entrance to the VC underground hiding place was under the sacred house, and another was under a nuc mam fermenting pot. The third entrance was next to the local shithouse. The ARVNs caught the local commander and his senior lieutenant trying to escape out through that third entrance. However, because of a slight miscalculation concerning which boards were to be removed, the commander and his aides had to be cleaned up before they were fit to be carried away.

With the aid of the villagers, we caught around 18 to 20 hard-core Victor Cowards in our subsequent raid. Some of them were turned in by their families, including the loud-mouthed sergeant whose brother turned him in. His brother was none other than the owner of Blue Max.

While the ARVN teams conducted the search, we made sure that no one got past us. Our medevac birds came in with doctors and medical personnel. They treated the baby for a fractured arm and returned it to its father. Although Doc B. did all that he could for her, the baby's mother did not survive. Wilson had suffered damage to one of his lungs, and he was taken back to the States. Our other wounded troopers went to either Phu Bai or to the hospital ship, the USS *Repose*. The ARVNs promised to come back and care for the other wounded villagers.

When the operation was finished, we got ourselves ready to move on down the line. Before we left, some of the villagers kindly gave our soldiers cooked crabs, rice cakes, home-made brew, and fresh coconuts and bananas. The owner of the real hero of that operation – Blue Max, the skinny, old dog – had to be tied up so that he would not follow Caldwell. It broke our hearts to hear Blue Max crying and yodeling sadly. We hated to leave him there. He was a real trooper in the purest sense of the word.

Angels of Mercy

The extraordinary stress of fighting a guerrilla-terrorist type war in the flatlands was surely taking its toll on us. When the enemies fired at us, they typically did it from an ambush position or from a village full of civilians. In the latter case, the cowardly bastards knew that if we came after them, all they had to do was hide their weapons and they were instantly "civilians". In such situations, we could do nothing to them.

Even if we knew who they were and could positively identify them, we could not touch them because our news media would scream foul play and label us as murdering drug-heads. The VC would hide behind whatever afforded them concealment or cover and shoot at us. They used every dirty trick possible. They mined and booby-trapped the trails, rice paddies, and any path that they thought we might use. They designed most of their fiendish snaps and traps to break our minds and our bodies rather than to kill us instantly.

It was safe to say that the VC were carrying on a war of attrition against our minds, and I must admit that they were having some marginal success because we hated them more with each passing day. On the upside, however, we knew that, with crystal-clear minds, we had to use our hate against the VC, along with our ability to think like them. In that way, the VC were helping rather than hurting us. During our entire time in the flatlands, we never once lost a trooper to the thousands of snaps and traps we encountered almost daily along our way. That says a lot about us, considering that our company strength was over 100 men.

Each soldier of Black Knight Alfa possessed the learned ability to actually become the VC. We transformed into their collective, foul character so that those bastards could never slip up on us or catch us napping. We projected our minds all around us in all directions at all times, and we noticed immediately when something was out of place. We noticed if the leaves on the trees lay unnaturally or their colors were different in the same area. We were suspicious if the odor borne by the same wind suddenly changed or if birds were disturbed from their natural state. We could feel when hostile eyes were watching us.

We also imagined where the VC would ambush us from a certain piece of terrain, and then we would thump that terrain. More often than not, we would be rewarded by the gratifying screams of the Viet Cong, and they would have to shoot back before they were ready. Of course, once they started shooting at us, the cat was out of the bag, and we would chew up their asses. Then we left their bodies lying around too proud to speak, as a warning to the other VC bastards that if they pulled on us, they would have to be prepared to pay the piper. There were times when some of us or our point men would give the signal to take cover, just seconds or minutes before we were hit or fired upon, or before we came upon a mine, booby trap, spiked whip, punji pit, or spider hole. When we had time and our situation permitted it, we "adjusted" the enemies' snaps and traps. In other words, we would change the location of a land or an anti-personnel mine, completely rearrange the layout of their trip wires, or back up some of their fiendish devices with some of ours.

Can you imagine the enemies' surprise when they traveled through the path they had deliberately left clear of mines and suddenly there was a BOOM! Yes, we did such things after we learned to think like the VC.

We also learned early on to avoid the villages and other areas of civilian population, which included the rice paddies and the working fields of the Vietnamese. We also avoided setting a pattern to anything we did, and we certainly never did the same thing twice. I do not believe the VC ever got a handle on us. Sure, they watched us every day, but we knew they were watching and we did things to send them false messages.

We must have been doing something right because after our first two or three encounters with them, the VC would never stop to fight us, even if we hit them. Whenever it was possible, they ran away. On the other hand, many of the other American companies who were working in the areas adjacent to ours were suffering casualties every day and night. One day, during the same time span, the VC hit Bravo and Charlie companies on either side of us, but they did not pop a single round at us.

Later that same afternoon, we went back to a good dirt road that was sometimes used by American convoys traveling between Khe Sanh and Phu Bai. Those convoys always traveled with escorts – armored personnel carriers (APCs) and air support. That day, we suspected the VC were going to hit one of those convoys, and after looking at our maps and thinking like the VC, we had a good idea of where the hit might occur, and we decided to "horn in".

The CO sent teams along both sides of the road while we organized a position on the high ground. Our teams reported that no VC were in sight, and the CO told them to come home, admitting that maybe our suspicions had been incorrect.

The team returning on our side of the road came across something interesting. While inspecting a position that would have been the best place to hit a convoy, they noticed a section of the road that looked abnormal, so they sent Worthington down to investigate.

The road was mined with enough C-4 and other less manageable explosives to take out a good section of the road. While inspecting the set-up from a distance, Worthington discovered that the explosives were command-detonated. After reporting his find, both teams traced the wires to the detonator. They found a pretty little girl appropriately dressed in black pajamas and a traditional Vietnamese straw hat. Our teams requested Tran, and I accompanied him while the CO stayed with the rest of the company.

The young girl was sitting with a pack of four flashlight batteries taped together, and one of the wires to the explosives was already secured to the negative post. All she had to do to trigger an explosion that would kill a lot of American soldiers was to touch the naked end of the other wire to the positive end of the battery pack, and BOOM!

That was neither the first nor the last time that we encountered a child in control of the VC's explosives. That was how they fought the war in the flatlands. What could we do? We certainly could not shoot or arrest the girl. She was just a child, very similar in age to my daughter, Doris. Her only possessions, other than the battery pack, were her lunch of cooked rice, a banana, and some water.

Redleg pushed up to Battalion and told them what we had. They responded that an American convoy was soon scheduled to pass that point on the road. Redleg gave them our position so the gunships would not pop caps on us. Of course, if they saw the VC, they were cleared to light up his ass.

The little girl said she was 10 years old and Viet Cong. When we discovered two markers alongside the road, she admitted they were hers. She had been instructed to wait until the lead vehicles of the convoy (not the escort) were in between the markers. Then she was to touch the lead wire to the positive end of the battery and duck, waiting until most of the debris fell back to the ground. Then she must run away. She was told that she was far enough away that no one would see her, and if someone did, he would not dare to shoot at her because she was just a girl.

Worthington and another man made sure that the connecting wires at the little girl's end were safe. I did not let them go near the explosive charge. Battalion reported that a helicopter with an Explosive Ordnance Demolition (EOD) team aboard was headed for our location.

I pushed up to the CO and asked him what we should do with our little detonator. She was very much afraid of us because her VC bosses had told her a long string of tales describing what we "degenerate Americans" would do to her if she was caught, and none of those stories were very nice.

By that point, she had resigned herself to her cruel fate and squatted down, her lips held tight but trembling. Clearly, she was expecting us to pounce on her young female body as her instructors had assured her we would.

Now I guess I will never know if we did the right thing, but after talking it over, we agreed to let her return to her village. Tran told her of our decision, and she was definitely unprepared for that response. She was completely confused. After a long flow of Vietnamese between Tran and her, she finally understood. She picked up her lunch and took a long look at each of us standing there. Then, she smiled as if she was not used to smiling, and all of us understood her Vietnamese "thank you". There were tears of joy in her eyes as she ran away.

Maybe we were suckers for children and perhaps that is why the VC chose her to do the job. Now that little girl would be free to blow up some other Americans. I am not sure what happened to her because I never saw her again. I do know that we let her go, untouched and unharmed.

We later learned that the gunslingers and Blue Max caught a VC unit coming out of the treeline on the other side of the road where the little Vietnamese girl was supposed to have hit the convoy with the explosives. That VC unit had been lying dog some distance away until their lookout told them that the convoy was on its way. Then they moved into position along the road to hit the convoy after the explosion occurred. Their plan did not work out, however, because old Blue Max caught them in the opening and stomped their butts all over the landscape.

Two days later, we were working a new area in the foothills of the mountains. Another company had been in that same area before us, and Charlie and the VC had chewed them up very badly. Battalion decided that we would switch areas because we had not seen the VC since we had encountered their pretty little detonator.

We were happy in our AO because it reminded us of the highlands. During our briefing we were also pleased to learn that a lot of NVA were working with the Cong in that area because they shared the nearby infiltration route. Battalion believed that the enemy units who had previously hit the American units to our right and left had come down that route.

Up to that point in time, the ARVN and American artillery units were placing a lot of artillery fire in the area at different times. They had hit the area the night before we slicked in. Our mission was to determine if their steel ambushes were having any effect. The units we were replacing had inflicted casualties on the VC, which had slowed them down but had failed to stop them. We were there to stop them – period!

Once our lift birds were safely away, Blue Max also had to leave. We were all alone and packing heavy. We did not know if our reputation had preceded us, and we were hoping that the VC did not know our team's identity. We could feel the VC's eyes all over us, so we stumbled along as if we were fat, dumb, and happy. Of course, every man of Black Knight Alfa was alert and waiting. Our formation was well spread out, and our mortars were ready to shoot at a moment's notice.

The VC cut loose with at least two light machine guns, thinking that we were like the unit before us. That was their first mistake, and for some of the bastards, it was their last mistake. It was most gratifying to hear the VC's shrieks of pain because we knew that we were hurting them. They had never before been the victims of our thump-gun serenade, and they were slightly confused. Instead of hitting the ground and running, they tried to fight us, and we lit into them. We were like Holyfield when he sat Iron Mike down on his ass in the boxing ring. I guess those VC had owned the ring for too long, and they thought they were bad, when in fact the only thing that was bad was their breath.

Just like clockwork, the VC hit the first squad of our lead platoon (Two-Six), and our squad and the rest of the platoon immediately returned fire. At the same time, Two-Six became our base of fire, and the CO, along with the Headquarters section, moved up behind them. Our Weapons Platoon fell into the rear of Headquarters; they could not shoot because the enemy was too close. Three-Six became the "maneuver platoon", and they took off to the left and went around behind the Weapons Platoon. The First Platoon was running drag and formed to cover our rear and to link up with the base-of-fire platoon. These changes happened almost instantly and without any shouting between our men.

I went with Mac and the maneuver platoon. The base-of-fire platoon kept the VC's heads down, and we ran like hell to get into position before the VC figured out what was going down. It was a classic maneuver left, or the old squeeze play. Both of our other rifle platoons were thumping the VC, in addition to the area in front of and behind us, just in case there were VC in those directions.

I could see the VC moving around, but they did not see us. However, one of them fired an RPG in our direction. I saw it coming, and somehow I landed in a big shell crater half full of water. It took me a second to realize that I had not jumped or fallen into the crater. I had been knocked into it.

Something struck me in the chest, and it felt like a big gray Mississippi mule had kicked me. My chest hurt like hell, and I was having trouble breathing. The muddy water in the crater was turning red. Oh dear God, I am hit! I looked down at my jungle fatigue jacket, but it was not bloody in the area where I felt pain. Still, the water was getting redder by the second. What the hell?

Then, I smelled the sweet aroma of strawberries, and I figured that I had finally blown my stack and had gone all the way around the bend. I checked my cargo pocket, which was soaked through, and there I found a few worn and leaking packets of pre-sweetened, strawberry-flavored Kool-Aid.

My chest was almost completely numb, and although I felt some pain, it was not as if I had a big hole in my heart. I was hit, but I was not sure where. I figured that if I had been hit in the heart, I would not be standing there trying to figure out what had just happened.

Suddenly, I started to giggle. Then I howled with laughter as if I had won the big lottery. Even I recognized the hysteria of my laughing antics. The crack grew wider.

I fought to regain control of whatever I had left in order to get on with the mission. I scrambled out of the crater and ran to catch up. My chest felt as if it belonged to someone else. There was a sharp pain right in the center, along with another strange feeling. I decided that I did not want to know what had hit me. I was moving again under my own steam, and that was all that mattered.

Soon, I felt a slight bulge in my chest, and when I gently touched the swollen area, I realized what it was. Out of revulsion, I slapped it and could feel the warm blood running past my crotch and down my leg. I knew I had a blood-sucking leech, but the leech was not making my chest hurt.

There was no other way; I had to look at it. As soon as I could, I opened my jacket to find that I did have a foul, blood-sucking leech attached to my chest. There was a small puncture to the right of where the leech was still holding on as my blood continued to flow through him. I smashed him wide open. There was something obscene about him sucking my blood and then having that same blood of mine oozing out of his broken body.

I was still under fire and did not have the luxury to tend to my wound, so I braced myself and pushed on. It looked as if I had taken some shrapnel almost dead center but slightly to the left of my breastbone. I buttoned my jacket and ran to catch up to the others.

By that time, old Victor Coward was getting wise to our squeeze play and decided he did not want to play any more. He picked up his marbles and took off, leaving close to 20 of his former comrades behind. We had three men down but not out. They would live to fight again some other day. Thank you, God.

The Charley-Charley bird was the first bird in, followed by dust-off. The CO and the battalion commander were engaged in a serious conversation, and I did not butt in. Instead, I accompanied my wounded troopers to medical aid. The remaining VC and NVA pulled on us, and we flew into them, killing nine. Those who ran away found themselves in the direct path of a Cav LURP team, and they lost another five men. The LURP team reported that the few VC who made it up the mountain had left a lot of blood trails. I guess it was not a good day for the VC. They should never have pulled on Black Knight Alfa.

Before we left that area and while we were being resupplied, I asked Doc B. to get the damned leech off me. When he did, he immediately spotted my shrapnel wound and wanted to tell the CO. I advised him not to breathe a word of it to anyone. He was pretty upset with me but promised to hold off until he could get a better look at the wound. It was swollen but not terribly.

We pushed on longer than normal because we wanted to FOB in a location where we could get artillery support if the VC came to get even with us. It was almost dark by the time we moved to a good location and set up temporarily. After it was completely dark, we slid over to another location and formed our usual lager.

I avoided Doc B., but he came looking for me and insisted on dressing my wound. He threatened to tell if I refused his help.

"Top, you are crazy as hell," he said. "And I'm crazy, too, for going along with this shit. You should have gone out on our last dust-off. I'll look at it again in the morning and ... well, First Sergeant, I'll do what I have to do."

The way he said it, I knew he meant business. The pain in my chest had subsided, and I told myself the swelling would be gone by the next morning.

I could not admit it to Doc B., but I did not want to leave Black Knight Alfa, as long as I could carry my own weight. That company was my whole life, and those magnificent young men were the heart in my body that kept me alive. Somewhere along the way, somebody upstairs took a liking to all of us. That was the only way to easily explain how we had walked the length of the Valley of Death without losing a man. Since that time, we had locked up with the NVA and the VC, and we continued to come away smelling like a garden of roses. How long would it or could it last? Black Knight Alfa was my company, and the only way I was going to leave was flat on my back or wrapped in my poncho liner. I would have to bury the farm and help the dead bury the dead.

Around 0130 hours the VC came to visit us. Sliding to another FOB location after it was completely dark had paid off for us. When the VC moved up to hit us, they were aiming at our previous location. They stumbled upon our second location only because it was where they wanted to set up their mortars. We caught them cold turkey. I would not call our run-in with the VC a fight; it was more of an ass-kicking. I have to give them some credit, though, because they adjusted very well after realizing their mistake. Of course, they lost their mortars. We had them. Maybe that was why they refused to go away. They were afraid to run off and leave their mortars, so they hung around and kept shooting at us for most of the night.

The CO, Redleg, and I thought the VC might be trying to keep us in that location until they could mount a wholesale attack or hit us with some other mortars. Their firing at us served no other purpose except to hold us or to tell us they were still out there. We decided not to call in artillery fire unless we really needed their help, and at that time, we were sitting pretty.

Soon, one hell of a downpour started. It rained so hard we could hardly see, and the darkness made matters worse. The CO was thinking of having us move to another location and letting the downpour cover our movement. However, our lager was up tight and all right, and Redleg had us locked in tightly with Birth Control. No! If the VC wanted us, they were going to have to come get us. Getting out of our positions was not the answer.

Meanwhile, the VC were steadily popping caps at us, and they also sent some RPGs our way. We responded by thumping the blast signals. It was soon clear that they were losing too many RPG gunners because they stopped using their RPGs.

Our fighting holes were filled to the brim with rainwater. Fortunately, Pete and I had separate holes because I had to relieve myself, and I was forced to do it in my hole. To get out of my well-dug fighting position was to ask for a hole in my head or my butt. Either the VC would shoot me or I would be hit by friendly fire. Needless to say, I spent the rest of the night almost completely submerged in a hole full of water and my own filth, which was a far cry from pre-sweetened strawberry Kool-Aid.

The next morning I was impossible to be around, but I was alive, which was quite contrary to the way I smelled. (That was akin to being dead for a few months.) Man oh man, I stunk so badly that I made myself sick.

At the first rice paddy we found, the CO halted the company while this first sergeant took a much-needed bath. I jumped into the paddy where the water was deepest, and I bathed with a small bar of soap that someone had kindly given to me.

Incidentally, my little episode in the flatlands earned me the nickname "Rice Paddy Daddy". Some of my old Army buddies still call me that.

We moved with extreme caution and tried to distance ourselves from our last contact area. We also avoided coming within rifle range of any villages or civilians. Let's face it; up to that time, we had really dumped on the VC, which had damaged their exalted positions of power over the frightened Vietnamese villagers and others who were afraid of them.

Each time the VC were foolish enough to pull on us, we blew them away because we were not afraid of them. The VC's situation was not good, so they had to do something very soon. Since we moved into that area, we felt them watching us. Under normal circumstances we would have dropped off a kill team to eliminate the watchers. However, in that case, we actually wanted them to spy on us. As long as we were sure they were watching us, we showed them what we wanted them to see.

We were happy working alone in the foothills. Our AO was quite a distance away from any civilian populations, which greatly relieved us and reduced our stress. In the foothills it was possible for the men of the Grand Company to get down to some serious ass-kicking.

Our formation was beautiful. We were very well spread out and moving into an area where there were enough large trees and irregular terrain features to offer us protection in case we hit some shit. We had not felt the eyes of the VC upon us for some time, and I passed the word for our point man to be especially watchful. The area we were in was a good place for the enemy to put us in a mortar or rocket ambush. Maybe that was why our tail had dropped back so far that we no longer felt him. I truly believe that every one of us had a tree picked out to get down behind in case the VC opened up with a mortar attack.

However, all was quiet – too quiet – and warning signals were going off among us. Pete slid up closer to me, and as he started to speak, our peaceful environment was interrupted by the harsh sounds of gunfire, battle, and the reverberating hoof beats of the four horsemen of the Apocalypse. The troopers of our lead platoon had suddenly encountered the enemy, and we knew the VC had come to fight and were determined to do a job on us. What they did not know was that we were even more determined to do a job on them.

The CO had already issued instructions governing what we would do in case our lead or any other platoons were suddenly hit. In that situation we performed a perfect sucker play. It is too bad that the Hollywood Films Oscar committee was not there to judge our performance because our act was first class, and I think we might have won at least two or three Oscars.

Boy oh boy, our opening act was perfect. Everyone acted as if we had been completely caught off guard. We hollered and screamed, and some of the guys in our lead platoon hollered that their weapons were jammed. To top that off, only our lead platoon returned fire.

While the lead platoon was busy doing what we were expected to do, the remainder of the company did what we were NOT expected to do. We formed into our fighting lager and held our fire. We did not even thump the trail behind us. Instead, we formed rock-steady and waited. I heard the clanging sounds as our mortars set up, and I heard the satisfying reports coming in to me over Pete's radio. They were void of proper SOI[90] procedures, because the platoons had no time to get fancy with their reports.

"Two up. One up. Four up."

I nodded my head, and Pete went right back to them.

"Five Alfa. Roger. Out."

The reports from our Second, First, and Weapons platoons verified that our lager was ready. We left a hole open in our circle for the Third Platoon to enter; then they turned and closed the gap.

"Oh my God! Let's get the hell out of here. Pull back! Pull back!" yelled the CO, as if he was scared to death. At that "signal", our lead platoon jumped up and ran back toward us like scared jackrabbits, yelling and screaming all the way.

The VC fell for our little act – hook, line, and sinker. They were so happy that they finally "had" us that they actually jumped up from their safe positions and chased our lead platoon. I could not believe that the VC could be so stupid. They should have known us better than that, but I guess the sweet smell of success had gone to their heads.

The CO and I stood on opposite sides of the opening, and we instructed our troopers where to go as they passed by us. The platoon sergeant had to be last in the maneuver, and when Mac ran by us, he gave the CO a thumbs up to signal that his entire platoon was in front of him. We quickly closed the gap, and the happily approaching VC ran into a solid wall of effective fire. Our thump-gun serenade began as our thump gunners fired shot into the enemies' path while the others fired HE.

We were on the VC like stink on cat shit, and they soon discovered that we had only pretended to be as weak as our news media had said we would be. Of course it did not matter since it was too late for them to save themselves. The only time left open to them was the time to die.

Someone started our battle cry, and the victims knew they were up against Black Knight Alfa. We locked up with them and waltzed down the road to hell, with them fully in the lead. Because they were hard hats with a lot of NVA fill-ins, they thought they could push us around. Wrong! As wrong as two left shoes!

The tie-up was short and sweet. We cut them down like dirty weeds, and as usual the VC and the NVA followed their cowardly modus operandi by tucking their tails and running full out to break contact with us and to get away to the high grounds. Once again, they did not stop to drag away their dead, because there were more dead than living cowards.

The fight was over in a very short time, and quietness fell like a ton of bricks. When I called for my sit-reps, I heard: "Alfa Five. Alfa Three. You have to see what we got, and still kicking. Six is on the way to our 10-10. Over."

Pete was quick to answer: "Alfa Three. This is Five Alfa. What have you got? Come on back."

"Women, and they are still alive. Over."

"Alfa Three. Be advised. We are on our way. Over."

Pete's speaker was on, and I clearly overheard his conversation with Mac's RTO. Without bothering to ask me if we were going to Three's location, Pete started running, so I followed. We ran to where the first caps were popped, and along the way we saw the terribly high price the VC and the NVA had paid for fucking with Black Knight Alfa. Their dead were all over the terrain, and I wondered why they had not used their mortars.

As we passed the dead VC soldiers, we cautiously checked to make sure they were truly in the state of no return. We had already experienced sad times when some of our enemies only played dead so they could shoot us in the back.

When we reached the initial contact area of our firefight with the VC, we found some of the men of the Third Platoon guarding two rather pretty, female VC soldiers. I say "rather pretty" because it had been so long since we had seen a woman that even an Egyptian female mummy would have looked good to us.

Both women were dressed in their black pajamas, and they carried AK-47s and medical aid bags. Otherwise, they were traditional Vietnamese women in size and appearance. They had other emblems that further identified them as medical personnel, in addition to the aid pouches they carried. However, there was something distinctly different about one of the women. Something about her medical aid bag, her little insignia pin, and the incorrectly positioned band around her arm did not ring true.

As soon as I saw her, I felt pain. I had the feeling that she was not a medic at all. Actually, I suspected she was the leader of the unit that had hit us. She seemed to be wearing a mask, and there was nothing sweet about her. She was as hard as nails, and when our eyes met, I could tell that she knew I could see through her. Just looking at her made me hurt, and it was not from wanting her as a woman, but from … When I read her, I saw Evil Incarnate.

The "leader" was squatting down in typical Vietnamese fashion, as if resigned to her fate. Her uniform revealed that she had been hit. Blood was running down her leg and collecting in her shoes. She was wearing the full web-gear harness with AK-47 magazine pouches. Our trooper who had taken her AK said she had fired it at them. They had also taken two grenades and a map pouch from her. Those pieces of evidence told me that we had a VC leader. The absolute hatred that blazed in her eyes was unmistakable. She was our 100-per cent sworn enemy.

The other female VC soldier appeared to be a real medic, and she stood there unharmed. Our troopers had already taken her medical pouch, and one of them told me that she had been carrying a weapon but did not have the same web gear as the other woman. Then, I knew that I was right in my assessment of the female VC unit leader.

Our troopers kept our two female prisoners well separated. The female leader tried not to show her pain as Doc B. tried to help her, but she kept refusing his aid. It was obvious that she understood English. He begged her to let him help her, and she eventually gave in because she was almost unconscious. He removed her web gear and tore away her pajamas so he could reach her wound.

By that time, she was stretched out on the ground, and Doc B. was down on his knees beside her, working silently and concentrating on saving her life. He ignored the hatred in her eyes and her face. Her worst injury was a nasty gunshot wound to the left side of her stomach, and it was clear to us that Doc B. knew he could save her.

"Now you just hold on, young lady, and this old Doc will have you fixed up like new," he said as he applied his craft to keep his solemn promise.

She seemed to accept his predictions, and even smiled, which was contradictory to the hatred that was still coming from her eyes. As Doc B. leaned over to get something out of his medical bag, the bitch shot him. Poor Doc! With a surprised look on his face, he grunted twice and rolled over dead.

Seemingly out of nowhere, that miserably evil, ungrateful VC bitch had pulled a French-made .9mm MAB P15s automatic. I will never know where she had managed to conceal such a large weapon. It was similar to our own caliber .45 pistol. The bitch had made her weapon bark twice in rapid succession, but her second shot was unnecessary. The first cowardly shot took the life of the man who had been trying so hard to save her worthless ass.

Time stopped and stood stark still, as I screamed in pain. Oh dear Lord, she just shot Doc B. Why? Why? Why?

The trooper standing closest to the woman and Doc B. dropped his M16 and grabbed her by the arm, twisting it so violently that he wrenched it from its socket. The dirty bitch screamed and cursed in Vietnamese as she tried to swing her weapon around for another shot at us.

Then everything seemed to occur in slow motion. In unison, all of us, except for the two men who were guarding the other woman, moved forward with the intention of killing the bitch who had just shot Doc B.

I hated her so much that I could have bitten her to death like a ferocious dog. However, I could not get to her, so I held Doc B., our senior company medic, in my arms, and I died with him. During that moment I think I lost a lot more of the little mind that I had left.

Still I tried in some insignificant way to share what life I had left with him. Sweet Jesus, there I was crying again. It seemed like I was always crying. I simply could not stop. My heart was nearly bursting with pain, and my mind reeled. There I was getting paid back for all of the times we had done a job on the NVA and the VC, after which we had walked away smelling like roses. Finally, we were not going to walk away clean from a firefight. The VC took Doc B., an unforgivable act that I would never forget.

"Top, he's dead. Doc is dead. There's nothing any of us can do for him. He's gone home to God. It's all over for him. Top, let him go. It's okay. It's okay."

Doc California's gentle voice came to me from far away, and I heard myself say: "*Credo in unum Deum, Patrem omnipotentem, factorem caeli et terrae.*"[91]

Someone had the presence of mind to call for dust-off, and I sadly noted that every man was crying for our beloved Doc B. They quickly and thoroughly searched the murderess, and that time they did it right, not caring that she was a woman. We really wanted to blow her ass away, and she knew it. The hatred in her eyes was quickly replaced by abject fear.

However, no one attacked the murderess. Doc California set her arm after he finished what Doc B. had started. We truly wanted to pull her guts out and dance on them, but none of us put our violence on that murdering bitch.

We men of Black Knight Alfa proved more than ever that day that we were truly a Grand Company of the finest American soldiers who have ever lived. We loved Doc B. with all of our hearts, but even in our great sadness, we could not stoop so low as the VC. We had not been raised to act that way.

I held Doc B. until it was time to get him ready to start his long journey home. We wrapped him neatly in his poncho liner. When we heard that our medevac birds were inbound, I let Long Claw bring them in. I clenched my teeth so hard that I tasted blood.

There were tears in the CO's eyes, and Captain Norris was crying. In fact, all of us shed many tears that day. When it was time, we slid our M16s under Doc B.'s body to form a makeshift stretcher, and we lifted him up. One of the platoon medics moved Doc B.'s brown hair aside and placed his small American flag over his eyes to keep the sunshine out and let old Doc see where he was going.

A whole rifle platoon lined up to face each other, and they formed the honor guard all the way to the dust-off bird. As the men with the rifle stretcher carried Doc B., the CO and I followed, and I carried Doc B.'s gear.

The crew of the dust-off bird was silent, and the door gunner saluted as everyone shouted: "Before us there were none, and while we are here, there are no others. After we are gone, there shall be no more! Black Knight Alfa. Alpha and Omega!"

It was impossible for us to exist as we had and not bear scars for life. Take it from me – the pain never goes away.

Doc B. had certainly done his best to save the life of the miserable scum who shot him, and there she was on the other dust-off bird going back to an American surgical unit who would put the finishing touches on Doc B.'s attempts to save her life. Damn her foul soul to eternal hell!

Doc, I am trying to tell the world how it really was, and my friend, I still feel the sorrow of that day and that time in the flatlands of South Vietnam when you were shown such disrespect. I shall love and respect you forever. I thank God for allowing me the privilege to walk through the Valley of Death with you. Someday, we will share a hot beer together again. May God grant you and all of the US "peace in the valley".

One final note about the female VC medic: Tran told us the last thing she said before leaving was, "I am very sorry that my commanding officer murdered your doctor." She knew that Doc B. was primarily responsible for saving the female officer's life.

After the Fact

Some of you who read this story might say that we should have killed the female enemy soldier who murdered Doc B. On the other hand, some of you might agree with our actions. Keep in mind that at the time of the incident, everyone except me thought the woman was an enemy medic rather than a VC unit leader. Of course, the fact that she was a woman might prompt some people's sympathy. Some of you might say that killing her would have been pointless because it could not bring Doc B. back to life. Some of you might say that we should have used the woman's pistol to blow her ass away. Perhaps you are thinking that Doc California was wrong to try to save her life. After all, she was our enemy who had been armed with an AK-47, had sought to kill us, and had succeeded in killing Doc B.

What was right and what was wrong? Should we have shot that little girl who patiently waited to blow up one of our convoys? Was it right or wrong to turn her loose and allow her to return to her family and her village?

Were we the good guys in the white hats, or were we the bad guys in the black hats? Was there an issue of morality? Was there an issue of Duty, Honor, Country?

Should we have killed both angels of mercy right there on the spot? If we had, perhaps Doc B. would still be alive today. Both women had been armed and had participated in the fight against us. They had pulled on us and had lost. We could have shot them and then used this excuse: "After all, it was war. It was combat, and they were clearly the enemy. We were just following orders."

Truly, there was right and there was wrong. I sincerely hope we made the right decisions in all of the difficult situations we faced in the Nam.

It is so easy, after the fact, to say what was right and what was wrong, and what you should have done or should not have done.

Later, I was informed that the female soldier who had shot Doc B. was, in fact, the leader of the unit that had hit us. After her stay in the hospital, she was held in a detention center near Bien Hoa. Within a few days after she arrived there, her VC comrades murdered her. The South Vietnamese never discovered who had taken her out or why.

Sometimes, evildoers are justly rewarded.

"Vengeance is mine, and retribution, in due time their foot will slip;
For the day of their calamity is near."   (Deuteronomy 32:35)

"Signs of the end of the age;
Brother will betray brother to death."

But in those days, following that distress,

**"THE SUN WILL BE DARKEN,
AND THE MOON WILL NOT
GIVE US LIGHT;**

**THE STARS WILL FALL FROM
THE SKY, AND THE HEAVENLY
BODIES WILL BE SHAKEN."**

Mark 24 and 25

R-E-S-P-E-C-T

The cold, hard fact that we were in almost daily eyeball-to-eyeball contact with the enemy proved that our mission in the flatlands was successful. Every time the VC popped caps on us, they paid right up front with one or more of their numbers. Belly-up. Graveyard dead.

Because of our learned ability to detect their presence and to think like they did, the VC had not yet been able to catch us cold, and I think that bothered them a lot. When they put people on our tail to dog us, we always doubled back and took them out of the game, permanently.

One time they came very close, and I knew that God was watching over our Grand Company. We were moving along, and everything was too quiet. There was a wooded area to our left, and we avoided it because it looked like snap-and-trap heaven.

The CO said to Redleg and me, "Top, you know, of course, if I were the VC, I would shoot at us in the hope that we would head for the trees and the wood line. Then I would mortar the woods. If they pop caps on us, we run like hell, but in the same direction we are heading. Pass the word."

Almost as soon as Pete received an "up" from the drag platoon, the VC acted according to the CO's prediction. Instead of popping caps, though, they dropped two 82mm mortar rounds in the clearing behind us to our right. Their little maneuver was clearly designed to force us to run to our left into the wooded area. The VC mortar men were pretty good.

"Move! Move!" shouted the CO.

We ran straight ahead, doing the unexpected, just like always. Of course, that would mean the VC mortar men would have to try to bring us down while we were on the run. It came down to how good the VC mortar men really were. Our formation was already well spread out; therefore, we only had to run faster than the VC mortar crews could. As we ran, we tried to find their forward observers and to determine whether or not they were shooting line-of-sight.

The next two rounds impacted the area that we had recently vacated. The VC mortar men were good. We guessed that their next rounds would be in front of us.

As soon as we were up again, the CO had us moving straight to our right. The Second Platoon reported that they had a probable location for the enemy forward observer, and the CO replied with the order to "put his lights out". I heard our thump guns firing and our machine guns working, as we continued moving as quickly as possible.

The VC mortar crews did shoot in the direction we were originally heading, and they dropped everything they had. They used only one mortar to register, and they shot only two rounds when they could have easily shot more. We were already ahead of them in our planning because we had thought like them and had anticipated their actions. Therefore, we were able to get behind them without much effort.

They really screwed up the countryside and lost a lot of ammunition, but we had already made a radical change in our direction of movement, and we kept on getting up! Moving like the wind and like Broadway Joe carrying the ball, we showed them a big-time ghost.

Either the Second Platoon had been successful in neutralizing their forward observer, or we were moving too fast for them. In any case, the enemy mortar rounds stopped falling just as suddenly as they had started. We never knew what happened, just that we had survived the only real mortar attack the VC mounted against us. We suffered three wounded but no KIAs. Once again, our ability to think like our enemy saved us, along with our quick reactions to the enemies' actions.

We continued with our mission as if nothing had happened. It was no big thing to US.

We found a safe place to send our wounded out on dust-off and to replace the ammo that we had fired during our last contact. Then we returned to the task of getting up.

Later that evening, we held and commanded the best high ground location in the area. It was far enough away from any known village. From there we planned our defensive/fighting positions very well, and we dug in deeply enough to get below ground level. We used everything we could possibly find as protective shields, and we spread out as far as we could while maintaining the required solidarity of our combined all-around defensive posture.

Within our defensive circle, a made-to-order, natural depression provided our mortars about 4 feet of depth below the natural ground level. Its generous width enabled them to organize very well. After each platoon sent the ammunition they were carrying to that central location, our mortar men were up tight and all right.

They were able to fire in any direction and under any possible situation. They placed their aiming stakes out in a circle and lit them for night firing. Setting up those 360 degrees was as easy as Mama's apple pie! That position supported the required mask clearance, and we had no-fail backup because our mortar men were the world's best hip shooters.

Late that evening, I had the opportunity to show my troopers some of the tricks of the trade that my old Buffalo Soldier mentors had taught me. Thank the dear Lord that I had been privileged to serve with and to listen to some of the proud men of the 92nd Division. What those old black Buffalo Soldiers had taught me was helping to keep us men of the Grand Company alive. "Sgt. Hezekiah Bones, I do thank you so much, and all of the other old Buffalo Soldiers of the 92nd Division."

Two of the old Buffalo Soldier tricks that I explained to my troopers that evening were the sly practice of faking a FOB position and the learned ability to pretend not to notice an enemy tail. The piece of high ground on which we were organized was not too far from another similar piece of terrain. In fact, that other area was the hill where we had initially begun our set-up. However, we did not stay at that initial location because we had a tail and we discovered a more advantageous piece of terrain (i.e., our current position). Because our tail had been dogging us since the mortar incident, we decided not to take him out. Captain Norris and the CO thought it would be advantageous to let the VC think we were unaware of their presence. Our tail had observed us moving onto the first hill. However, he had not noticed that we only pretended to set up there. When it was dark enough, we slid off the back side of the hill and moved over to the other higher and better position. That proved to be one of the best decisions we ever made.

What we did not know but found out later was that the local VC commander had gathered a strong fighting force to put an end to our problematic presence. We had already iced too many of the VC, so under the orders of his headquarters, the local VC commander gathered a full battalion of Victor Cowards and augmented it with an NVA unit that was conveniently in the area. The NVA command headquarters pressed that NVA unit into the service of the VC commander, especially knowing that we American hell raisers in the flats were the same troops who had walked the entire length of the A Shau Valley in broad daylight right under the noses of their men. We had taken one hell of a toll on them while doing it, not to mention what we had done to those fools who had tried to delay our departure from the mountaintop.

Obviously, the NVA were more than happy to be involved in bringing us down. Because there were no villages or innocent civilians in the area, we had plenty of artillery fire on call. Redleg had planned well. We had 105mm artillery fire available, and it had us locked in very tightly.

All of us had the distinct feeling that the VC were going to hit us that night. We had called them out, and there was nothing left for them to do but to engage in a firefight with us. Both sides were going to duel to the death.

We were short a few good men. Doc B. was gone, and our memories of him were bittersweet. I tried not to think of it because it was still too painful. Despite our slightly smaller number, we were still one of the best fighting infantry companies in the 1st Air Cavalry Division. Actually, knowing that we were at reduced strength made us meaner than junkyard dogs. We were even more determined to beat the odds and to stay alive when we next kicked off on the VC's ass. Victory would be ours, plain and simple!

Once we were locked in tightly, we decided to place snaps and traps rather than human listening posts. Doing so would permit us to have all of our personnel within the confines of our lager. As usual, we placed our snaps and traps in positions that would tell us where our enemies were, as well as the direction from which they were approaching our positions.

We had all of our starlight scopes up and working and all of our outer ring of flares attached to claymores. Additionally, we set up antipersonnel mines in the most likely avenues of enemy approach. Because we only had four left, we placed them wisely and recorded their positions so that we could retrieve them if the VC did not spring them.

As soon as I received an "up" from all of my platoons, I passed the word to the CO that we were settled in to wait. By that time, it was completely dark, and the moonlight was minimal. There was no jungle canopy to block the light, so we had already fully adjusted our night vision and could see well enough to accomplish our given tasks. Before Katie barred the door, I checked some of the positions nearest ours and found them to be nice and deep. Our troopers knew it was a good time for the VC to come calling, and even if they put rockets and mortars on us, we would survive. However, we might have a problem if they decided to use their big mothers – their 122s and their large mortars. Generally, the VC saved those big ones for major fights, and we hoped they were underestimating our capabilities and assuming our lockup would be a minor fight.

There were a few distinctive locations around our perimeter where there were tall bushes and perfect places for the enemy to hide if they snuck up closer to us. Our troopers hung noisemakers (C-ration cans containing small stones) on some of the bushes, and they booby trapped others with all kinds of fiendish do-me-goodies.

We had our shit together, so we settled in to wait.

Later, I noticed that Pete was snoring. He lay curled up like a big baby on the ground behind our fighting position, and he was using his radio as a pillow. I hate to admit it, but the CO and I were also dozing a little. That day had been a trying one; we had moved around so much that it felt as if we had dug our way to Hong Kong. No matter how hard we tried, we could not resist nodding a little. I was certain, though, that if we were hit, every man would be instantly alert and ready to fight.

The normal sounds of nature filled the warm, muggy night. I knew that all of us had become acclimated to the sounds, smells, and feelings of our surroundings, so that if something suddenly did not fit, we would know immediately that there was a problem. Naturally, we were not supermen or in possession of super powers, but we had returned to nature and had reverted to our original animal existence out there in the bush. We had become one with our environment.

The CO and I shared a fighting position so that we could plan an emergency escape route. With Redleg's assistance we planned our artillery fire. Once Redleg moved over to his position, I remained with the CO to allow Pete to get some sleep.

We were dozing when the next event happened, and by the grace of God, our seventh survival sense kicked in fully and ran smoothly like the purring of a big cat. As the CO and I looked at each other, he whispered, "Top, we're fixing to have company. Victor Charlie is on his way, and there are a lot of the little bastards with blood in their eyes. I can feel them. Can you feel them too?"

"Yes, Sir. Old Victor Coward is out there, and he is packing heavy. He is coming to bring us down, once and for all. His presence woke me up too," I replied.

As I whispered to the CO, I held tightly onto my little black Bessie as I went to wake up Pete. I found him fully awake and already in the process of making sure our platoons were on full alert. They were!

We felt and smelled the VC as they tried to sneak up on us. Their heavy stink permeated the muggy, night air. The jungle symphony was interrupted, and the sounds of it changed, even though we could not yet hear the VC's movements. They were still too far away. Yet we smelled the stink of their unwashed bodies, the oil they used on their weapons and other equipment, their tobacco, fish, and nuc mam. There was definitely a whole shit pot of them. They were not coming to harass us; they were coming to take us down and to do it at all costs.

I wondered if Black Knight Alfa's Final Battle was approaching. Redleg and his RTO moved to our positions, and I slipped into a hole with Pete. Redleg shared the CO's hole. We agreed that if we were going down, we would do so by the last artillery salvos that were shot out for us. We would not fall into the hands of the Viet Cong.

Normally, under such conditions, our company communications consisted only of keying the mikes with our codes. However, because of the gravity of the situation, the Third Platoon reported by voice over the company net.

"Alfa Five, Alfa Five. Alfa Three, over."

I knew it was Mac, and Pete gave me his mike.

"Alfa Three, Alfa Five, over," I whispered.

"Five, this is Three. Be advised; we got trouble coming. Now I'm not positive because of the distance, but I swear the VC are setting up a mortar in front of our positions. We can see them well enough to take them out. What to do? Over."

311

"Three, this is Five. Wait. Out."

I passed the information to the CO and Redleg. It certainly did not make sense for the VC to set up their mortars in plain view. It was not completely dark, and we could see a short distance from our vantage point.

We formed our lager with the Third Platoon facing away from and almost on line with the first high ground area we had pretended to set up on. The high ground where we were organized was between where our enemies were setting up their mortars and the first hill that we had only temporarily used.

Captain Norris was the first to figure out the situation. He said, "The VC think we are on that first high ground. They don't know that we are here. I'll bet that Cong who was watching us as we moved onto the first hill only waited around to be sure he was right. Then he ran off to spread the news. He did not know that we moved into our present position, which puts us between where Three-Six said the mortars are setting up and the hill the VC think we are on. They are fixing to hit the other hill, not ours. The VC mortars are using our hill to hide behind, so they cannot be hit with fire from the other hill."

I was close enough to see the CO smile. Then he turned to me and said, "Top, once again, you and your old Buffalo Soldiers have proven your worth. Tell Three-Six to just sit tight and wait and to be ready to shoot the bastards when I give the word." He smiled with glee as he thought of what we were going to do to the VC.

Redleg pushed up to Mac to request the location of the enemy mortars. Then, he pushed up to Birth Control and planned a concentration on the enemy mortar positions. When the CO gave the word, the VC were going to unexpectedly do a lot of bleeding and burning. We were sneaky!

We already knew the main enemy attack force was moving into a position where they could launch their night attack against that unoccupied hill. We were in a good position to observe the proceedings, even with the limited visibility. Using their starlight scope, the Second Platoon reported movement that seemed to be directed toward the vacant hill, which proved what Redleg had figured out. The VC were massing to hit the wrong hill.

There was a joker in the deck, and all would go well as long as the enemy moving into position did not use our positions as jumping-off points and did not set off any of our flares or traps, especially those closest to us. If they popped some on the outer ring, it would be less harmful to us as long as we did not pop caps on them to give away our positions. Once again, old Fate and good planning were well on our side.

The CO passed the word that we were not to pop caps unless we were directly threatened. We waited patiently while the CO got on the radio to Battalion to inform them that the shit would soon be hitting the fan.

Every man in the Grand Company was fully alert and poised like the magnificent killing machines and predators we had become. We experienced the "true state of grace" that was bestowed only on true predators, and it had been that way since the beginning of time when our world was still young.

"Captain Brooks, I have good news. In addition to our 105s, we can also have a battery of 155s, and I can initially put the 155s on the enemy mortars and keep the 105s protecting us," Redleg said happily.

There was no doubt in my mind that the VC had one hell of a surprise coming. We were going to put something very heavy on their collective butt.

The CO smiled and said, "That's very good, Redleg. I'll give you the word when. Meantime, go ahead and put your big guns on the enemy mortar positions. Battalion is getting us a Fire Fly mission on station. We just don't know when it will be able to get here."

"Top, I have an uncanny feeling, and I'm wondering if you and Redleg are getting the same vibrations?" the CO whispered.

"Sir, if you are thinking about or feeling K-5, then I have the same bad vibrations. I think K-5, or rather what we left of K-5 Battalion, is out there seeking revenge for what we did to them. They are here to help pick our bones clean. I tell you truly, I can feel their presence," I said.

Redleg agreed.

"How many do you think are out there?" the CO asked.

"Well, Sir, I think we got us at least a VC-augmented battalion. I believe they have NVA and Chinese advisors with them. From what McKinnon and Maggio[92] reported, the VC don't seem to be afraid. They have come to stay," whispered Redleg.

We gave a lot of thought to what he said, knowing full well that he was as right as rain.

All three of the rifle platoons in our defensive circle reported seeing enemy movement. We were surrounded.

Three of the flares on our outer ring were popped. One must have gone off directly in the face of an enemy soldier, because a man screamed and ran headlong into another trap, and that claymore put him out of his misery.

That incident signaled the beginning of the VC's mortar barrage. Man oh man, did they put some heavy stuff on that vacant hill. They must have lowered it considerably. The VC had mustered at least eight 82mm mortars.

Mac called us to confirm the enemy mortar positions. There were two separate positions, but Redleg had them covered.

Old Victor Charlie really unloaded on that poor vacant hill. When there was a lull in their firing, we knew what was coming next. They charged toward the hill, yelling and screaming slogans and profanities. Because the right end of their charge was going to pass right over our Second Platoon's positions, we had to stop being observers and engage in some action.

Redleg called for the 155mm barrage that would take out all of their mortars. The CO ordered the Second Platoon to shoot as soon as the attacking VC hit our inner ring of snaps, traps, and flares. The cat was out of the bag. It was time for the dead to bury the dead!

"Shot out!" Redleg yelled over the din of the Second Platoon's opening fire.

The intensity of their fire indicated how close the enemy troops were to their positions. Although the VC were caught off guard, they recovered quickly. They thought they had hit one of our forward security positions. As the Second Platoon fired, the rest of our perimeter held our fire until we had positive targets.

The 155mm barrage landed dead on its target. Redleg was already calling in a shift in order to widen the impact area. There was another earth-shaking barrage, and Redleg yelled, "Fire for effect!"

The enemy knew their shit was out because our 155mm projos that were taking out their mortars told them they had some major miscalculations. The First Platoon reported that their outer ring of flares was being popped.

Of course, our enemies were up to their old tricks. A "hero" among them jumped on a burning ground flare to extinguish the light it gave off. I will admit it was a brave thing to do, especially since we often booby-trapped our flares to discourage such measures. That heroic dude went and lost his head, literally; it was blown cleanly off.

The First Platoon opened fire, and I think that, by that time, the VC were adjusting to the fact that they were being sucked in. This knowledge had them jawed up really tight.

They came out of the darkness, screaming and yelling. It looked as if their entire front line of soldiers was armed with RPDs. Our outer ring of flares was popping everywhere, and the light cast a weird glow over the killing ground. We saw the three distinct uniforms worn by our enemies – the black pajamas, the variety of ragtag (i.e., civilian) attire of the Viet Cong, and the khaki-colored uniforms of the regular NVA soldiers. Their head coverings included steel pots, pith helmets, cloth headgear, and bandannas.

Of course, their uniforms were unimportant. What was significant was that they were finally attacking us in the right place, and the unit heading straight for our positions along our perimeter was a very large unit that was massed to roll right over us. I was hoping that Fire Fly would come in time to help us, especially before our flares lost their valuable light.

"Top, I got Killer Junior coming in. You better pass the word. It will be here in no time!" Redleg yelled to me.

Pete put the word out immediately.

"Kill Junior" was the actual name we had given to artillery rounds with super-sensitive fuses that were set to explode the projectile above ground and to rain sudden death upon our enemies. Naturally, some of the rounds had the normal impact-detonating fuses.

Redleg and Birth Control were unleashing the hounds of hell on the VC. Now there was a real Iron Curtain, just like we always used. The accuracy of our artillery support was brilliant. I do not remember how many batteries we had firing for us that night, but I do remember that their combined firepower was awesome.

We hunkered down in our holes while Mother Birth Control did her thing. Captain Norris was truly in his world. He talked to the Birth Control Fire Direction Center (FDC), and the FDC talked to the cannoneers. Those wonderful artillery pieces then talked to the VC. I do not think the VC liked the direction the conversation was going, but that was just too bad. We bit the ground while the Victor Cowards died en masse.

Our platoons talked directly to Redleg as he made the necessary adjustments to our protective wall of steel. That perfect coordination was paying off. We had neutralized the enemy mortars and broken the enemy charges. The VC movement was losing momentum, and our troopers dropped the few enemies who managed to reach our perimeter.

The VC attack came closest to the First Platoon's portion of our perimeter, and Long Claw and his men did an outstanding job of stopping the VC dead in their tracks. The VC hit them twice, but at no time did the enemy come close enough that the First Platoon had to pop their protective claymores. Long Claw proved to be the good leader and warrior that I always thought of him as being.

The CO told Redleg to put the 155s on what was left of the vacant hill that the VC element was mistakenly attacking. Over the crescendo of battle, we heard the faint screams of our dying enemies as the hot steel of the 155mm projos further reduced the height of that hill and the number of enemy soldiers who had come to kill us that night.

"Top, we're hurting the bastards a thousand times more than they are hurting us. I think they are getting ready to do what they do best, and you know what that is," the CO said, after he finished talking to the Second Platoon.

On behalf of the VC, I must say that they fought like real soldiers. They came at us, determined to make us fall, but we were even more determined, and we did not fall. The Viet Cong fought us as if they were NVA soldiers, which helped us a lot because we knew very well how to fight the NVA.

The VC knew when to back off. They had tasted our resolve, which was flavored with the hot steel of Birth Control, and they knew they could not win. Redleg was hoping that Spectre and Fire Fly were on the way. If they came, the VC would receive another unwanted bloodbath. The VC stopped pushing us, and Redleg called a halt to our artillery supporting fires. An eerie quietness prevailed and was broken only by the rhythmic popping of the illumination rounds fired by our artillery to shed a little light on the situation.

A few minutes passed, and then the VC buglers suddenly began blowing their crazy notes. It sounded like there were two buglers widely separated, with one following the lead of the other. I detected a note of sadness in their refrains.

The CO grabbed Danzig's mike and alerted the company to get ready, but to wait until their kill was certain. Then he shook his head and said, "Damn it to hell, I thought the bastards had enough. Redleg, I really want to cream them this time!"

The bugles were typically used to signal the start of a big banzai-like charge. The VC had already used that tactic twice on us that night. However, the VC attack did not materialize. The sour notes of their bugles faded away into the night and were not replaced with the sounds of charging men and small arms fire. The eerie quietness returned.

All of our platoons reported movement to their front, but the movement was not hostile. Not one enemy shot was fired; in turn, we held our fire. The next artillery illumination round shed its flickering light on the battlefield around our perimeter, where we saw our enemies tending to their wounded and actually dragging away their dead.

Not one of our troopers fired on the enemy. It was like watching a stage play or a Hollywood production of a scene from the days and nights of the bubonic plague era, when a tremendous number of dead bodies had to be moved and buried. Truly, it was the time for the dead to bury the dead, but this happened with some assistance from the living. We watched in silence, and our medics moved about within our lager, caring for our wounded.

We called for dust-off, and fortunately, they came and went without a single round being popped.

We could have easily dropped more artillery fire on the VC as they tended to their wounded and dead soldiers. However, we were American soldiers who did not do such things. I am very proud of that fact.

Our enemy failed to bring us down. They failed! They failed!

After our dust-off birds flew away, we settled in to await the dawn.

Spectre and Fire Fly never came because they were involved with another mission. However, it did not matter to us because we had prevailed alone.

The VC worked very hard at removing their wounded and dead soldiers. Even as first light crept in, they continued to move silently about their task. They knew they had been beaten, and we no longer had anything to fear from them.

No matter how hard and quickly they worked, the clear dawn turned into the light of a new day, and the sunlight came out slowly, putting an end to what had happened during the night. We remained quiet as we went about our essential tasks. We did not bother the VC, and they did not bother us.

Silently, the enemy melted away. They were forced to leave behind some of their dead because they lacked the time and effort to remove all of the bodies. The mute testimony of death ran rampant, and it illustrated what they came to do and could not do. They had certainly paid a terrible price for pulling on Black Knight Alfa.

Blue Max was on station, and our Charley-Charley bird was inbound. Our supply birds also came, bringing everything we needed to continue our mission. Meanwhile, we had teams removing our intact claymores, snaps, and traps.

There were still a lot of dead bodies lying around. I guess the VC had to be selective about which ones they dragged off. The blackened pools of dried blood, the bits of shattered bodies, the weapons, and the equipment left on the scene told the story of all that we had not seen.

A lone and broken tree stood near the middle of the battlefield and in front of us along our perimeter. As we neared it, we noticed something white attached to the side that faced us. Once we were standing around the tree, we could plainly see that it was one of our calling cards. Wedged beside it was one of the black-and-gold shoulder patches of the 1st Air Cavalry Division. None of our troopers had been near that tree before, so I knew that none of us had placed the card there. We concluded that the VC must have placed those items on the tree. I shall always believe that it was our enemies' way of paying us their R-E-S-P-E-C-T.

Go Tell it on the Mountaintop

Five days later, we cleaned out the K-5 Battalion. I remember the incident as if it were yesterday. We left our FOB and moved toward a VC infiltration route south. The VC used that particular route because they controlled most of the small villages along it, and it passed through a rather large hamlet. Those villages that were not under their complete control were at least sympathetic to the VC cause.

Battalion gave us a briefing of information and intelligence gained from some of the prisoners we had taken after our rumble with K-5. The route we were planning to ambush was one that the VC believed to be so secure that they used it during daylight hours. Of course, the nearness of small villages afforded them a safe haven to run to if the American units working in the area happened to stumble upon them.

The villages were heavily populated with women, old folks, and those too young to be pressed into the services of the Cong. Therefore, it was nearly impossible for the American and South Vietnamese armies to occupy those areas without bearing the huge risk of injuring or killing innocent people. I suppose the VC had chosen that route because it passed through what was essentially a "no-fire zone", which made the area even safer than Hanoi. However, the no-fire rule was restricted primarily to artillery, mortars, and air attacks. Small arms could be used with extreme caution.

With those restrictions in mind, we traced the route on our maps and came up with three possible locations where we could best spring a surprise party on old Victor Charlie. After scouting the three areas, we decided on the location that would give us the best advantages and offer the least possibilities of hitting a civilian or a water buffalo.

We took a carefully selected route to our ambush location, and we arrived there without being seen. Then we set up and waited. It was still early morning, and most of the villagers were probably still sleeping or having coffee.

Our S-2 gained intelligence that a messenger from the VC Headquarters normally passed by that location on his way south every week. However, no time was given for his passing any particular point. Therefore, we planned to stay in that location as long as we could remain there without being seen. If we were discovered, it would be all over, leaving us with only one option – to diddy mau the area and to return at a later date.

The situation was touch-and-go, and our chances of making a hit were very small – one in a thousand, perhaps. However, because we had mauled the last unit that had hit us, Battalion figured that the VC Headquarters would be forced to do something.

Looking at the route through the eyes of our enemy, we chose the location that they would deem the safest portion along their route, which would naturally be the best place for us to attack. The CO had the First Platoon form a blocking position between the nearest village and us, and he had the Second Platoon stay along one side of the trail to prevent the VC from running to the village or doubling back. He used the Third Platoon as the ambush platoon, and he had the Weapons Platoon and the Headquarters section organize within the ambush site as part of our defensive lager. I went with Mac and Lt Zen. Zen wanted to be in on the action.

We were all set in and waiting. The First Platoon was positioned along our escape route, where they could give us covering fire if the VC decided to chase us. The CO, Redleg, Lt Zen, and I discussed the best way to pull out if we were discovered. The route was a rather nice trail that was used by the villagers, which made our mission more challenging. If the VC were not wearing their uniforms or were not carrying their weapons, we could do nothing but watch them stroll by us. We were discussing such possibilities when the Third Platoon's lookouts came on the radio to tell us that the VC were coming toward us, diddy bopping down the trail like nobody's business. Not only were they fully armed, but they were also wearing complete uniforms and packing heavy.

"Damn, Top, our luck is still holding. Let's bring those fuckers down and get the hell out of here, like it never happened," the CO whispered, just as Lt Zen and I were bellying along the ground down to where Mac was already in position.

"There are six of them. That's all. We don't see any more following them. They seem to be alone. There is an NVA officer with them, and they have two RPDs. They are alert."

"The lead man is carrying an AK, the man behind him has an RPD, and the next man has an AK. The next man is some kind of an officer in an NVA uniform. He has an AK and a side arm. There is one other RPD and an AK, and that's all."

Our lookouts reported these important details about our target, and Mac's decision to have them posted far enough up the trail was a blessing that gave us time to decide what to do. Our first thought was to just ice them and run like hell. However, Battalion wanted whatever information the messenger might be carrying, and if at all possible, the living messenger himself.

Mac, Lt Zen, and I were running through some possible strategies when the CO slid into our huddle and solved the problem by saying, "There are only six of them, so let's take them by surprise if we can. Remember how close we are to the village. If we light them up, we may take hits from the village, and we cannot shoot back. Let the lookout security remain in place until we call them in. In the meantime, we simply take out the six men as silently as we can. Then, we will roll up and get the hell away from here."

Moving as quickly as possible, we reorganized our ambush to take the enemy down. Soon, we heard them approaching our positions. As fate would have it, our security teams reported that a group of villagers (mostly women and children) was coming down the same trail from the opposite direction.

"How far away from our position are the civilians?" I asked the security team.

Their reply was heartening. If everyone continued to move at the same speed, the VC would reach us well ahead of the villagers.

Tran stepped boldly out on the trail and started rattling off a string of Vietnamese words at the VC. He said something about his water buffalo being in heat. That certainly got their undivided attention. They pointed their weapons at him, but they did not shoot. Then we jumped them from both sides of the trail. Mac laid one of the machine gun-carrying VC out cold. The poor guy never knew what hit him. The little NVA officer was the first one to try to yell for help. As he pulled his side arm, one of our guys laid him out, too. There was a lot of scuffling and cursing but no shooting. Not one round was popped.

Disarming and subduing the enemy took a few minutes longer than we had planned. They were little but strong men, and they put up a good fight. Nevertheless, they lost, and we dragged them off the trail and picked up what was dropped during our brief struggle. Our last man had barely cleared the trail before the approaching female civilians appeared on their way to their rice paddies.

We did not have enough time to run with our additional baggage of two prisoners (who were out cold) and three rather heavy enemy rucksacks. We got down as close to the ground as possible and prayed for our luck to continue.

The women appeared to be very ordinary, much like the average women of the world. They walked along, laughing and talking. They did not seem to notice that anything was out of order as they slowly passed us by. We waited until it was safe to move before we had both of our lookout security teams come home. Then, we moved very quickly out of the area.

Before we left, however, we revived the two VC soldiers whom we had knocked out. The little officer's lip was busted, and his pride was wounded because he had been captured alive. That poor little bastard begged us to kill him.

Once we were in the clear, we assumed our running-and-fighting formation and moved on down the line. When we were safely out of the area, we formed into our lager and waited for the battalion commander's arrival. During that time we studied our VC captives.

We had not caught the messenger; instead, we had the VC paymaster. That little guy had been around for a long time according to his official identification papers. He had been at the Battle of Dien Bien Phu and had earned a lot of Red Stars. He also had papers signed by Uncle Ho and Giap. A real hero. We threatened to cut out his tongue if he did not stop wagging it. He was carrying a small pouch containing a number of official-looking documents, which the CO took from him. The little officer pleaded even more to be shot, but we did not intend to accommodate his wish.

323

Three of the rucksacks turned out to be quite a boon. The little VC group was carrying a lot of heroin, skag, and opium – all bound for any American drug addicts they could reach. They had twice as much paper money in various denominations, and their currencies included South Vietnamese piasters, North Vietnamese dong, and twice as many bundles of good-old American greenbacks in 20-, 50-, and 100-dollar bank notes. Of course, there were also a few bundles of American ones and fives.

Our troopers had quite a time searching, binding, and gagging our prisoners. We searched them as soon as we caught them. Not one of us forgot what had happened to Doc B. One of the VC prisoners was an NCO, and he was caught trying to get one of his men killed (i.e., by encouraging the man to make a move on us). To prevent any other disruptions from him, we stripped him buck naked and hid his clothes. He then became very quiet.

The CO told Battalion about the drugs and the money, and we turned all of it over to two Special Forces captains and a Spook. I was later told that they took the paymaster and most of the stuff all the way to Saigon and Long Binh. They let us keep the weapons. It is also noteworthy to mention that not one of those guys we had brought down was wearing racing slicks. In fact, they were all very well dressed, and I wondered if they were combat troops or carriers.

Once those VC were removed from our hair, we relocated to a more secure area and set up so that we could finally have a decent meal. We had left too early that morning to even consider eating.

Speaking of eating, two of the enemy rucksacks contained a lot of good chow, including large, cooked crabs; hunks of roast pork; cooked cabbage wedges; good black nuc mam; and some large balls of cooked rice wrapped in banana leaves. At Doc California's advice, we skipped the pork and ate everything else.

That was not the first time we had taken out one of the VC's paymasters and captured a shit pot full of money. However, that was the first time we had bagged such a "distinguished" paymaster and with such credentials signed by the VC's top men. He was indeed a great catch!

Everyone wondered what was so important about the papers he was carrying. The paymaster had certainly tried hard to conceal his little pouch from us, and after giving it up very reluctantly, he had begged us to kill him.

324

On the following day we received answers to some of our questions about the pouch.

During that next day Battalion pushed up to us and requested our location. We gave it to them, and some minutes later they told us where to meet them. We lagered and waited. Fortunately, there were locations in the flatlands where it was not necessary to cut an LZ.

Our battalion commander arrived with gunship escorts, who remained on station in the air while he was on the ground with us. He seemed very happy and asked that the company be pulled in so they might hear what he had to say. This was unusual, but as long as the gunships were in the air above us, it was fairly safe for us to come so closely together.

Once the company was assembled, the battalion commander spoke to us. Above his head he held a sheet of paper inside a plastic document protector. When he had our attention, he said:

"Captain Brooks, Captain Norris, Lt Zen, Top Steen, and all of you wonderful Skytroopers of Black Knight Alfa. I am holding in my hand a copy of an original enemy order sent down to the NVA and Viet Cong troops in this and other areas. Men, this order originated at the top level of the Viet Cong Headquarters and bears the signature of their commander. The order was discovered among the many important documents carried by the VC paymaster. I want you to know what is in this order because it specifically concerns you, all of you men whom we call our Grand Company. Listen, everyone, to what the translation of this order says:

'To all the commanders and troops operating in Areas 16, 18, and 20a. You are to avoid all contact with the American 1st Cavalry Division unit code named Black Knight Alfa. If they fire on you, you may return fire in an effort to break contact. They are a special CIA-trained, very highly motivated unit of skilled assassins using advanced technologies and secret deceptive methods in an attempt to destroy us ...'

"There was more to the order, but I just wanted you to hear the most important part of it. Needless to say, I am proud of every one of you. This order is a first of its kind, and according to the paymaster, the order is already in the field.

"In addition to this order, you are blamed for a lot of things that you did do. As an example, there is written proof that your little sojourn through the A Shau Valley really did hurt them, so much so that the NVA actually believed that you were TWO UNITS. One unit acting as a decoy to draw fire, and when they drew fire, another GHOST UNIT, Black Knight Alfa, would suddenly materialize and fly into and destroy them."

Of course, the enemy document failed to explain or to even suggest how that ghost unit, Black Knight Alfa, managed to magically appear and disappear at will. If the other unit was not ours, how was it that they were always there when we needed them?

Clearly, the top brass of the NVA and the VC were totally unsuccessful in their rather comical attempt to explain why they were unable to bring us down.

Happily, Battalion passed the word that the enemy had admitted in writing to the deadly accuracy of our artillery supporting fires. Our commander said that Birth Control was very happy to know that they were "shooting good". The other "secret" VC documents, which were scheduled for the eyes-only reading of our Battalion's top leaders, also revealed that each VC unit that had encountered Black Knight Alfa had been badly hurt.

Here is a translation of the enemies' own words:

"The great losses suffered by the NVA and Viet Cong units due to their having contact with the berserk, criminal, drug-using (lone) American berserk killer unit, was found by General Giap to be totally unacceptable."

Notice that they used the word "berserk" twice in the same sentence and also that they used the word "lone" after saying they had been in contact with two of our units.

The enemies' higher commands even accused us of testing some new types of American weapons that we certainly knew how to use. They also said we were elite troops in the field and a one-of-a-kind infantry unit that was very deadly.

I think their references to our "new" weapons were addressing how we used our thump guns and claymores. We used both of these weapons in an entirely effective, but unorthodox, manner, and our methods had really hurt our enemies.

The battalion commander thanked us and said he would see that our commanding general received copies of the enemy documents that we had captured from the paymaster, in addition to his own special report.

"First Sergeant, I'm sure we have collected enough AKs to get some beer and ice, so we can wet down all of those nice comments from our enemy," the CO said loudly so that everyone could hear him.

In response, our entire company raised their voices in unison: "Black Knight Alfa. Alpha and Omega!"

After the Charley-Charley bird was gone, we waited for our birds because Battalion was pulling us out of that area.

We were slicked into LZ Barbara for some well-earned rest. Cold beer and a meal fit for a boatload of kings awaited us. As a dedicated chowhound, I engaged in some serious eating, and I played hell with the giant, hot rolls that were served to us. I did not indulge too much in the beer, though.

My company clerks brought my backlogged paperwork to me, and the CO submitted recommendations for all of our medevac troopers to receive awards that they so justly deserved. He requested that Doc B. be given the highest award possible. He also wrote award recommendations for all of the men who left the company at that time. Some of our troops left for R & R, and others headed for The Land.

We received some new guys, and I had the time to give them my standard inbriefing and to make sure that each new man was partnered with an old soldier.

The battalion commander sent a photocopy of the enemy order to our orderly room, which made me very happy. It was great to have in writing what the men of the Grand Company, along with the other members of our magnificent team, had WROUGHT.

JoJo Is Down

As part of a major First Team combat operation, our company was slicked into LZ Jane. From there we were part of a massive Charley Alfa back into one of our old AOs, which was in the Nui Mien Mountains. It was so good to be back in the mountains, even though we were not there in our usual mode of being alone. After three days of pulling security missions in preparation for another operation Jeb Stuart, which numbered somewhere around the third or fourth time an operation was given that official name, Black Knight Alfa was assigned to cover one flank of the operation. To accomplish our new mission right the first time, we had to be there in position 25 hours a day. There was no downtime and no time to sleep because a large number of Charlies seemed determined to occupy the area at all costs.

Late one evening, our battalion S-2 officer met us in a fairly secure area to give us a new mission that was right down our alley. We had been looking forward to such an assignment for a long time. We were given the task of finding the 18th NVA Regiment, fixing them in a holding position, and fighting them until our big brothers rushed to the scene to take them out permanently.

Battalion had a strong indication of where they were planning to hole up and where they would be in motion trying to get across the border into Laos. We would have air support and Rolling Thunder from Birth Control available at all times, which meant that our Redleg forward observer had to stay in constant contact with Birth Control, to provide them with our changing locations. This method of regular contact between our Redleg and our artillery fire support was designed to greatly reduce the time lapse between our first call for help and the time on target (TOT) of our first supporting fire round that actually hit our enemy. We often used this method of fire support when our company was moving, and it always worked for us because our artillery forward observer teams and our wonderful cannoneers were well above the best.

Sure, I am an old cannon cocker, and I know TOT is not officially in the book as I have just explained it, but that is what it meant to us, and it worked out very well. If it had not, I would not be alive to tell you our story.

Early the next morning we moved out with Black Knight Alfa in the lead and JoJo on point. The rest of the battalion task force fell in behind us. In that operation we had a full battalion, minus our company, running drag for us. The battalion commander wanted us to pay close attention to our front and sides. Basically, we had the ball, and the rest of the battalion was covering our plays.

We took our positions in our best running-and-fighting formation. One-Six was our lead platoon, followed by the Headquarters section, Two-Six, Four-Six, and Three-Six. Because our battalion units behind us were not within our seeing and hearing distance, we maintained positions and contact strictly by radio. Our positions provided enough distance for Charlie to sneak in between our units. Although it was not a good way to operate, the terrain and our situation temporarily dictated that method of movement. The possibility of Charlie intervening prompted the CO to put Mac and his Third Platoon in their familiar drag position.

We did not change platoon positions in our formation. Once we picked up the rhythm, security and control were of the utmost importance. JoJo was our best tracker, and when Rod or Nat backed him up, the pair was an unbeatable team. In a situation like that, we worked two point men and switched off on the backup points. As a rule, we never had all three of our best point men forward at the same time. We moved in that manner for two days. The units following us had trouble keeping up, and they called at least four times to ask us to slow down.

Around 1000 hours on our third day out, JoJo picked up the trail of the 18th, and when he was sure he had his quarry, we stuck to them like glue. JoJo was like an old, experienced Mississippi coon dog hot on the trail of a young, inexperienced, half-smart coon who was destined to fall.

The CO pushed up to Battalion with the news that we were on our enemy's trail. The battalion commander asked if the CO was sure it was the 18th, and the CO replied that he was damned sure because his point man said it was the 18th.

Battalion responded, "Go get them, Black Knight Alfa. We are dropping back some more so you guys can do your thing like you do best. We don't want to cramp your style. Good hunting, and save some for us. Out."

I remember it well because I could not find my watch. When I asked Pete for the time, we discovered that he had my watch, and his watch was in the bag with his long antenna. We had no idea how the switch had occurred. We laughed about our watch problem, and he said, "Top, both of our watches show 1400, give or take a couple of minutes."

We had been dogging the 18th's butt for nearly four hours. If they knew we were tail-grabbing them, they were deliberately not showing it.

The CO gave the word for us to announce our presence, and he moved up with the lead platoon sergeant. Long Claw was allowed to formulate his own plan of attack, and when he was ready, the CO ordered him to "Do it!"

Black Knight Alfa grabbed the unsuspecting 18th NVA Regiment, and we chewed on them a little bit, cleanly dropping 12 of them upon first contact. While screaming our battle cry, One-Six dealt a decisive blow to the trailing enemy unit. We surely wanted them to know who was knocking on their back door.

I believe they truly had not known we were there because they seemed to be in a hurry, even before we hit them, and when we rammed into their rear, they did not turn to fight us. Instead, they opted to keep moving, leaving their 12 dead soldiers scattered in their wake. Shortly before dark, we bit them again and took out four more of their men. Still, those bastards refused to stop and lock up with us.

"Top, I think those Charlies have something much bigger than us on their minds. It's not right or like them not to stop and fight us. They did fire a few rounds and two RPGs, but they kept on going. First Sergeant, mark my words, there's something big in the wind. I've already told Long Claw to slow JoJo down. Maybe our red friends up front are trying to get cute! Top, I think we should pull JoJo back. He's been up front too long. Don't you agree?"

I fully agreed with him, and in fact, I had already alerted Mac that he was going up front. One-Six would take up the drag platoon's position.

That night we made the switch. Old JoJo was not too happy about it, but he finally admitted that he was a bit tired. Nat moved to the point position with a new man as backup because I wanted to hold Rod in reserve.

All troopers in our three line platoons were fully capable of filling the point man position and doing it very well. However, it was pucker time, and everyone fully understood the value of having the best point men on the job. There were no better point men in all of creation than JoJo, Rodriguez, and Natkowski.

Here, I want to explain some details about our situation. When we began that operation, we Charley Alfa-ed into the Nui Mien Mountains, almost halfway between their highest point and the foothills. Then our operation took us down into the foothills. The 18th NVA Regiment, or elements of it, and the Viet Cong were operating freely in those foothills, where according to our intelligence information (gained mostly from our very own Cav LURP teams), the 18th had come south from the Ho Chi Minh Trail, and they were packing heavy as if they were going to a big fight. Although Cav Division knew of their location, they did not know why the enemy was there. Additional reports indicated that there were other NVA units packing heavy and moving south. We were there to shake the tree and to see what fell out.

When we latched on to the ass of the 18th, they tucked their tails and ran back toward the safety of the high ground. When darkness fell, we stopped our chase and found a nice FOB location, where we went to ground, formed our normal lager, and waited for the new day. If old Charlie wanted us, he would have to come to us. The advantage was ours, and we kept it that way.

The 18th did not come looking for us, which indicated that they were not foolish. They must have figured out that hitting us that night would have been an invitation to their disaster. Old Charlie surely knew that, with assistance from Birth Control, we would have torn him a new asshole. Therefore, both the 18th and our company had a peaceful night.

We left early that morning with the Third Platoon leading out and Nat on point with another trooper from the Third Platoon covering his ass. The CO had the Second Platoon screening to our right because the formation of the terrain and our best route of travel made our right flank vulnerable to an ambush or a hit. We traveled more slowly and cautiously because the enemy already had a full night's opportunity to prepare and place a lot of deadly snaps and traps behind them.

The Second Platoon called a halt while they checked a suspicious area. The rest of the company lagered and informed Battalion of our plans to hold up. Four or five minutes later, Gonzalez asked the CO and me to come to his position to see "something very interesting."

The objects of interest were six 122mm enemy rockets, each weighing well over 100 pounds. The enemy had fixed the rockets in firing positions on a mobile launching rack and had expertly camouflaged and rigged them to fire automatically. (Here, I have stressed the word "automatically" because not only was it a beautiful, automatic system, but it was also the third time we had come across that type of deadly rocket with the same automatic triggering device.)

Those automatic firing devices were exceptionally beautiful because they allowed the rockets to be fired accurately at any time without the nearby presence of an enemy soldier. The enemy could be miles away when the Americans came looking for them, and they would lose only the mobile rocket launchers, most of which were hand-made and expendable – a small price to pay considering all of the death and destruction the rockets were capable of causing.

It was unforgettable that a single 122 had taken out that first marine ammunition dump on "Day One" of the siege of Khe Sanh. That NVA 122mm rocket had taken out well over 1,500 tons of high, explosive ammunition.

The firing devices were quite simple in design. Their electrical power was gained from improperly discarded American batteries, ranging from everyday flashlight batteries, to radio (PRC-25) batteries, to Jeep and truck batteries. In some cases, the batteries were linked together to provide enough electrical charge to set off the rocket's motor propellant in one or more of the 122mm rockets.

Most of those simple firing devices consisted of basic rice bowls that contained a measured amount of water. On top of the water sat a simple wooden or cork float that was rigged with thin bamboo twigs to keep it stationary. The positive lead wire was securely tied to a U-shaped piece of medium-gauged copper wire that was attached to the float. Another piece of copper wire was formed along the rim of the rice bowl, and the negative lead was attached to it. The batteries were properly positioned to form the circuit, which was open as long as there was enough water in the bowl for the float. Hot weather would cause the water in the bowl to evaporate, thereby lowering the water level and the float until the positive and negative lead wires touched. When the electrical circuit was complete, the battery charge would fire the initiator charge, which then fired the main charge of the solid propellant that launched the rocket.

I take my helmet off to the designer of those firing devices. They were items of pure beauty, simplicity, and creativity. The designer was obviously very good at THINKING and DOING.

Because we were familiar with the wiring setup and no snaps or traps were present, we found it easy to locate the batteries and trace the wiring. Within a short time we disarmed all six rockets and safely shut them down.

There we were again, as we had been in The Valley with that M46 130mm Gun-Howitzer. However, this time, we had ownership (finders-keepers) of six of General Giap's 122mm rockets. Now what were we going to do with them?

It did not take the CO and Redleg long to determine (with utmost accuracy) the rockets' American target. The CO immediately pushed up to Battalion with the news. The American "target" already had the feeling that they were going to be hit, but they did not know when it might happen. The presence of the rockets strongly suggested that there had to be enemy ground units poised to attack the American target, and those enemy troops did not know that we had discovered their mission.

The American command – our gunships and troops – were already in motion to catch the enemy wherever they were "poised". Soon, it was a done deal – our guys found the enemy and did them in.

The CO radioed Battalion the correct coordinates to the location of the rockets, and we made sure the firing chain was permanently destroyed. We also rigged one of the rockets with a special trap that was designed to surprise anyone who attempted to rewire the firing chain.

In the meantime, a flight of F-4 Phantoms in Da Nang was being prepared to come and destroy all six rockets. This happened once we were safely away. The air strike was well on time and on the money.

Our battalion commander said that our discovery of those six rockets had surely saved many American lives. During the time we had spent disarming them, however, we had lost our prey – the 18th. Nevertheless, we did not regret our decision to stop those 122s from flying.

We decided to make a mad dash to try to catch up with our quarry, but we did not move so fast that we disregarded the primary rules for staying alive in hostile NVA and Cong country. We knew it was possible that our enemy had stopped to prepare to bushwhack us. With that in mind, we pushed on, following their trail before it became too cold.

The first group of enemy soldiers we encountered must have been the group responsible for the six rockets, because they were running in the direction of the rockets, which was straight into our path. We were not sure why they were going back to the rockets; they certainly could have done better by going the other way. We felt them before we actually saw them, but we had no time to plan an ambush. Therefore, we just dropped down and hit them. They never knew what happened.

After greasing the entire group, we got our shit back together and continued on the trail of the big boys. We wanted the head of the snake. We wanted the 18th.

Unfortunately, that last group we dropped and the big bang of the air force taking out their "toys" must have spooked our enemy and made them even more elusive.

Battalion ordered us to push on and reminded us of the possibility that our enemy might scatter or go to ground. On the other hand, they might just stand and fight. If they did, we were to hold them until the rest of the battalion could get into position to finish them.

We moved only a short distance forward, when Battalion ordered us to stop where we were and to shackle them our location. We lagered and did as instructed. Something was wrong!

After a few minutes, we got the word.

The unscheduled air strike and our hitting those guys who had been running toward us had caused our enemy to break into smaller groups and scatter. However, just like always, there was a joker in the deck in the form of a large Viet Cong unit accompanying the 18th. They did not break up but continued toward higher ground. They were hanging tough as if they wanted a fight. Perhaps they were acting as decoys to take the heat off the 18th or to draw us into a trap. By that time, however, they would be crazy not to know there was a full battalion, assisted by air power, dogging their butts.

We found out what the enemy was doing after learning that one of our Cav LURP teams was also dogging the 18th. They were shook up because we had just missed taking them out when we bit the 18th in the ass. Someone had dropped the ball and had forgotten to tell the LURP teams that we were also after the 18th. I was so relieved that we had not hit any of our own men.

Battalion decided that the rest of our battalion would go after that large VC unit and that we would continue to dog the majority of the 18th because they believed the leader was there. (He was a full NVA colonel who was soon expected to become a general.) In that mission, Black Knight Alfa became the closest American unit to the largest piece of the action.

However, before the companies moved out, our battalion commander changed the game plan to have only two companies take up the chase. I think he decided to hold one company and some of his attached units in reserve because we had replaced our combat support company with a Delta company. I also believe that Division and Battalion knew they were on to something big, and the mission given to Black Knight Alfa was very important to the goal of bringing down the enemy element that offered the largest threat. Our battalion commander knew that once we were on the enemy's tail and after the smell of the enemy's blood was on us, we would not stop until we brought our prey all the way down.

Much later, it was revealed that the NVA and the Viet Cong were trying to get their forces into positions for a spectacular offensive, which explains why the NVA had avoided a fight with us. If they had dug in and fought us, it would have resulted in a large gathering of American forces in the areas where they were planning their build-up and positioning.

The NVA's partners in crime were primarily the Viet Cowards. The planned major operation/offensive was right down the VC's alley, and they had been given the same "don't fight because it will draw unwanted attention" order. Nevertheless, they were still a mob whom their NVA masters had a hard time controlling because the VC wanted to grab all of the glory heaped upon them by the American press.

The VC made an abrupt change of direction and turned back down to the foothills. We did not fall for their tired old shit because we already knew the bastards were heading for the safety of the high grounds. Our CO even figured out approximately where they would make another drastic turn before heading back for the high ground, and that is where we went to cut their asses off.

Chasing the Cong was a bit more difficult than chasing the NVA because the Cong was mainly composed of out-of-work bums who had grown up in that area. I guess one could say the average local Cong member knew each tree and blade of grass on a first-name basis.

I had read a lot articles in our American newspapers in which the reporters and writers admiringly described the VC as outstanding and very elusive freedom fighters. The "elusive" bit was not always true, especially if one knew how and where to look for them. After a person learned that skill, it was easy to find them. After all, the mob was just a noisy group of people, and finding any such group was no big thing. We were old hands at finding Victor Charlie because we had acquired the capability of thinking like them. They could run and they could hide, but we could damned well find them, no matter how well they hid.

Once they made their last drastic change in direction and headed back for the high ground, we fell in on their asses, and they realized that we had not fallen for their old bag of tricks. The going was rough because we were climbing the side of a mountain, and both the VC and our company were packing heavy.

According to our map, there was a beautiful piece of defendable high ground a little farther up the mountain. The VC were sure as hell heading straight for that piece of terrain. The CO and I agreed that if we were the VC, that is where we would turn and fight because the terrain would give them a clear advantage.

We had to catch them before they reached that terrain, so we pushed them really hard and lit their rearguard up. We dropped them every step of the way. We nipped at their asses, and they lost both men and equipment, which was evident by the growing amount of equipment and bodies we found in the path of our advancement. Like us, they were tired, and we could smell their growing fear mingled with their sweat and blood. I had the disturbing feeling that we had locked up with them somewhere before. When I shared my suspicions with the CO, he said he would keep that in mind.

Soon, the ground became flat for a while, and the jungle became thicker and more difficult to negotiate. One might say that the VC found themselves facing a wall of nearly impenetrable jungle entanglements, with Black Knight Alfa behind them.

Victor Charlie had to stop and pull "quail tactics". We knew that they were cornered rats with big, sharp teeth, and like always, we did not make the mistake of underestimating them. We went straight for their jugulars.

It was still daylight on a typical bright, sunny Vietnamese day, and the overrated Viet Cong fighters had nowhere to hide. Although I say they were overrated, the group that we were dealing with was not the usual bunch of ragtag Viet Cong conscripts who were pressed into the services of the people. Hell no! It was evident by looking at those enemy soldiers whom we had already dropped that we were up against a full-size, hard-hat VC unit. They were old, experienced, full-time Viet Cong soldiers, fully equipped and fully uniformed. Also, they had been traveling during daylight hours, and they were packing heavy, which told us that something was definitely afoot, Normally, a hard-hat unit of that size would not be moving so boldly in broad daylight.

I mentioned earlier that the VC had no options but to fight us. Actually, there were other options. They could have run away, but whoever the VC commander was at that time had decided to fight us. In fact, he tried his best to draw us into a well-planned trap, but it did not work because we had already thought of the same trap, only in reverse.

Because of the high location and the trees, it was difficult for Redleg to get our 175mm long-range artillery in to help us where we most needed their support. However, he did bring our supporting fires in well beyond our front, and then he had them walk the fire back in toward our positions.

We suddenly stopped chasing the VC and turned their asses over to Birth Control. We did that before the VC had the opportunity to spring their well-planned trap on us. They realized that we had Rolling Thunder coming down on them, and we were in the only good path left open to them. They were in the process of setting up their mortars, but they had the same problems that we had, and Redleg added to their problems by determining with reasonable accuracy where they would set up their mortars. Birth Control was causing them a lot of pain, and when they finally tried to run, it was too late. We had them cornered, and we were ramming those big 175mm projos down their throats.

Long Claw saw four of the VC trying to muscle a heavy machine gun into a firing position that would hurt us, and he quickly informed the CO of that danger. The gun would be too close to our positions for our own mortars to fire back, and we dared not bring our artillery supporting fires in any closer to us. The VC who were setting up that gun knew the score; however, they failed to add to that score Black Knight Alfa's proud determination to survive.

Accompanied by some of his brave lads, Long Claw went into the raging inferno of our battle to prevent that enemy machine gun from entering the firefight. When the VC soldiers saw our men coming, they abandoned their machine gun and cut loose with their AKs. Fortunately, they missed Long Claw because JoJo and Sp4 Jones spoiled their aim and blew away all four of them, in addition to two more who were on their way to assist the original team. While bringing the VC down, JoJo overexposed himself and turned his back on a dying enemy soldier. That dying bastard shot JoJo in the back.

"Aw shit. Top! Top! JoJo is down. He just got hit. The Cong got him!" Pete yelled over the din, and I heard another voice calling to me almost at the same time.

"Top, JoJo is calling for you!" Pete hollered.

I took off running, and I heard the CO yelling at me. He was trying to tell me something, but I did not hear him.

"Oh my dear, sweet Lord. God, don't let him die. Please God, not JoJo."

I don't know whether I was praying aloud or just thinking those words.

As I ran headlong for the First Platoon's position, I heard some of my troopers screaming at me. "Top, get down, get down. Ya wanna get yourself killed?"

The piece of shrapnel in my chest was causing it to swell a little and to hurt rather badly. No one knew about my wound. Of course, I had told Doc B., but he was dead. Although the shrapnel began to kick my ass royally, I charged on like a madman. I was going to JoJo come hell or high water, and only old Death had the power to stop me and keep me away from my downed friend and fellow soldier.

I always went to my troopers when they were down, unless it was an impossible situation. It was one of the many duties of the first sergeant in the field, in combat, and in a firefight. It was even more special with JoJo and a few of the other troopers who were there when I took over the company. We had been together a long time.

The First Platoon was far away on our extreme right flank, so I had quite a distance to run. However, I did not get tired, and through the raging battle, I made it to JoJo in good time, all things considered and with the supreme help of the good Lord watching over me. I guess He was also watching over Pete because he was right behind me. I had not wanted him to follow my lead because I did not want him to risk getting hit. I knew that what I was doing was somewhat crazy, but I do believe we were all just a little crazy (or perhaps insane) during our time in the Nam.

When I arrived, some of the troopers reassured me: "Top, he's not dead. Dust-off is already on the way, so he has a good chance."

I heard Pete say that Redleg had already stopped our supporting fires to allow our medical evacuation birds to come in.

Doc Hopkins, who had replaced our beloved Doc B., had already cut most of JoJo's jungle fatigues off and had him lying face-down in the grass. His wounds were already bandaged, so I could not see how badly he was hurt. That he had been hit more than once was very apparent. Doc Hopkins verified that fact.

"Top, he was hit more than once. He took one of those rounds in his back – in his right shoulder – and it's real bad. That round hit the bone and did a lot of damage before it lodged in the muscle tissue. I think he's going to make it okay. Old JoJo is too damn mean a Cajun to die."

I reached out to touch the young man with the funny name, the young soldier who had taught me how to live in the jungle, eyeball-to-eyeball with our enemies. And there he was lying face-down and bravely trying not to show how much he must have been hurting. I knelt and put my face close to his. His eyes were cloudy and darker than usual. Still, he tried to smile at me and to look into my eyes as he whispered, "Top, you remember all I taught you, and keep your head down, ya heah. And, Top, you know damn well you are my one and only First Sergeant."

JoJo mumbled something else that I could not hear over the noise of the ongoing battle. He closed his eyes, stopped talking, and relaxed his hold on my hand.

"Doc! Doc!" I screamed.

Doc replied, "It's okay, Top. That last load of happy juice just kicked in fully, and that Cajun is floating on a white cloud. He's okay."

"First Sergeant, we got birds inbound. Dust-off is coming in, and smoke is already popped!"

I clearly heard our 81s shooting from the hip. A standard set-up was impossible.

"Top, there is nothing more any of us can do for him. It's all in God's hands now, just like it is for every one of us, and it ain't going to do any of us any good grieving. We got to stay alive. Now, Top, you get down now, 'cause you still got all of us left."

Nat's calm, cool voice reminded me of what I should have been doing. He was as right as rain. I still had almost 100 of the best Skytroopers of all times depending on me, and we were still locked up in a fight to the finish with our old enemy, the Viet Cong. To say that we needed each other was an understatement.

Johnny Johnny LeCroix was safe because he was in the same hands that held the whole world. Who was I to question the owner of those hands? As I helped to lift and carry JoJo to the dust-off bird, I briefly smelled the Louisiana Bayou, heard some sweet Cajun music, and tasted gator tail and rice served in a bowl of hot garlic and tomato sauce.

Yes, I cried again, as one more friend and wonderful trooper was taken away. I hurt for him.

"So long, JoJo, my young friend. I'll see you again on the flip side. SUOIeeeeeeeeeee!"

At that moment I wanted to kill as many VC as I could line up in my sights or get my hands on. Instead, I knelt to pick up some of the stuff that had fallen out of JoJo's pockets. Before I had a chance to follow the guys carrying JoJo to the dust-off bird, Pete was forcefully thrown on top of me, and both of us went down. I heard the air whoosh out of Pete's lungs, and I smelled the odor of sweat, blood, gunpowder, and death.

For the second time since Pete and I had been together, the enemy shot his radio off his back, and his radio saved his life – again. Of

340

course, the poor PRC-25 did not fare well. It was blown into a million pieces by a full burst of slugs fired from an enemy AK-47.

Pete was relatively unharmed, although he momentarily lost his breath from the impact of the hit on his radio, and his ears were ringing because a piece of the radio had gone under his steel helmet and parted his hair down to his scalp. He was also rather upset about losing his radio.

After Long Claw took out the VC shooter who had tried to take Pete down, some of the men of the First Platoon rushed to help Pete and me get up. As Pete and I faithfully thanked God for our lives and His help, the next call came in to Long Claw's RTO, who happened to have his speaker turned on. We heard:

"One-Six Alfa, this is Three-Six Alfa. Is Alfa Five at your location? Come back."

"Three-Six Alfa, this is One-Six Alfa. That's most affirm. Come on back."

"One-Six. We have a man down. Caldwell. And he is calling for Five. He said, 'Tell Five to hurry 'cause there ain't much time!' Out."

Sp4 Romanski pointed in the direction of the Third Platoon, and Pete and I were off running again. I do not know why Pete insisted on dragging the remains of his radio along, but he did.

Pete yelled back to Romanski as we took off, "Tell Three-Six we are on the way and not to pop caps on us."

I was saddened that I did not have the opportunity to say a proper farewell to JoJo, but our dust-off birds had to leave the area very quickly because they were under enemy fire.

"JoJo, I'm still so sorry that I wasn't there to see you off, but I know the good Lord was with you then, and He is still with you, wherever you are. Suoieeeee!"

On our way to see Caldwell, I was still praying to God, and I am happy to say that I did not wait until my balls were in the sand to talk to Him. I often took the time, when the situation was favorable, to say "Thank you, Father."

During our run, I prayed for Caldwell's life. He was one of my old troopers who had been with me since the Battle of Hue and during all of our valley campaigns. I begged God not to take him, but I was aware of the fact that "God's will shall be done".

Caldwell had been hit badly. Although the medics were putting forward a superhuman effort to save him, his blood refused to stop flowing. I looked into the face of my young trooper and saw the reflection of the familiar face of old Death. Sweet Jesus! Sweet Jesus! You cannot live with old Death on a daily basis and not be able to clearly recognize his cold touch and feel his ominous presence. Old Death was certainly there, larger than life.

I felt really sick, and I could not keep my hands from shaking. I was aware that some of my troopers were looking first at Caldwell and then back at me. Dear Lord, what was I to do?

I knelt down beside my badly wounded trooper, and in the background, I overheard the medics trying to get one of the dust-off birds to turn around and come back. I did not move Caldwell, fearing that any movement would cause the blood to flow freely again from his wounds. My guts were tied in knots, and I was determined to hold back the tears. I had already cried so much since being in the Nam, and I had to keep my cool because other troopers might be down and asking for Top to come to their sides. I was running out of tears, and I knew that my mind was going to be the next thing to leave me.

I came as close to Caldwell as possible and was suddenly shocked when he opened his eyes. They appeared to be a dull brown, rather than their normal blue color. In a loud, clear voice, Caldwell asked, "That you, Top?"

When I responded in the affirmative, he smiled and said, "Top, will you sing my favorite song for me, one more time?"

"Damn right I will, but I gotta warn you. It's going to be out of tune a whole lot."

"That's okay, Top."

I was all choked up, but Lord, I had to try.

"Kentucky, you are the dearest land outside of heaven to me."

As I started to sing the song that he and I had sung many times before, my voice cracked. The fight was still going on around us, but right there in that sacred spot, there was peace in the valley. I tried again because one of my magnificent troopers was preparing to embark on the longest journey of his life. He asked me to do something for him, and I was going to do it or die trying.

"Kentucky, I miss the hound dogs chasing coon.

When I die, I want to rest upon a distant mountain so high, For there is where God will look for me.

Kentucky, I will be coming soon ..."

I sang my heart out and was moved beyond words when all of our troopers who heard my voice raised theirs to join in a moving tribute to one of our own. Soon, even over the sounds of our battle with the Viet Cong, one could hear the beautiful melody as we sang as loudly as we could, "Kentucky, I will be coming soon!"

We really let go, and the rest of the company took up the beat. Our voices floated upward on the smell of the sweet bluegrass of the great state of Kentucky, and the sounds of "Kentucky" rose high enough for the Good Shepherd to hear us.

My memories of that time are foggy, and I cannot tell you exactly what happened after our wonderful outburst of song. My vision was blurred with all of the tears I had been holding back, and although his grip on my hand did not relax, "Kentucky" (i.e., Caldwell) was gone from us. Mother of God, Kentucky slipped quietly away to that mountain so high.

My wonderful troopers helped me to my feet, and together we went to finish bringing Victor Charlie down. I was consumed with a red haze as we went directly to the heart of the matter, to where the last pocket of VC were holed up.

Sixteen of the VC threw in their towels, and within minutes, our backup company was there, along with a lot of ARVNs and even some marines. By the time our supporting elements arrived, the battle was over. Black Knight Alfa had already brought the enemy all the way down. I gathered my report, and I helped to load Caldwell on the bird so he could return home and hear the hound dogs chasing coon.

My chest and heart ached terribly. That damned battle had cost us, but one damned thing was certain: the VC suffered a much greater loss than we did. JoJo and Kentucky did not fall in vain. Victory, undisputed Victory was ours.

Someone said to me, "It's all right, Top. We got the bastards good. Top, listen to me. It's all over!"

I had to lean against a tree for support.

When the CO approached me later, he said, "First Sergeant, you are something else. You run through hell to comfort one of our downed troopers, then you come close to getting your head blown off by standing up and singing like you were at some kind of hoedown. And you follow that little act by leading a charge right down the VC's throats. Top, they had to think you were crazy, that we were all crazy Americans. Man oh man, you are one hard act to follow, but, First Sergeant, I wouldn't have you any other way, so I guess that makes us both crazy as hell."

The CO was both mad and glad, and he told me never to do that again. Then he shook my hand and told me to get my report to him so he would know how we stood.

Eventually, I learned that JoJo had lost most of the normal use of his right arm and leg, but he survived. I imagine that he is still hunting alligators down in the deep Louisiana swamps. As for Caldwell, well … God found him just where he wanted to be found – on a distant mountain so high in the beautiful state of Kentucky!

Retrospection

Isn't it peculiar? The Russians, Chinese, Cubans, East Germans, and only the good Lord knows who else were in Vietnam trying their best to kill all of American soldiers, and all the while, the news media of the world were involved in a feeding frenzy to pick our bones clean. Through the untiring efforts of the media, the world was outraged against American soldiers. Why, in some cases, they were even blaming the bad weather conditions on American soldiers in Vietnam. Worldwide, the newspapers, radio, and television stations struck out at the US as much as they possibly could, and they declared that the American soldiers fighting in Vietnam were the worst soldiers the world had ever seen.

However, when two of the good-old boys who were killing us in Vietnam had a falling-out, Red China "invaded Vietnam" on 17 January 1979. Yes! Ho Chi's and Giap's old buddy, Red China, sent two full armies into Vietnam to fight the NVA. Their 41st and 42nd Armies consisting of 85,000 well-armed troops, which were later augmented to 200,000 troops, made a run on Vietnam at three widely separated points "to teach the NVA a lesson".

Those three points of invasion were Lao Cai, Cao Bang, and Lang Son. The mighty People's Liberation Army was stopped and held motionless by the 60,000-strong Vietnamese regional forces. Sure, the Chinese soldiers briefly took Lang Son, but the Chinese paid up front for their actions with over 20,000 casualties. The number of soldiers Giap lost was a mystery; those statistics were kept hush-hush.

Isn't it peculiar that there were no loud cries and big, bold headlines, no condemnation by the same world news media who had so effectively crucified American soldiers? Was it the old Barabbas thing revisited, or was it that the news of China invading Vietnam did not have much market value?

On the other hand, 200,000 Chinese soldiers went into Vietnam and returned to China minus 20,000. I wonder ... would the world call that a Chinese victory, or ... ?

Then, there was that American Cav unit of only 100 Skytroopers who called the NVA out and kicked their collective ass. I might add that they did it with great style and amazing grace. Moreover, when the ass-kicking was called because of rain, that American unit was still intact, having suffered only four KIAs and seven casualties.

Black Knight Alfa. Alpha and Omega!

Up on the Mountain

According to the scuttlebutt, our whole battalion was scheduled to move south to III Corps and into the rubber plantations. Follow-up word said that we were going to Phuoc Vinh, which was not far from Saigon. However, until that possibility became a reality, I Corps was still our home and AO, and once again, we were moved right up to the DMZ. We were assigned to an area in a quadrangle formed by the ancient city of Hue, the combat base of Khe Sanh, Phu Bai, and the border of Laos. Our AO was somewhere within, but not limited to, that rough quadrangle.

We chased Charlie on a daily basis. He had become somewhat bolder, especially after his devious success during Tet. Partnering with the Victor Cowards, old Charlie showed his "bravery" by terrorizing the civilian population and blowing up some aircraft. Big deal! Neither the civilians nor the inanimate aircraft was armed.

Thinking they were bad, the VC and the NVA let their cowardly success go to their heads. When they thought they had the upper hand, they would pull on us, and we would blow their asses away. Clearly, they were not used to fighting well-organized and determined predators like us. Still, our enemy continued to send their forces south, especially after our good folks back home persuaded the President to stop the B-52 raids on the Ho Chi Minh Trail "'cause those raids were immoral". Of course, those same anti-war demonstrators did not care that more enemy soldiers and supplies coming down the trail meant a greater number of dead American soldiers.

The enemy often planned their trails south to pass near or through villages, because they knew we would not dare to hit them near a village of innocent civilians for fear of creating another My Lai. Believe me, the enemy milked the My Lai story for all it was worth. The villages situated nearest to the foothills of the mountains were all primary routes for the NVA and their VC guides. Such was the case concerning the village bordering our area.

The NVA were boldly moving large units down the trail to the foothills in close proximity to that village, which was, for them, advantageously close to the Laos border. Our mission was to ambush the NVA coming down that particular trail before they reached the safety of the village. However, we were not going to try to ambush them on any section of trail in the foothills. The marines had tried that twice, but both times they had come out bloody and on the shitty end of the stick, just like that unit who had ambushed the river before we came to square things away.

That evening, we had plenty of time to plan our ambush. The ambush was an art form to us, and as usual, we did not operate by the book. Battalion told us to get the job done, and they let us do things our way. Because the trail had been ambushed twice in the foothills and because the enemy likely believed that we would not dare hit them in the flats close to the village, we did just that. We dared. In fact, we went all the way and set up our ambush site in the local village cemetery.

The cemetery sat in a wide-open field approximately 800 yards further along the trail and away from the high grounds of the foothills. Frankly, the cemetery was so obvious it practically screamed at you, and this fact became our ally. We chose the cemetery as our ambush site because it was so obvious that our enemy would hardly notice it. Around the cemetery, the terrain was as flat as a pancake. Even the rice paddy dikes were unusually flat.

We could make our kill zone as wide as we desired, and once we hit old Charlie, he would have absolutely no place to hide. If he ran toward the village, we would cut him down before he could get halfway there, to avoid endangering the villagers. We also planned our site to prevent Charlie from running back to the high ground of the foothills, and we agreed to grease anyone who might come from the high grounds to help him. The cemetery was an excellent location for what we wanted to do. If Charlie came down the trail that night, his ass would be ours.

We could not physically go down to the cemetery for a better inspection because we might be seen. Therefore, we lay dog during the remainder of the daylight hours and planned. From a position where we could view most of the terrain with our field glasses, the CO and I made a detailed map study of the area. After determining that the cemetery would not accommodate our entire company, we decided to send only a reinforced platoon.

The CO selected a good location for our home base, and he chose a position from which he could cover us in case any VC soldiers came from the village to join the fight. Also, from that position, the rest of the company could offer us maximum protective fires, and we could come home under those fires if it became necessary.

Because radio communications were very good in that portion of the flatlands, we planned to maintain constant radio contact. Although our starlight scopes were working, we did not need them because the moon was nearly full. The night was typically warm and so clear that we really did not think Charlie would be moving about much. Nevertheless, we planned as if we were expecting the whole damned NVA.

Our chances of getting artillery-supporting fires were nil because we were too close to a village. Battalion authorized us to use our own mortars "only in an extreme emergency". Captain Norris wanted to go with us in case we did need to use them. The CO was unhappy with this arrangement because he knew that if push came to shove, Captain Norris would get his buddies to shoot for him. Though reluctant, he agreed to let Captain Norris go along with us on our ambush.

In support of our ambush arrangement, we originally approached the village from the hilly side. Then we snuck down through the foothills until we had a good view of the village and the surrounding area below us. The cemetery was between our position in the foothills and the village at a greater distance.

Once darkness came to cloak our movements, we moved in a direct line toward the village, keeping the cemetery between the village and us. At my suggestion, we left a security team with a radio in our original location to protect our back door and possible escape route. We took the rest of the company down to a slightly lower level not far from our rear security. From that position the CO established our home base as a box-shaped ambush with the heavy side toward the route we expected

348

the NVA to take and the cemetery where the Third Platoon and I would be set up to ambush Charlie.

As soon as we made the necessary arrangements on our codes and planned the return route that my unit would take, I talked with Sfc. Tuzo about our mortar-supporting fires, which we had already planned on our maps. After everything was set, we took the reinforced Third Platoon, and keeping the cemetery between the village and us, we moved down and occupied the Vietnamese cemetery.

Before entering the cemetery, Mac sent an R & R team forward to check for late-night mourners. We received an "all clear" and quickly moved in and began to hastily, but positively, set our weapons in position. We also dug in well.

I will be the first to admit that it was more than a little bit weird to be digging holes in an old cemetery at night with an almost-full moon. We were planning a graveyard bash, and we were inviting the NVA and the VC to our surprise party. We were very careful not to disturb the graveyard's occupants, and I apologized to them for our intrusion and explained that our incursion into their domain was necessary. I also assured them that we would clean up after our party ended.

Once again, we had sufficient time to do everything right the first time, which was a huge plus for our side. We troopers felt like grave robbers in a B-type Hollywood movie. Nevertheless, we remained devoted to our mission, and without desecrating the cemetery or any of the graves, we set up in our classic lager-type ambush. The cemetery was shaped like a large, round mound, which nicely complemented our ambush formation.

We were machine gun-heavy, and we positioned our guns to give us all-around protection and one hell of a kill zone. Most of us on the ambush had humped at least two bandoleers of 100 rounds of machine gun 7.62mm ammunition to the cemetery. We also had as much 40mm high-explosive thump-gun ammunition as we could carry.

Our kill zone stretched across open and flat terrain, where a few trees and some rice paddies dotted the landscape, along with two or three small shacks that we had completely covered. We employed our machine guns in high-gun and low-gun positions, and our grazing fire was a machine gunner's dream. The downside was that we would not use our flares and claymores as we normally did. Instead, we had to use most of them as close-in support and could place them to our front only as far as we thought it safe to move forward. Of course, we also removed all tracer rounds from our machine-gun ammo.

Redleg spent a few minutes pushed up to Birth Control, and they agreed to shoot illumination rounds for us if we needed them. Sfc. Tuzo had our pre-planned fires set in as backup support.

When we had our shit together, we settled in to wait.

Our most serious drawback was having a no-fire area. Given our company's position, such an area was necessary to prevent a friendly fire accident. The CO and I safeguarded the no-fire areas that affected both of our positions.

I think it was shortly after 0100 hours when our security team contacted us from their position up the trail in the direction we expected the NVA to come. First, they keyed the mike using our planned signal. Then they came on the radio in a whisper. Our enemy had not stayed at home on such a beautiful moonlit night. They were on their way. The hit was going down!

Mac made sure everyone was awake and alert. He said, "Five, be advised old Charlie is right now in the process of thoroughly checking out the areas near the last ambush site, and from what we can see, old Charlie is packing heavy, and you won't catch him napping. These guys got their shit together, and they look as mean as hell!"

So, our enemies were at those "textbook" ambush sites, making sure they would not be caught napping. That was what we wanted to hear because it strongly indicated that they did not suspect our "obvious" location.

Mac very wisely pulled his security into our positions. They had to run to get ahead of the oncoming enemy unit. Redleg made sure Birth Control had their ears on, and I let the CO know that the shit was going to hit the fan.

Of course, we were not so crude as to have the enemy lead man set off a flare. No! All of our flares were command-controlled. Besides, the night was so clear and the moon was so bright that we had no trouble seeing our enemy. We waited until they filled our kill zone, and Mac looked at Redleg and me. When I nodded my head, Mac whispered, "Shoot."

We opened up only with our M16s and thump guns. There was a slight delay after we fired our thump guns and before the grenades hit their targets.

YES!

When springing an ambush, the ambushers should open up with all of their might to try to take out as many enemy soldiers as possible during the initial surprising burst of fire. As written, that part is very true. What was different in our case, however, was that we tried to get the enemy to either hit the ground or to move out of the kill zone. That is exactly what they did, and our low machine guns fired first, followed by our high guns. My old Buffalo Soldier mentors had taught me that trick, which they had learned from the German Army.

The enemy yelled commands and shot at the wind as we killed many of them. Despite their failure to hit us, their initial reactions had told us clearly that we were not up against a bunch of ragtag soldiers. Although they were good, we were better. We had to be.

"The cemetery! The cemetery!" their leaders yelled in disbelief.

Redleg shot our first illumination rounds to improve the stage lighting, and we could see the enemy as if it were broad daylight. Our troopers were bringing them down as if they were shooting electronic targets on a train-fire range in the States. However, when the enemy targets went down, they were definitely not getting back up.

The enemy was packing mortars, which we did not allow them to set up. Our machine guns were walking their fire up and down where our enemies were dying, and we had no idea how many they numbered. We had other things on our minds. We were cutting them to ribbons, and it was almost like a daylight ambush. They tried to fall back, but our thump guns played hell with their rear.

They were only able to attack the cemetery to make a run on us. Just as we had planned for them to do, they sent some of their numbers to try to outflank us. However, their maneuver failed, and they ran into more of our machine gun-fire. Those left on their feet opted to run for the village. Having already anticipated that move, we dumped on them heavily in a wholesale slaughter. No matter how good the VC and the NVA thought they were, we had them dead to rights, mostly dead. Our illumination rounds revealed a ground littered with motionless forms. Some of our enemies escaped, which was okay because they would run home and tell General Giap that Black Knight Alfa had chewed on them.

Our early morning fight with that enemy unit was short, sweet, and fierce. Although the enemy did not just roll over and play dead, we had them by the short hairs and gave them only two options – to run like hell or to stay and die. Because we were all over them, they never had a chance to bring their mortars into play. Naturally, that was why we were all over them.

Within minutes, our fight was reduced to an occasional burst from an enemy AK. One enemy soldier foolishly shot an RPG. It took the enemy too long to figure out that the muzzle flashes from their AK-47s gave them away and that we had simply waited for them to shoot to reveal their positions.

Soon, that strange, but old and familiar, quietness came. The CO called to report no enemy movement as far as he could see. That old cemetery had been one hell of an ambush site, but it was not a good place to be caught during an enemy mortar or rocket attack. Mac's soldiers were busy filling in their prone fighting positions and pulling in their snaps, traps, flares, and claymores. In a few minutes, we were ready to leave. We ran for home and moved into our positions with the rest of the company.

From the direction of the village, the enemy hit the cemetery with a few 82mm mortar rounds. The VC certainly did not respect their dead. Silence came quickly again, and the VC did not come after us.

First light brought a beautiful flight of Blue Max and dust-off birds, but the men of the Grand Company required no assistance.

And Down to the River

Our cemetery ambush had been a success. Only one of our men was taken out by medevac because his eyes had caught some of the particles from an RPG explosion.

We held our home position until later that morning when we received supplies and chow. The ARVNs moved into the village and found 17 NVA soldiers who were too seriously injured to be moved. They also discovered many blood trails leading in various routes back into the foothills. Our security team came home without a scratch. They reported that several Charlies had passed by them, with some carrying their wounded.

The ARVN commander and his American advisors wanted to meet the Cav company commander who had pulled the ambush on the NVA unit. After verifying that all was well in the village they occupied, they came to visit us. They had a first-hand view of the destruction we had brought down on the heads of the NVA without disturbing the civilians or their village. The cemetery was certainly damaged, but not by our hands. The village chief knew that the Cong had fired the mortars, but he was afraid to talk, except to say, "The mortars were set up and fired outside the village."

Proof of our effective ambush tactics was everywhere. The American senior advisor (a Special Forces major) said there was indisputable proof that we had taken out a large number of enemy soldiers. They had been fresh troops and a special cadre unit – the equivalent of an American Special Forces unit – composed of seasoned, hand-picked veterans left over from the NVA 325C Division and the 304th Division. That special unit had come down from Dong Ha into Laos to Sepone and back into South Vietnam along Route 23 and into Quang Tri.

The ARVNs had found a local VC guide who was in need of medical attention. While they tended to his wounds, he told them everything he knew about the unit he was guiding. (That is how they gathered so much information in a short amount of time.) The VC guide had also claimed that his unit had been "ambushed by an American battalion with a couple of companies set up in the cemetery." He added that we had shown no respect for his ancestors.

The advisors saw the carnage and believed that the VC guide was telling the truth, except for his exaggeration that two companies had occupied the cemetery. They could see that the old cemetery was far too small, even for one company.

Major Davidson, our Special Forces Green Beret major, said he had felt compelled to meet with our commander and our men who had wrought all of that well-focused destruction. After learning that we were still in the area, he and the Vietnamese troop commander had decided to jump a bird and come out to see us and our recent battleground. He admitted to having hoped that we were Special Forces, as was originally reported to him.

"And you guys tied in to that much larger unit without air or artillery support? It's plain you didn't know what unit you were hitting. Those guys you hit were the cream of their crop, but you could not have known that," Major Davidson smiled and said.

In addition to what he said, his smiles and those of the other advisors implied that if we had known our recent enemy's identity, we would have passed on the hit.

The CO was really pissed off by their sarcasm. He stood close to the Green Beret major and spoke right into his face:

"Sir, I assure you that we are Cav, and as you can plainly see, we are only one company. We are not a battalion, and we are not reinforced. Only one third of our unit was in that cemetery. Right on down front, it was only one rifle platoon – my Third Platoon – who ambushed old Charlie. The rest of our company was right where you see us now. If our whole company had hit them, all of them would have most certainly died. Actually, we wanted some of them to run back to their headquarters and tell the story of what it was like to have Black Knight Alfa on their asses."

354

The CO handed the major one of our calling cards.

"Oh shit! So you guys *are* Black Knight Alfa. Sir, I'm sorry if I have offended you because your reputation precedes you, all the way to Pentagon East. You guys are a bunch of mean mothers," the major said with new-found respect.

"Damn straight!" the CO said, smiling proudly.

Our troops took up the standard and yelled our battle cry: "Black Knight Alfa. Alpha and Omega!"

Major Davidson threw us a very respectful salute.

The talkative enemy guide gave the ARVNs some good information, but he only talked when he was separated from his comrades, to prevent them from knowing that he was singing. The ARVNs also gathered some random information from the other wounded enemy soldiers that confirmed what the enemy guide had told us.

The ARVNs gave a body count to the guide, and he estimated the number of potential escapees, saying he was never told how many troops he would be guiding. He did know that he had been guiding a very special unit who had intended to hurt the Americans badly, for the glory of the People's Army.

The ARVN officer said that the enemy body count, which was steadily increasing as his units continued searching the foothills, suggested that the number of troops left to that elite enemy unit, after their rumble with Black Knight Alfa, was very small. He also reported that those enemy soldiers found alive were as ragged as a nickel mop.

The ARVNs who were following the blood trails in the foothills were expecting to have contact momentarily with the fleeing, wounded enemies. I passed the word on to our Air Cav troopers.

Then, we moved on to another area and another series of contacts with Charlie.

The bit of shrapnel in my chest had formed a sizeable lump that was giving me trouble. I tried hard not to give in to the pain, but I finally decided to let Doc California in on my secret. He promptly chewed me out and threatened to tell the CO if I did not. I promised I would, just to shut him up. Despite his threats, he kept quiet, and he gave me a shot of penicillin under the guise of my needing it for my leech and skeeter bites.

The CO watched me suspiciously. We slept in the same shithole together, ate from the same tin can, and saw the same mind-bending sights. We were the company commander and the first sergeant in the truest sense of our titles. I would go to hell with or for him without a concern for how I might get back. I was truly sorry about the day when JoJo was hit and we lost Caldwell. I know it was a crazy thing to do, but I just had to sing "Kentucky". The CO was also upset with me because I had turned down my chance to ensure that my name was on the E-8 list going to MILPERSN. At that time, I was one of the most senior E-7s in the US Army. However, I promised my troops that I would walk through the Valley of Death with them, and I did. My promise to them was far more important than getting my name on the E-8 list to DA.

Everyone was weary from our ambush, and despite the CO's attempt to get some rest time for us, we were forced to move on before long. Rest was an elusive commodity in our business, and the price was very high even for a few minutes.

Two days later, we had a run-in with Charlie, and he put up a fight in order to break contact with us. We took out a few enemy soldiers and believed the rest had run for the hills. When Blue Max radioed their discovery of the same Charlies in a nearby village, which was a well-known VC stronghold, we were ordered to go there to remove them.

Some of the slicks that had brought the ARVNs in to that operation gave us a quick ride to the village. I remember that day very well because it was the first time we were told to use the Chieu Hoi (Open Arms) program in an effort to win the hearts and the minds of the people. It did not matter that most of them were already loyal NVA and VC. The ridiculous part of the program was the required task of shouting "Chieu Hoi" to the enemy "before" we shot at them. They, however, were not required to follow that stupid protocol.

I have often wondered if any other army in the field has received such an absurd order. Imagine! I could not shoot at an enemy without first warning him of my presence.

Anyway, we rushed in to intercept the NVA and the Viet Cong, and before long, we were again in contact with them. There were far more VC soldiers than we had expected, and they suddenly turned "bad" because they knew that we could not use our artillery or air power.

I had no idea how many NVA and VC were in that village. All appeared to be armed with AK-47s, and they tried their best to bring us down. One thing was certain; it was not the right time to start the Chieu Hoi program.

356

My platoon managed to maneuver themselves between a group of Charlies and the village. We had them cornered, and the ARVNs were between them and the high ground. A large number of those Charlies broke for the high ground but were immediately cut down by the ARVNs.

As we yelled "Chieu Hoi," the enemy was already answering with AK fire. Therefore, we stopped yelling and got down to some serious ass-kicking. It was crunch time, and we had the enemy cut off from the relative safety of the village. We stood between them and their escape routes into the foothills. The CO was with the bulk of the company, forming our base of fire and effectively preventing the enemy from escaping. I was with the single-platoon maneuvering element, and we were mopping up the last of the enemy resistance. Clearly, we had broken the enemy's back.

From the last rice paddy closest to the village, I could see the nearest street, two houses, and some of those little religious stone monuments that stand about 4 or 5 feet high. Those "shrines" were scattered about, and some stood alone in the fields. They were too small for the average Charlie to hide behind, but I decided to keep a close eye on them because I had encountered some Charlies who could easily pass for midgets.

When three or four NVA soldiers made a run for the nearest house in the village, I alerted one of our machine-gun teams. Together, we made sure those enemy soldiers did not make it to the house.

As I dropped my empty magazine and fanned in a full one, I made the stupid mistake of averting my eyes and attention from the current situation. God knows, I had changed a million magazines without once looking down to find the hole. I could and still can change magazines on an M16 rifle in record time without watching what I am doing. However, that day I completely blew it.

A split second of negligence was all it took. An NVA soldier suddenly appeared out of nowhere, and he pointed his AK-47 at me. I could smell his sweat and body odor. My survival senses screamed their warnings, and even though it was too late for self-recrimination, I mentally kicked my own butt for making such a stupid error.

I was staring into the cold, deadly eyes of old Death. Time stood stark still, and I knew it was finally my time. Sweet Jesus!

Born of my many years of training and combat experience, my survival instincts kicked in, and I slipped sideways to become a smaller target. At the same time, I shot from the hip because I had no time to take aim.

I knew I would hit the enemy soldier, and I did, dear God. I was close enough to see the puffs of dust fly from his NVA uniform as my 5.56mm slugs tore into him, stitching him from gut to shoulder. The force of the little slugs threw him violently sideways and then over backward, as his AK spewed its slugs upward after dancing off one of the shrines that stood somewhere between us. One of those slugs slammed into me, spun me around, and threw me backward into the rice paddy. At the time, I did not understand why I was down in the water of the rice paddy.

When people who have been shot try to explain the sensation, they will often say, "It was like the kick of a full-grown mule or like being hit by a fast-moving truck." I am sorry to say that for me, it was rather like being slapped.

I remember struggling around in the cool water of the rice paddy, trying in vain to get out of the water and on my feet again. At the same time, I was looking around for my steel pot. I was alert and still holding onto my little black Bessie. I was also aware that our fight with the enemy was winding down.

I could not get up, and it was suddenly very cool. This time, it was definitely my blood and not strawberry Kool-Aid that mingled with the rice paddy water. I rose about halfway to a standing position before my legs buckled and I landed in the rice paddy water again.

With every effort left in me, I gave it one more try, but nothing happened. I was as weak as a newborn kitten, and I felt ashamed for being down and unable to get back up on my feet.

"Damn it all to hell!" I tried to yell, but I heard only a bubbling, coughing sound.

I gagged on the foul-tasting, muddy water, and I was shocked to see that what I had spit out was my own bright red blood. I looked down at the front of my jungle fatigues and saw that they were also bloody.

My foggy mind had trouble accepting the fact that I had been hit, that Charlie had hit me just as he had JoJo, Doc B., Caldwell, and some of our other troopers. I was not going to get up and waltz away from the hit. My time had finally come, and there was not a damned thing I could do about it. The giant wave I had been surfing had finally petered out.

Nothing much seemed to work on my body, and those functions that were still active were operating in slow motion, even to my foggy thinking. I had seen plenty of downed soldiers to know that my body was shutting down all of its non-essential systems. Surprisingly, I was not feeling any pain, except for my shrapnel wound.

My legs were numb, and my mouth and the right side of my head felt as if a dentist had just given me an overdose of Novocain. I could not understand why my legs did not work. Full reasoning eluded me.

I rolled over onto my hands and knees and threw up some water and a lot of blood. I gagged and choked, and then I pitched face-first back into the water. I think I tried to call for help as I began to drown in my own blood and the dirty water of the rice paddy.

Pushing with the small amount of strength that I had left in my arms, I managed to turn myself slightly. I could not roll over onto my back because of my rucksack, and I could not figure out how to untangle myself from my load, which consisted of two rounds of 81mm mortar ammunition, two claymores, a LAW, and 200 rounds for our M60 machine guns. Every movement was a huge effort, and from somewhere, pain and a cold numbness crept up on me. Sweet Jesus, I was dying.

"Come on, Fred, stop fighting it. It's all over and you know it. Let go!" something alien inside of me said in a smooth, used-car salesman's voice.

Soon, my body was completely numb, except for the feeling of having the whole world sitting on my chest.

It was my time to help the dead bury the dead, and I was scared.

A mind-numbing chill slowly crept over me, and I felt as if I were soaking in a tub of ice water. My eyesight grew cloudy. I was slipping slowly down, and the cold, murky water of the rice paddy was coming to engulf me. I gagged. I was drowning.

Damn! I thought. I should have worn a flak jacket, but everyone knows those damned things are more trouble than they are worth. I had seen some of my men faint from the weight of the jackets. Well, I had been caught with my pants down, and now my mind was going amid crazy thoughts.

I still had no positive idea where I had been hit, and I was too scared to look. That Charlie must have gotten me good. Way to go, Charlie! I complimented him silently. Then, I remembered the slap of the slug that had set me on my ass, and I refused to think about where I had

359

been hit. I was bleeding heavily, like a stuck hog. I could not help but visualize scenes where guys lay dead with their guts hanging out and where human body parts flew through the air. I remembered a time when I had seen human brains spattered over the walls of bunkers. Oh God, oh God. I was tripping.

I could no longer hold my head above water. Water and blood filled my mouth and my nose. I was drowning and helpless to stop it. That is when I saw her, wading in the water toward me. Oh dear God, it was my own dear mother coming to me all the way from 41st Street on the south side of Chicago. I swear to God, she came to me in that muddy, bloody rice paddy all the way over in South Vietnam.

Sis reached down and took my head in her warm, loving hands. Then she lifted and held my head above the water so that I would not drown. I coughed up more blood and water. With the index finger of her right hand, she gently touched the center of my forehead, and she spoke one Zulu word: "Im-Amba!"

Then Sis smiled and said, "Boy, you gonna be all right, ya heah me. Now you just hold on. One of your men is coming heah to help. Meanwhile, I'll hold you till he gets heah."

A warm calmness engulfed me, and I experienced more peace than I had ever felt before. (Only you who have "been there" will understand what I mean.) I felt no pain, no more killing, only sweet PEACE. There was peace in the valley.

Sweet Jesus, I smelled the wonderfully sweet aroma of freshly ground nutmeg.

From across the universe, I heard somebody scream, "Oh, my dear God. Here he is. Top! MEDIC! MEDIC! Doc, Doc, Top is down! Top is down!"

A squad leader from the Third Platoon jumped into the rice paddy with me and took over the job of holding my head up. He held me like a baby. I wanted to thank him, but I could no longer speak because I was numb all over.

It was Sgt. Blanchard who held me in his arms and screamed for a medic. He rocked back and forth a bit, as if trying to comfort me. As he cried, his tears splashed down onto my face and mixed with the water and the blood already there.

I could hear him, even though there was still some sporadic rifle fire.

"Oh God, Top. That bastard hit you. I saw it but I could not get here in time. But, Top, you got him good. He ain't ever going to shoot anyone again. Top, I'll get his bayonet for you. Now don't you worry. Doc is coming, and you're going to make it. You'll see.

"Top, First Sergeant, please don't let go. That's what you always say to us. You said no damn NVA or VC soldier would ever put you down all the way," Blanchard said.

I heard someone else yell, "Over here, Doc. He's over here!"

Many willing hands lifted me and carried me to dry land. By that time, I was hurting all over, and the stark coldness was rapidly returning to my body. I wanted to tell them not to forget my little black Bessie and my steel pot, but I was past saying anything to anyone. Only my mind, ears, and eyes were working, although they were rapidly failing me, too.

They laid me flat on the ground and gathered around to look at me. I saw pain and sorrow in their eyes, and I saw their tears through mine. Yes, there I was crying again and probably for the very last time. However, I was not crying out of pain; rather, I was crying for my soul and the fact that I was dying. I did not want to leave those magnificent men, those outstanding troopers and soldiers of Black Knight Alfa. Sweet Jesus, I loved them with all of my heart. I decided that Mac or Long Claw should take my place when I was gone.

Pete was crying, too, as he repeatedly said, "Top, Top."

Doc Hopkins gave me my first shot of happy juice, and he yelled for everyone to get back to give him room to work. Doc California was on my other side, and I knew that I was safe. I could see Long Claw but not Mac, and I hoped to God that he was okay because I knew he would be there if he could.

I still heard some caps being popped.

The medics ripped my jacket off, and I think I felt another sting of golden dreams.

Doc Hopkins yelled, "Top, hold the bandage with your right hand. Man, I can't stop the blood, and you have lost too much already!"

I could not do as he asked because I no longer had control of my limbs, or anything else for that matter.

After some time, Doc California said smiling, "Top, we've stopped the bleeding. You are going to be okay! First Sergeant, you know we can't let you get away from us."

The CO asked, "Doc, I want to know right up front and no bullshit, how bad is Top hit?"

Doc California repeated that I would be fine, and Redleg announced that dust-off was on its way.

I was tripping in a big way. At first, they were there; then they were gone. I saw Mac, who was saying something to me, but I was deaf in my right ear and my head felt like a big balloon. I heard the CO yell for the First Platoon to hold their positions, and he assured them that I was okay.

"Sir, we have to move him now. He's lost a lot of blood," Doc Hopkins said to the CO, and then he mentioned something about shock.

I felt myself being loaded aboard one of the slicks that had brought us in. (I knew that because I recognized the door gunner.) I smelled hot cherry juice and the odor of hot brass rolling around on the floor. I saw some of the faces of the men of the Grand Company, and then I passed out.

When I came around, I saw the door gunner smiling down at me, offering words of encouragement. Soon, we were in the air, and I passed out again.

As the last shot that Doc Hopkins had given me wore thin, I slipped back into the world of the living and found myself lying on a stretcher wearing only my birthday suit. I had been cleaned up, and there was a plastic tube down my throat and a lot of other tubes and wires hanging from me. I had no idea how I had gotten there.

A corpsman who noticed that I was awake put a warm blanket over me. I wanted to thank him, but I could not talk. He asked how I felt, and I tried to smile, but it hurt too much. The corpsman said that I was in Phu Bai.

The first doctor I became aware of immediately got my attention because he was so professional-looking and he displayed a no-nonsense approach to my situation. He seemed to know what he was doing, and he immediately gained my complete trust. The nurse with him was a very beautiful woman with rather short, chestnut-colored hair. She also appeared to be completely competent. They expressed concern and a desire to do all they could to help me.

"Well, Sergeant, I really should chew you out about that small bit of shrapnel you were carrying around in your chest. Now you and I know it didn't just get there. And because you didn't do what you should have, it made our jobs a bit harder, but not to worry, it's going to be okay."

The nurse chimed in, "Sarge, if you understand what the Colonel is saying, close your eyes twice. If the answer is no, then close them only once."

I closed my eyes twice.

The doctor continued, "Sergeant, I'm afraid we can only make you comfortable here. At this station we can give you some relief by taking away your pain, but that's all we can do."

Someone called urgently to the doctor, and he excused himself. For some reason, my head was beginning to feel like the Goodyear Blimp, and I was having an increasingly difficult time breathing. I was frightened because I could not feel any part of my body. The only thing I felt was extreme coldness.

I could not turn my head, so I had a limited view of my surroundings. A few minutes later, a different man, who also looked like a doctor, came to examine me. He looked at me very sadly as he gave me the bottom line. He told me that they did not have something that was necessary to repair the damage that had been done to me. Then he said, "Sergeant, you are going to die."

Lord, I was scared. I thought about my mama, my wife, my children, and Chicago. I also thought of Doc B., Caldwell, Smitty, and all of my other friends and fellow soldiers and brothers-in-arms who had been taken from me by the Vietnam War. Then I decided that I was fully ready to go down to the great river. I forgave the enemy soldier who had shot me, and I asked him to forgive me for shooting him. I felt no hatred in my heart. Thank you, sweet Jesus.

The doctor who had told me I was checking out also explained that I would not be able to breathe without the tube in my throat. By then, I had already figured out that small detail.

The tube did not make me feel any better about my situation. In fact, I began to panic because I was having more and more trouble breathing. I was also doing a lot of tripping.

"Sarge, they shot you in the right side of your neck, and there is some damage. Because of the extensive swelling, we are going to perform a ... [some big medical word that eluded me]. Basically, we must make some incisions so you can breathe."

The word "incisions" certainly got my attention. I was not so dumb or so spaced out of my mind that I did not know the dude was telling me that they were going to cut my throat.

I promptly passed out.

When I came to, I heard them discussing what to do with me. I could no longer talk, and no one asked me anything. I was moved into an operating area, and I started to pray. The next thing I could clearly understand was that I was being moved again. I tripped out.

I was on a medevac helicopter with a lot of things sticking out of me. A friendly corpsman hovered over me. He was a Southerner from South Carolina, and he told me that I was lucky they had come along when they did, "'cause, Sarge, they were getting ready to slit your throat, but then they decided to send you out to the *Repose* 'cause there they are a lot better equipped for that kind of operation. Now you just hold on. We will have you there in a minute."

With the sun shining into my eyes and my heart, I broke into song: "There's a place in the sun where there's room for everyone. Moving on. Moving on."

I continued with: "Mother, mother, why are you crying? Brother, brother, brother, there's far too many of you dying." Naturally, I was singing only in my mind and in my heart.

And, there old Fred was, crying again!

I did not feel our landing on the helipad of the USS *Repose*; however, I felt myself being moved, and I felt the cold breeze of the South China Sea. The friendly corpsman held my hand and told me everything was going to be all right.

Although it has taken quite some time to relate to you the details of my story, realize that no time was wasted in transporting me from where I had been hit to Phu Bai and then on to the USS Repose.

At this time, I would like to thank those pilots and the crews who transported me, as well as all of my wounded and dead fellow soldiers. Thank you! I surely do hope that the young corpsman from South Carolina made it safely back home.

On the USS *Repose*, I was taken to an operating room that was much different from the one at Phu Bai. I knew I was being X-rayed. The blanket was removed, and I was freezing. The table was cold and hard, but the giant lights were warm. For some reason, I was more lucid, but only my mind, hearing, and eyesight were working. Everything else had gone fishing.

A medical team was busily attending to me when a male voice said, "Someone, stop the bleeding."

Then, a female voice called for some type of clamp.

"Sergeant, can you hear me? If you can, open your eyes," said a muffled male voice.

I opened my eyes.

"Sarge," a doctor wearing a surgical mask said. "I know that you are experiencing some pain and discomfort, but because of the location of your wound, we cannot give you any anesthetics or painkillers right now, so just bear with us."

After some minutes, or perhaps hours, I saw the doctor rip his surgical mask away. His face was drawn and sad. He looked at me briefly and then looked away quickly.

A Catholic priest hovered over me, whispering gently. Having once been an altar boy, I knew that I was receiving my last rites. Before he finished, I caught sight of and felt someone attaching a tag to my toe.

I was lifted onto a metal stretcher and then wheeled along a corridor where I was placed on the floor. I do not know how long I had lain there, but I was definitely not alone. I was naked and cold, and my pain was bearable. I think most of the hoses and wires had been removed from my body. I passed out again.

After becoming conscious again, I thought each breath that I took would be my last, and the mental anguish was almost unbearable. Sweet Jesus, I was suffocating. My mind was clear, but I could not move anything other than my eyes. I was in some kind of refrigerator.

I could still move my eyes around, and what I saw caused my blood to run cold. I felt an absolute horror like never before – one that no man should ever experience.

I thought frantically, oh dear God, I'm lying with the dead. I don't think I'm dead yet, but I'm already here.

My mind screamed continually.

"Sergeant, wake up! Come on back to me! Don't you dare go out on me now! Breathe, damn you, breathe. You can do it! Breathe!"

A doctor was down there with me, holding my head in his hands. I saw someone else, but my mind was almost gone. The doctor put his face down next to mine and screamed at me. I remember smelling his breath against that other stark odor. The doctor was a pipe smoker, and he used rum and maple tobacco. I was certain of that because I used to smoke the same tobacco.

"Don't you leave me now. I can help you, but you have got to help yourself. You look like a fighter. Well, now is your time to fight. I'm going to slowly turn your head. Forget about the pain, and when you can breathe on your own, just close your eyes real tight and I will know. That's all you got to do!"

The pain was mind-blowing, but I endured it because the chance to live was a powerful painkiller. I closed my eyes as tightly as possible, and the doctor slowly turned my head as far as he could in one direction and then back the opposite way. I was breathing on my own. Of course, it hurt like hell, but I could breathe. Even the air surrounding the dead became sweet.

Yes, I was crying again. Great tears of joy flooded my eyes, and I tried but could not say "thank you" to that wonderful doctor who had saved my life.

"Somebody, give me a hand to get this man out of here. How did he get down here? Oh, and grab those X-rays. He's very weak, but ... Hurry, hurry, hurry!"

As they moved me, I saw more of my surroundings and those who shared that silent, cold place with me. Oh, sweet Jesus and Mother of Mercy.

Even to this day, I often wake up screaming over and over.

Somewhere along the pitch-black corridor, I thanked God that I was Cav, a Skytrooper, and a member of the 1st Air Cavalry Division. I thanked Him that I had served with the true men and the best infantry rifle company in the world.

If it was my time and I was going to heaven or to hell, one thing was certain. I was going standing up and walking like a man because I was Cav.

The small ward was spotlessly clean. The air was fresh, and my neighbors were alive. I lay on a clean white sheet, and unlike before, I was in a hospital bunk. I wondered if the tag was still on my toe.

Somewhere not too far away, a radio played, and I could plainly hear with my left ear the country voice of Charlie Pride as he sang, "What's going to happen to the little folks?"

Thank you, dear God, and thank you, dear doctor.

I was alive!

"One has never lived till he has almost died.
Life has a sweetness the protected will never know."

Author unknown[93]

The personnel who worked aboard the hospital ship the USS *Repose* AH-16 deserve a special "thank you" from many people and most especially from me. To all of you: "I thank you, and you have my undying gratitude forever." To the doctor who made a special trip downstairs to get me: "Sir, I thank you for saving my life."

I am not sure how long I was downstairs before the doctor who saved me and the man in charge of the room downstairs who referred to me as "the one who got away" visited me. Both men talked with me briefly, and they shook my hand.

When I was well enough to have solid food, they gave me a jar of baby food – "Strained Beef Heart". Of course, I did not have the heart to eat it. When the guy in the bunk next to me was served meatloaf, mashed potatoes, and green peas, he did not eat all of it because I took his tray and tried to eat his food. That was clearly an indication that I was getting better. Of course, big tears formed in my eyes as I ate because it was terribly painful to swallow. The nurse on duty got so mad at me that she snatched the food away and threatened to hit me over the head with the tray.

Later, a high-ranking navy officer came aboard the ship and pinned a medal on my robe during a simple ceremony. I did not know how long I had been there, but I was allowed to visit other patients and to see some of the wondrous results of the hard-working, dedicated medical personnel. Many American soldiers returned home alive as a direct result of the brilliant accomplishments of those women and men aboard the USS *Repose*. To them and to all of the unsung American heroes who were positively involved in the Vietnam War, I say, "Thank you."

Some personnel from the 1st Cavalry Division were aboard the *Repose*, and they took great care of us Cav troopers by writing letters on our behalf and doing other things that we were not yet capable of doing.

When I, along with many other soldiers, left the USS *Repose*, our first stop was Japan. From there, we were flown aboard a medical evacuation aircraft back to Travis Air Force Base in the good old USA. Man oh man, it was so good to touch the green grass of home and to admire the still-beautiful state of California. It was wonderful to be back in God's country. Even though I arrived flat on my back, I was home again and aching to see 41st Street.

Being back home in America was a very good feeling, and despite all that had happened, I never lost faith in my country. Clearly, I would go through it all again. (That thought could certainly become a reality because the turnaround time for us grunts was down to about six months.)

My greatest loss was the privilege of being with the men of the Grand Company. My heart, mind, and soul were and are forever with them, the magnificent men of Black Knight Alfa. Physically, I was in a medical rack, but in spirit, I had my load on my back and my little black Bessie in my hands as I humped the bush with the men of the best infantry-fighting company the world would ever see.

> Black Knight Alfa. Alpha and Omega! May God in His infinite wisdom bless you one and all, wherever you may be today.

When those of us who were bound for the East Coast reached our final debarkation point, we were loaded onto army buses for further transportation to an army hospital, where we would undergo some final tests before we were released to go home.

During that short run, our convoy slowed to a crawl under local police escort because several anti-war demonstrators were blocking our route. Some carried placards and threw eggs at our buses. Others burned small American flags. The eggs and signs were tolerable, but the flag-burning hurt a lot, especially when I thought of those small flags that each of us carried and the ones that we had placed over the faces of Doc B., Caldwell, and the others.

I shared a window with another soldier, and we watched helplessly as a pretty young girl broke away from the police and jammed her placard against our window. It read something like this:

> MURDERERS. BABY KILLERS.
> RAPISTS. DRUG-HEADS.
> We don't want you here!!!!!!!!

She screwed up her young face with hatred, and she flipped us the bird.

That was our welcome home. **GOD BLESS AMERICA!**

Our God and the soldiers we alike adore
Ev'n at the brink of danger; not before.
After deliverance, both alike requited,
Our God's forgotten, and our soldiers
Slighted.

Francis Quarles 1592–1644
Divine fancies (1632) of common devotion

I still say:

"GOD BLESS AMERICA!"

Glossary

While fighting in the Vietnam War, we American soldiers created an entirely different and colorful language. Our vernacular was a mixture of military terminology, old and new GI slang from World War II and Korea, good-old-boy talk from the South, and the black tongues of the ghettos all over America.

During my three tours in the Nam, I became proficient in our new language, which I felt was necessary because I was a grunt all the way. Over the years, our way of speaking took on many names for easy identification, such as Gruntspeak and Nam'spk. I prefer to call it Namguage.

I am aware that Namguage may seem a bit harsh and perhaps offensive to some people. Therefore, I have made an honest effort to soften it whenever possible. Nevertheless, to tell the story of Black Knight Alfa properly, there are times when I have to let it all hang out. For instance, there is no way to soften the general-purpose expletive "motherfucker" because it was a sign of the times.

Though a whole dictionary of Namguage terms exists, my glossary includes primarily those terms that I used to tell the story of my Grand Company.

ACs .... Aircraft Commanders.

AGENT ORANGE   A chemical defoliant used to deny the enemy the ability to use the natural environment as concealment.

AIR CAV   Air Cavalry. Helicopter-borne infantry assault troopers.

AK or **AK-47**   The Kalashnikov assault rifle.

ALFA   The first letter of the military phonetic alphabet. "A" is translated into Alfa, "B" into Bravo, "C" into Charlie, and so on. "Z" represents Zulu.

AMBUSH   To lie, well hidden, in wait for an unsuspecting enemy and to destroy him.

AO   Area of operation(s).

ARC-LITE   The code name for a B-52 raid.

ARVN   Army of the Republic of Vietnam.

BIRD   Any aircraft. In our case, this was usually a helicopter.

BIRTH CONTROL   Our code word for any artillery unit who shot for us.

BLOOD   A black soldier. Derived from "blood brother".

BLUE MAX   The Bell AH-1G assault helicopter(s). Air Cobra(s). Snake(s).

BOX   To form the company or unit into a box-shaped formation in order to ambush, fight, or defend. Normally, the side facing the enemy threat was referred to as the heavy side.

BRING DOWN   To kill the enemy. Other terms include dust, pop, ice, grease, hit, chill, zap, and do.

BUG JUICE   Insect repellent in a white plastic bottle that was often worn on the steel helmet and held in place by an expanding camouflage band.

BUSH   In the combat area anywhere outside a heavily defended area, city, or town.

CHARLEY ALFA   Combat assault. A helicopter-borne assault onto an enemy area, position, or landing zone.

CHARLEY-CHARLEY BIRD   The command-and-control bird, or helicopter.

CHARLIE   The enemy soldier(s). The same term was used when referring to one or more of them. Our company used Charlie mostly to refer to the NVA.

CHERRY JUICE   Automatic transmission fluid and/or hydraulic fluid, usually red.

CHIEU HOI   The Open Arms program designed to win friends and to influence the enemy.

CHOPPER   A helicopter.

CLAYMORE   The M18 Al anti-personnel device; the best little friend a trooper could have.

CO   Commanding officer, or company commander.

CONTACT   A firefight with the enemy.

CP   Command post. Where one could often find the CO. The Headquarters section is also usually in or near the same location.

C-RATS   Combat rations (food).

DELTA-DELTA or **DOUGHNUT DOLLIES.**   Beautiful American girls who brought us doughnuts and coffee.

DIDDY BOPPING   Walking or strolling along carelessly.

DIDDY MAU   To run like hell, pulling for all you are worth.

DIG IN   To dig a hole or a fighting/defensive position, whichever the tactical situation dictated.

DMZ   Demilitarized zone, on the 17th parallel. As the name implies, no military personnel were supposed to fight in such an area, but someone forgot to tell Charlie about this rule.

DOC   The term of endearment given to all of our company medical personnel. Normally there was a senior company medic located in the Headquarters section; he was school-trained, and the most experienced of all medics. There was also one school-trained medic per platoon.

DOG or **DOGGING**   To follow without being seen.

DRAG   The last unit, element, or man in the rear of a combat formation. (Running drag.)

DUST-OFF   Medical evacuation of wounded personnel, mostly by helicopter.

EOD   Explosive Ordnance Demolition.

FAC   Forward Air Controller(s), usually air force personnel, who are attached for specific missions.

FDC   Fire Direction Center.

FIRE BRIGADE   Our code word for identifying our maneuvering unit.

FIRE FLY   An AC-47 flareship dropping forty-five 200,000 candle-power flares.

FIREBASE   In general, an artillery base of fire in a forward position from where the artillery can fire in support of infantry ground operations. Sometimes a firebase provided only temporary support during a specific operation. Normally, the infantry secured all firebases and landing zones.

FIREFIGHT   To exchange small arms fire with the enemy.

FNG   Fucking new guy. A term applied to all new or incoming personnel.

FOB   The code name for a position established while spending the night in enemy territory.

GRUNT   The combat infantry soldier, the cornerstone of the US Army.

GUNSHIP or **GUNSLINGER**   A combat helicopter armed with various weapons.

HANG-IT   To hold a mortar round that was ready to be dropped down the tube.

HARD HAT   A full-time Viet Cong soldier.

HAUL ASS   To run like hell.

HE or **HIM**   Often used to designate the enemy, no matter how many there were.

HIP SHOOTING   To fire a mortar without using the standard army-prescribed firing methods. Hip shooting was used for super-quick firing at line-of-sight targets.

HIT   To kill the enemy, to bring him down.

HOME   Our code word to indicate where the main part of the company or the CP was located.

HOOK   A CH-47 Chinook (cargo) helicopter.

HOT   An area or position under enemy fire.

HUMP   To walk or to move while carrying a load.

INCOMING   Incoming, high-angle, enemy fire, such as an enemy mortar or rocket attack.

KIA   Killed in action.

KILL ZONE   A designated area in which the desired result is to kill 95 per cent of the enemy, such as on an ambush. Our desired result was always a 100 per cent kill.

LAGER   Our code word for forming the company or unit into a circle where our positions of troops and weapons formed a perimeter that provided us with an all-around defense. We could fight and defend from our lager position.

LOACH   A light observation and reconnaisance helicopter, the Hughes OH-6A.

LOG MAN   Logistical (supply) personnel.

LT   A lieutenant, a company grade officer.

LURP RATS   Field or combat rations that were designed for the long-range reconnaissance patrols. The beef and rice ration was outstanding.

LURPS   Long-range reconnaissance patrols.

LZ   Landing zone. A secured position in enemy territory with either a cleared and prepared landing field for fixed-wing aircraft or a landing pad for rotary wing aircraft (helicopters). This term was sometimes used to designate an area or a position held by the enemy.

MACV   Military Assistance Command/Vietnam.

MIKE-MIKE or **mm**   The term used to express millimeters.

MORTAR A short-barreled or tube weapon designed for high-angled fire.

MOS   Military Occupational Speciality.

MOTHER or **MOTHERFUCKER**   General-purpose expletive.

MRF   Mobile Riverine forces.

NAM   Vietnam.

NCO   Non-commissioned officer.

NVA   The North Vietnamese Army.

PAYBACK   To get revenge.

PHY-OPS   Physiological warfare.

POP CAPS   To fire a weapon.

POP SMOKE   To activate a smoke grenade or canister.

PROJO   The projectile fired from an artillery weapon. It was usually high explosive.

PUFF THE MAGIC DRAGON   An AC-47 gunship armed with the GAU-2A minigun, which had a rate of fire that ranged from 6000 rpm (high) to 200 rpm (low). Sometimes referred to as Spooky. The AC-130 gunship took on the same role; called Spectre, it employed weapons and electronic sensors.

PUNJI PIT   A hole dug in the ground and lined with sharpened and hardened bamboo stakes that were driven into the bottom and the sides. The pit was carefully concealed and positioned where an unsuspecting American soldier might fall in and have the sharpened stakes driven into his body. The VC smeared human feces on the sharpened stakes to serve as a poison.

PUSH   Our code word to talk on the radio. This term also meant frequency.

QRF   Quick reaction force. Also known as the fire brigade.

R & R   Rest and recuperation.

RADIO   Our main radio was the battery-operated ANPRC-25, or PRC-25.

REDLEG   Our code designation for our artillery forward observer. In our case, he was an artillery officer, a lieutenant, or a captain. He and his RTO were attached to our company. In every case, the redleg and his RTO were outstanding soldiers and an important part of our company.

ROCK AND ROLL   Automatic fire.

RPG   rocket-propelled grenade.

RTO   Radio telephone operator.

S-2   Our intelligence officer or section.

S-3   The battalion-level operations officer or section

S-4   The battalion-level supply officer or section.

SAPPER   An enemy engineer soldier who was specially trained to breach our defensive systems and to blow up our most important locations, such as ammunition dumps, fuel supply dumps, and other critical areas. Sappers would also kill as many of us as they could. However, they were NOT invincible or indestructible; they went down when hit, just like anyone else.

SATCHEL CHARGE   A small bag, usually made of canvas, loaded with an explosive charge and some form of firing or detonating device. Composition-4 (C-4) was most often used, but sometimes TNT was used.

SHACKLE   To encode a series of new numbers to a known code/series of numbers.

SIX   The numerical designation code for our company commander.

SLICK   A UH-1 troop-carrying helicopter.

SLICKED OUT or **SLICKED IN**   Moved by helicopter.

SNOOPY   Aerial surveillance teams.

SOG Special Operations Group operating within the enemy positions. Ghosts.

SOP Standard Operating Procedure.

SPIDER HOLE A well-concealed enemy foxhole used to fire from and to hide in.

STAND-DOWN To go to a secured area for a short rest.

STARLIGHT SCOPE A device for viewing targets during times of darkness and reduced visibility.

STEEL POT The steel helmet.

STONER M63A1 WEAPONS SYSTEM The elite weapons system. Nothing could equal the Stoner; it was far superior to the Kalashnikov AK-47.

TET The Vietnamese New Year.

THUMP GUN The M79 grenade launcher. The term "thump" was derived from the sound made when the M79 was fired.

TOC Tactical Operations Center.

TOP The first sergeant.

TOT Time on Target.

TWO STEP A bamboo viper. If one bit you, you had only two steps left before dying.

VICTOR CHARLIE The Viet Cong, or Viet Coward.

WAIT-A-MINUTE VINES Jungle vines that hold, cling, and entangle.

WILLIE PETE White phosphorus. This chemical agent was also known as the Whispering Death.

Notes

1. "What's Going On" – Marvin Gaye
2. Foxhole
3. 105mm and 155mm artillery pieces
4. the lead man
5. command and control, the battalion commander's helicopter
6. the lead platoon
7. We tuned our radio to the same frequency as the loach
8. location
9. communications wire (WD-8)
10. Napoleon
11. "Countdown" was our code word that informed everyone to duck.
12. the area of destruction
13. a pit
14. the nickname for the 7th US Cavalry
15. logistics personnel
16. there were holes in the canopy
17. out and back in
18. a trail
19. a full-time, elite soldier
20. Charlie usually carried ammunition with as many as six or seven lot numbers.
21. the Russian-made light machine gun, most commonly used by Charlie
22. a lightweight, helmet-shaped hat made of pith or cork

23. our artillery support
24. aircraft that came to our aid at night and dropped illuminating flares
25. three types of rapid-fire guns
26. situation reports
27. "What's Going On" – Marvin Gaye
28. a secret agent; a CIA agent
29. my official army records file
30. Tactical Air-Strikes
31. the words "Victor" and "Charlie" represent the letters "V" and "C" in the army's phonetic alphabet.
32. a claymore that was robbed of its C-4 explosives
33. designed for controlled detonation
34. set off by the enemy
35. they pressed the Press-to-Talk button on their radio microphone
36. peseta, the common currency in South Vietnam
37. a single artillery or mortar round that is fired to mark a location
38. our code word for illumination
39. surface-to-air missile
40. a hand-held survival radio used by downed pilots to signal for rescue
41. HH-53C air/sea rescue helicopters
42. jet fuel
43. also the colours of our insignia
44. his replacement
45. there were some radio operators in Vietnam who took it upon themselves to play music "illegally" for the troops and to do it over the known combat frequencies
46. lyrics from Stevie Wonder's song "Moving On"
47. a nickname for the 1st Infantry Division
48. to prevent the enemy from penetrating our right flank, or end
49. a land-line for telecommunications
50. "What's Going On" – Marvin Gaye
51. this line is taken from one of Sis's favorite old Mississippi Delta gospel songs.
52. a line from the "Whiffenpoof Song" (one of Rudy Vallee's radio and stage theme songs)
53. our code word for chow

54. strong, metal, temporary landing-strip sections
55. it was customary for the NVA soldiers to wear rope or string around their ankles and wrists to make it easier for their buddies to drag their bodies away if they were killed
56. words of wisdom from my grandpa
57. the army's phonetic alphabet uses the words "Charley" and "Alfa" to represent the letters "C" and "A" respectively. "Charley" (the army "C") is not to be confused with "Charlie" (the enemy)
58. an operation
59. our morning report
60. the pilot
61. if the enemy was still there and capable of placing accurate fire on your troops
62. Physiological Warfare Operations
63. JoJo's real name
64. our term describing the sound of our artillery fire when it was shifted without a break in the firing
65. white phosphorus
66. Our battalion commander directed and controlled the entire operation from this bird.
67. "What's Going On" – Marvin Gaye
68. a Russian abbreviation that translates to "self-loading rifle"
69. often referred to as Saint Vitus's dance
70. I puked my guts out
71. Latin for "I believe in one God" (from the "Credo")
72. short for Saigon
73. the public saw their first M-46 during the May Day parade in 1954
74. On Vehicle Maintenance
75. an explosive detonations cord used in demolition
76. the burning grease and oil were the sources of most of the smoke
77. an old Mississippi Delta expression that meant it was far too late to pray
78. to retreat or withdraw
79. "Praise the Lord" was our code phrase to distribute existing ammunition among the company so that everyone would have an approximately equal amount. We borrowed this code phrase from an old song that was popular during World War II – "Praise the Lord and Pass the Ammunition"

80. our code word for location or position
81. this heavy seat was designed like an anchor to penetrate a jungle canopy. The seat was attached to a lifeline and lowered from a hovering helicopter
82. the thump-gun ammunition
83. roughly translated, "Ba-muey-Ba" refers to the Vietnamese Beer 33, and "Chow-co-dep" is a term used to address a beautiful girl
84. a small shovel
85. a brother unit to Black Knight Alfa, the 2nd Brigade
86. better known as Ho Chi Minh
87. the Vietnamese version of soy sauce
88. "What's Going On" – Marvin Gaye
89. a line from an old gospel song by the same name
90. Signal Operating Instructions
91. "I believe in one God, the Father almighty, maker of heaven and earth". (a translation from the Creed)
92. Sergeant E-5 Maggio had recently replaced Sp4 Gonzalez as the sergeant of the Second Platoon. Gonzalez went back to the Big Apple
93. this quote has been with me for a long time and has served as one of my standards of living